IN THE AGE OF THE SMART MACHINE

IN THE AGE OF
THE SMART MACHINE

The Future
of
Work and Power

SHOSHANA ZUBOFF

A Member of the Perseus Books Group

Library of Congress Cataloging-in-Publication Data

Zuboff, Shoshana, 1951–
   In the age of the smart machine.

   Includes index.
   1. Automation—Economic aspects.
2. Automation—Social aspects.   3. Machinery
in industry.   4. Organizational effectiveness.
I. Title.
HD45.2.Z83   1988   338'.06   87–47777
ISBN   0–465–03212–5 (cloth)
ISBN   0–465–03211–7 (paper)

To Bob,
Who hears the world's heart
And has taught me much about how to listen.

CONTENTS

Contents

PREFACE

THIS BOOK was born of serendipity and silence and a passionate curiosity. There is a story to it. . . .

By the autumn of 1978, I had spent more than nine months deep in the stacks of a mammoth university library. I had been reading literature on the history of the industrial revolution as part of the preparation for completing my Ph.D. degree at Harvard University and a specialization in the history of work. Through this literature, I tried to grasp how everyday life had been altered by the profound material change in the means and methods of production. By "everyday life" I mean those things that we usually take for granted—the cast of our feelings, sensibilities, and expectations; the intimate details of eating, drinking, and socializing; the things that make us cry or laugh; and the things that make us mad. Yet I found the historical investigation frustrating. In many cases it provided rich detail about behavior, or the interpretations of behavior by observers, but offered inadequate insight into the subtleties of human experience. Constructing an idea about the inward sensibilities of ordinary people during those volatile times required painstaking effort and imagination. As my work progressed, I was ever more fascinated with the very different social constructions of reality that characterized workers then and now. I was fascinated by the ways in which older sensibilities are lost to a kind of social amnesia, crowded out by our adaptations to the demands of changing times.

While working on my research, I continued to develop my practice as a consultant to organizations. My practical work had been in the areas of organizational change and the evaluation of workplace innovations. Late in 1978, a Wall Street bank asked me to assess its first application of advanced information technology to clerical work. It had dramatically restructured its approach to the production of several key products, such as loans and letters of credit. Clerks who had performed one small operation in a long paper chain were, for the first time, using computer technology to accomplish all the functions associated with a single product. Visiting the bank's offices, I witnessed a sight that would eventually become so familiar as to defy notice—an entire floor of people seated at their partitioned workstations, staring into the screens of desktop terminals. At that time the experience was still peculiar enough, for both the clerks and their managers, as to provoke concern. The clerks seemed to have more difficulty adapting to these conditions than anticipated, and the first phase of the new effort resulted in sky-rocketing error rates. Managers believed that they had enriched the clerical job, and they could not explain the sense of malaise that had swept over the back office. I proposed to interview a broad sample of clerks and managers and to determine the sources of these troubles.

The technological change was one among many subjects we discussed during these interviews, but it was the one for which their responses were the most puzzling. Many people voiced distress, describing their work as "floating in space" or "lost behind the screen." They complained that they were no longer able to see or touch their work. Many felt that they no longer had the necessary skills or understanding to function competently. I did not know how to make sense of these comments, but I could not stop thinking about them either.

Within a month I had accepted another assignment, this time with a large daily newspaper. It wanted to understand more about the human and organizational issues raised in the computerization of their typesetting operations, a transition from "hot" type, which depended upon the manual operation of Linotype machines, to "cold" type, which was set with computer keyboards and printed out on photoprocessors. I spent several nights interviewing Linotype operators and hanging out, watching them work. To my surprise, their comments paralleled those of the bank clerks, sometimes quite precisely.

After one such night I left the building at about 9:00 A.M. and paced the city in a state of agitation. I finally ended up in an art museum where there was an exhibit of the sculptor David Smith's Voltri series. These powerfully expressive figures of burnished iron had been created in an abandoned factory workshop in the Italian village of Voltri, for exhibition in the 1962 Spoleto festival. Many of the figures reminded me of old hand tools; some were reminiscent of familiar industrial objects. Extracted from their worldly context, cast in the enduring silence of iron, enveloped by the pure white silence of the museum amphitheater where they were on display, these figures seemed like strangely beautiful fossils, wordless relics of a dying time. Their silence was as tantalizing and poignant as that of the historical documents I had been reading; it beckoned and pointed but left me yearning to hear them speak.

Before I knew it, I was writing furiously in my notebook. A vision came together for me that morning, one that has been brought to fruition only now, with the completion of this book. I realized that the people I had been interviewing were on the edge of a historical transformation of immense proportions, as important as that which had been experienced by the eighteenth- and nineteenth-century workers about whom I had read so much and imagined even more. I had long fantasized about what it would have been like to take a tape recorder into the workshops and factories of Britain in 1789 or 1848 and had considered the questions I would have asked in order to elicit the kind of insight I hungered for. Now there was an opportunity to do just that. The qualities of knowledge for which I had combed two-centuries-old documents were available here, now, in the hearts and voices of those people who were experiencing these new circumstances of production for the first time.

The statements that had puzzled me in my interviews with the bank clerks and Linotype operators began to make more sense. The material alterations in their means of production were manifested in transformations at intimate levels of experience—assumptions about knowledge and power, their beliefs about work and the meaning they derived from it, the content and rhythm of their social exchanges, and the ordinary mental and physical disciplines to which they accommodated in their daily lives. I saw that a world of sensibilities and expectations was being irretrievably displaced by a new world, one I did not yet understand. The question that held me centered on the nature of the differences between the two. The world of industrialism, its means and methods, was about to succumb to the same silence that had already engulfed the tools of the craftsman's workshop. What kind of world would emerge from this silence and how would we feel in it? Would it be possible, at this early stage in the historical process, to learn enough to frame the choices that would be laid open? Might a clearer grasp of these choices enable us to avoid the worst mistakes of the past? Would it be possible to take hold of new opportunities rather than simply repeat old patterns?

Based on the illumination of that morning, I began to outline the research program whose results are presented in this book. I wanted to interact with people at every level of a variety of organizations engaged in disparate forms of work. The approach would combine participant observations with semiclinical interviews and small group discussions. I intended to use my clinical skills to help people articulate their still-implicit experiences in the new work settings. With such data it would be possible to identify generic patterns of psychological and organizational experience associated with the emerging technological conditions of work.

I also hypothesized that history would offer only a brief window of time during which such data could be gathered. The jolt of unfamiliarity had to be exploited for the heightened sensibility it brings. I thought of the early American mill workers who expressed outrage at the thought of reporting to work at a fixed hour. Yet in less than a generation, such work rules had become routine. The workers' outrage betrayed a conception of daily life different from our own, one that was only made explicit in the confrontation with an unexpected set of demands. It seemed likely that in the apparently maladaptive responses of workers to computer-based technology (what many called "resistance to change"), it would be possible to trace a lineage of ordinary assumptions that referred back to the realities of the past and their points of disjuncture with the future. Like many other scholars of my generation, I had been struck by Daniel Bell's formulation of the post-industrial society, but discussions of these social changes were frequently limited to sociological abstractions. I wanted to discover the flesh and blood behind the concepts, the interior texture rather than the external form. I wanted to understand the practical problems that would have to be confronted in order to manage the new computerized workplace in ways that would fulfill the lofty promise of a knowledge-based society and to generate knowledge that would be instructive to those charged with that managerial responsibility.

I could not have known in 1978 that it would be ten years between that moment of insight and the publication of this book. The research process proved to be richly studded with opportunities for discovery. My understanding of the phenomena in question continued to change and grow with each year of field investigation, as I struggled to make sense of my data, particularly those that were unexpected or could not be explained with the concepts I had already developed. I learned that while resistance to the new technology is a valuable source of knowledge, it is not the only one. It became equally challenging to understand the indifference or enthusiasm or resignation that can greet the new technological conditions of work. My experience on the faculty of the Harvard Business School further sensitized me to the many complexities of managers' behavior, both as participants in and as proponents of technological change. My continuing efforts as a consultant to organizations teach me never to underestimate the magnetism of the past and the forces of inertia upon which it thrives. As a result, the data presented here reflect not only the emergence of new patterns in the workplace but also the concrete ways in which old patterns and assumptions assert themselves and can dull the impact of change. The themes are those of continuity and discontinuity, juncture and disjuncture, what is past and what is possible.

ACKNOWLEDGMENTS

FِّıRST, thanks to those who were my teachers—the women and men of Piney Wood, Cedar Bluff, Tiger Creek, Metro Tel, DrugCorp, Universal Technology, Global Bank Brazil, and Consolidated Underwriters Insurance. They were generous with their time and much more. As new computer-based technologies entered their work lives, they allowed me to accompany them in an exploration of much that was inwardly felt but still unnamed. I listened as they discovered their voices. With them I learned what was at stake in this technological transformation and how to identify the threat and the promise of what might emerge. I learned what it would take to make the promises come true. I would gladly thank them individually were it not for my commitment to maintain the confidentiality of all our discussions and interviews.

Thanks to Robert Schrank. Long before I first formally proposed the idea for this book, the questions I wanted to engage were given definition in years of joint contemplation and searching conversation. His vast knowledge of work and workers formed a crucial piece of my education. With his fertile, ranging mind he has been a companion to my thoughts—sounding board, critic, and source of unfailing support and inspiration. His friendship has provided one of my life's greatest blessings.

I owe an intellectual debt to the philosopher-psychologist Eugene Gendlin and the historian Jonathan Z. Smith, both of the University of Chicago. Smith helped me learn to take the long view, to see phenomena in the context of their histories. Gendlin helped me learn to decipher the interior structure and texture of experience, the play of feelings and situations that gives life its meaning and depth. They understood how to discern a worldly context from a shard or a sigh, and each of their methods is employed here.

Thanks to two colleagues who helped me at an early stage of my work on this book. The social historian Herbert Gutman read an early version of my work on the industrial revolution and insisted that I pursue my approach to the history of the work. Eliot Liebow of the National Institute of Mental Health believed in this project early on and was midwife to a major NIMH grant in 1981 that was vital in expanding my field research.

Thanks to Jack Rockart of the Massachusetts Institute of Technology's Center for Information Systems Research and Peter Keen and Richard Beckhard, both formerly of MIT. They too provided crucial financial and intellectual support long before the value of my subject and my approach was widely recognized. They helped me gain access to some preliminary research sites in 1980; these early data provided the basis upon which I was able to design the architecture of my research and to identify crucial lines of inquiry.

My gratitude goes to many other colleagues. Gloria Schuck collaborated with me in several field sites, including Global Bank Brazil, DrugCorp, and Cedar Bluff. Her work has been an invaluable contribution to this book. As if that were not enough, her friendship and intellectual passion have provided comfort and strength during the many years it took to complete this manuscript. Richard Walton has been a steadfast friend and critic. He gave generously of his time, reading the manuscript during its many drafts and providing careful, penetrating critiques at each stage. His energy and dedication did much to sustain me during these past years of writing. Steve Fraser of Basic Books, my deeply gifted editor, has been tireless in providing extensive commentary on each draft and in his perpetual enthusiasm. With his early and unequivocal commitment to this book he has been an intellectual touchstone and a crucial source of motivation. My colleagues Chris Argyris, George Lodge, Edgar Schein, Warren McFarlan, Thomas McCraw, Jay Lorsch, and John Kotter each read the manuscript at crucial stages and provided extremely helpful comments.

Thanks to those who have contributed in other ways. Brent Mansen provided twenty-four-hour-a-day technological support and patient encouragement. David Delong provided diligent assistance in the library research effort. Benzion Chanowitz did a masterful job of collating the data from DrugCorp. Pam Lovell helped with library research and with great dedication organized files, helped construct bibliographies, and heroically typed the first draft of the manuscript. Marybeth Donahue Ferrante took charge of manuscript production with care, efficiency, and grace. Gloria Buffonge has helped see the chapters through many drafts with patience and professionalism.

Thanks to the Harvard Business School Division of Research, which has provided me with generous support during these past years.

Thanks to the many friends who have showed good cheer in spite of my writer's distraction and absorption.

Many thanks to my family—Marilyn and Maurice and Steven and Linda Zuboff, and Sophie Miller. For more years than I care to count they have accepted my abandon to this book, never chiding me for missed celebrations or opportunities to share quiet time. I hope they know how much I missed them, too.

And finally, a prayer for my grandfather, Max Miller, who first taught me about the dignity and joy and pain of work.

In the Age of the Smart Machine

The names and identifying characteristics of the corporations discussed in this book have been changed.

DILEMMAS OF TRANSFORMATION

IN THE AGE OF

THE SMART MACHINE

The history of technology is that of human
history in all its diversity. That is why specialist
historians of technology hardly ever manage to
grasp it entirely in their hands.

—FERNAND BRAUDEL
The Structures of Everyday Life

We don't know what will be happening to us
in the future. Modern technology is taking
over. What will be our place?

—A Piney Wood worker

PINEY WOOD, one of the nation's largest pulp mills, was in the
throes of a massive modernization effort that would place every aspect
of the production process under computer control. Six workers were
crowded around a table in the snack area outside what they called the
Star Trek Suite, one of the first control rooms to have been completely
converted to microprocessor-based instrumentation. It looked enough
like a NASA control room to have earned its name.

It was almost midnight, but despite the late hour and the approach
of the shift change, each of the six workers was at once animated and
thoughtful. "Knowledge and technology are changing so fast," they
said, "what will happen to us?" Their visions of the future foresaw
wrenching change. They feared that today's working assumptions could

not be relied upon to carry them through, that the future would not resemble the past or the present. More frightening still was the sense of a future moving out of reach so rapidly that there was little opportunity to plan or make choices. The speed of dissolution and renovation seemed to leave no time for assurances that we were not heading toward calamity—and it would be all the more regrettable for having been something of an accident.

The discussion around the table betrayed a grudging admiration for the new technology—its power, its intelligence, and the aura of progress surrounding it. That admiration, however, bore a sense of grief. Each expression of gee-whiz-Buck-Rogers breathless wonder brought with it an aching dread conveyed in images of a future that rendered their authors obsolete. In what ways would computer technology transform their work lives? Did it promise the Big Rock Candy Mountain or a silent graveyard?

> In fifteen years there will be nothing for the worker to do. The technology will be so good it will operate itself. You will just sit there behind a desk running two or three areas of the mill yourself and get bored.

The group concluded that the worker of the future would need "an extremely flexible personality" so that he or she would not be "mentally affected" by the velocity of change. They anticipated that workers would need a great deal of education and training in order to "breed flexibility." "We find it all to be a great stress," they said, "but it won't be that way for the new flexible people." Nor did they perceive any real choice, for most agreed that without an investment in the new technology, the company could not remain competitive. They also knew that without their additional flexibility, the technology would not fly right. "We are in a bind," one man groaned, "and there is no way out." The most they could do, it was agreed, was to avoid thinking too hard about the loss of overtime pay, the diminished probability of jobs for their sons and daughters, the fears of seeming incompetent in a strange new milieu, or the possibility that the company might welsh on its promise not to lay off workers.

During the conversation, a woman in stained overalls had remained silent with her head bowed, apparently lost in thought. Suddenly, she raised her face to us. It was lined with decades of hard work, her brow drawn together. Her hands lay quietly on the table. They were calloused and swollen, but her deep brown eyes were luminous, youthful, and kind. She seemed frozen, chilled by her own insight, as she solemnly delivered her conclusion:

I think the country has a problem. The managers want everything to be run by computers. But if no one has a job, no one will know how to do anything anymore. Who will pay the taxes? What kind of society will it be when people have lost their knowledge and depend on computers for everything?

Her voice trailed off as the men stared at her in dazzled silence. They slowly turned their heads to look at one another and nodded in agreement. The forecast seemed true enough. Yes, there was a problem. They looked as though they had just run a hard race, only to stop short at the edge of a cliff. As their heels skidded in the dirt, they could see nothing ahead but a steep drop downward.

Must it be so? Should the advent of the smart machine be taken as an invitation to relax the demands upon human comprehension and critical judgment? Does the massive diffusion of computer technology throughout our workplaces necessarily entail an equally dramatic loss of meaningful employment opportunities? Must the new electronic milieu engender a world in which individuals have lost control over their daily work lives? Do these visions of the future represent the price of economic success or might they signal an industrial legacy that must be overcome if intelligent technology is to yield its full value? Will the new information technology represent an opportunity for the rejuvenation of competitiveness, productive vitality, and organizational ingenuity? Which aspects of the future of working life can we predict, and which will depend upon the choices we make today?

The workers outside the Star Trek Suite knew that the so-called technological choices we face are really much more than that. Their consternation puts us on alert. There is a world to be lost and a world to be gained. Choices that appear to be merely technical will redefine our lives together at work. This means more than simply contemplating the implications or consequences of a new technology. It means that a powerful new technology, such as that represented by the computer, fundamentally reorganizes the infrastructure of our material world. It eliminates former alternatives. It creates new possibilities. It necessitates fresh choices.

The choices that we face concern the conception and distribution of knowledge in the workplace. Imagine the following scenario: Intelligence is lodged in the smart machine at the expense of the human capacity for critical judgment. Organizational members become ever more dependent, docile, and secretly cynical. As more tasks must be accomplished through the medium of information technology (I call this "computer-mediated work"), the sentient body loses its salience as a source of knowledge, resulting in profound disorientation and loss of meaning. People intensify their search for avenues of escape through drugs, apathy, or adversarial conflict, as the majority of jobs in our offices and factories become increasingly isolated, remote, routine, and perfunctory. Alternatively, imagine this scenario: Organizational leaders recognize the new forms of skill and knowledge needed to truly exploit the potential of an intelligent technology. They direct their resources toward creating a work force that can exercise critical judgment as it manages the surrounding machine systems. Work becomes more abstract as it depends upon understanding and manipulating information. This marks the beginning of new forms of mastery and provides an opportunity to imbue jobs with more comprehensive meaning. A new array of work tasks offer unprecedented opportunities for a wide range of employees to add value to products and services.

The choices that we make will shape relations of authority in the workplace. Once more, imagine: Managers struggle to retain their traditional sources of authority, which have depended in an important way upon their exclusive control of the organization's knowledge base. They use the new technology to structure organizational experience in ways that help reproduce the legitimacy of their traditional roles. Managers insist on the prerogatives of command and seek methods that protect the hierarchical distance that distinguishes them from their subordinates. Employees barred from the new forms of mastery relinquish their sense of responsibility for the organization's work and use obedience to authority as a means of expressing their resentment. Imagine an alternative: This technological transformation engenders a new approach to organizational behavior, one in which relationships are more intricate, collaborative, and bound by the mutual responsibilities of colleagues. As the new technology integrates information across time and space, managers and workers each overcome their narrow functional perspectives and create new roles that are better suited to enhancing value-adding activities in a data-rich environment. As the quality of skills at each organizational level becomes similar, hierarchical distinctions begin to blur. Authority comes to depend more upon an appropriate fit between knowledge and responsibility than upon the ranking rules of the traditional organizational pyramid.

The choices that we make will determine the techniques of administration that color the psychological ambience and shape communicative behavior in the emerging workplace. Imagine this scenario: The new technology becomes the source of surveillance techniques that are used to ensnare organizational members or to subtly bully them into conformity. Managers employ the technology to circumvent the demanding work of face-to-face engagement, substituting instead techniques of remote management and automated administration. The new technological infrastructure becomes a battlefield of techniques, with managers inventing novel ways to enhance certainty and control while employees discover new methods of self-protection and even sabotage. Imagine the alternative: The new technological milieu becomes a resource from which are fashioned innovative methods of information sharing and social exchange. These methods in turn produce a deepened sense of collective responsibility and joint ownership, as access to ever-broader domains of information lend new objectivity to data and preempt the dictates of hierarchical authority.

This book is about these alternative futures. Computer-based technologies are not neutral; they embody essential characteristics that are bound to alter the nature of work within our factories and offices, and among workers, professionals, and managers. New choices are laid open by these technologies, and these choices are being confronted in the daily lives of men and women across the landscape of modern organizations. This book is an effort to understand the deep structure of these choices—the historical, psychological, and organizational forces that imbue our conduct and sensibility. It is also a vision of a fruitful future, a call for action that can lead us beyond the stale reproduction of the past into an era that offers a historic opportunity to more fully develop the economic and human potential of our work organizations.

THE TWO FACES OF INTELLIGENT TECHNOLOGY

The past twenty years have seen their share of soothsayers ready to predict with conviction one extreme or another of the alternative futures I have presented. From the unmanned factory to the automated cockpit, visions of the future hail information technology as the final

answer to "the labor question," the ultimate opportunity to rid ourselves of the thorny problems associated with training and managing a
competent and committed work force. These very same technologies
have been applauded as the hallmark of a second industrial revolution,
in which the classic conflicts of knowledge and power associated with
an earlier age will be synthesized in an array of organizational innovations and new procedures for the production of goods and services,
all characterized by an unprecedented degree of labor harmony and
widespread participation in management process.[1] Why the paradox?
How can the very same technologies be interpreted in these different
ways? Is this evidence that the technology is indeed neutral, a blank
screen upon which managers project their biases and encounter only
their own limitations? Alternatively, might it tell us something else
about the interior structure of information technology?

Throughout history, humans have designed mechanisms to reproduce and extend the capacity of the human body as an instrument of
work. The industrial age has carried this principle to a dramatic new
level of sophistication with machines that can substitute for and amplify
the abilities of the human body. Because machines are mute, and because they are precise and repetitive, they can be controlled according
to a set of rational principles in a way that human bodies cannot.

There is no doubt that information technology can provide substitutes for the human body that reach an even greater degree of certainty
and precision. When a task is automated by a computer, it must first be
broken down to its smallest components. Whether the activity involves
spraying paint on an automobile or performing a clerical transaction, it
is the information contained in this analysis that translates human
agency into a computer program. The resulting software can be used
to automatically guide equipment, as in the case of a robot, or to execute an information transaction, as in the case of an automated teller
machine.

A computer program makes it possible to rationalize activities more
comprehensively than if they had been undertaken by a human being.
Programmability means, for example, that a robot will respond with
unwavering precision because the instructions that guide it are themselves unvarying, or that office transactions will be uniform because
the instructions that guide them have been standardized. Events and
processes can be rationalized to the extent that human agency can be
analyzed and translated into a computer program.

What is it, then, that distinguishes information technology from earlier generations of machine technology? As information technology is used to reproduce, extend, and improve upon the process of substituting machines for human agency, it simultaneously accomplishes something quite different. The devices that automate by translating information into action also register data about those automated activities, thus generating new streams of information. For example, computer-based, numerically controlled machine tools or microprocessor-based sensing devices not only apply programmed instructions to equipment but also convert the current state of equipment, product, or process into data. Scanner devices in supermarkets automate the checkout process and simultaneously generate data that can be used for inventory control, warehousing, scheduling of deliveries, and market analysis. The same systems that make it possible to automate office transactions also create a vast overview of an organization's operations, with many levels of data coordinated and accessible for a variety of analytical efforts.

Thus, information technology, even when it is applied to automatically reproduce a finite activity, is not mute. It not only imposes information (in the form of programmed instructions) but also produces information. It both accomplishes tasks and translates them into information. The action of a machine is entirely invested in its object, the product. Information technology, on the other hand, introduces an additional dimension of reflexivity: it makes its contribution to the product, but it also reflects back on its activities and on the system of activities to which it is related. Information technology not only produces action but also produces a voice that symbolically renders events, objects, and processes so that they become visible, knowable, and shareable in a new way.

Viewed from this interior perspective, information technology is characterized by a fundamental duality that has not yet been fully appreciated. On the one hand, the technology can be applied to automating operations according to a logic that hardly differs from that of the nineteenth-century machine system—replace the human body with a technology that enables the same processes to be performed with more continuity and control. On the other, the same technology simultaneously generates information about the underlying productive and administrative processes through which an organization accomplishes its work. It provides a deeper level of transparency to activities that had been either partially or completely opaque. In this way information technology supersedes the traditional logic of automation. The word that I have coined to describe this unique capacity is *informate*. Activities, events, and objects are translated into and made visible by information when a technology *informates* as well as *automates*.

The informating power of intelligent technology can be seen in the manufacturing environment when microprocessor-based devices such as robots, programmable logic controllers, or sensors are used to translate the three-dimensional production process into digitized data. These data are then made available within a two-dimensional space, typically on the screen of a video display terminal or on a computer printout, in the form of electronic symbols, numbers, letters, and graphics. These data constitute a quality of information that did not exist before. The programmable controller not only tells the machine what to do—imposing information that guides operating equipment—but also tells what the machine has done—translating the production process and making it visible.

In the office environment, the combination of on-line transaction systems, information systems, and communications systems creates a vast information presence that now includes data formerly stored in people's heads, in face-to-face conversations, in metal file drawers, and on widely dispersed pieces of paper. The same technology that processes documents more rapidly, and with less intervention, than a mechanical typewriter or pen and ink can be used to display those documents in a communications network. As more of the underlying transactional and communicative processes of an organization become automated, they too become available as items in a growing organizational data base.

In its capacity as an automating technology, information technology has a vast potential to displace the human presence. Its implications as an informating technology, on the other hand, are not well understood. The distinction between *automate* and *informate* provides one way to understand how this technology represents both continuities and discontinuities with the traditions of industrial history. As long as the technology is treated narrowly in its automating function, it perpetuates the logic of the industrial machine that, over the course of this century, has made it possible to rationalize work while decreasing the dependence on human skills. However, when the technology also informates the processes to which it is applied, it increases the explicit information content of tasks and sets into motion a series of dynamics that will ultimately reconfigure the nature of work and the social relationships that organize productive activity.

Because this duality of intelligent technology has not been clearly recognized, the consequences of the technology's informating capacity are often regarded as unintended. Its effects are not planned, and the potential that it lays open remains relatively unexploited. Because the informating process is poorly defined, it often evades the conventional categories of description that are used to gauge the effects of industrial technology.

These dual capacities of information technology are not opposites; they are hierarchically integrated. Informating derives from and builds upon automation. Automation is a necessary but not sufficient condition for informating. It is quite possible to proceed with automation without reference to how it will contribute to the technology's informating potential. When this occurs, informating is experienced as an unintended consequence of automation. This is one point at which choices are laid open. Managers can choose to exploit the emergent informating capacity and explore the organizational innovations required to sustain and develop it. Alternatively, they can choose to ignore or suppress the informating process. In contrast, it is possible to consider informating objectives at the start of an automation process. When this occurs, the choices that are made with respect to how and what to automate are guided by criteria that reflect developmental goals associated with using the technology's unique informating power.

Information technology is frequently hailed as "revolutionary." What are the implications of this term? *Revolution* means a pervasive, marked, radical change, but *revolution* also refers to a movement around a fixed course that returns to the starting point. Each sense of the word has relevance for the central problem of this book. The informating capacity of the new computer-based technologies brings about radical change as it alters the intrinsic character of work—the way millions of people experience daily life on the job. It also poses fundamentally new choices for our organizational futures, and the ways in which labor and management respond to these new choices will finally determine whether our era becomes a time for radical change or a return to the familiar patterns and pitfalls of the traditional workplace. An emphasis on the informating capacity of intelligent technology can provide a point of origin for new conceptions of work and power. A more restricted emphasis on its automating capacity can provide the occasion for that second kind of revolution—a return to the familiar grounds of industrial society with divergent interests battling for control, augmented by an array of new material resources with which to attack and defend.

The questions that we face today are finally about leadership. Will there be leaders who are able to recognize the historical moment and the choices it presents? Will they find ways to create the organizational conditions in which new visions, new concepts, and a new language of workplace relations can emerge? Will they be able to create organizational innovations that can exploit the unique capacities of the new technology and thus mobilize their organization's productive potential to meet the heightened rigors of global competition? Will there be leaders who understand the crucial role that human beings from each organizational stratum can play in adding value to the production of goods and services? If not, we will be stranded in a new world with old solutions. We will suffer through the unintended consequences of change, because we have failed to understand this technology and how it differs from what came before. By neglecting the unique informating capacity of advanced computer-based technology and ignoring the need for a new vision of work and organization, we will have forfeited the dramatic business benefits it can provide. Instead, we will find ways to absorb the dysfunctions, putting out brush fires and patching wounds in a slow-burning bewilderment.

THE PLAN OF THIS BOOK

The choices for the future cannot be deduced from economic data or from abstract measures of organizational functioning. They are embedded in the living detail of daily life at work as ordinary people confront the dilemmas raised by the transformational qualities of new information technology. For this reason the research presented here focuses upon the texture of human experience—what people say, feel, and do—in dealing with the technological changes that imbue their immediate environment. I studied eight organizations during the five-year period from 1981 to 1986. Each was well known as a model of technological sophistication within its particular industry. In each, information technology was implemented in ways that fundamentally altered how people were required to accomplish their daily work. In most cases, employees found themselves having to operate through the computer medium in order to perform their tasks, and in almost every instance, this was their first direct experience with information technology.

The most treacherous enemy of such research is what philosophers call "the natural attitude," our capacity to live daily life in a way that takes for granted the objects and activities that surround us. Even when we encounter new objects in our environment, our tendency is to experience them in terms of categories and qualities with which we are already familiar. The natural attitude allows us to assume and predict a great many things about each other's behavior without first establishing premises at the outset of every interaction. The natural attitude can also stand in the way of awareness, for ordinary experience has to be made extraordinary in order to become accessible to reflection. This occurs when we encounter a problem: when our actions do not yield the expected results, we are caught by surprise and so are motivated to reflect upon our initial assumptions.[2] Awareness requires a rupture with the world we take for granted; then old categories of experience are called into question and revised. For example, in the early days of photography, the discrepancies between the camera's eye and the human eye were avidly discussed, but, "once they began to think photographically, people stopped talking about photographic distortion, as it was called."[3]

In the organizations I have studied, the introduction of information technology provided just such a sense of crisis. I found a "window of opportunity" during which people who were working with the technology for the first time were ripe with questions and insights regarding the distinct qualities of their experience. As time passed (usually twelve to eighteen months), they would find ways to accommodate their understanding to the altered conditions of work, making it more difficult to extract fresh insights from beneath a new crust of familiarity. For this reason, I also sought out men and women who had experience accomplishing the same tasks in both the context of an earlier technology—pneumatic controls, paper and pencil, face-to-face interaction, mechanical equipment—and the context of information technology—integrated information and control systems, on-line transaction systems, real-time information systems, and computer-conferencing systems. This provided an experiential frame of reference and heightened their awareness of the continuities and discontinuities in the quality of their work experience.

No sector of the economy is exempt from the technological changes under way or the dilemmas they create. This book seeks to understand the generic themes of this transformation as they cut across a range of organizations engaged in what appear to be wholly distinct kinds of work and to compare and contrast the issues that arise within diverse sectors, such as the offices of a large service organization and an automated manufacturing process. As a result, the following chapters portray a diverse set of organizations—from pulp and paper mills to insurance offices to the elite precincts of an international bank. This attention to similarity and difference also bears upon my observations of the various occupational levels within a given organization—workers, clerks, managers, and professionals were each involved in my research effort. There are generic themes that unify their experiences as well as important sources of difference between them.

The organizations studied include two pulp mills and one pulp and paper mill (located in separate divisions of the American Paper Company); Metro Tel, an operating unit of a telecommunications company; the dental claims operation of Consolidated Underwriters Insurance; the offices for stock and bond transfer of a large corporation known as Universal Technology; the Brazilian offices of Global Bank, a major international financial institution; and a large pharmaceutical company called DrugCorp. (See appendix B for a more complete description of the field methodology.) Each site is not equally represented in the thematic discussions within each chapter because the nature of the technological application in a given organization or the particular kind of work in which people were engaged illuminated certain sets of themes in a particularly important way. This study sought to use the range of sites to build a comprehensive map of the territory in question, rather than to perform a comparative analysis between each organization.

The three mills studied were each in the process of implementing a new control interface based upon microprocessor technology. The level of technological innovation in each case represented the state of the art for process control technology. Two of the mills, Piney Wood and Tiger Creek, had traditional work systems with unionized work forces. They were old mills, and the conversion process represented a radical technological change. The third mill, Cedar Bluff, had been recently constructed and was considered to be one of the most automated pulp mills in the world. Its work force had been newly recruited and thus had no prior experience with other forms of pulping technology. Cedar Bluff's work system had been designed to achieve high levels of employee involvement and commitment; it emphasized worker teams and a pay-for-skills approach to compensation.

Metro Tel had recently implemented a computer-based administrative system that linked managers in a central office to workers in field locations. This was an attempt to create a technologically based administrative infrastructure to support their centralized technical operations, such as switching and repairs. The organizational structure was traditional, hierarchical, and highly centralized. Workers were members of the Communications Workers of America union, and most enjoyed long years of service with the company.

In both Consolidated Underwriter Insurance's dental claims operation and the stock and bond transfer offices of Universal Technology, clerical workers were using information technology for the first time. Each of these offices had installed high-volume transaction systems in which clerks used desktop terminals to receive and enter data.

The Brazilian offices of Global Bank represented 20 percent of the parent corporation's international revenues. Like many other banking institutions, Global Bank Brazil had shifted its strategic thinking from an emphasis on loans to an emphasis on the development of new technology-based products and services. Information, rather than money, was now recognized as the bank's most valuable commodity. As a result of Global Bank Brazil's technological sophistication and financial importance, it was chosen as a site for a pilot program developing a new generation of information technology. This technology, technically referred to as the "data base environment," was regarded as an innovation that would profoundly affect the nature of banking, with consequences for the skills and forms of organization appropriate to each banking function. Though Global Bank Brazil had not fully completed its transition to this new stage of technological deployment, this study documents the organization's efforts to grapple with the likely consequences of the technological change.

Finally, the managerial precincts of DrugCorp provided an opportunity to study one of the world's most extensive computer-conferencing systems. Managers and professionals were linked by a computer network that allowed ongoing dialogue, electronic meetings, and rapid communication. Their experiences with this technology reveal much about the emerging structure of communication within the computerized organization.

This book is structured to reflect the succession of dilemmas that typically accompany an organization's transformation to advanced computer-based technology. Part 1 is directed toward the dilemmas associated with the changing grounds of knowledge as a result of the computer mediation of work. It explores the historical role of the body in both industrial and white-collar work and depicts the emerging demand for intellective skills, that frequently supplant the body as a primary source of know-how. Drawing together data from the mills and the offices, part 1 offers a broad conceptualization of the cognitive and social-psychological requirements for developing and expressing knowledge in the computerized workplace.

Part 2 focuses upon the dilemmas of authority that develop as the new demands for intellective skills blur traditional distinctions between operational and managerial roles. It begins by tracing the historical evolution of managerial authority and proceeds to explore the way in which the managerial hierarchy can subvert the forces of change, using the experiences of the three mills as examples. The mills also illustrate how, despite these attempts to resist change, new roles and relations of authority begin to take shape.

Part 3 concerns the attempts to shore up these threatened authority relations with new techniques of control that draw upon the technology's tendency to heighten the visibility of organizational processes. Managers who doubt the strength of authority-based bonds or who prefer technical certainty to the rigors of managing face-to-face relationships are drawn to the technology as a new source of techniques for shaping the behavior of their subordinates. Their efforts engage a series of organizational responses that, ironically, weaken managerial authority even more profoundly.

The conclusion sets out a portrait of a hypothetical informed workplace. It defines a direction for managerial efforts that would take up the challenge of this historical moment and strike out on a new path. It suggests landmarks as well as pitfalls. It offers a vision.

PART ONE

KNOWLEDGE AND
COMPUTER-MEDIATED
WORK

CHAPTER ONE

THE LABORING BODY:
SUFFERING AND SKILL
IN PRODUCTION WORK

We had pleased ourselves with the
delectable visions of the spiritualization of
labor. . . . Each stroke of the hoe was to
uncover some aromatic root of wisdom. . . .
But . . . the clods of earth, which we so
constantly belabored and turned over and
over, were never etherealized into thought.
Our thoughts, on the contrary, were fast
becoming cloddish. Our labor symbolized
nothing and left us mentally sluggish in the
dusk of the evening.

—NATHANIEL HAWTHORNE
The Blithedale Romance

THE AUTOMATIC DOORS

The bleach plant is one of the most complex and treacherous areas of
a pulp mill. In Piney Wood, a large pulp plant built in the mid-1940s,
railroad tank cars filled with chemicals used in the bleaching process
pull up alongside the four-story structure in which dirty brown digested
pulp is turned gleaming white. Each minute, 4,000 gallons of this brown
mash flow through a labyrinth of pipes into a series of cylindrical vats,
where they are washed, treated with chlorine-related chemicals, and

bleached white. No natural light finds its way into this part of the mill. The fluorescent tubes overhead cast a greenish-yellow pall, and the air is laced with enough chemical flavor that as you breathe it, some involuntary wisdom built deep into the human body registers an assault. The floors are generally wet, particularly in the areas right around the base of one of the large vats that loom like raised craters on a moonscape. Sometimes a washer runs over, spilling soggy cellulose knee-deep across the floor. When this happens, the men put on their high rubber boots and shovel up the mess.

The five stages of the bleaching process include hundreds of operating variables. The bleach operator must monitor and control the flow of stock, chemicals, and water, judge color and viscosity, attend to time, temperature, tank levels, and surge rates—the list goes on. Before computer monitoring and control, an operator in this part of the mill would make continual rounds, checking dials and graph charts located on the equipment, opening and shutting valves, keeping an eye on vat levels, snatching a bit of pulp from a vat to check its color, sniff it, or squeeze it between his fingers ("Is it slick? Is it sticky?") to determine its density or to judge the chemical mix.

In 1981 a central control room was constructed in the bleach plant. A science fiction writer's fantasy, it is a gleaming glass bubble that seems to have erupted like a mushroom in the dark, moist, toxic atmosphere of the plant. The control room reflects a new technological era for continuous-process production, one in which microprocessor-based sensors linked to computers allow remote monitoring and control of the key process variables. In fact, the entire pulp mill was involved in this conversion from the pneumatic control technology of the 1940s to the microprocessor-based information and control technology of the 1980s.

Inside the control room, the air is filtered and hums with the sound of the air-conditioning unit built into the wall between the control room and a small snack area. Workers sit on orthopedically designed swivel chairs covered with a royal blue fabric, facing video display terminals. The terminals, which display process information for the purposes of monitoring and control, are built into polished oak cabinets. Their screens glow with numbers, letters, and graphics in vivid red, green, and blue. The floor here is covered with slate-gray carpeting; the angled countertops on which the terminals sit are rust brown and edged in black. The walls are covered with a wheat-colored fabric and the molding repeats the polished oak of the cabinetry. The dropped ceiling is of a bronzed metal, and from it is suspended a three dimensional structure into which lights have been recessed and angled to provide the right amount of illumination without creating glare on the screens. The color scheme is repeated on the ceiling—soft tones of beige, rust, brown, and gray in a geometric design.

The terminals each face toward the front of the room—a windowed wall that opens onto the bleach plant. The steel beams, metal tanks, and maze of thick pipes visible through those windows appear to be a world away in a perpetual twilight of steam and fumes, like a city street on a misty night, silent and dimly lit. What is most striking about the juxtaposition of these two worlds, is how a man (and there were only men working in this part of the mill) traverses the boundary between them.

The control room is entered through an automatic sliding-glass door. At the push of a button, the two panels of the door part, and when you step forward, they quickly close behind you. You then find yourself facing two more automatic doors at right angles to one another. The door on the right leads to a narrow snack area with booths, cabinets, a coffee machine, and a refrigerator. The door to the left leads into the control room. It will not open until the first door has shut. This ensures that the filtered air within the control room is protected from the fumes and heat of the bleach plant. The same routine holds in reverse. When a man leaves the control room, he presses a button next to the frame on the inner door, which opens electronically. He then steps through it into the tiny chamber where he must wait for the door to seal behind him so that he can push a second button on the outer door and finally exit into the plant.

This is not what most men do when they move from the control room out into the bleach plant. They step through the inner door, but they do not wait for that door to seal behind them before opening the second door. Instead, they force their fingertips through the rubber seal down the middle of the outer door and, with a mighty heft of their shoulders, pry open the seam and wrench the door apart. Hour after hour, shift after shift, week after week, too many men pit the strength in their arms and shoulders against the electronic mechanism that controls the doors. Three years after the construction of the sleek, glittering glass bubble, the outer door no longer closes tightly. A gap of several inches, running down the center between the two panels of glass, looks like a battle wound. The door is crippled.

"The door is broke now because the men pushed it too hard comin' in and out," says one operator. In talking to the men about this occurrence, so mundane as almost to defy reflection, I hear not only a simple impatience and frustration but also something deeper: a forward momentum of their bodies, whose physical power seems trivialized by the new circumstances of their work; a boyish energy that wants to break free; a subtle rebellion against the preprogrammed design that orders their environment and always knows best. Yet these are the men who also complained, "The fumes in the bleach plant will kill you. You can't take that chlorine no matter how big and bad you are. It will bleach your brains and no one (in management) gives a damn."

Technology represents intelligence systematically applied to the problem of the body. It functions to amplify and surpass the organic limits of the body; it compensates for the body's fragility and vulnerability. Industrial technology has substituted for the human body in many of the processes associated with production and so has redefined the limits of production formerly imposed by the body. As a result, society's capacity to produce things has been extended in a way that is unprecedented in human history. This achievement has not been without its costs, however. In diminishing the role of the worker's body in the labor process, industrial technology has also tended to diminish the importance of the worker. In creating jobs that require less human effort, industrial technology has also been used to create jobs that require less human talent. In creating jobs that demand less of the body, industrial production has also tended to create jobs that give less to the body, in terms of opportunities to accrue knowledge in the production process. These two-sided consequences have been fundamental for the growth and development of the industrial bureaucracy, which has depended upon the rationalization and centralization of knowledge as the basis of control.

These consequences also help explain the worker's historical ambivalence toward automation. It is an ambivalence that draws upon the loathing as well as the commitment that human beings can experience toward their work. Throughout most of human history, work has inescapably meant the exertion and often the depletion of the worker's body. Yet only in the context of such exertion was it possible to learn a trade and to master skills. Since the industrial revolution, the accelerated progress of automation has generally meant a reduction in the amount of effort required of the human body in the labor process. It has also tended to reduce the quality of skills that a worker must bring to the activity of making something. Industrial technology has been developed in a manner that increases its capacity to spare the human body, while at the same time it has usurped opportunities for the development and performance of skills that only the body can learn and remember. In their treatment of the automatic doors, the bleach plant workers have created a living metaphor that reflects this ambivalence toward automation. They want to be protected from toxic fumes, but they simultaneously feel a stubborn rebellion against a structure that no longer requires either the strength or the know-how lodged in their bodies.

The progress of automation has been associated with both a general decline in the degree of know-how required of the worker and a decline in the degree of physical punishment to which he or she must be subjected. Information technology, however, does have the potential to redirect the historical trajectory of automation. The intrinsic power of its informating capacity can change the basis upon which knowledge is developed and applied in the industrial production process by lifting knowledge entirely out of the body's domain. The new technology signals the transposition of work activities to the abstract domain of information. Toil no longer implies physical depletion. "Work" becomes the manipulation of symbols, and when this occurs, the nature of skill is redefined. The application of technology that preserves the body may no longer imply the destruction of knowledge; instead, it may imply the reconstruction of knowledge of a different sort.

The significance of this transposition is impossible to grasp without reference to the grounds of knowledge for workers in the past. In the factory, knowledge was intimately bound up with the efforts of the laboring body. The development of industrial technology can be read as a chronicle of attempts to grapple with the body's role in production as a source of both effort and skill and with the specific responses these attempts have evoked from workers and managers. The centrality of the body's historical meaning for production has informed the self-understanding of managers and workers and the relationship between them. It has also been a salient force guiding the development and application of manufacturing technology. A better understanding of what the body has meant for industrial work and how it has been linked to the logic of automation will sharpen an appreciation of the character of the current transformation and its capacity to provoke comprehensive change in the relationships that structure the workplace. Before deciphering the present or imagining the future, it is first necessary to take ourselves out of the twentieth century and return, if only briefly, to a time when the nature of work was both simpler and more miserable, a time when work was above all the problem of the laboring body.

THE FRONTIER OF CONTEMPT

The world of production, where primary materials are processed and goods are manufactured, has long been marked by a great divide between those who give of their bodies and those who are exempt from physical depletion. Yet those exempted from bodily alteration may give of themselves in other ways. Their physical presence may be required for purposes of interpersonal influence, communication, and coordination. They may give of their time and attention in both supervisory and analytical activities, or they may give of themselves more abstractly as sources of investment capital or expert knowledge. However, the groups that stand on either side of this divide constitute fundamentally distinct modes of involvement with the production enterprise. The experiential distance between them is one important living source of the divergent interests in terms of which workers and managers have tended to define themselves. Workers facing the physical requirements of labor seek ways to preserve their bodies from exertion, while managers are charged with extracting the maximum feasible effort from the work force.

This divide has been an important characteristic of social hierarchies in virtually every culture known to the historical record. Wealth and power have everywhere meant an escape from toil: the unequal distribution and concentration of wealth and power within a small group is a phenomenon of such universality that the French historian Fernand Braudel has called it a "constant law of societies, a structural law that admits of no exception."[1] In the societies of preindustrial Europe, the decisive challenge of social mobility was to permanently rid oneself of the stigma of physical labor and then to repudiate the commercial activities that made such an escape from work possible. European nobility defined itself by the gulf it created between its members and the hardship of labor. Of the bourgeois families who gained access to the highest ranks of society Braudel writes that "the only feature they had in common with the authentic nobility was their rejection of trade or labor, their taste for idleness or rather leisure, which was for them synonymous with reading and learned discussion with their peers."[2]

This repugnance toward labor rides a long wave in Western history, a wave that has not, even yet, reached its crest. In the religious zeal of the early Middle Ages, trades that trafficked in money were considered illicit, materialism being an indication of a lack of faith. With the growing urbanization, more detailed division of labor, and accelerated mercantilism of the late Middle Ages, however, this view of economic activity took an important turn: "A new frontier of contempt arose right in the midst of the new classes and even within professions. . . . Work itself no longer constituted the distinction between respectable and contemptible categories; instead, it was manual labor that had come to be the key factor in the frontier between respect and contempt. . . . Across from the *manouvriers* and *brassiers* who worked with hands and arms, was the patrician world, the new aristocracy, consisting of all those who did no manual labor: employers and rentiers."[3] Even the guilds were influenced by the contempt toward manual work. Some of them required entrants to have relinquished their trade for twelve months before admission. In 1241 a municipality in Flanders excluded from the urban magistracy all robbers, coiners, and "those who have not given up all manual work for at least one year."[4]

The Middle Ages produced a conception of labor infused with a loathing drawn from three traditions: (1) the Greco-Roman legacy that associated labor with slavery, (2) the barbarian heritage that disdained those who worked the land and extolled the warrior who gained his livelihood in bloody booty, and (3) Judeo-Christian theology that admired contemplation over action. For centuries European literature and iconography depicted peasants as huge-headed monsters or wild beasts lurking the depths of Europe's dark forests.[5] Labor came to humanity with the fall from grace and was at best a penitential sacrifice enabling purity through humiliation. Labor was toil, distress, trouble, fatigue—

an exertion both painful and compulsory. Labor was our animal condition, struggling to survive in dirt and darkness.

Freedom from the necessity of labor has been a prominent feature of most utopian thinking. English civil war sects awaited the coming of the Fifth Monarchy because it was said that it would abolish painful labor. Bishop Godwin's *Man in the Moone*, published in 1638, reported on a society in which "food groweth everywhaer without labour," while all the necessities of life were amply provided. Other utopian writers of the period, Campanella, Winstanley, Bellars, and More, saw the reduction of labor as an important feature of a wholesome moral life.[6] Sir Thomas More's *Utopia* limited the consumption of commodities to the "necessary" and the "comfortable," in order that any surplus labor could be devoted to learning. The six-hour work day was seen as adequate, and if it turned out to be excessive, the community would further curtail the number of hours assigned to work: "What time may possibly be spared from the necessary occupations and affairs of the Commonwealth, all that the Citizens should withdraw from the bodily service to the free liberty of the mind and garnishing of the same."[7]

The recent English translation of the historian Norbert Elias's *The Civilizing Process* has helped shed light on a deeper explanation for this repugnance toward work.[8] While a full description of Elias's pathbreaking analysis is beyond the scope of this discussion, it is worth highlighting the skeleton of his discoveries as they contribute to an understanding of the enduring relationship between the universality of social hierarchy and the fact that physical labor is everywhere considered to constitute its lowest echelons.

Elias studied books of etiquette and other documentation of daily life from the early Middle Ages through the eighteenth century. He discovered that norms of daily conduct, particularly those that bear upon bodily functions, have changed radically throughout the course of the centuries. When in 1530 Erasmus wrote his treatise *On Civility in Children,* he provided a portrait, refracted through his admonitions, of contemporary standards of behavior. Our own sensibilities are overcome with repugnance and horror at behavior that was accepted as routine in the sixteenth century. Elias points out the "infinite care and matter-of-factness" with which Erasmus addressed habits concerning bodily functions in his effort to encourage more "civilized" standards: "There should be no snot on the nostrils. . . . A peasant wipes his nose on his cap and coat, a sausage maker on his arm and elbow. It does not show much more propriety to use one's hand and then wipe it on one's clothing. . . . It is more decent to take up the snot in a cloth, preferably while turning away. If when blowing the nose with two fingers something falls to the ground, it must be immediately trodden away with the foot. The same applies to spittle."[9]

Elias found that behaviors related to table manners, bodily functions, nose blowing, spitting, sleeping, sex, and aggression that we have come to consider barbaric and disgusting were once routine. He argues that the process of curbing these behaviors was set into motion by, and in turn helped to promote, stable, centralized forms of social organization. The embryo for these modern forms was evident in the court societies that by the end of the Middle Ages, had begun to spread across Europe.

> Here were created the models of more pacified social intercourse which more or less all classes needed, following the transformation of European society at the end of the Middle Ages; here the coarse habits, the wilder, more uninhibited customs of medieval society with its warrior upper class, the corollaries of an uncertain, constantly threatened life, were "softened", "polished" and "civilized". The pressure of court life, the vying for the favour of the prince or the "great"; then, more generally, the necessity to distinguish oneself from others and to fight for opportunities with relatively peaceful means, through intrigue and diplomacy, enforced a constraint on the affects, a self-discipline and self-control, a peculiarly courtly rationality. . . . This increased restraint and regulation of elementary urges is bound up with increased social constraint, the growing dependence of the nobility on the central lord, the king or prince.[10]

Elias reminds us that violence was inscribed into the very structure of medieval society. Rape and death, the hunting of men and animals, were part of everyday life. "The documents suggest unimaginable emotional outbursts in which—with rare exceptions—everyone who is able abandons himself to extreme pleasures of ferocity, murder, torture, destruction, and sadism."[11] Everyday objects like the fork (at first a source of mockery and still a rare luxury in the seventeenth century), the handkerchief, and the nightgown, or the new sense of repulsion felt at the sight of humans defecating, spitting a piece of food back into the common bowl, or picking their teeth with the communal knife, all symbolized the progress of the civilizing process—an increased control over and distance from the animal life of the human body: "People have begun to construct an affective wall between their bodies and those of others. The fork has been one of the means of drawing distances between other people's bodies and one's own. One repulses the body, isolates it, feels ashamed of it, tries to ignore it. . . . For many centuries, this wall did not exist."[12]

Elias's discoveries illuminate an unconscious dimension of Western history. The consolidation of stable social hierarchies based upon centralized power and the rule of law demanded a new level of behavioral control. The body had to be reinterpreted as a source of disgust and as an object of discipline.[13] This reinterpretation, and the forms of conduct that developed from it, first took root at the highest levels of the emerging society, where the pressures of interdependence and political opportunism were most acute. These in turn became the models for behavior that successively lower social strata would imitate and finally assimilate.

It is easy to see that gradations in status are related to gradations in power, but Elias's work alerts us to the fact that such differences in status parallel another axis of social comparison whose levels are marked by degrees of distance from the body's own animal life and the animal life of surrounding bodies. The ability to maintain one's distance from the body developed as an important sign of hierarchical position. It has served to intensify the repugnance toward forms of activity that involve the body in sweating, heaving, grunting, hauling, and carting; that expose the body to pain and discomfort from extreme temperature, extended muscular effort, inclement weather, or hurtful substances; and that so immerse human consciousness in the sentient surroundings of effort and fatigue that one fails to notice (or care) whether the nose is dripping, the sweated body is giving off an unbearable stench, or filthy fingers have been used to grab a piece of food—the very proprieties that came to be seen as part of a complex of behaviors distinguishing the barbaric from the civilized.

There is reason enough to want to avoid exhausting work, but the constancy of repugnance was not confined to forms of labor that were extremely punishing. As noted earlier, in the membership practices of some guilds, even the craftsworker was liable to be an object of contempt because of the manual nature of that work. Such repugnance is in itself an act of distancing. It is both a rejection of the animal body and an affirmation of one's ability to translate the impulses of that body into the infinitely more subtle behavioral codes that mediate power in complex organizations. Once this translation occurs, the body is no longer the vehicle for involuntary affective or physical displays. Instead, it becomes the instrument of carefully crafted gestures and behaviors designed to achieve a calculated effect in an environment where interpersonal influence and even a kind of rudimentary psychological insight are critical to success. In the interpersonal world of court society, the body's knowledge involved the ability to be attuned to the psychological needs and demands of others, particularly of superiors, and to produce subtly detailed nonverbal behavior that reflected this awareness.

> The court is a kind of stock exchange; as in every "good society", an estimate of the value of each individual is continuously being formed. But here his value has its real foundation . . . in the favour he enjoys with the king, the influence he has with other mighty ones. . . . All this, favour, influence, importance, this whole complex and dangerous game in which physical force and direct affective outbursts are prohibited and a threat to existence, demands of each participant a constant foresight and an exact knowledge of every other, of his position and value in the network of courtly opinions; it exacts precise attunement of his own behavior to this value. . . . "A man who knows the court is master of his gestures, of his eyes and his expression; he is deep, impenetrable. He dissimulates the bad turns he does, smiles at his enemies, suppresses his ill-temper, disguises his passions, disavows his heart, acts against his feelings."[14]

The tension between hierarchical status and the animal body also may be sustained by the psychologic need to defend oneself from the fact of the body's tragic weakness. The animality of the body is a source of repulsive events that must be controlled, and the most repulsive and least controllable of these events is death itself. Death is the inevitable conclusion ordained by the animality of the body and poses a series of challenges (in addition to the central challenge, which is the cessation of life). Death underscores the commonality of all who share life; death highlights the vulnerability of the body; death reminds the living of the ultimate uncontrollability of the body. Each of these problems is in a way addressed by the act of distantiation. Hierarchical distance rejects the display of animality that is common and deindividualized for civilized conduct, intricately fashioned by personality, wit, and will. Distantiation, in promoting forms of control over the body, can protect its fragility and, in some ways, its health. Finally, distantiation allows us to avoid reminders of animality, thus making it possible to suppress an awareness of the body's inevitable decline.

The close relationship between the rejection of animality and the progress of civilization is at the heart of our modern conception of work. Marx expressed this relationship when he argued that mastery of the material world was the basis upon which man humanized himself and developed culture. This in fact is the civilizing process; *humanization* means tempering animality with rationality, aesthetic grace, and moral choice. It is a process that has informed much of the impetus toward the extension of material culture powerfully exemplified in the development of industrial technology, which simultaneously frees the production process from the organic limits of the body, frees consumers from having to exercise bodily effort in order to enjoy the panoply of goods produced by the machine system, shapes workers who are capable of exercising considerable control over their own spontaneous impulses (and so can conform to the behavioral demands of mechanized production), and gradually diminishes the most painful forms of exertion associated with the work of making things.

Indeed, the worker's body posed a complicated set of problems for industrial management. Industrial work depended upon the laboring body as much for its raw energy as for its special gifts. In many industries, the worker's body remained central to production well into the early decades of the twentieth century. Only then, in many cases, was labor-saving technology diffused widely enough to substantially alter the role of the body in the production process. If work was to be performed economically and effectively, then the impulsive behavior associated with the body's animality would have to be disciplined. The members of court society were required to turn their bodies into instruments of interpersonal influence, instruments for *acting-with*. Industrial workers were also required to turn their bodies into instruments, but instruments for *acting-on*—for producing calculated effects on material and equipment. In the following section, we will see how the first generations of factory owners and their managers were frustrated, confounded, and sometimes ruined as they searched for the methods by which to translate the animal body into a more precise instrument that could be applied to increasingly systematized processes of production.

THE EARLY FACTORY AND THE PROBLEM OF THE BODY

There is ample evidence that throughout the fifteenth and sixteenth centuries, workers were not silent in their degradation. Social cleavage took its toll in thousands of peasant insurrections as well as violent disturbances among urban workers.[15] It was not until the industrial revolution, however, that the focus of the conflict between worker and employer came to rest on the detailed performance of the worker's body and the degree of discipline to which the body might legitimately be subjected.

Consider the case of Britain at the brink of industrialization during the second half of the eighteenth century. For all the bone-crushing labor demanded of the agricultural worker or the cottage weaver, the traditional rhythms of exertion and play were a world removed from the behavioral demands of industrial production. Work patterns were irregular, alternating between intense effort and idleness. Most work activities emanated from the home, and the distractions of the family, the taverns, and the social web of the community limited any undivided commitment to work.

Cottage workers, upon whom most textile production depended, were relatively impervious to the middleman's demand for heightened productivity. Their inclination to physical exertion was guided more by their own immediate needs than by acquisitive ambitions. Throughout the eighteenth century, the British Parliament passed legislation requiring ever-shorter turnaround times for finished goods from domestic workers and imposing increasingly severe sanctions on those who did not comply. Such sanctions were difficult to enforce; finally, only the pressure of immediate supervision was able to induce a greater level and consistency of effort from workers.[16] The need to intensify production was the driving force behind the establishment of the early factories and workshops, even before the widespread diffusion of the steam engine.[17] There is evidence that workers submitted to the physical rigors of factory discipline only when other alternatives had been exhausted.[18] But even those employers who were able to recruit a labor force still faced the haphazard and spasmodic rhythms with which their new employees approached their work.

The employers deplored the fact that the old subsistence mentality had carried over into the new work settings. Of the piece-rate worker they complained, "At the precise inch of cloth he stopped, in the mines, at the necessary pound of coal."[19] Workers in their turn bemoaned the loss of freedom and rebelled at the prospect of long confinement and steady production. The highlander, it was said, "never sits at ease at a loom; it is like putting a deer in the plough."[20] Attendance was irregular; workers would sometimes stay away from the job for days and send for their wages at the end of the week. In South Wales during the 1840s it was estimated that workers were absent 20 percent of the year, a figure that reached as high as 33 percent during the fortnight after their monthly payday.[21]

One study of Birmingham, England, from 1766 to 1876, found that well into the nineteenth century, workers continued to celebrate Saint Monday—a weekly day of leisure spent in the alehouse enjoying drink, bar games, entertainments, "pugilism," and animal fights.[22] The tradition of Saint Monday followed from the bouts of weekend drinking and represented deeply held attitudes toward a potential surplus of wages: "The men . . . [are] regulated by the expense of their families, and their necessities; it is very well known that they will not go further than necessity prompts them."[23]

The industrial entrepreneurs tried, usually without success, to prohibit the observance of Monday as a holiday. Boulton and Watt's first enterprise foundered on the continual drunkenness of their work force.[24] The owner of a button-making factory decided that although he would not be able to control his workers, he would make an effort to train his apprentices in more industrious work habits. His diary records his frustration: "This evening Edward Lingard's misconduct in going to the Public House in the afternoon for drink, contrary to my inclination and notwithstanding I had forbidden him from it only yesterday—this I say, and meeting him on his way back, induced me hastily to strike him. With which my middle finger was so stunned as to give me much pain."[25] In addition to the time lost through observing Monday as a holiday, harvest time and other traditional feast days kept workers away. In 1776 the famous Josiah Wedgwood who pioneered new techniques of pottery production and business management, wrote to a colleague: "Our men have been at play 7 days this week, it being Burslem Wakes. I have rough'd and smoothed them over, & promised them a long Xmas, but I know it is all in vain, for Wakes must be observed though the World was to end with them."[26]

Nineteenth-century American industrialists faced a similar set of problems when it came to honing the worker's body as an instrument of production. The owner of a Pennsylvania ironworks complained of frequent "frolicking" that sometimes lasted for days, along with hunting, harvesting, wedding parties, and holiday celebrations. One manufacturer filled his diary with these notes: "All hands drunk; Jacob Ventling hunting; molders all agree to quit work and went to the beach. Peter Cox very drunk and gone to bed. . . . Edward Rutter off a-drinking. It was reported he got drunk on cheese."[27] In 1817 a Medford shipbuilder refused his men grog privileges and they all quit.[28] The ship's carpenter in one New York shipyard describes the typical workday: cakes and pastries in the early morning and again in the late morning, a trip to the grog shop by eleven for whiskey, a big lunch at half past three, a visit from the candyman at five, and supper, ending the workday, at sundown. He recalled one worker who left for grog ten times a day. A cigar manufacturer complained that his men worked no more than two or three hours a day; the rest of the time was spent in the beer saloon, playing pinochle. Coopers were famous for a four-day work week; and the potters in Trenton, New Jersey, immigrants from Staffordshire, were known to work in "great bursts of activity" and then lay off for several days.[29]

We can see that the early apostles of industrialism had to confront the still-rudimentary progress of the civilizing process as it bore upon work behavior. The spontaneous, instinctually gratifying behavior of the new industrial worker had to be suppressed, and that energy channeled into the controlled behavior demanded by the intensification of production. The factory became a pedagogic institution where the new standards of conduct and sensibility, generally referred to as "labor discipline," would be learned. The exhaustive measures that employers took to thwart the animal body are a sign of its very intractability.[30]

The notion of labor discipline signaled a very concrete problem: how to get the human body to remain in one place, pay attention, and perform consistently over a fixed period of time. Elaborate systems of fines were developed, minutely tailored to extinguish particular expressions of the impulsive body. For example, many fines sought to keep the body stationary. One work rule at Haslingden Mill about 1830 read, "Any person found from the usual place of work, except for necessary purposes, or talking with anyone out of their own alley, will be fined."[31] The Hammonds report fines at a textile mill near Manchester for "going further than the roving room door when fetching rovings" and for "any spinner found in another's wheel gate."[32] Ashworth fined his weavers for being found "out of the room."[33] Other fines addressed the sounds that emitted from the body at work: punishable infractions included singing, whistling, swearing, and yelling. Some fines, intended to enforce a fixity of gaze and attention, punished workers for opening a window. Still other fines concerned the body's smell and appearance: workers were fined for being dirty, for not changing their shirts at least twice a week, and for spitting. Finally, there were fines to discourage aggressiveness, sexuality, and disorderliness—throwing water, seducing females, being drunk, arriving late, or not showing up at all.[34]

American employers also found that only the severest fining policies had an effect on work habits. Workers were routinely fined up to half a day's pay for singing, talking, visiting, or being late.[35] In 1859 a mill agent in Chicopee, Massachusetts, complained of the general indisposition of factory hands toward steady work, and in the years preceding World War I, it was still not unusual for as much as one-tenth of the work force to be missing on a given day.[36] Quit rates around the turn of the century were high—textile mills, meat-packing plants, automobile plants, steel mills, and machine works often showed annual turnover rates of 100 percent.[37] One survey showed that between 1905 and 1917, the majority of industrial workers changed jobs at least once every three years. Between 1907 and 1910, turnover in the woolen industry was between 113 percent and 163 percent. It reached 232 percent in New York City garment shops in 1912, 252 percent in a sample of Detroit factories in 1916, and 370 percent in the Ford Motor Company in 1913.[38]

These quit rates reflect not only the ambivalence and enduring orneriness of American workers but also the increasingly severe pressure that employers and managers brought to bear on dysfunctional, uncontrolled, and irregular behavior. Many scholars have argued that the introduction of steam power (and, later, other forms of expensive equipment) did more to consolidate the new behavioral norms than the earlier systems of fines alone.[39] This was in part because employers, in an effort to fully utilize their capital investment, became more ruthless in their willingness to dismiss workers who did not comply with the regularity of effort required to efficiently exploit the new machinery and in part because workers had to conform to a pace and quality of production increasingly driven by the machine, rather than by their own traditions and habits of organization.

As traditional working conditions grew scarce, worker resistance to labor discipline itself became more rationalized. The trade union movement set itself to limiting working hours, maintaining employment levels, and protecting wages, but a parallel approach of greater informality and striking continuity with older traditions also emerged. Workers began to act self-consciously to limit their efforts and so preserve their bodies. As early as 1757, Josiah Tucker wrote in a pamphlet entitled "Instructions for Travelers" a description of domestic weavers transplanted to factory life. He provides one of the earlier descriptions of what was to become a central strategy for the industrial worker—withholding effort: "They think it no crime to get as much wages and to do as little for it as they possibly can, to lie and cheat and do any other bad thing, provided it is only against their master whom they look upon as their common enemy, with whom no faith is to be kept. . . . Their only happiness is to get drunk and make life pass away with as little thought as possible."[40]

Though skilled workers were indignant at the idea of deliberate slacking, by the end of the nineteenth century the British unions had come to recognize the characteristics of the trade cycle and to think of their effort as a commodity to be withheld or controlled in the service of free market bargaining.[41] Work banking, goldbricking, soldiering, are the modern terms that convey the legacy of this earlier clash between two wildly different conceptions of the standard of work discipline to which a body should conform.

In the American factory at the turn of the century, the foreman had primary responsibility for implementing management's goals: he was the "undisputed ruler of his department, gang, crew, or ship."[42] When in 1912 a congressional committee investigated the United States Steel Corporation, they attempted to understand just how the foreman functioned. They learned that foremen throughout American industry practiced something known as the "driving method," an approach to supervision that combined authoritarian combativeness with physical intimidation in order to extract the maximum effort from the worker. The driving method was well suited to work that depended upon the consistent exertion of the human body. The foreman's profanity, threats, and punishments were complemented by the workers' methods for limiting output. Methods of withholding labor varied somewhat from industry to industry and might be modified according to economic conditions, but the underlying spirit was everywhere the same—to protect the body by tempering exertion.

There were numerous stories of new employees who were approached by older, presumably wiser, workmen. "See here, young
fellow, you're working too fast. You'll spoil our job for us if you
don't go slower." If a friendly admonition did not have the desired
effect and the man was judged a "rooter" or "rusher," social pressure, threats, and even violence might follow.[43]

The protective response of so many workers to the demands made
on their bodies is also the source of many work procedures that have
been formalized and institutionalized in labor contracts and work rules.
Studies by Lloyd Ulman and Sumner Slichter have shown how glassworkers', textile workers', and metalworkers' unions used agreements
on production standards to restrict the driving method of supervision.[44]
Work rules codified restrictive labor withholding practices, transforming them from informal methods of self-protection to deliberate contractual agreements.[45]

THE PARADOX OF THE BODY

Until now we have treated the body in one of its aspects—as the scene
and source of effort. This was the body that had to be disciplined if
effort was to be drawn forth in a way that complemented the demands
of an intensified, collectivized, and regulated production process. But
the body as the scene of effort, the body to be protected, held a special
paradox. For it was also through the body's exertions that learning
occurred, and for those who were to become skilled workers, long
years of physically demanding experience were an unavoidable requirement. This was the reward of physical involvement, since there was
virtually no access to the craftsperson's skills short of an investment in
years of effort. The body's meaning for production was not just to be
an animal source of motive power or a pair of hands for an endless
series of monotonous performances. Where the skilled worker was concerned, the body's sentience was also highly structured by a felt knowledge of materials and procedures. These twin functions of the body—
as a source of skill and as a source of effort—complicated the way in
which employers confronted the problems of labor discipline and the

speed with which they invested in labor-saving technology, just as they complicated workers' responses to that technology.

The historian Raphael Samuel has demonstrated that the body continued to play a central role in production, as a source of both effort and skill, throughout the nineteenth century in activities as diverse as mining, and quarrying, agriculture, gardening, and other forms of food production, construction, glass, pottery, and leather trades, woodworking, and metallurgy.[46] His examples are drawn from nineteenth-century Britain, but many of the labor processes he describes were prevalent in America as well.

There were few segments of the mid-Victorian British economy that steam power and machinery had not touched, but fewer still did not depend upon hand technology. Many factors impeded the progress of labor-saving machinery. Many trade unions were successful in resisting the encroachment of machinery on their crafts. From the employers' side, however, there were other compelling reasons. Wages were low, and the possibilities of increasing productivity with hand technology had not yet been exhausted. Employers often found other sources of efficiency in an increasingly minute division of labor and in the use of cheaper labor-saving materials. Market uncertainties made capital investment risky; besides, there was still a plentiful supply of cheap labor. Skill was also an important part of the problem. Ebullient descriptions of the new forms of "self-acting" machinery dominated trade journals of the day, but the new, more automatic machines were often fraught with technical difficulties and could not be relied upon as a substitute for skilled work. Moreover, consumers continued to value the quality of work that only a craftsworker could produce.

Samuel describes the wide variety of jobs that required nothing more than the effort of the laboring body. Coal was excavated by pick and shovel—"tools of the most primitive description, requiring the utmost amount of bodily exertion."[47] Clay-getting required working with a heavy pick. Masses of slime had to be stirred and trampled into the right consistency. Bakeries produced bread almost entirely by manual labor, the hardest operation being that of preparing the dough, "usually carried on in one dark corner of a cellar, by a man, stripped naked down to the waist, and painfully engaged in extricating his fingers from a gluey mass into which he furiously plunges alternately his clenched fists."[48]

There were many occupations in which the pain and physical alteration that resulted from such exertion were inseparable from the subtle and complex skills from which a craftsperson derived pride and economic power. One account of candy making in an Edinburgh factory ends this way: "The whole process . . . requires great skill in the manipulation and it also requires the most severe and continuous muscular labor. We know, indeed, of no other kind of labour that requires more. Not a muscle or joint of the whole body remains inactive. It has quite a marvelous effect in taking down superfluous fat. It is well know that a stout man taken perhaps from lozenge making, and put to work on the hot pan, becomes in six weeks converted into a living skeleton."[49]

In glassmaking, everything was done by hand, "the gatherers taking the 'metal' from the furnace at the end of an iron rod, the blower shaping the body of the bottle with his breath, while the maker who finished the bottle off . . . tooled the neck with a light spring-handled pair of tongs. Each bottle was individually made no matter what household, shop or tavern it was destined for."[50] There were steady inroads made by machinery in this industry, but despite its labor-saving potential, glassmakers and their union organizations bitterly resisted and successfully impeded its progress. In 1878 one observer summarized the glassmakers' ambivalence: "If in many industries the substitution of mechanical for manual labor offers important advantages because . . . it decreases a man's fatigue, we do not think it will have the same effect on the absolutely special work of the glass industry, and we fear that in depriving glassworkers of difficult tasks we will destroy their skill as well as the artistic talents of which glassmakers have the right to be proud."[51]

Pottery work was very physical and involved personal handling of the clay at every stage of production. Hands, thumbs, fingers, and palms were the sources of a delicately nuanced skill that guided the throwing and shaping of each item: "Dippers prepared the ware for firing by steeping it in a glaze tub. The right hand and arm are plunged nearly up to the elbow as he passes the piece of ware through the liquid. . . . Then with a rapid circular movement of the hand . . . a movement that only years of practice can teach . . . he makes the glaze flow thin and even over the surface."[52]

In the leather trades, the process of currying, which softened the leather for saddlery, coach linings, and shoes, was a highly skilled trade that required a laborer's strength to perform the heavy work of slashing, shaving, and pummeling the hide. Ironmaking was another industry that depended upon combinations of skill and strength. New technology utilizing steam power to pound and roll metal together, and new puddling furnaces based on chemical reactions rather than mechanical action, had made the production process cheaper and had increased output. These innovations were not entirely labor-saving, however. In many cases they required new skills, even as they increased the physical demands of work. "The puddler, who had the key role in the new process, was given a task that was simultaneously highly skilled and exhausting, turning a viscous mass of liquid into metal. He worked in conditions of tremendous heat, violently agitating the metal as it boiled, rabbling it from side to side in the furnace, and then gathering it at the end of a rod while the molten liquid thickened. . . . The men had to relieve each other every few minutes, so great was the exertion and so intense the heat, but even so it was said that every ounce of excess fat was drained from them. . . . Few puddlers, it was said, lived beyond the age of 50."[53]

These are just a few examples of the body's central presence as the source of both effort and skill in myriad industrial operations throughout the nineteenth century. In many cases, machinery was used to replace humans in supplying the motive power for various subprocesses of production. In most trades, though, labor-saving machinery developed slowly, and many factors inhibited its progress. Sometimes the new machinery, in amplifying the capacity of the human body to perform a given operation and thus increasing output, could also intensify the human participation that was required and thus exacerbate the problems of physical depletion.

Samuel notes that labor-saving machinery spread more rapidly in America, owing to a scarcity of labor and consequent higher wages. However, the historian of technology David Hounshell has recently shown that in some of the largest and most successful American firms, handwork and skilled machine work prevailed during most of the nineteenth century. For example, the Singer Sewing Machine Company was not able to produce perfectly interchangeable parts. As a result, they relied on skilled fitters to assemble each product. The McCormick Reaper Works employed crude manufacturing techniques. Production depended upon skilled machinists, blacksmiths, carpenters, and molders.[54] In 1911 an observer of the American steel industry tried to convey the notion that skilled work did not imply diminished physical exertion: "New skills, like the puddler's, the catchers, or the machinists

included very heavy manual work. As one worker speaking about working in a steel mill declared: 'Hard! I guess it's hard. I lost forty pounds
the first three months I came into the business. It sweats the life out
of a man!' The differences between the work performed by the skilled
workers and the laborers was not of an "intellectual" versus manual
activity. The difference lay in the content of a similarly heavy manual
work: a content of rationality of participation for skilled workers versus
one of total indifference for laborers.[55]

The work of the skilled craftsperson may not have been "intellectual," but it was knowledgeable. These nineteenth-century workers
participated in a form of knowledge that had always defined the activity
of making things. It was knowledge that accrues to the sentient body
in the course of its activity; knowledge inscribed in the laboring body—
in hands, fingertips, wrists, feet, nose, eyes, ears, skin, muscles, shoulders, arms, and legs—as surely as it was inscribed in the brain. It was
knowledge filled with intimate detail of materials and ambience—the
color and consistency of metal as it was thrust into a blazing fire, the
smooth finish of the clay as it gave up its moisture, the supple feel of
the leather as it was beaten and stretched, the strength and delicacy of
glass as it was filled with human breath. These details were known,
though in the practical action of production work, they were rarely
made explicit. Few of those who had such knowledge would have been
able to explain, rationalize, or articulate it. Such skills were learned
through observation, imitation, and action more than they were taught,
reflected upon, or verbalized. For example, James J. Davis, later to
become Warren Harding's Secretary of Labor, learned the skill of puddling iron by working as his father's helper in a Pennsylvania foundry:
"None of us ever went to school and learned the chemistry of it from
books. . . . We learned the trick by doing it, standing with our faces in
the scorching heat while our hands puddled the metal in its glaring
bath."[56]

Though this form of knowledge evades explication, it is not fragile;
on the contrary, it is extremely robust. The swimmer who has been
away from the water for a year, the woman who has not ridden a bicycle
since childhood, the grandmother who has not held an infant since she
weaned her last, the carpenter who has retired his tools, the guitarist
who abandoned her instrument, each of these can confront the object
of their skills—the sea, the bicycle, the crying infant, the wood, the
guitar—and find that the knowledge they once possessed remains,

ready to be activated. Such knowledge is hard won and not easily lost. Within moments, the arms, and legs find their angle and rhythm as they cut through the water, the bicycle moves swiftly, the child is calmed, the chisel, plane, hammer, and saw find the pathways and resonance of the wood, and the fingers rediscover their agility against the strings of the guitar.

Effort may have signaled sacrifice and self-protection, but it was also the occasion and context for the development of this intimate, robust, detailed, and implicit knowledge. Such knowledge formed the basis of the worker's power. Historian David Montgomery has called this the "functional autonomy" of the craftsperson, derived through decades of sustained physical involvement during which the knowledge of each craft was systematized, not in explicit rules, but in the course of practical action.[57] It is appropriate that such knowledge be referred to as "know-how," for it was knowledge that derived from action and displayed itself in action, knowledge that meant knowing how to do, to make, to *act-on*.

The craftsworker's know-how was also an important source of social integration. The foreman was typically a worker who had turned his wide experience into superior competence. He achieved his position by virtue of his technical skill, and such opportunities were a real source of mobility for an ambitious worker.[58] The fact that workers were required to "use up" their bodies kept them distinct from those who employed them, but the skills mastered in physical activity provided an opportunity for independence, mobility, and identification with superiors.

Such experience-based knowledge had its weaknesses, too. When it came to improving work methods or adapting them to new techniques and business conditions, the practical know-how of the traditional craftsworker could be limiting.[59] With the growing complexity and size of factories, expanding markets that exerted a strong demand for an increase in the volume of production, and a rising engineering profession, there emerged a new and pressing concern to systematize the administration, control, coordination, and planning of factory work.

The man who emerged as the chief symbol of the rational approach to management was Frederick Taylor. Though much has been written on Taylor and the philosophy and methods of scientific management, it is worth highlighting a few central themes for three reasons.[60] First, Taylorism explicitly treats the worker's body in its two dimensions—

as a source of effort and as a source of skill. Second, workers' responses to Taylorism reveal the ambivalence that this dual role of the body can create, as it did among the bleach plant operators or the nineteenth-century glassmakers. Third, the logic that motivated the early purveyors and adapters of scientific management has continued to dominate the course of automation in the twentieth-century workplace. As will be argued later, it is a logic that must undergo a fundamental reevaluation as information technology is widely adapted to productive activity.

THE PURIFICATION OF EFFORT

The agenda for scientific management was to increase productivity by streamlining and rationalizing factory operation from cost accounting and supervision to the dullest job on the shop floor. Efficiency was the mania, and to achieve efficiency, it would be necessary to penetrate the labor process and force it to yield up its secrets. In order that effort be rationalized, the worker's skills had to be made explicit. In many cases, workers' perceptions of their own interests prevented them from articulating their know-how, but there was yet another involuntary barrier. These skills did not easily yield themselves to explication; they were embedded in the ways of the body, in the knacks and know-how of the craftsworker.

Proponents of scientific management believed that observing and explicating workers' activity was nothing less than scientific research. Their goal was to slice to the core of an action, preserving what was necessary and discarding the rest as the sedimentation of tradition or, worse, artifice spawned by laziness. Taylor's disciples were driven by a vision of truth that would place managerial control on a footing of absolute objectivity, impervious to the commotion of class conflict or the stench of sweating bodies.[61] The principal method of acquiring such knowledge was the time study and, later, with the influence of Frank Gilbreth, the time-and-motion study. Here, "expert" observations of worker performance made it possible to translate actions into units of time and reconstruct them more efficiently.

The data from the time-study sheets became the possession of management and helped to fuel an explosion in the ranks of those who would measure, analyze, plan, report, issue orders, and monitor the various aspects of the production process. Armed with such data, planners, time-study experts, and production specialists (frequently organized as a staff group for the plant manager) became responsible for analyzing and organizing work tasks, controlling and monitoring their execution, coordinating functions, managing the flow of materials, and keeping records.[62]

Taylor despised wasted effort at work, whether it resulted from deliberate self-protection or from ignorance. His single-minded devotion to the purification of effort gave rise to a set of practices that, whether adopted in whole or in part, transformed the nineteenth-century factory into the modern mass-production facility. The essential logic of his approach followed three steps. First, the implicit knowledge of the worker was gathered and analyzed through observation and measurement. Second, these data, combined with other systematic information regarding tools and materials, laid the foundation for a new division of labor within the factory. It became possible to separate planning from task execution, to increase the fragmentation and thus the simplicity of production jobs, and so to minimize the amount of skill and training time associated with efficient operations. Third, the new system required a variety of specific control mechanisms to ensure the regularity and intensity of effort while continuing to supply managers and planners with the data necessary for adjustment and improvement. These mechanisms included the development of incentive payment schemes, monitoring systems, and standard operating procedures.

Taylorism meant that the body as the source of skill was to be the object of inquiry in order that the body as the source of effort could become the object of more exacting control. Once explicated, the worker's know-how was expropriated to the ranks of management, where it became management's prerogative to reorganize that knowledge according to its own interests, needs, and motives. The growth of the management hierarchy depended in part upon this transfer of knowledge from the private sentience of the worker's active body to the systematic lists, flowcharts, and measurements of the planner's office.[63] In 1912 a prominent naval engineer writing in the *Journal of the American Society of Naval Engineers* listed the seven laws of scientific management. His first law, from which all the others followed, stated that "it is necessary in any activity to have a complete knowledge of what is to be done and to prepare instructions as to what is to be done before the work is started . . . the laborer has only to follow direction. He need not stop to think what his past experience in similar cases has been."[64]

Another contemporary interpreter of scientific management took pains to outline the quality of knowledge upon which this approach was based:

> Instead of depending upon judgment, scientific management depends upon knowledge in its task of administration. Judgment is the instinctive and subconscious association of impressions derived from previous experience . . . but even the best judgment falls far short of knowledge. . . . This knowledge is carefully and systematically collected and the data so obtained are classified and digested until the knowledge is instantly available whenever a problem is presented to management. Back of the form of organization is a knowledge of the needs and the work of the plant. Back of the plan of wage payment is a knowledge of psychology and sociology. Back of the instruction sheet is a knowledge of the sciences of cutting metals and of handling work.[65]

Another industrial engineer addressing a conference at Dartmouth University's Amos Tuck School of Management in 1912 stressed the difference between scientific management and the more general movement known as systematic management. The scientific management approach rested on complete knowledge of materials, equipment, routing, job assignments, tools, task organizations, time standards, and performance methods. Each phase of an operation was to be planned completely before anything was done: "By this means the order and assignment of all work, or routing as it is called, should be conducted by the central planning or routing department. This brings the control of all operations in the plant, the progress and order of the work, back to the central point. Information, which even in the *systematized* plant is supposed to be furnished by the knowledge of the workman or the gang-boss or foreman, is brought back to the planning room and becomes a part of the instruction card."[66] This transfer of knowledge both necessitated and legitimated a new conception of managerial (line and staff) responsibility in coordinating and controlling the complexities of the factory as it entered the era of mass production.

The complexity of workers' responses to scientific management has much to do with the dilemmas created by the body's dual role in production. As rationalization depleted the worker's skill base, there were reactions of loss and threat. These were not without contradiction. Where rationalization did offer less strenuous ways to accomplish physical tasks while improving tools, working conditions, and wages, there is evidence to suggest that many workers who were suspicious at first later accepted and even welcomed the innovations.[67]

Men like Taylor and Gilbreth, who were firmly committed to raising the total level of worker output by easing the arduousness of physical tasks, looked both to new equipment and to new principles of work organization in order to accomplish their goal. For example, after a meticulous study of bricklaying, Gilbreth introduced an adjustable scaffold for piling up bricks. His invention eliminated the worker's bending over and lifting the weight of his body "a thousand times a day," and increased a worker's output from 1,000 to 2,700 bricks daily. Gilbreth claimed that workers typically responded to his innovations with gratitude, as their jobs were made easier.[68]

Taylor believed it was necessary to share the fruits of such productivity increases and saw the differential piece-rate system, a central tenet of scientific management, as a method of uniting workers and managers in a bond of common interest. But incentive wages are devilishly hard to administer, and all too often, managers attracted to differential wage schemes succumbed to shortcuts that promised fast gains. Managers would frequently change piece rates as workers learned to meet the standards. This lead to the complaints of overwork with which unions relentlessly dogged proponents of Taylorism. Scientific management frequently meant not only that individual effort was simplified (either because of labor-saving equipment or new organizational methods that fragmented tasks into their simplest components), but also that the pace of effort was intensified, thus raising the level of fatigue and stress. Effort was purified—stripped of waste—but not yet eased, and resistance to scientific management harkened back to the age-old issue of the intensity and degree of physical exertion to which the body should be subject. As long as effort was organized by the traditional practices of a craft, it could be experienced as within one's own control and, being inextricably linked to skill, as a source of considerable pride, satisfaction, and independence. Stripped of this context and meaning, demands for greater effort only intensified the desire for self-protection.[69]

Taylor had believed that the transcendent logic of science, together

with easier work and better, more fairly determined wages, could integrate the worker into the organization and inspire a zest for production.
Instead, the forms of work organization that emerged with scientific
management tended to amplify the divergence of interests between
management and workers. Scientific management revised many of the
assumptions that had guided the traditional employer-employee relationship in that it allowed a minimal connection between the organization and the individual in terms of skill, training, and the centrality of
the worker's contribution. It also permitted a new flexibility in work
force management, promoting the maximum interchangeability of personnel and the minimum dependence on their ability, availability, or
motivation.[70] The time-study expert became the new focus of workers'
antagonisms.[71] Informal production quotas persisted and, in many
cases, took on an overtly anti-management spirit. The union contract
became the most important means for institutionalizing workers' in-
stincts for self preservation, as rationalization routed out the ordinary
graces with which the workday had been laced. Concern over wages
and hours, work rules, and working conditions began to replace the
craftsworker's culturally embedded practices of effort regulation.[72]
Overall, the purification of effort meant a heightened standard of labor
discipline, and as such it widened the gulf between those who gave of
their bodies in the service of production and those who did not. Yet
even into the second decade of the twentieth century, a more traditional sensibility toward work, one that suffused it with the rhythms of
a chatty, sensual, and fun-loving humanity, could still be articulated.
A machinist gained prominence when he debated Taylor in 1914 and
remarked, "we don't want to work as fast as we are able to. We want
to work as fast as we think it's comfortable for us to work. We haven't
come into existence for the purpose of seeing how great a task we can
perform through a lifetime. We are trying to regulate our work so as
to make it auxiliary to our lives."[73]

A GLASS HALF FULL

As the logic of Taylorism took hold, the substitution of machine power
for human labor became the obvious method of increasing the speed
and volume of production. In an important way, however, the inno-

vations of mass production added a new dimension to work relationships. Beginning with the highly mechanized Ford Highland Park auto assembly plant, technology would be relied upon to complement or supplant human direction: "The instruction cards on which Taylor set so much value, Ford was able to discard. The conveyor belt, the traveling platform, the overhead rails and material conveyors take their place. . . . Motion analysis has become largely unnecessary, for the task of the assembly line worker is reduced to a few manipulations. Taylor's stop-watch nevertheless remains measuring the time of operations to the fraction of a second."[74]

The fragmentation of tasks characteristic of the new Ford assembly line achieved dramatic increases in productivity due to the detailed time study of thousands of operations and the invention of the conveyor belt and other equipment that maximized the continuity of assembly. H. L. Arnold, an industrial journalist who wrote enthusiastically about Ford's innovations, summarized some of the key elements of this cost-reduction strategy. First, all needless motions were eliminated from the worker's actions; second, the task was organized to require the "least expenditure of willpower, and . . . brain fatigue."[75] This formula has dominated the design of mass-production techniques throughout the twentieth century. Effort is simplified (though its pace is frequently intensified) while skill demands are reduced by new methods of task organization and new forms of machinery.

A distinction can be made between the new technologies for the organization of production, which allowed management to control the pace of the assembly line (and, thus, the intensity of effort), and the introduction of new forms of machinery that could reduce the requirements for both effort and skill. The continuity of assembly depended upon the production of interchangeable parts for uniform products. A new generation of automatic and semiautomatic machine tools moderated the physical demands on the machinist as they transferred skill from the worker to the machine. The new workers hired to operate these machines "had no skills and simply placed a piece in and removed it from the machine."[76]

In the second decade of the twentieth century, when these developments were being debated, the fast-growing automobile industry faced shortages of skilled workers. Cheap labor was in abundance, particularly as unskilled rural laborers and new immigrants flocked to cities like Detroit in search of employment. Ford's engineers attempted to construct machine tools suited to the skill level of this labor force. The economic rewards of this approach were so great that with the spread of mass production, this pattern of design choices was carried over from the particular historical situation that had engendered them. For the majority of industrial workers in the generations that followed, there would be fewer opportunities to develop or maintain craft skills. Mass production depended upon interchangeability for the standardization of production; this principle required manufacturing operations to free themselves from the particularistic know-how of the craftsworker. Ford was the first to succeed in this endeavor on a massive scale, where others had failed.[77]

Thus, applications of industrial technology have simplified, and generally reduced, physical effort, but because of the bond between effort and skill, they have also tended to reduce or eliminate know-how.[78] This paradox of the body's dual role in production is nowhere better illustrated that in James Bright's 1958 study of automation in American industry and the subsequent reinterpretation of his findings by social critic Harry Braverman in 1974.[79] Bright studied thirteen manufacturing facilities, including automobile engine plants, a refinery, a bakery, an electrical-part manufacturer, plating plants, and others. He observed varieties of automation in production and materials handling (though it should be noted that applications of computers in manufacturing were virtually nonexistent at the time of his study).[80]

Bright concluded that throughout the thirteen plants he studied, workers were receptive and, in many cases, enthusiastic toward the new automated equipment. Why? "Automation takes the heavy labor out of a job. . . . The gain to management is productivity; the gain to labor is a much easier job. . . . In one engine plant a grizzled veteran manning a push button signal light control panel governing some hundred feet of machinery was interviewed. . . . He said, 'Sure I like it better. It's a lot easier. I can tell you one thing—I'll last a lot longer on this job.' "[81] Self-preservation would induce the worker to accept automation. Bright also clearly stated automation's effect on skills: "As the controls become more sensitive and responsive to the requirements of the operation, environment, and the task, the machine assumes responsibility, just as it has already assumed skill, knowledge, and judgment requirements."[82] He noted that this was one of labor's biggest "headaches" with automation,[83] but he believed that new wage determination systems, coupled with sensitive implementation processes, could overcome any resistance engendered by skill dilution. As he put it, "the principal shortcoming . . . is that very few firms truly do 'sell' the automated equipment to the worker."[84]

In Braverman's influential critique of what he called the "degradation of work" in this century, he used Bright's study to make a very different point. Where Bright saw the glass half full because the physical demands of work were curtailed, Braverman saw the glass being drained, as workers' skills were absorbed by technology. For Braverman, the transfer of skill into machinery represented a triumph of "dead labor over living labor," a necessity of capitalist logic. As machinery is enlarged and perfected, the worker is made puny and insignificant. By substituting capital (in the form of machinery) for labor, Braverman believed that employers merely seized the opportunity to exert greater control over the labor process. As the work force encountered fewer opportunities for skill development, it would become progressively less capable and, thus, less able to exert any serious opposition.[85]

Although most analyses of industrial organization during the middle decades of the twentieth century have taken up one of these viewpoints, worker ambivalence toward automation has been a persistent theme.[86] Since skilled work is less automated, it also tends to involve more exertion, bodily alteration, dirt, and discomfort. Chinoy's 1955 study of automobile workers found few unskilled men harboring goals of becoming skilled workers. To a certain extent, this finding reflected the real and perceived lack of opportunities to move into skilled positions, but it also reflected a desire to avoid jobs that were physically demanding. "The values which played the greatest part in determining the order of preference among nonskilled jobs were regulation of employment and the relative absence of physical and psychological strain. . . . Men wanted work which was 'not too hard,' 'not too heavy,' 'not too dirty,' and 'not too noisy.' . . . They did not like jobs in which 'you got to keep your hands in oil and grease all day.' "[87]

In his account of the skilled auto worker, Bill Goode, a sociologist and former autoworker, reflects on the attitudinal gulf between skilled and unskilled workers in that industry. Most unskilled production workers are not interested in skilled jobs, he contends, because they are not as much fun: "One aspect of skilled work that production workers do not usually experience is dirt . . . skilled work is filthy. . . . The skilled worker carries the marks of his trade under his fingernails and in the creases of his hands. . . . Assemblers . . . have more fun. There is a spontaneity about the play on a line that is unmatched by skilled work."[88]

Similarly, another worker-turned-sociologist-of-the-workplace, Robert Schrank, reports that workers in a machine shop where he was employed routinely rejected opportunities to become skilled machinists. As these workers expressed themselves to Schrank: "What the hell do you want all the responsibility for? I just stand by this machine, watch it, adjust it once in a while, load it, and I can think about anything I want. I don't have to worry about all those tools and tolerances."[89] Later, Schrank became a set-up man on a turret lathe, a highly skilled position. He began to question the sacrifices he had made to develop and practice his skill: "As I worked in the turret lathe department, my doubts about being a skilled worker increased. The operators seemed to be having more fun than me, playing the races, fooling with the girls, and feeling free . . . the pay differential . . . did not seem to be worth the added responsibility."[90]

In the early days of industrialization, skill development was an important source of social integration, as the most skilled workers were often promoted to management ranks. As production jobs offered less opportunity for skill development, they came to have little relevance for the kinds of expertise needed at supervisory levels, and the boundary between these classes of organization members became more rigid. Chinoy's study of the ABC auto plant again speaks to this historical shift: "The structure of opportunity in the ABC plant gives most workers little reason to 'think of the corporation as a pyramid of opportunity.' . . . The pattern of working one's way up from the ranks was seen as largely a thing of the past."[91]

THE SEARCH FOR A SOLUTION

By the early 1960s, scholars had begun to ask whether this tendency would continue to grow with increasing levels of automation. As the range and depth of automation increased, further limiting the contribution of physical effort to the production process, would it continue to reduce skill requirements and thus widen the gulf between workers and management?

Robert Blauner's 1964 study *Alienation and Freedom* contrasted workers' attitudes and experiences in four types of industrial organizations—craft-based (the printing industry), machine-tending (the textile industry), mass production (the auto industry), and continuous-process (the chemical industry). Because of its advanced degree of automation, the continuous-process form of production was considered to "portend the conditions of factory work and employment in a future dominated by automated technology."[92] Would the experiences of continuous-process workers simply repeat the disturbing trade-offs in the mass-production industries? Or would these highly automated workplaces offer an alternative?

Blauner's report on the social-psychological dynamics associated with the continuous-process form of production revealed a very different relationship between the labor process and the body of the worker (for a description of continuous-process production and how it differs from other manufacturing processes, see appendix A, p. 415). Skill and effort finally seemed to be uncoupled. In the chemical industry, the focus of Blauner's research on continuous-process operations, production depended upon capital investment in highly automated equipment. Workers were called upon to physically exert themselves only when the equipment broke down, thus creating an inverse relationship between manual effort and productivity. The technology had helped to shape a work environment that freed the worker's body from the kinds of disciplinary pressures that had been routine features of industrial life.

For example, operators required to make the rounds of the equipment in a part of the plant in order to read instruments and monitor plant functioning could control the pace of their activities. As one operator told Blauner, "You can eat the soup first and do the work later, or take the readings at 1:45 and then eat your soup."[93] The very act of making equipment rounds provided a physical variety and freedom of movement that contrasted sharply with the machine-paced work of the assembly line. This mobility typically placed the continuous-process operator out of the range of an immediate supervisor and made it possible to escape scrutiny. As a result, the operators in Blauner's study felt they had "considerable scope to do their jobs in their own way."[94]

In other industrial settings, the close relationship between effort and skill meant that a reduction in the amount of physical involvement required of the worker tended to mean a reduction in the amount of skill he or she had to bring to the job. Did the reduction of effort in continuous-process operations also mean a reduction of skill? Blauner himself had some difficulty answering this question. In general, he argued that the shift from a job-centered to a process-centered form of work organization meant that the individual contribution changed from one of providing skills to one of assuming responsibility. The operator was responsible for the trouble-free operation of the process, the quality of product being produced, and the preservation of expensive automated equipment. Yet the head operator, in whom the greatest responsibility was invested, had achieved his position by virtue of long years of experience in the plant. Presumably, such experience was important because of the opportunities for skill development it afforded. Another fact makes Blauner's logic difficult to accept—the workers themselves felt that the skills demanded of them were considerable: "Virtually all of the workers interviewed said that their tasks required skill, even lots of skill, yet they were unsure of what was involved."[95]

Research by British investigators during the late 1950s and early 1960s provided a better understanding of the kinds of skills that workers had to bring to bear in a continuous-process environment. E. R. F. W. Crossman headed a research team that developed the first comprehensive description of the process operator's skills and activities, based on field visits within a variety of industries. Crossman found that the work of the process operator fell into four main categories. The most important of these was "control," followed by "special procedures and drills," "routine maintenance," and "recording and reporting." Activities related to controlling the process were described this way: "The process-operator . . . must monitor the various gauges, attend to the signs coming from the plant itself, such as noises, smells and vibration, and occasionally carry out special tests on the product. . . . Apart from the 'official' controls, there are often special ways of influencing the process, such as propping doors open to give greater cooling, or tapping pipes to loosen deposits."[96]

Crossman went on to analyze what he called the "five components" of process-control skill: sensing ("the smells and appearance which indicate how the plant is running"), perceiving, prediction, familiarity with controls, and decision making. It was this final component that Crossman considered to be the most crucial, and he identified three principal ways in which an operator might approach decision making: by rule of thumb, by having an intuitive feel of what is best, or by pursuing an explicit and logical analysis. Crossman concluded that "on the whole, discussions with operators have suggested that the first, or 'rule-of-thumb,' method is common among the less good operators, and the second, or 'intuitive,' method is often characteristic of the better ones. But few operators seem to use a fully rational or conceptual approach. . . . The intuitive understanding which enables him to deal with subtle changes and unusual situations seems to come with experience alone."[97]

Blauner's discussion of operator skills lacks the depth and nuance of Crossman's observations, but his conclusions are similar. Blauner noted that although the worker in such an operation may have a wide range of knowledge about the factory, that knowledge is concrete rather than conceptual: "Whereas continuous-process production increases the worker's breadth of knowledge and awareness of the factory as a totality, it does not necessarily enhance the worker's depth of understanding of the technical and scientific processes . . . the very complexity of the scientifically-based reaction means that there is more that is unknown to the average worker in the continuous-process industries than to the all-competent printing craftsperson or the automobile assembler."[98]

What are the implications of this skill profile? To most observers, the continuous-process operation appears to present a significant discontinuity with other forms of production work. It would seem that this sense of uniqueness derives in large measure from the way in which these environments have achieved a de facto resolution of the paradox of the body in the labor process. Skill and effort are no longer inextricably linked. The operator must put forward a minimum of strenuous physical exertion, but the most critical skills he or she brings to the process still depend on the subtle and inarticulate know-how that a body accumulates with years of experience. In this respect, the skills of continuous-process work are in a direct line of descent from earlier generations of craft knowledge. The implicit action-embedded quality of such skills (remember James Davis on learning to puddle iron) would help to explain why the operators Blauner interviewed had a difficult time describing what precisely their skills were.

Based on his comparative studies, Blauner formulated the now-classic U-curve hypothesis. Comparing levels of social integration across industries at distinct stages of automation, he found the highest levels within those industries that had the least (printing) and the most (chemical) automation. He found that workers in these craft-based and continuous-process industries were considerably less socially alienated and more socially integrated than their counterparts in the mass-production industries of textiles and automobiles. He further argued that rather than exacerbating industrial tensions according to some presumed linear function, higher levels of automation actually begin to reverse some of the most prominent negative tendencies associated with the rationalization of manufacturing work. Continuous-process operators experienced a greater degree of identification with their managers and more loyalty toward their companies, resulting in a heightened sense of mutuality and collaboration.

In the twenty years since Blauner published his study, other researchers have replicated his findings.[99] They observed higher levels of social integration among workers in the most automated industries. Yet some other scholars, notably Mallet, Braverman, and Gallie, have argued to the contrary.[100] Duncan Gallie's empirical work in particular shows that the line distinguishing the interests of the continuous-process operator and the manager can remain very clearly drawn.

To understand why and to what degree the continuous-process organization is likely to reveal a strong tendency toward social integration (particularly when compared to the mass-production industries), consider again the body's dual meanings for the production process—as a source of effort and skill.

Continuous-process operators are spared much of the exertion, exhaustion, and depletion that typifies factory work in less automated industries. Because automation has reduced the amount of physical sacrifice required of such workers, the antagonism between those who give of their bodies and those who do not has been muted. Continuous-process operators are driven by neither the foreman nor the machine system. They are not forced to conform to a narrow behavioral standard. Like their managers, they feel that they are in control of their bodies as they move through time and space.

However, the nature of the operators' skills both contributes to and ultimately limits the potential for social integration in a continuous-process operation. Blauner saw the level of responsibility that characterized the operator's role as a crucial factor accounting for the high degree of social integration. If the technology necessitates that an operator assumes responsibility for monitoring and controlling broad sections of the plant, how can management regard its workers as adversaries? Hence, "the alienation curve begins to decline from its previous height as employees in automated industries gain a new dignity from responsibility and a sense of individual function.[101]

The level of responsibility to which Blauner and others have pointed remains firmly linked to an implicit judgment of the operator's skill. It is the operator with the most experience who becomes the head shift operator or crew leader. This is because the skills he or she must have, the "intuitive feel" described by Crossman, are developed only through many years of working at a variety of jobs in the plant and of observing a wide range of equipment operating under diverse conditions. The fact that this competence is experience-based helps orient the operator toward the stratified occupational structure within the work force. Because skill is cumulative, know-how gathered at the lower status levels is relevant to performance at higher levels, and the prospect of advancement serves as an important integrating mechanism. The extended temporal horizon necessary for skill development provides the opportunity for an individual to develop an identification with and loyalty to the organization.

Responsibility not only is a measure of the skill level of the operator but also denotes the dependence of management on the worker. The worker's bodily involvement with the production process over many years provides exclusive access to the subtle and specific knowledge required for competent operations. Blauner's observation of small work teams imposing their own standards of work discipline is reminiscent of the work groups in the early factory, whose unique craft knowledge empowered them to exert their own vision of appropriate work organization and behavior.[102] Like those early craftspeople, the exclusive knowledge of the workers in a continuous-process operation lashes them to their managers with bonds of reciprocity.

That the worker's body, through the sensual information it accumulates with physical involvement in the production process, remains a crucial source of skill both defines and limits the extent to which the worker is likely to be a fully integrated member of this kind of organization. The operator's knowledge continues to depend upon sentience, and it is the personal, specific bodily character of this knowledge that persistently differentiates the operator from the management superstructure. As long as their knowledge is concrete and specific rather than conceptual and technical, workers will tend to be confined to a certain set of roles. Without a conceptual understanding of the process in which they work, indeed, of their own actions, workers will find it difficult to make a contribution to that domain of more comprehensive functions typically labeled "managerial."

Thus, despite the high level of social integration in many continuous-process organizations, a fundamental aspect of Tayloristic logic has been preserved. The much-touted collaborative atmosphere of continuous-process industries derives in large measure from the minimal emphasis placed upon the need for physical sacrifice from the worker. However, the body as the operator's source of skill remains a strong link to the industrial past and continues to demarcate the boundary between those who give of their bodies in the service of production and others who do not. Should operators perceive any devaluation of their skills, it is likely that this boundary would deepen and the sense of mutuality would diminish.

The history of work has been, in part, the history of the worker's body. Production depended on what the body could accomplish with strength and skill. Techniques that improve output have been driven by a general desire to decrease the pain of labor as well as by employers' intentions to escape dependency upon that knowledge which only the sentient laboring body could provide. Skilled workers historically have been ambivalent toward automation, knowing that the bodies it would augment or replace were the occasion for both their pain and their power. In Blauner's model, the problem seemed to have been solved; automation was able to minimize exertion without depleting skill. Yet even within this optimistic rendering, the body's role in the labor process continues to describe the distance between managers and the managed.

From this vantage point it is possible to see that the progress of automation has been a result of a transfer of knowledge and has, in turn, further enabled that transfer. However, the term *transfer* must be doubly laden if it is to adequately describe this process. Knowledge was first transferred from one quality of knowing to another—from knowing that was sentient, embedded, and experience-based to knowing that was explicit and thus subject to rational analysis and perpetual reformulation. The mechanisms used to accomplish this transfer were themselves labor intensive (that is, they depended upon first-hand observation of time-study experts) and were designed solely in the context of, and with the express purpose of, enabling a second transfer—

one that entailed the migration of knowledge from labor to management with its pointed implications for the distribution of authority and the division of labor in the industrial organization. In the case of Blauner's chemical plant, operators' sentient knowledge could not be explicated. Their skills were left intact but in a way that continued to circumscribe their role in the organization.

As information technology is applied to the production process, what effect will it have upon the grounds of knowledge? What will it take "to know"? What kind of knowledge will enable competent participation in the processes associated with making things? History alerts us to the fact that answers to these questions will require some understanding of the relationship between the new technology and the sentient body. Will information technology continue to diminish physical effort but allow the retention of experience-based skills as in Blauner's scenario? Will effort and skill, indeed the very presence of the worker, be wiped out altogether as Braverman (or Bright) would lead us to predict?

The following chapter presents a third, relatively uncharted, alternative, suggesting that this latest technological transformation can indeed alter the terms of the centuries-old paradox concerning effort and skill. By redefining the grounds of knowledge from which competent behavior is derived, new information technology lifts skill from its historical dependence upon a laboring sentient body. While it is true that computer-based automation continues to displace the human body and its know-how (a process that has come to be known as *deskilling*), the informating power of the technology simultaneously creates pressure for a profound *reskilling*. How are these new skills to be understood? What might be their implications for the differences that have separated workers from their managers, differences that have, in an important way, depended upon the necessity of the body's labor and the body's learning.

CHAPTER TWO

THE ABSTRACTION OF

INDUSTRIAL WORK

Without a doubt, the part of mankind which
has advanced intellectually is quite under the
spell of technology. Its charms are twofold.
On the one hand, there is the enticement of
increasingly comfortable living standards; on
the other, there is a reduction in the amount
of work which is necessary to do. . . . The
irresistible pull toward technological
development . . . is caused, we should
remember, by the unconscious and deep-
rooted desire to free ourselves from the
material oppression of the material world.

—FOLKERT WILKEN
The Liberation of Capital

THE BODY'S VIRTUOSITY AT WORK

In the older pulp and paper mills of Piney Wood and Tiger Creek, where
a highly experienced work force was making the transition to a new
computer-based technology, operators had many ways of using their
bodies to achieve precise knowledge. One man judged the condition
of paper coming off a dry roller by the sensitivity of his hair to electric-
ity in the atmosphere around the machine. Another could judge the
moisture content of a roll of pulp by a quick slap of his hand. Immediacy
was the mode in which things were known; it provided a feeling of

certainty, of knowing "what's going on." One worker in Piney Wood described how it felt to be removed from the physical presence of the process equipment and asked to perform his tasks from a computerized control room:

> It is very different now. . . . It is hard to get used to not being out there with the process. I miss it a lot. I miss being able to see it. You can see when the pulp runs over a vat. You know what's happening.

The worker's capacity "to know" has been lodged in sentience and displayed in action. The physical presence of the process equipment has been the setting that corresponded to this knowledge, which could, in turn, be displayed only in that context. As long as the action context remained intact, it was possible for knowledge to remain implicit. In this sense, the worker knew a great deal, but very little of that knowledge was ever articulated, written down, or made explicit in any fashion. Instead, operators went about their business, displaying their know-how and rarely attempting to translate that knowledge into terms that were publicly accessible. This is what managers mean when they speak of the "art" involved in operating these plants. As one manager at Piney Wood described it:

> There are a lot of operators working here who cannot verbally give a description of some piece of the process. I can ask them what is going on at the far end of the plant, and they can't tell me, but they can draw it for me. By taking away this physical contact that he understands, it's like we have taken away his blueprint. He can't verbalize his way around the process.

In this regard, the pulp and paper mills embody a historical sweep that is unavailable in many other forms of work. Unlike other continuous-process industries, such as oil refining or chemical production, the pulp-and-paper-making process has not yet yielded a full scientific explication. This has retarded the spread of automation and also has worked to preserve the integrity of a certain amount of craft know-how among those operators with lengthy experience in the industry. Like other continuous-process operations, the technological environment in these mills has created work that was more mediated by equipment and dependent upon indirect data than, say, work on an assembly line. However, discrete instrumentation typically was located on or close to the actual operating equipment, allowing the operator to combine data from an instrument reading with data from his or her own senses. Most workers believed that they "knew" what was going on at any particular moment because of what they saw and felt, and they used past experience to relate these perceptions to a set of likely consequences. The required sequences and routines necessary to control certain parts of the process and to make proper adjustments for achieving the best results represented a form of knowledge that the worker displayed in action as a continual reflection of this sentient involvement. Acquired experience made it possible to relate current conditions to past events; thus, an operator's competence increased as the passing of time enabled him or her to experience the action possibilities of a wide variety of operating conditions.

In Piney Wood and Tiger Creek, the technology change did not mean simply trading one form of instrumentation for another. Because the traditional basis of competence, like skilled work in most industries, was still heavily dependent upon sentient involvement, information technology was experienced as a radical departure from the taken-for-granted approach to daily work. In this sense, workers' experiences in these mills bridge two manufacturing domains. They not only illustrate the next phase of technological change within the continuous-process industries but also foreshadow the dilemmas that will emerge in other industrial organizations (for example, batch and assembly-line production) with the transition from machine to computer mediation.

When a process engineer attempts to construct a set of algorithms that will be the basis for automating some portion of the production process, he or she first interviews those individuals who currently perform the tasks that will be automated. The process engineer must learn the detail of their actions in order to translate their practice into the terms of a mathematical model. The algorithms in such a model explicate, rationalize, and institutionalize know-how. In the course of these interviews, the process engineer is likely to run up against the limits of implicit knowledge. A worker may perform competently yet be unable to communicate the structure of his or her actions. As one engineer discovered:

> There are operators who can run the paper machine with tremendous efficiency, but they cannot describe to you how they do it. They have built-in actions and senses that they are not aware of. One operation required pulling two levers simultaneously, and they were not conscious of the fact they they were pulling two levers. They said they were pulling one. The operators run the mill, but they don't under-

stand how. There are operators who know exactly what to do, but they cannot tell you how they do it.[1]

Though every operator with similar responsibilities performs the same functions, each will perform them in a unique way, fashioned according to a personal interpretation of what works best. A process engineer contrasted the personal rendering of skill with the impersonal but consistently optimal performance of the computer:

> There is no question that the computer takes the human factor out of running the machine. Each new person who comes on shift will make their own distinct changes, according to their sense of what is the best setting. In contrast, the computer runs exactly the same way all the time. Each operator thinks he does a better job, each one thinks he has a better intimate understanding of the equipment than another operator. But none of them can compete with the computer.

These comments describe a particular quality of skill that I refer to as *action-centered*. Four components of action-centered skill are highlighted in the experiences of these workers:

1. *Sentience.* Action-centered skill is based upon sentient information derived from physical cues.
2. *Action-dependence.* Action-centered skill is developed in physical performance. Although in principle it may be made explicit in language, it typically remains unexplicated—implicit in action.
3. *Context-dependence.* Action-centered skill only has meaning within the context in which its associated physical activities can occur.
4. *Personalism.* It is the individual body that takes in the situation and an individual's actions that display the required competence. There is a felt linkage between the knower and the known. The implicit quality of knowledge provides it with a sense of interiority, much like physical experience.

THE DISSOCIATION OF SENTIENCE AND KNOWLEDGE

Computerization brings about an essential change in the way the worker can know the world and, with it, a crisis of confidence in the possibility of certain knowledge. For the workers of Piney Wood and

Tiger Creek, achieving a sense of knowing the world was rarely prob-
lematical in their conventional environments. Certain knowledge was
conveyed through the immediacy of their sensory experience. Instead
of Descartes's "I think, therefore I am," these workers might say, "I
see, I touch, I smell, I hear; therefore, I know." Their capacity to trust
their knowledge was reflected in the assumption of its validity. In the
precomputerized environment, belief was a seamless extension of sensory experience.

As the medium of knowing was transformed by computerization, the
placid unity of experience and knowledge was disturbed. Accomplishing work depended upon the ability to manipulate symbolic, electronically presented data. Instead of using their bodies as instruments of
acting-on equipment and materials, the task relationship became mediated by the information system. Operators had to work through the
medium of what I will call the "data interface," represented most visi-
bly by the computer terminals they monitored from central control
rooms. The workers in this transition were at first overwhelmed with
the feeling that they could no longer see or touch their work, as if it
has been made both invisible and intangible by computer mediation.

> It's just different getting this information in the control room. The
> man in here can't see. Out there you can look around until you find
> something.
>
> The chlorine has overflowed, and it's all over the third floor. You see,
> this is what I mean . . . it's all over the floor, but you can't see it. You
> have to remember how to get into the system to do something about
> it. Before you could see it and you knew what was happening—you
> just knew.
>
> The hardest thing for us operators is not to have the physical part. I
> can chew pulp and tell you its physical properties. We knew things
> from experience. Now we have to try and figure out what is happen-
> ing. The hardest part is to give up that physical control.

In a world in which skills were honed over long years of physical
experience, work was associated with concrete objects and the cues
they provided. A worker's sense of occupational identity was deeply
marked by his or her understanding of and attachment to discrete tangible entities, such as a piece of operating equipment. Years of service
meant continued opportunities to master new objects. It was the immediate knowledge one could gain of these tangible objects that engendered feelings of competence and control. For workers, the new

computer-mediated relationship to work often felt like being yanked away from a world that could be known because it could be sensed.

> Our operators did their job by feeling a pipe—"Is it hot?" We can't just tell them it's 150 degrees. They have to believe it.

> With computerization I am further away from my job than I have ever been before. I used to listen to the sounds the boiler makes and know just how it was running. I could look at the fire in the furnace and tell by its color how it was burning. I knew what kinds of adjustments were needed by the shades of color I saw. A lot of the men also said that there were smells that told you different things about how it was running. I feel uncomfortable being away from these sights and smells. Now I only have numbers to go by. I am scared of that boiler, and I feel that I should be closer to it in order to control it.

It is as if one's job had vanished into a two-dimensional space of abstractions, where digital symbols replace a concrete reality. Workers reiterated a spontaneous emotional response countless times—defined by feelings of loss of control, of vulnerability, and of frustration. It was sharpened with a sense of crisis and a need for steeling oneself with courage and not a little adrenaline in order to meet the challenge. It was shot through with the bewilderment of a man suddenly blind, groping with his hands outstretched in a vast, unfamiliar space. "We are in uncharted water now," they said. "We have to control our operations blind." This oft-repeated metaphor spoke of being robbed of one's senses and plunged into darkness. The tangible world had always been thick with landmarks; it was difficult to cast off from these familiar moorings with only abstractions as guides.

One operator described learning to work with the new computer system in Tiger Creek's pulping area. "The difficulty," he said, "is not being able to touch things." As he spoke, his hands shot out before him and he wiggled all his fingers, as if to emphasize the sense of incompleteness and loss. He continued:

> When I go out and touch something, I know what will happen. There is a fear of not being out on the floor watching things. It is like turning your back in a dark alley. You don't know what is behind you; you don't know what might be happening. It all becomes remote from you, and it makes you feel vulnerable. It was like being a new operator all over again. Today I push buttons instead of opening

valves on the digester. If I push the wrong button, will I screw up? Will anything happen?

Many other descriptions conveyed a similar feeling:

> With the change to the computer it's like driving down the highway with your lights out and someone else pushing the accelerator.

> It's like flying an airplane and taking all the instruments out so you can't see. It's like if you had an airplane and you put pieces over each instrument to hide it. Then, if something went wrong, you have to uncover the right one in a split second.

> Doing my job through the computer, it feels different. It is like you are riding a big, powerful horse, but someone is sitting behind you on the saddle holding the reins, and you just have to be on that ride and hold on. You see what is coming, but you can't do anything to control it. You can't steer yourself left and right; you can't control that horse that you are on. You have got to do whatever the guy behind you holding the reins wants you to do. Well, I would rather be holding the reins than have someone behind me holding the reins.

The feeling of being in control and the willingness to be held accountable require a reservoir of critical judgment with which to initiate informed action. In the past, operators like those at Piney Wood derived their critical judgment from their "gut feel" of the production process. Becoming a "good" operator—the kind that workers and managers alike refer to as an "artist" and invest with the authority of expertise—required the years of experience to develop a finely nuanced, felt sense of the equipment, the product, and the overall process. With computerization, many managers acknowledged that operators had lost their ability "to feel the machine." Without considering the new skill implications of this loss, many managers feared it would eliminate the kind of critical judgment that would have allowed operators to take action based upon an understanding that reached beyond the computer system.

Piney Wood's plant manager, as he presided over the massive technology conversion, asked himself what the loss of such art might mean:

> In the digester area, we used to have guys doing it who had an art. After we put the computers in, when they went down we could go to manual backup. People remembered how to run the digesters. Now if we try to go back, they can't remember what to do. They have lost the feel for it. We are really stuck now without the computer; we

can't successfully operate that unit without it. If you are watching a screen, do you see the same things you would if you were there, face-to-face with the process and the equipment? I am concerned we are losing the art and skills that are not replenishable.

There were many operators who agreed. In one area of Piney Wood, the crew leader explained it this way:

> The new people are not going to understand, see, or feel as well as the old guys. Something is wrong with this fan, for example. You may not know what; you just feel it in your feet. The sound, the tone, the volume, the vibrations . . . the computer will control it, but you will have lost something, too. It's a trade-off. The computer can't feel what is going on out there. The new operators will need to have more written down, because they will not know it in their guts. I can't understand how new people coming in are ever going to learn how to run a pulp mill. They are not going to know what is going on. They will only learn what these computers tell them.

Sam Gimbel was a young production coordinator in Piney Wood. Though trained as a chemical engineer, he had been particularly close to the operators whom he managed. He had shepherded them through the technology conversion and construction of the new control room, and worked closely with them as they grappled with new ways of operating:

> We are losing the context where hands-on experience makes sense. If you don't have actual experience, you have to believe everything the computer says, and you can't beat it at its own game. You can't stand up to it. And yet who will have the experience to make these kinds of judgments? It will surely be a different world. You lose the checkpoints in reality to know if you are doing it right; therefore, how will anyone be able to confront the computer information?

Piney Wood's management had approached the technology conversion with the following message: "We are simply providing you with new tools to do your job. Your job is to operate the equipment, and this is a new tool to operate the equipment with." Managers repeatedly made statements such as, "We told them this was a tool just like a hammer or a wrench." One manager even went so far as to say, "We hoped they wouldn't figure out that the terminal we were giving them was really a computer."

As experience with the new operating conditions began to accumulate, many managers began to see that treating the computer system like a physical object, "just another tool," could lead to chronic suboptimization of the technology's potential. A powerhouse worker with over twenty-five years of experience had developed a special way of kicking the boiler in order to make it function smoothly. He used the same approach with the terminal; if he hit a certain button on the keyboard, a particular reading would change in the desired direction, but he did not know why or how. Piney Wood's powerhouse manager put it this way:

> The guy who kicks the boiler is the same guy who mashes the button a certain way just to make the line go down. This person will never optimize the process. He will use too much chemical and too high pressure. He will never make you money because he doesn't understand the problem.

Just as the digester operators had lost their ability to cook manually, other workers throughout the mill felt equally powerless:

> In the old way, you had control over the job. The computer now tells you what to do. There is more responsibility but less control. We lost a boiler that was on computer control. We just had to sit there and stare. We were all shook up.

> Sometimes I am amazed when I realize that we stare at the screen even when it has gone down. You get in the habit and you just keep staring even if there is nothing there.

Ironically, as managers and operators across the mill watched the level of artistry decline, the senior technical designers continued to assume that manual skills would provide the necessary backup to their systems.

The problem was even more acute in Cedar Bluff, where most of the work force lacked the experience base from which felt sense and critical judgment are developed. Managers at Cedar Bluff engaged in a quiet debate as to how much of a problem this lack of experience would ultimately be. On one side of the argument were the "old-timers"— managers with years of experience in the industry:

> I like to smell and feel the pulp sometimes. It can be slick, it can be slimy, it can be all different consistencies. These are the artistic aspects of making pulp that the computer doesn't know about. Some of the operators have been picking up these aspects, but there are so many numbers so readily accessible, we have to shortcut it at times

and solve more problems from the office. The information is so good and rapid we have to use it. . . . You have got to be able to recognize when you can run things from the office and when you have to go and look. Yet, I recognize that I am not as good a pulp maker as the people who trained me, and the new operators are not as good as I am. They are better managers and planners. I am very happy with the new managers, but not with the new pulp makers.

The younger engineers, schooled in computer-based analytic techniques, had little patience with anxious laments over the loss of the art of pulp making. They were relentlessly confident that a good computer model could reproduce anything that operators knew from experience—only better. Here is how the process engineers articulated the argument:

Computer analysis lets us see the effects of many variables and their interactions. This is a picture of truth that we could not have achieved before. It is superior to the experience-based knowledge of an operator. You might say that truth replaces knowledge.

People who have this analytic power do not need to have been around to know what is going on. All you need is to be able to formulate a model and perform the necessary confirmation checks. With the right model you can manage the system just fine.

Most Cedar Bluff managers agreed that the computer system made it possible to do a better job running the plant with an inexperienced work force than otherwise would have been possible, though some wondered whether the levels of expertise would ever be as high as among workers with hands-on exposure to the pulping process. Yet even as managers argued over the essentiality of action-centered skill, technology was irreversibly altering the context in which the operators performed. The opportunities to develop such skills were becoming increasingly rare as the action context was paved over by the data highway.

Many of Cedar Bluff's managers believed that the traditional knowledge of the pulp mill worker would actually inhibit the development of creativity and flexibility. Under the new technological conditions, the young operators would develop their capacity to "know better" than the systems with which they worked as they struggled with the complexities of the new technology and the data it provided. The data interface would replace the physical equipment as the primary arena for learning.

Yet as months passed, other managers observed a disturbing pattern of interactions between the operators and the computer system. Some believed that the highly computerized task environment resulted in a greater than usual bifurcation of skills. One group of operators would use the information systems to learn an extraordinary amount about the process, while another group would make itself an appendage to the system, mechanically carrying out the computer's directives. These managers complained that the computer system was becoming a crutch that prevented many operators from developing a superior knowledge of the process. One "old-timer" provided an example:

> When there is a shift change and new operators come on, the good operator will take the process from the computer, put it on manual, make certain changes that the operator thinks are necessary, and then gives it back to the computer. The average operator will come in, see this thing on automatic control, and leave it with the computer. Sometimes that operator won't even realize that things are getting bad or getting worse. They should have known better, but they didn't.

Most Cedar Bluff operators spoke enthusiastically about the convenience of the computer interface, and some freely admitted what they perceived to be a dependence on the computer system:

> The computer provides your hands. I don't think I could work in a conventional mill. This is so much more convenient. You have so much control without having to go out to the equipment and adjust things.

> We can't run this mill manually. There are too many controls, and it is too complex. The average person can only run four or five variables at once in a manual mode, and the automatic system runs it all. If the computer goes down, we have to sit back and wait. We sit and we stare at the screens and we hope something pipes in.

Many managers observed with growing alarm the things that occurred when operators neither enjoyed the traditional sources of critical judgment nor had developed enough new knowledge for informed action.

> In a conventional mill, you have to go and look at the equipment because you cannot get enough data in the control room. Here, you

get all the data you need. The computer becomes a substitute tool. It replaces all the sensual data instead of being an addition. We had another experience with the feedwater pumps, which supply water to the boiler to make steam. There was a power outage. Something in the computer canceled the alarm. The operator had a lot of trouble and did not look at the readout of the water level and never got an alarm. The tank ran empty, the pumps tripped. The pump finally tore up because there was no water feeding it.

We have so much data from the computer, I find that hard drives out soft. Operators are tempted not to tour the plant. They just sit at the computer and watch for alarms. One weekend I found a tank overflowing in digesting. I went to the operator and told him, and he said, "It can't be; the computer says my level is fine." I am afraid of what happens if we trust the computer too much.

At least since the introduction of the moving assembly line in Ford's Highland Park plant, it has been second nature for managers to use technology to delimit worker discretion and, in this process, to concentrate knowledge within the managerial domain. The special dilemmas raised by information technology require managers to reconsider these assumptions. When information and control technology is used to turn the worker into "just another mechanical variable," one immediate result is the withdrawal of the worker's commitment to and accountability for the work. This lack of care requires additional managerial vigilance and leads to a need for increased automatic control. As this dynamic unfolds, it no longer seems shocking to contemplate an image of work laced with stupefaction and passivity, in which the human being is a hapless bystander at the margins of productive activity. One young operator in Cedar Bluff discussed his prior job as a bank clerk. I asked him if his two employment experiences had anything in common. "Yes," he said, "in both cases you punch the buttons and watch it happen."

As automation intensifies, information technology becomes the receptacle for larger and larger portions of the organization's operating intelligence. Algorithms become the functional equivalent of a once diffuse know-how, and the action context in which know-how can be developed and sustained vanishes. Because many managers assume that more technology means a diminished need for human operating skill, they may recognize the waning of worker know-how without becoming concerned enough to chart a different course. Left unchallenged, these systems become more potent, as they are invested with an escalating degree of authority. Technical experts temporarily serve as resources, but once their knowledge has been depleted, and converted into systematic rules for decision making, their usefulness is attenuated. The analysts and engineers, who construct programs and models, have the capacity to manipulate data and, presumably, to make discoveries. Ultimately, they will become the most important human presence to offer any counterpoint to the growing density and opacity of the automated systems.

There is an alternative, one that involves understanding this technological change as an occasion for developing a new set of skills—skills that are able to exploit the informating capacity of the technology and to become a new source of critical judgment. In order to assess the likelihood of this alternative—the forces that will drive organizations in this direction and those that will impede them—we first have to understand the nature of these new skills. What can the experiences of workers in these three mills teach us about the emerging requirements for competence at the data interface?

FROM ACTION-CENTERED TO INTELLECTIVE SKILL

The pulp and paper mills reveal the shift in the grounds of knowledge associated with a technology that informates. Men and women accustomed to an intimate physical association with the production process found themselves removed from the action. Now they had to know and to do based upon their ability to understand and manipulate electronic data. In Piney Wood, a $200 million investment in technology was radically altering every phase of mill life. Managers believed they were merely "upgrading" in order to modernize production and to improve productivity. Tiger Creek was undergoing a similar modernization process. In both cases, informating dynamics tended to unfold as an unintended and undermanaged consequence of these efforts. Cedar Bluff had been designed with a technological infrastructure based on integrated information and control systems. In that organization, managers were somewhat more self-conscious about using the informating capacity of the technology as the basis for developing new operating skills.

The experiences of the skilled workers in these mills provide a frame of reference for a general appraisal of the forms of knowledge that are required in an informated environment. My contention is that the skill demands that can be deciphered from their experiences have relevance for a wider range of organizational settings in both manufacturing and service sectors. Later chapters will compare the experiences of clerks and managers to those of the mill operators. This joint appraisal will help to unravel the intrinsic and the contingent aspects of change and to gauge the generalizations that follow from the dilemmas of transformation described here.

A fundamental quality of this technological transformation, as it is experienced by workers and observed by their managers, involves a reorientation of the means by which one can have a palpable effect upon the world. Immediate physical responses must be replaced by an abstract thought process in which options are considered, and choices are made and then translated into the terms of the information system. For many, physical action is restricted to the play of fingers on the terminal keyboard. As one operator put it, "Your past physical mobility must be translated into a mental thought process." A Cedar Bluff manager with prior experience in pulping contemplates the distinct capacities that had become necessary in a highly computerized environment:

> In 1953 we put operation and control as close together as possible. We did a lot of localizing so that when you made a change you could watch the change, actually see the motor start up. With the evolution of computer technology, you centralize controls and move away from the actual physical process. If you don't have an understanding of what is happening and how all the pieces interact, it is more difficult. You need a new learning capability, because when you operate with the computer, you can't see what is happening. There is a difference in the mental and conceptual capabilities you need—you have to do things in your mind.

When operators in Piney Wood and Tiger Creek discuss their traditional skills, they speak of knowing things by habit and association. They talk about "cause-and-effect" knowledge and being able to see the things to which they must respond. They refer to "folk medicine" and knowledge that you don't even know you have until it is suddenly displayed in the ability to take a decisive action and make something work.

In plants like Piney Wood and Tiger Creek, where operators have relied upon action-centered skill, management must convince the operator to leave behind a world in which things were immediately known, comprehensively sensed, and able to be acted upon directly, in order to embrace a world that is dominated by objective data, is removed from the action context, and requires a qualitatively different kind of response. In this new world, personal interpretations of how to make things happen count for little. The worker who has relied upon an intimate knowledge of a piece of equipment—the operators talk about having "pet knobs" or knowing just where to kick a machine to make it hum—feels adrift. To be effective, he or she must now trade immediate knowledge for a more explicit understanding of the science that undergirds the operation. One Piney Wood manager described it this way:

> The workers have an intuitive feel of what the process needs to be. Someone in the process will listen to things, and that is their information. All of their senses are supplying data. But once they are in the control room, all they have to do is look at the screen. Things are concentrated right in front of you. You don't have sensory feedback. You have to draw inferences by watching the data, so you must understand the theory behind it. In the long run, you would like people who can take data and draw broad conclusions from it. They must be more scientific.

Many managers are not optimistic about the ability of experienced workers to trade their embodied knowledge for a more explicit, "scientific" inference.

> The operators today know if I do "x," then "y" will happen. But they don't understand the real logic of the system. Their cause-and-effect reasoning comes from their experience. Once we put things under automatic control and ask them to relate to the process using the computer, their personal judgments about how to relate to equipment go by the wayside. We are saying your intuition is no longer valuable. Now you must understand the whole process and the theory behind it.

Now a new kind of learning must begin. It is slow and scary, and many workers are timid, not wanting to appear foolish and incompetent. Hammers and wrenches have been replaced by numbers and buttons. An operator with thirty years of service in the Piney Wood Mill described his experience in the computer-mediated environment:

Anytime you mash a button you should have in mind exactly what is going to happen. You need to have in your mind where it is at, what it is doing, and why it is doing it. Out there in the plant, you can know things just by habit. You can know them without knowing that you know them. In here you have to watch the numbers, whereas out there you have to watch the actual process.

"You need to have in your mind where it is at"—it is a simple phrase, but deceptive. What it takes to have things "in your mind" is far different from the knowledge associated with action-centered skill.

This does not imply that action-centered skills exist independent of cognitive activity. Rather, it means that the processes of learning, remembering, and displaying action-centered skills do not necessarily require that the knowledge they contain be made explicit. Physical cues do not require inference; learning in an action-centered context is more likely to be analogical than analytical. In contrast, the abstract cues available through the data interface do require explicit inferential reasoning, particularly in the early phases of the learning process. It is necessary to reason out the meaning of those cues—what is their relation to each other and to the world "out there"?

It is also necessary to understand the procedures according to which these abstract cues can be manipulated to result in the desired effects. Procedural reasoning means having an understanding of the internal structure of the information system and its functional capacities. This makes it possible both to operate skillfully through the system and to use the system as a source of learning and feedback. For example, one operation might require sixteen control actions spread across four groups of variables. The operator must first think about what has to be done. Second, he or she must know how data elements (abstract cues) correspond to actual processes and their systemic relations. Third, the operator must have a conception of the information system itself, in order to know how actions taken at the information interface can result in appropriate outcomes. Fourth, having decided what to do and executed that command, he or she must scan new data and check for results. Each of these processes folds back upon a kind of thinking that can stand independent from the physical context. An operator summed it up this way:

Before computers, we didn't have to think as much, just react. You just knew what to do because it was physically there. Now, the most important thing to learn is to think before you do something, to think about what you are planning to do. You have to know which variables are the most critical and therefore what to be most cautious about, what to spend time thinking about before you take action.

The vital element here is that these workers feel a stark difference in the forms of knowledge they must now use. Their experience of competence has been radically altered. "We never got paid to have ideas," said one Tiger Creek worker. "We got paid to work." Work was the exertion that could be known by its material results. The fact that a material world must be created required physical exertion. Most of the operators believed that some people in society are paid to "think," but they were not among them. They knew themselves to be the ones who gave their bodies in effort and skill, and through their bodies, they made things. Accustomed to gauging their integrity in intimate measures of strain and sweat, these workers find that information technology has challenged their assumptions and thrown them into turmoil. There was a gradual dawning that the rules of the game had changed. For some, this created panic; they did not believe in their ability to think in this new way and were afraid of being revealed as incompetent.

Such feelings are no mere accident of personality, but the sedimentation of long years of conditioned learning about who does the "thinking"—a boundary that is not meant to be crossed. As a Tiger Creek manager observed:

> Currently, managers make all the decisions. . . . Operators don't want to hear about alternatives. They have been trained to *do*, not to *think*. There is a fear of being punished if you think. This translates into a fear of the new technology.

In each control room, a tale is told about one or two old-timers who, though they knew more about the process than anyone else, "just up and quit" when they heard the new technology was coming. From one plant to another, reports of these cases were remarkably similar:

> He felt that because he had never graduated high school, he would never be able to keep up with this new stuff. We tried to tell him different, but he just wouldn't listen.

Despite the anxiety of change, those who left were not the majority. Most men and women need their jobs and will do whatever it takes to keep them. Beyond this, there were many who were honestly intrigued with the opportunity this change offered. They seemed to get pulled in gradually, observing their own experiences and savoring with secret surprise each new bit of evidence of their unexpected abilities. They discussed the newness and strangeness of having to act upon the world by exerting a more strictly intellectual effort. Under the gentle stimulus of a researcher's questions, they thought about this new kind of thinking. What does it feel like? Here are the observations of an operator who spent twenty years in one of the most manually intensive parts of the Tiger Creek Mill, which had recently been computerized:

> If something is happening, if something is going wrong, you don't go down and fix it. Instead, you stay up here and think about the sequence, and you think about how you want to affect the sequence. You get it done through your thinking. But dealing with information instead of things is very . . . well, very intriguing. I am very aware of the need for my mental involvement now. I am always wondering: Where am I at? What is happening? It all occurs in your mind now.

Another operator discussed the same experience but added an additional dimension. After describing the demand for thinking and mental involvement, he observed:

> Things occur to me now that never would have occurred to me before. With all of this information in front of me, I begin to think about how to do the job better. And, being freed from all that manual activity, you really have time to look at things, to think about them, and to anticipate.

As information technology restructures the work situation, it abstracts thought from action. Absorption, immediacy, and organic responsiveness are superseded by distance, coolness, and remoteness. Such distance brings an opportunity for reflection. There was little doubt in these workers' minds that the logic of their jobs had been fundamentally altered. As another worker from Tiger Creek summed it up, "Sitting in this room and just thinking has become part of my job. It's the technology that lets me do these things."

The thinking this operator refers to is of a different quality from the thinking that attended the display of action-centered skills. It combines abstraction, explicit inference, and procedural reasoning. Taken together, these elements make possible a new set of competencies that I call *intellective skills.* As long as the new technology signals only deskilling—the diminished importance of action-centered skills—there will be little probability of developing critical judgment at the data interface. To rekindle such judgment, though on a new, more abstract footing, a reskilling process is required. Mastery in a computer-mediated environment depends upon developing intellective skills.

Trusting Symbols

To understand the significance of intellective skills and how they differ from action-centered skills in this new environment, some appreciation of the nature of symbols is required. The data interface is a symbolic medium through which one produces effects and on the basis of which one derives an interpretation of "what is happening." These symbols are abstractions; they are experienced as remote from the rich sensory reality to which people are accustomed. Because of this remoteness, the new medium is not spontaneously felt to be legitimate. People confront this new world of symbols and ask, what does it mean?

In a symbolic medium, meaning is not a given value; rather, it must be constructed. This is a problem that action-centered skills are not required to address. The medium of equipment and materials conveys its meaning in its own immediate context. An example can be found in any object. Consider a pot handle: the handle means that human hands grasp objects in particular ways, and the handle exists as an acknowledgment of how hands can best grasp pots. When the handle is made of a nonconductive material, it further means that heat is dangerous for the human hand. Hands can best accomplish the work of pot grasping when the handle is of a temperature congenial to the skin. Alternatively, one can see that the meaning of objects is contained within their situations when objects are lifted out of their ordinary contexts and placed in a different or "abnormal" environment. Photographers, painters, and sculptors frequently juxtapose familiar objects with unfamiliar contexts in order to evoke a deeper sense of reflection from the viewer. Once lifted from its meaningful context, the object can be regarded "in-itself." Its meaning becomes problematic and must be constructed by the observer.[2]

The civilizing process has increased the distance between behavior and the impulse life of the animal body. It has also produced symbolic media (for example, the alphabet, mathematic notation, printed text) that can both convey and absorb human meaning unfettered by the contextual limitations of embodied presence. With each new medium people have had to revisit the problem of meaning. Rich historical and anthropological materials testify to a profound initial disjuncture between symbol and experience; they reveal the mental effort with which human beings have had to construct the linkages that connect a new kind of symbolic medium to a meaningful context. With time, these linkages become so tightly wrought that it is difficult to recover the original problematic quality of the relationship.

Language itself is an excellent field with which to demonstrate this historical process. The spoken word represents one medium that human beings have developed to convey experience; it preserves a close relationship between the word and bodily presence. Spoken words emit from and are shaped by the body's immediate interior condition (for example, breathlessness, fright, grief, joy). Their communicative power was bounded by the presence of both speaker and listener. The historical progression to the written word plainly shows the crisis of meaning that emerged as language took on a life of its own at a distance from experience and independent of speakers and listeners.

The medieval historian M. T. Clanchy has illustrated the reluctant acceptance of written documentation in place of first-person witness as it occurred over more than three centuries of early English history. "Documents," he tells us, "did not immediately inspire trust." People had to be persuaded that written documentation was a reliable reflection of concrete, observable events. To the modern mind, the evanescence of the spoken word seems more plastic, quixotic, and undependable than the printed word. To members of a highly oral culture, however, the spoken word was connected to the incontrovertible realities of bodily experience, while the written word was a thin, substanceless scratching whose two-dimensionality seemed highly arbitrary. Clanchy quotes one twelfth-century scholar who struggled to define the relationship between the written word and the palpable reality associated with the spoken word: "Fundamentally letters are shapes indicating voices. Hence they represent things which they bring to mind through the windows of the eyes. Frequently they speak voicelessly the utterances of the absent."[3]

The skepticism and mistrust that greeted the advent of the written word were evident in the procedures used to legitimate legal transactions. For example, a land transaction required witnesses who heard the donor utter the words of the grant and saw him make the transfer with a symbolic object, such as a knife or a piece of turf from the land. If there was a dispute, the accounts of these witnesses provided the evidence with which to settle it.

> Before documents were used, the truth of an event or transaction had been established by personal statement, often made on oath, by the principals or witnesses. If the event were too far in the past for that, the oldest and wisest men were asked what they could remember about it . . . the establishment of what passed for truth was simple and personal, since it depended on the good word of one's fellows. . . . Both to ignorant illiterates and to sophisticated Platonists, a written record was a dubious gift, because it seemed to kill living eloquence and trust and substitute for them a mummified semblance in the form of a piece of parchment. Henry I's partisans in the dispute with Anselm, who had called a papal bull a sheepskin "blackened with ink and weighted with a little lump of lead," were arguing for the priority of the personal testimony of the three bishops who exercised memory over the mere "external marks" of a writing.[4]

In a completely different context, J. R. Clammer's study of literacy in the Fiji islands reveals the same skepticism and bewilderment as people confronted the relationship between "external markings" and their wordly experience. He recounts the experience of a missionary who had written a note to his wife on a wood chip and asked a Fijian chief to deliver the message: "The Chief was scornful of the errand and asked, 'What must I say?' . . . You have nothing to say, I replied. The chip will say all I wish. With a look of astonishment and contempt, he held up the piece of wood and said, 'How can this speak? Has this a mouth?' "[5]

In the modern world, literate minds have long become accustomed to a comfortable unity of the written word and the world to which it refers. When we read, we barely confront the problem of meaning. As long as a word is understood, our minds are well adapted to experience the word in terms of what we know it "means." But when we come upon a word, *fardel*, for example, whose definition we may not know, the problem of meaning suddenly wells up. We look at the word, and it seems to be an arbitrary collection of letters—there is no sense to it. That combination of letters becomes a meaningful symbol only when we discover what it refers to. Then we can reenter the sense of connectedness between the word and the world—the same comfortable "sense" of a word that we have when we read *chair* or *book*. In order to achieve this comfort, it was first necessary to encounter the word as a problem and to make its meaning explicit. Once that explicit recognition is accomplished, it is possible to develop a more implicit sense of the word, knowing that, should it become necessary, it will be possible to reconstruct an explicit definition from our reservoir of implicit knowledge.

We have made our peace with the problem of meaning in other ways as well. The voice over the telephone, the image in a photograph, the scene on a television screen—each of these is tacitly treated as though they fully convey a reality. We no longer puzzle over their connectedness to the "real" thing, though it is still possible to find individuals who remember when people were frightened of telephones or looked behind the television set hoping to discover the source of its images.

COMPUTER-MEDIATED WORK AND THE PROBLEM OF MEANING

Data and Concrete Reality

Intellective skills are necessary when action is refracted by a symbolic medium. They are used to construct appropriate linkages between a symbol and the reality it means to convey. The operators who were learning to effect the production process through the manipulation of electronic data were acutely aware of the problem of meaning, and their early experiences were laden with doubt regarding the representational power of that medium.

As they began to develop and apply intellective skill, I observed two distinct levels of complexity in terms of which the problem of meaning was organized. One involved the relationship of the electronic symbols to a concrete world. The second concerned symbols as a reflection of abstract functions, variables, and systemic relationships.

At the first level, operators experienced a blunt mistrust of the electronic data. Their initial efforts were geared toward establishing, psychologically and intellectually, the legitimacy of the data and their representational power. In other words, operators had to feel certain about what the data signified before they could approach the more complex aspects of their meaning.

Isaac was a Piney Wood manager, one of the few individuals promoted from the ranks, who was widely respected by workers and managers alike. He was a soft-spoken and gentle man who conveyed a sense of whimsy and serene wisdom in his conversation. With the massive technology conversions under way, Isaac had lobbied for and won a tiny appropriation to pull together a technology training laboratory where mock-ups of the control room terminals were available to improve operators' sense of familiarity and comfort with the new technology. He had pressed upper management for the modest funds after sensing the psychological dislocation caused by the new technology. Isaac spent long hours listening to worker's reactions to the new technology, observing how they interacted with it, and trying to help them learn. He discovered that:

> They haven't learned to trust the machine to tell them what to do. This trust does not come naturally. It will only come when they really understand how it works.

Isaac states the problem as if the fault lies in the operators' hardheaded reluctance to trust the machine. It is as if the machine is *supposed* to tell them what to do. If the men would only relinquish their suspicion, they would be free to enter into a more harmonious relationship with the computer. However, many operators sensed that the relationship between data and reality is a matter for inquiry, inherently problematic. As a man with over twenty years of experience in Piney Wood put it:

> You can ask for 50 percent output to your damper, but even if the screen says you have got it, how can you be sure unless you have turned the damper yourself and can see that it is open? You have to depend on the computer to tell you the truth, just like a fellow working for you. But it is not necessarily the truth. You are dependent on that machine. If that machine lies to you, you cannot do your work. You can learn to rely on an individual, but you can't learn to rely on a computer machine.

There are at least two dimensions to this crisis of trust. The first is captured by the question, what does this mean? Significance is not a transparent feature of the data from the system; rather, significance is a construction that emerges from the application of intellective skill to the available data. Only through interpretation can data become a vehicle for the experience of the mastery, certainty, and control that was routinely available in the world of action-centered skill. The need for competent interpretation as a prerequisite for trust hits at the core of the difference between action-centered and intellective skills.

> The computer makes your job easier . . . but it also makes things more complicated. You have to know how to read it and what it means. That is the biggest problem. What does that number actually mean? You have to know this if you want to really learn how to trust the technology.

Even when interpretation is competent, meaning is open to vulnerability in new ways that concern the technology's reliability. Algorithms can be wrong or improperly programmed; a faulty circuit can cause an incorrect instrument reading and render a set of worthless data. Before, knowledge was immediate. Now, any slender sense of certainty is prey to a hundred invisible dependencies.

> You haven't proved to me that I can trust the system. The men who programmed the system can make mistakes. . . . When you put your hands on things, you knew what you were doing. Instead of the process becoming simpler, it's become more complex.

The second dimension of this crisis involves the ambiguity of action. It is conveyed in the question, what have I done? The computer system now interpolates between the worker and the action context, and as it does so, it represents to the worker his or her effects on the world. However, reading symbols does not provoke the same feeling of having done something as one gets from more direct, organic involvement in execution. There is a continual questioning of action—Have I done anything? How can I be sure? Computer mediation seems to bathe action in a more conditional light: perhaps it happened; perhaps it didn't. Without the layered richness of direct sensory engagement, the symbolic medium seems thin, flat, and fragile. At the outset, the precariousness of the relationship between cause and effect is perplexing. Isaac observes:

> One of the real stumbling blocks in learning to trust is that if you are in a room with a screen, you have a hard time convincing yourself that something is really happening.

Other operators also give voice to this experience:

> In learning to work with this new equipment, it takes a while to believe that when you push a button something is actually taking place somewhere else. You don't get the feeling that things are connected. How can pushing a button in here make something happen somewhere else?

> What strikes me as most strange, hardest to get used to, is the idea of touching a button and making a motor run. It's the remoteness. I can start it from up here, and that is hard to conceive. I can be up in the control room and touch the keyboard, and something very far away in that process will be affected. It takes a while to gain the confidence that it will be OK, that what you do though the terminal actually will have the right effects. . . . It's hard to imagine that I am sitting down here in front of this terminal and running a whole piece of that plant outside. The buttons do all the work.

Piney Wood's operators are not the only ones who experience this epistemological distress. I attended a meeting in which plant managers discussed their technological needs with executives and technologists from one of the most prominent vendors of information and control technology. An executive from the vendor firm puzzled over "strange accounts" reported by several other clients: employees' complaints that they were "losing touch with reality" as they came to depend upon the new technology. "We should be able to respond to this," he lamented, "but we don't know how." He recounted a recent episode involving advanced automation in a new auto plant. A shop floor foreman was relocated to a control room, where he was expected to monitor the production process from a computer terminal:

> This foreman had lost his sense of what was going on down on the floor. He had to continually send someone down to the floor to check because he was losing the feel for what he was doing, even though he could call up anything he wanted in the data.
> Our response was—build in some redundancy so you can double-check things automatically. It was a technical solution that was irrelevant to the problem since the guy was sophisticated enough to already know the potential technical solutions. His problem was something different. He wanted to feel it, be involved with it, and he had lost that. We tend to dismiss this as defensiveness, but I am suspicious now that it is more than that.

The foreman's sense of unreality was the result of being cut off from the action context in which he had felt certain knowledge. The vendor's response was to provide yet more electronic data, but additional abstract cues simply intensify the need to ascertain their referential function, without providing new mechanisms that might aid in that process.

The vendors were aware of the problem of reference and the discomfort caused by the loss of physicality in task execution. Their expertise in designing technology led them to view this issue as a technical problem. In the discussion of design choices related to microprocessor-based process control technology, a senior designer noted:

> Technology will tend to prevail in the long run. We just have to supply the kind of information so that someone doesn't miss the shop floor. We see a greater use of graphics to replace the sense of a "hands-on" involvement.

Another design expert considered the difficulties introduced by the new reliance on a symbolic medium and, again, offered a technical solution for the problem of reference and the need to develop a psychological sense of trust in the computer system:

> The pressure is to get everything that is sensed and convert it to a symbol. In the long run, greater efficiencies of quick interpretation will depend upon greater symbolism. You can respond more quickly, and it's a more abstract and imagination-based approach. The crucial thing is that symbols must derive from reliable data. That is key. You must be able to trust your symbols. We are striving to make this true by relying on the machine's capability for self-diagnosis. Confidence in the symbols of operation is worth it, even if it takes brute-force measures like giving someone the job of maintaining one sensor. It is worth it if the value of that measure is high enough.

Again, the technologists address the problem of symbolic reference by further abstracting the data medium. Their cure for epistemological distress is more extensive use of symbols coupled with enhanced reliability.

The psychological discomfort that gives rise to doubt reflects the loss of an immediate knowledge for which there is as yet no replacement. Knowledge had depended in large measure upon the body and its experience of concrete cues. Now the operator feels both personally diminished and weakened by a loss of crucial contextual information. A new sense of certainty depends first upon clarifying the referential function of the data. Deductions are not read off the face of appearances; they are not transparent features of the terminal screen. Rather, they depend upon understanding, and understanding can be developed only from a solid intellective skill base that recognizes what symbols are supposed to represent and that has invented mechanisms for validating that they really *do* carry such force. This complexity is amply reflected in the following story told by a process engineer in Cedar Bluff who had been deeply involved in training the new work force to operate from the computerized control interface:

> One of the hardest pieces of training the new workers was to get them to understand the connections between the computer and the physical process. This connection does not happen spontaneously. When there is a discrepancy, they come back with things like: "The system said it was stable; I don't know why it was not right." They don't seem to handle upset conditions as well when they only have the computer and not the physical reality. I see them just pushing buttons, but they don't feel the consequences of that as they should. The other day they did not connect a reading of 105 percent to pulp flying across the street. There are ways to get out of that situation, but you have to be able to pick up on the alternatives. The information tells them that somewhere out there something is happening, but it doesn't seem to affect you because it is so remote. You have to learn how to make abstract judgments.

Because the referential function of electronic data is not taken for granted, operators began to invent ways to conquer the felt distance between electronic symbol and reality. Like the foreman in the auto plant, some created physical adaptations to solve the problem of reference. Each case involved finding new ways to connect the symbolic medium to the action context. This made it possible to compare distinct forms of data and increase the confidence they could feel about knowing "what's going on."[6]

> If I had to sit at the computer for twelve hours . . . I don't know, it's horrible thinking about it. When you walk around, you see things that make you think and ask questions. If you just sit back and look at the numbers all the time, you become a machine like the computer.

Sometimes operators teamed up, one person remaining in the control room, the other roving the plant, and the two communicating via walkie-talkie. Others would run back and forth between the control room and the production area in order to verify the system's readings.

> You should never put your faith into what these things tell you. If you believe in them and run off them, you will blow the place up. It requires continual checking.

In each mill, a series of changes was made in the control rooms in order to bring some remaining pieces of the old action context into the operator's visual reach. Video monitors were installed where lack of attention to equipment could have immediate physical consequences. In such instances, problems that were difficult to detect from remote data could be easily spotted from visual contact. For example, in Piney Wood's bleaching area, cameras trained on a surge tank enabled operators to monitor its levels easily and to prevent major pulp spillages:

> We've been running things blind, and it has been a shock. We just got a TV camera this year to prevent big pulp spills. The men can watch the cameras and keep the pulp off the floor. Unless the camera was there, he won't pay it no mind if it spills over because he's so busy. It would have to hit him on the head in the control room before he'd know it without the camera.

In Cedar Bluff, powerhouse operators faced a similar situation with their bark bins that held fuel for the furnace:

> There's a bin indicator on the computer and on the video. There's nothing better than sight. Those indicators can get stuck by just one piece of bark on it. The computer will say the bin is full when it's empty. Alarms go off all day long, so we always look at the video first. When that bark gets clogged on the assembly, it piles up real quick. If you don't catch it, it means that in just ten minutes, you'll have fifteen to twenty tons to shovel. That belt runs at 300 to 350 feet per minute. Before the video and special alarm, we wouldn't know it until the bark fell down the boiler right in front of this control room window. If you spill bark now, you have to be dead asleep—you'd have to sleep through four alarms. You would really catch hell for a bark spill now.

The more fundamental adaptations involve the quality of mind that a worker brings to the computer screen. In each mill, operators and managers alike described one important component of this quality of mind:

the capacity to paint an inward picture of the world to which the data refer. This inner vision, constructed out of a combination of memory and imagination, must take the place of a world that is ready-at-hand. When an operator becomes adept at this mental imaging, it is possible to respond more smoothly to the data. The portrait etched in thought helps to solve the problem of reference.

A Cedar Bluff process engineer with two years of experience training operators describes this quality of mind:

> I think being successful here has a lot to do with imagination. You have to be able to imagine things that you have never seen, to visualize them. For example, when you see a dash on the screen, you need to be able to relate that to a thirty-five-foot-square-by-twenty-five-foot-high room full of pulp. I think it has a lot to do with creativity and the freedom to fantasize. Sometimes I wonder if this eventually turns the operator into something like an autistic child with a closed circuit on their own imagination instead of actual sensory input.

Piney Wood's director of training makes a similar point:

> To be successful in this new environment you need a mental picture of what the systems refer to. It is easy to know when everything is right. You have to know what is happening when something is wrong by being able to relate the data you see to the actual process as you can envision it.

Operators describe what they go through mentally in order to grapple with the loss of immediacy and the feeling of confronting data whose connection to reality is experienced as problematic. In Cedar Bluff, one woman says:

> You have to have a mental picture of what is going on behind the indicators. When I plug into the screen, I try to imagine what is going on.

An old hand in Piney Wood explained it this way:

> In the back of my mind I can see what is going on in the mill (he grabs the back of his head with his left hand). The front of my head has to have the screens in it (he places the palm of his right hand over his forehead). You have to picture it all in your head. You have a lot going on in your head. If you have to shut down a pump, you can't do it unless you have it back here (he places the fingertips from

his left hand at the base of his skull above his neck). So I go back here (he points to the back of his head) to see the stock flow, and then to here (he points to his forehead and then to the screen) to fix it.

Operators at Cedar Bluff described a similar internal mechanism:

> When I look at the numbers I see the process. This controller is saying, "Hey, I don't need as much fuel in the boiler." That's what the numbers are telling you. The numbers talk to me.

> Each number is telling you about something, and you draw a picture in your own mind. Each number has a picture, and each number is connected to another number, et cetera, . . . and you get a map. You see the number, the equipment, and all the pieces of equipment related to it.

The act of visualization brings internal resources to bear in order to soften the sense of distance, disconnection, and uncertainty that is created by the withdrawal from a three-dimensional action context. Ironically, it means creating a doubly abstract world, where the reference function of the electronic symbols becomes less problematic because of yet another layer of abstractions (mental images) called up to serve as referents.

Operators did not appear equally adept at generating an inward image.[7] Many seemed unable to link data on the screen to a referential reality. Their interactions with the data were confined to the two-dimensional space of the terminal screen; the electronic symbols were deciphered according to the varying patterns in which they were arrayed. Typically, when asked what the data on the screen meant, these operators would point to distinct data elements and discuss them in terms of their spatial relationships on the screen, as if there were no external referents. Here is an example of such behavior as drawn from my field notes:

> Today I spent the afternoon in Piney Wood's bleach plant control room. Because it was Saturday, there were less people in the mill, and I had a great deal of time to speak with Gregory, who was in the control room most of the afternoon. He is a young man who wore a baseball cap made from black netting and canvas. Over the visor it said, "I may be dumb, but I'm not stupid." I asked Gregory, as I had asked so many operators, "How do you operate with the computer?" Each time he began to explain his answer, he used his index finger

to point to different readings on the screen and trace a path from
one reading to another. His utterances consisted exclusively of statements such as "When this (pointing to one reading) moves up here
(pointing to a location on the screen), then this one (another reading
indicated) will move down here (another location on the screen).
Each question I asked ("What is this? What does this mean?") elicited
more of the same. Finally, after about one half hour, Gregory seemed
agitated and frustrated. The agitation was not directed toward me,
at least I had no indication of that. Instead, he seemed frustrated by
the limits of his ability to explain anything to me. He stood up
abruptly and said, "Come on, I'll show you." With this, he guided
me out into the bleach plant and gave me a tour of the equipment.
He showed me the washers and the old instrument panels by the side
of each washer that used to be the way variables such as viscosity
levels were monitored. At each washer he stopped, stuck his hand
into the vat, and brought out a fistful of wet pulp. Rolling it between
his fingers, squeezing it, and sniffing it, he explained what stage each
sample was in. After the tour, his tone was that of someone speaking
in secrecy and confidence. "Using the computer might be easier if
the screens were arranged like the physical things on the floor. I don't
really work this computer stuff that well; I don't really understand it
all that well."

Gregory was unable to bring the external world of the plant into the
computer control room, either through visualization and the resulting
mental appropriation of that tangible reality or through formal language. His methods of explanation relied upon being able to touch and
exhibit the real thing. The screen was an encapsulated, formal space
unrelated to the plant beyond the control room door. He knew his way
around the screen, not because he could give meaning to what he saw
there, but because he had noticed through trial and error how data
elements were arrayed in relation to one another. Gregory could locate
himself knowledgeably in the action context but could not intellectually consolidate the connection between that context and the symbolic
medium. Instead, he turned the terminal screen into another sort of
action space by treating the symbols as mechanical moving parts whose
interaction could be sorted through the same kind of "trial-and-error"
and "cause-and-effect" active experimentation that one would engage
in while working on the shop floor.

The ability to supply a referential world for the electronic data is a
first and necessary step toward being able to invest the data with conceptual meaning. As the action context is obliterated by new technical

arrangements, there is less opportunity for recourse to action-centered skill as a source of immediate knowledge. This means that a return to feelings of certainty, competence, and control will depend more and more upon the quality of intellective skill and the invention of creative methods to tighten the connection between symbol and reality.

In the meantime, most operators felt pressured to resolve their sense of mistrust and bridge the gulf that had opened up between cause and effect, action and result. Many believed that as their intellective skill improved, they would learn to trust the computer, or that trial-and-error experience over a period of time would teach them to trust. There was a general sense that it was imperative to somehow get beyond the stressful feelings caused by the sense of uncertainty and disconnection. A Piney Wood operator reflected:

> I think being in this room with the computers is more mind work. But the longer you work with it, the more you will trust it. It is hard to learn to trust it. Right now, the men are afraid; they don't trust it, and so there is a lot of stress. They need to learn how to rely on it so they can relax.

Managers play an important role in this dilemma. They tend to perceive operator mistrust as an expression of resistance to technology change and so believe their interests will be served by exhorting workers to put their faith in the new systems. They view the withholding of trust and the refusal to rely on the technology as evidence of primitive thinking and look for ways to wean the worker away from a fixation with concrete reality. "Operators need to learn," summarized one manager, "that if you see the system indicates a flow, you can deduce that a pump is running." A Cedar Bluff operator relates:

> If you are in the situation where the computer reads one thing and the valve says another, we are told to believe the computer. . . . We did one time experience a runaway refiner. We had turned it off up here, and we believed that it was off. The fact is that it wasn't off, but the computer was telling us it was off. It's scary to believe in the computer, because that is all you have to go on unless something really goes wrong and you see it and you monitor it. But you have to get your confidence in the system, and usually the control is right.

Though these problems of meaning remained strong throughout the four years of my field visits, by the second half of year two, a new stream of sentiment had emerged, first at Cedar Bluff and somewhat more slowly at Piney Wood. It involved the age-old trade-off between skill and ease.

Cedar Bluff's work force, young and well educated (their average age was twenty-six, and almost half had completed one or two years of college-level training), was the first to perceive the opportunities offered by computer technology. Most of these workers had little industrial experience. Some had worked in farming or in light manufacturing, but most had been clerks or had held other low-paying service jobs. They were a group that seemed still unbowed by life. Most of those with whom I spoke did not associate work with suffering, at least they did not assume that doing a good day's work should leave them exhausted.

Their initial perplexity with the reference function of the information systems inspired curiosity and a need to understand the actual physical processes, while they withheld their trust from the computer. Mounting exhortations from many managers to increase their reliance on the computer, together with a certain amount of actual learning (both real conceptual appropriation and trial-and-error experience), allowed a new sensibility to take root. It was finally the ease offered by the computer system that induced many of these men and women to take the leap of faith that had been asked of them. The conditions of their work were consistent with their expectations for order, ease, control, effortlessness, cleanliness, and cogency. Though intellective demands could pose a real challenge and strain their ability, the freedom from physical exertion came to be perceived by these workers as irresistible and, finally, essential.

Most Cedar Bluff operators with whom I spoke shared the desires of so many workers in earlier generations—to preserve their bodies from depletion, to protect themselves from effort. Many seemed to expect the world to provide them with the means to "save" themselves. They shared an underlying sense that "technology is here to serve us." Technology could put the plant at their fingertips and wipe the sweat from their brows.

> I like this job. There are nice control rooms to sit in. You don't have to walk up and down the machines. When everything is running right, you don't have that much to do. It's very convenient. . . . You need to know how the system operates. You learn to look at the screen and detect when something is wrong. I depend on it. I can't imagine a paper mill running without it. We don't want to work any more than we have to.

> I used to be a jet mechanic, but this is better. It's easy and clean. I don't want to turn wrenches anymore, or get nasty and greasy. Once I had a taste of this, I didn't want to go back. I have changed my career path.

> I enjoy not having to go out and do manual labor. I can just punch in where I want the oil flow to go. I don't have to go anywhere or do anything.

> The computer makes our job easier. It takes the pressure off of us. You can have a snack, you can talk. I can leave this job and go home and relax.

The workers at Piney Wood were slower to develop an appreciation of this aspect of the computer system. They seemed, in general, more ambivalent. Even as the system displaced skills that had been their source of competence, certainty, and control, it permitted a degree of self-preservation that far exceeded their expectations. Most of them had never thought of themselves as being able to have an "easy" time at work. It was not that they wanted to work as hard as they did but that they never seriously considered any alternative. They did not expect to spend their days in comfort. Isaac shared his observations from the technology training room:

> They have begun to bring their wives to the room to see what they are working on. I have heard guys brag, "Look, I've almost got a tie on." I think they like the computer because they are sitting in a comfortable chair, in an air-conditioned room, and it's almost white-collar work.

Other operators noted the seductive advantages of the control room:

> People do use the computer as an opening to get out of physical work. Sitting here pushing buttons is more appealing than being out there doing something physical. There are some aspects of each job that people don't like. So now they are sloughing off the physical work. Going out into the process and checking things is more work, and it's hot, nasty, and wet. Most people would rather be in the control room.

> A man should enjoy his life. So why not take advantage of the computer?

Many managers, faced with their workers' initial mistrust of the new control systems, intensified their insistence that workers learn to operate by the computer. As the action context associated with their action-centered skills began to disappear with the new technical arrangements, more workers felt an inner need to escape the anxiety caused by the dogged feelings of mistrust and unreality associated with computer mediation. With the growing realization that working through the computer could be physically easier than anything they had ever known, many of the older workers were finally weaned away from their attachment to concrete objects. Many of the younger ones were persuaded that direct knowledge of a tangible reality was not, after all, crucial.

Inference and Insight

Once operators had established the referential function of the data, many moved to a higher level of complexity in dealing with the system of electronic symbols. At this level, the problem was not only to clarify the significance of individual data elements but also to construct from these elements, and particularly from their combinations, an interpretation of abstract properties of the production process. Instead of a problem of correspondence, the data now presented an opportunity for insight into functional relationships, states, conditions, trends, likely developments, and underlying causes, none of which can be reduced to a concrete external referent. In other words, data needed to be translated into information, and information into insight. At this stage, abstract thinking, explicit inference, and procedural reasoning are used both inductively and deductively in the service of building, testing, and refining hypotheses concerning the current functioning of the production process.

The Cedar Bluff start-up was one of the most advanced automation efforts throughout that mill's parent company and, as such, was the first opportunity to learn what might be involved in training an inexperienced work force to become competent in a high technology environment. Managers there spent a great deal of time trying to understand what operators "do" at the data interface. During the first years of operation, many managers had begun to appreciate the analytical demands exerted by the information presence. A systems engineer who had worked closely with the operators described the inductive reasoning that many developed in order to operate from the terminals:

> When you want to know what is going on in a part of the plant, you
> roll through several screens of data. You must keep important data

in your mind as you continue to scan. People learn how to organize
data in their minds. They build models in their minds about what is
really happening, and they build on the model with the data until
they have a complete picture.

The operators themselves had come to believe that analytical skills
were now essential elements of competence. As one young operator
put it,

> management wants to know how you are going to handle problems.
> They want to see your logical thinking, your reasoning. We need to
> be systematic; we need to analyze problems. The reasoning is all in
> your head.

The plant manager went one step further. He saw the technology as
a means of learning, a force that would educate workers to reason
systemically both inductively and deductively:

> We are depending on the technology to educate our people in ab-
> stract thinking. . . . You can no longer make a decision just based on
> local data. There is so much going on in the plant . . . you have to
> derive your decision from the interrelationships among the variables.

The physical process was represented by an interlocking set of variables, so that in order to "do" something, operators needed to know
how to make their way through this web of interdependencies. When
problems occurred, variations in these interdependencies were used as
the basis for formulating probabilistic statements and hypotheses that
might explain the event. Data from the screens, as well as from other
sources (for example, actual checking of plant equipment), were used
to disconfirm or refine these hypotheses.

The ability to engage in such analytical reasoning is complemented
by an overarching theoretical conception of the processes to which the
data refer. Such a theoretical grasp provides a basis for deduction. It
can guide operators through the data and inform hypothesis generation. Intellective competence at this level depends upon an explicit,
consciously articulated theory that can provide a framework for data
analysis.

The centrality of a theoretical understanding of the process had become one of the principal criteria with which Cedar Bluff's management evaluated its operators. Those with a theoretical grasp of the

process were most likely to be promoted to the higher pay curves. Top managers stressed the value of such theoretical knowledge among the operating work force and believed that without such knowledge, it would be impossible for operators to develop the quality of insight that would allow them to improve plant performance.

> The hope in Cedar Bluff is that people will discover ways to improve the process because they understand the basic theory.

Such emphasis was borne out among the workers themselves, who perceived theoretical knowledge as a salient factor in the development of their own competence:

> The more I learn theoretically, the more I can see in the information. Raw data turns into information with my knowledge. I find that you have to be able to know more in order to do more. It is your understanding of the process that guides you.

> We need to keep refining and defining what we have learned. There is a difference between knowing the instruments and knowing the relationships and theories that connect things. We need to understand the relationships between density and volume and flow and pressure. It's like knowing what it does versus knowing why and how. If you want to handle a problem, you have to want to know this.

In the traditional operating environment, such theoretical knowledge had been the exclusive domain of managers and engineers. Like the operators studied by Blauner and Crossman discussed in chapter 1, most of Piney Wood's workers knew how to do things, but they had little understanding of what they were doing and why. In the transition to data-based reasoning, they faced the need to learn theory as well. Many of Piney Wood's operators felt pressured to approach their work in a more explicit, systemic, and conceptual mode than they had ever before considered.

> To do the job well now you need to understand this part of the mill and how it relates to the rest of the plant. You need a concept of what you are doing. Now you can't just look around you and know what is happening; you can't just see it. You have to check through the data on the computer to see your effects. And if you don't know what to look for in the data, you won't know what's happening.

As a manager at Piney Wood explained:

We've never expected them to understand how the plant works, just to operate it. But now if they don't know the theory behind how the plant works, how can we expect them to understand all of the variables in the new computer system and how these variables interact?

Cognitive scientists have recognized two interdependent forms of perceptual processing. One proceeds by noticing and piecing together elements so that a coherent interpretation is constructed from the bottom up. The second proceeds by imposing a higher level of general knowledge on simpler perceptual units in order to arrive at an interpretation. Both "bottom-up" and "top-down" processing are vital. Without a capacity to impose order from the top down, our perceptual apparatus would be overwhelmed by stimuli. Without a capacity to take in living detail, all perception would be solipsistic and inflexible.

In the world of action-centered skill, the action context was the source of top-down processing. That context allowed a worker to know what kinds of details to look for and what kinds of data to expect. It provided an important framework for making sense of what was experienced. In the computer-mediated environment, theoretical understanding becomes a principal source of top-down perception. A theoretical conception of what might be happening in one's direct sphere of responsibility can be a guide through the data, providing criteria for allocating attention. It is a source of clues about where to dig deeper into the data base in order to disconfirm or refine hypotheses, and it makes the data base manageable by allowing a selective sampling from the available inputs in order to build a coherent diagnosis.

To summarize, the computerization process in these mills was undertaken in order to improve production control, process stability, and increase productivity. However, the new control technology had the parallel effect of informating the operators' task environment. Accomplishing work came to depend more upon thinking about and responding to an electronically presented symbolic medium than upon acting out know-how derived from sentient experience. The bundle of cognitive processes associated with these new activities—"thinking about," "responding to"—I have labeled *intellective skill*. It encompasses a shift away from physical cues, toward sense-making based more exclusively upon abstract cues; explicit inferential reasoning used both inductively and deductively; and procedural, systemic thinking. Intellective skill works through the problem of symbolic meaning at two levels. First, it establishes the referential power of symbols and thus provides them with legitimacy. Second, it uses the symbolic medium to ascertain the condition of "reality" in ways that cannot be reduced to correspondence with physical objects (for example, the ability to discern states, trends, underlying causes, relations, dynamics, predictions, sources of suboptimization, opportunities for improvement, et cetera). A theoretical conception of the total process is essential if intellective skill is to be successfully applied to the problem of meaning in this way.

What relevance might this transformation in the quality of knowledge required for competence in production work have for other forms of work? How do the dynamics associated with computerization in the offices of the service sector compare to those that have been described in the industrial settings of the three mills? In order to answer these questions, it will be necessary to turn once again to the historical record in order to examine the qualities of knowledge that have been associated with managerial and clerical activities during the past two centuries. This framework then will be used to consider the current dilemmas associated with the transformation of knowledge in clerical and professional settings.

CHAPTER THREE

THE WHITE-COLLAR BODY
IN HISTORY

When white-collar people get jobs, they sell
not only their time and energy but their
personalities as well. They sell by the week
or month their smiles and their kindly
gestures, and they must practice the prompt
repression of resentment and aggression. For
these intimate traits are of commercial
relevance.

—C. WRIGHT MILLS
White Collar

THE UNIQUE ETIOLOGY OF "WHITE-COLLAR" WORK

The use of the term *white collar* is, in a way, out of keeping with the
argument I have thus far presented. As the work of the sentient body
is displaced by the newer demands of intellective effort, who is to tell
the "white collars" from the "blue collars"? But it is precisely the way
in which these terms are dated that I want to draw upon in this chapter.
The difference they refer to is one that must be understood if we are
to explore the consequences of an informating technology for bureaucratic coordination—that is, the work of white-collared middle managers and their clerks.

Before closing in on the difference captured by these terms, we can
note their similarity. Both are about *collars*—about how people dress.

They evoke images of costume, physical bearing, and self-presentation. In each case, the term recognizes a body and the choices about how it is to be clothed. The difference between "white collar" and "blue collar" tells us much about what those bodies are likely to be up to. A blue collar indicates the probability of being soiled, while the white collar communicates the proud assumption that whatever stresses the white-collar body may endure, it will not be required to face the dirt and muscular exertion of animal effort.

It is evident that information technology can eliminate the utility of the blue-collar designation, the weight and consequence of which can be grasped only in light of the long, sometimes proud and sometimes sorry, history of the laboring body. It may well be that those individuals who remain in the manufacturing sector of the work force will be able to trade in their blue collars for ones that are gleaming white. However, this historical trajectory of the blue-collar body does little to inform our understanding of what has been white-collar work and what it is likely to become.

The evolution of white-collar work has followed a historical path that is in many ways the precise opposite of that taken by blue-collar work. Manufacturing has its roots in the work of skilled craft. In most cases, that work was successively gutted of the elements that made it skillful—leaving behind jobs that were simplified and routinized. An examination of work at the various levels of the management hierarchy reveals a different process. Elements of managerial work most easily subjected to rationalization were "carved out" of the manager's activities. The foundational example of this process is the rationalization of executive work, which was accomplished by ejecting those elements that could be explicated and systematized, preserving intact the skills that comprise executive craft. It was the carving out of such elements that created the array of functions we now associate with middle management. A similar process accounts for the origins of clerical work. In each case, the most easily rationalized features of the activities at one level were carved out, pushed downward, and used to create wholly new lower-level jobs. In this process, higher-level positions were not eliminated; on the contrary, they came to be seen more than ever as the depository of the organization's skills.

The role of the body in white-collar work is a further counterpoint to the experience of workers in manufacturing. Blue-collar workers used their bodies in the service of *acting-on*, to transform materials and utilize equipment. White-collar employees used their bodies, too, but in the service of *acting-with*, for interpersonal communication and coordination. It was not until the intensive introduction of office machinery, and with it scientific management, that this distinct orientation was challenged. During this period, an effort was made to invent a new kind of clerical work—work that more closely resembled the laboring body continually *acting-on* the inanimate objects, paper and equipment, that were coming to define modern office work. Automation in the factory had diverse effects, frequently limiting human effort and physical suffering, though sometimes exacerbating it. But the discontinuity in the nature of clerical work introduced with office machinery, together with the application of Tayloristic forms of work organization, did much to increase the physical suffering of the clerk. While it remained possible to keep a white collar clean, the clerk's position was severed from its earlier responsibilities of social coordination and was converted instead to an emphasis on regularity of physical effort and mental concentration.

In order to trace the unique etiology of white-collar work and the more recent discontinuities in the nature of clerical activity, it is necessary to start not only at the beginning but also at the top. It is in the nature of executive action that we can see the skillful domain from which middle-management functions were extracted. Similarly, the diversity and continued complexity of middle management provides the point of origin for clerical work as it once was and as it has become.

EXECUTIVE MANAGEMENT AS CRAFT

The first generations of industrial capitalists were owner-employers whose comprehensive, action-oriented, and undocumented know-how absorbed a wide range of management functions. As Sidney Pollard said of the early British entrepreneurs who founded many of the most important industrial works, "The typical entrepreneur was his own manager."[1] Or as Reinhard Bendix put it, "At one time individual entrepreneurs performed a large variety of routine administrative tasks in addition to their 'distinct economic function of undertaking new things.' "[2]

These owner-managers were engaged in activities ranging from invention to finance to direct supervision of their factories. Their knowhow was wrung from trial-and-error experience during a time when there were few resources for practical training. In fact, the term *management* had little meaning until well into the nineteenth century. Alfred Chandler reports that the owner-managers of that period were so immersed in the daily operation of their enterprises that they had little time or inclination left for objective evaluation and long-range planning: "The owner-managers prided themselves on their knowledge of a business they had done so much to build. They continued to be absorbed in the details of day-to-day operation. They personally reviewed the departmental reports and the statistical data. They had little or no staff to collect information and to provide expert advice. . . . Long-term planning was also highly personal . . . their moves were personal responses to new needs and opportunities."[3]

The dependence on oral communication was even more pronounced in a world where written documentation and correspondence were stored in boxes, pigeonholes, and difficult-to-read press books (bound volumes of tissue paper sheets onto which copies of letters had been impressed). Most business enterprises were small enough that orders, instructions, and reports could be given orally. The treasurer of one enterprise in 1887 defended the lack of written documentation in his organization: "We do not think printed rules amount to anything unless there is somebody around constantly to enforce them and if such a person is around printed forms can be dispensed with."[4]

The resistance to written communication is illustrated in a popular book published in 1896 by Seymour Eaton and called *How to Do Business as Business Is Done in Great Commercial Centers*. The volume is crammed with "hints and helps for Young Business Men," from banking and margin trading, to character, will, and cheerfulness, to grammar, arithmetic, or how to fold a letter, and his admonitions provide a clue to typical patterns of behavior. Eaton tries to cajole his readers to rely more upon written communication. "A letter is but a talk on paper," he says. "Things worth talking about are worth writing about."[5] The resistance to written communication must have been considerable if eager young businessmen required such encouragement to put pen to paper. Most calculations associated with commercial accounting were done mentally and communicated orally. Many successful merchants and entrepreneurs were well known for the speed of their mental calculations, and Eaton's how-to book provides a chapter on tricks and shortcuts to aid in rapid mental arithmetic.[6] Owner-managers frequently surrounded themselves with sons, nephews, and cousins—a move that facilitated oral communication through shared meaning and context and eased the pressure for written documentation.[7]

Detailed empirical studies of modern executives' work, several of which have been published over the last thirty years, are greeted with the curiosity and fascination usually reserved for anthropological accounts of obscure primitive societies. It is as if these researchers had brought back accounts from an organizational region that is concealed from observation and protected from rational analysis. Perhaps this sense of mystery surrounds top management activities because they derive from a set of skills that are embedded in individual action, in much the same way as those of the craftsperson. In both cases, skilled performance is characterized by sentient participation, contextuality, action-dependence, and personalism.

What is different is that the craftsperson used action-centered skills in the service of *acting-on* materials and equipment, while the top manager's action-centered skills are applied in the service of *acting-with*. Like the seventeenth-century courtier, the top manager uses his or her bodily presence as an instrument of interpersonal power, influence, learning, and communication. The know-how that is developed in the course of managerial experience in *acting-with* remains largely implicit: managers themselves have difficulty describing what they do. Only the cleverest research can translate such embedded practice into explicated material suitable for analysis and discussion.

In 1938, Chester Barnard, the executive turned scholar, wrote a lengthy treatise, *The Functions of the Executive*, that eloquently discussed the implicit, experience-based, action-centered quality of executive skills. In a summary description of the executive process, he wrote: "The process is the sensing of the organization as a whole and the total situation relevant to it. It transcends the capacity of merely intellectual methods, and the techniques of discriminating the factors of the situation. The terms pertinent to it are 'feeling,' 'judgment,' 'sense,' 'proportion,' 'balance,' 'appropriateness.' It is a matter of art rather than science, and is aesthetic rather than logical. For this reason it is recognized rather than described and is known by its effects rather than by analysis."[8]

Barnard believed that communication was the dominant function of

management and, as he put it, "the immediate origin of executive organization."[9] When he discussed an organization's communication system, however, he did not refer to technological devices, reporting procedures, or other methods of information gathering and dissemination.
For him, there were only two components of organized communication—the *means* and the *system*. In his view, people were the means of
communication, and the positions they held constituted its system:
"The center of communication is the organization service of a person
at a place." His reasoning, to put it in the language of this discussion,
was that an executive's place gave him or her exposure to a particular
action context. Each executive thus was responsible for grasping that
context and communicating it to the others. Executive communication
depended on each member of this small group giving voice to a facet
of the organization and so contributing to a shared sense of the whole.
Executive communication was expected to be largely oral, face-to-
face, and informal. For this reason, Barnard also emphasized the executive's bodily presence in its physical and characterological aspects, as
an instrument of *acting-with*:

> The general method of maintaining an informal executive organiza-
> tion is to operate and to select and promote executives so that a
> general condition of compatibility of personnel is maintained. Per-
> haps often and certainly occasionally, men cannot be promoted or
> selected, or even must be relieved, because they cannot function,
> because they "do not fit," where there is no question of formal com-
> petence. This question of "fitness" involves such matters as educa-
> tion, experience, age, sex, personal distinctions, prestige, race, na-
> tionality, faith, politics, sectional antecedents; and such very specific
> personal traits as manners, speech, personal appearance, etc. It goes
> by few if any rules, except those based at least nominally on other,
> formal, considerations. It represents in its best sense the political
> aspects of personal relationships in formal organization.[10]

The preeminence of action-centered skill has been stressed in several
recent studies of executive managers. John Kotter studied the daily
behavior of fifteen general managers and found that they spent most
of their time developing networks of relationships that provided the
insights they needed to develop their strategic agendas.[11] Kotter
stresses the implicit quality of the general managers' knowledge, noting
that their agendas tended to be informal, nonquantitative, mental road
maps highly related to "people" issues, rather than systematic, formal
planning documents.

Daniel Isenberg's research on "how senior managers think" has penetrated another layer of this, usually inarticulate, domain of executive management.[12] Isenberg found that top managers think in ways that are highly "intuitive" and integrated with action.[13] He concluded that the intuitive nature of executive behavior results from the inseparability of their thinking from their actions: "Since managers often 'know' what is right before they can analyze and explain it, they frequently act first and think later. Thinking is inextricably tied to action. . . . Managers develop thought about their companies and organizations not by analyzing a problematic situation and then acting, but by thinking and acting in close concert."[14] One manager described his own immersion in the action cycle: "It's as if your arms, your feet, and your body just move instinctively. You have a preoccupation with working capital, a preoccupation with capital expenditure, a preoccupation with people . . . and all this goes so fast that you don't even know whether it's completely rational, or it's part rational, part intuitive.[15]

Rosabeth Kanter's descriptive study of corporate life also underscored the salience of bodily presence in shared action contexts as the core of the manager's world.[16] Visible participation in the meanings and values of one's immediate group helps to build a joint experience base. In this way, managers can assume that they share a common language and understanding, which provides many shortcuts for communication in a pressured, rapid-fire world. Most of the managers she studied spent about half of their time in face-to-face communication. Kanter concluded that the manager's ability to "win acceptance" and to communicate was often more important than any substantive knowledge of the business. The feelings of comfort, efficiency, and trust that come with such shared meaning are triggered in a variety of ways by the manager's comportment. The nuances of nonverbal behavior and the signals embedded in physical appearance are an important aspect of such group participation. Because the tasks at the highest levels of the corporation are the most ambiguous, senior executives come to rely most heavily on the communicative ease that results from this shared intuitive world.

Henry Mintzberg authored a pathfinding empirical study of top managers' work in 1973.[17] He identified three role domains that account for most managerial activity: the interpersonal, the informational, and the decision-making roles. While there are intellective demands associated with each set of roles, the overwhelming emphasis in Mintzberg's data is on the action-centered skills that are at the core of each domain.

The interpersonal role, for example, relies upon the manager's bodily presence as an instrument of *acting-with*. Mintzberg stresses that actual leadership activity, as distinguished from the formal power derived from organizational status, is inseparable from the top manager's daily flow of interaction and communication. The most subtle elements of nonverbal behavior are treated as a window that exposes the manager's attitudes, values, and expectations. "In virtually everything he does, the manager's actions are screened by subordinates searching for leadership clues. In answering a request for authorization, he may encourage or inhibit a subordinate, and even in his form of greeting, messages (perhaps nonexistent ones) may be read by anxious subordinates."[18] Network building is based upon the manager's sociability in direct oral communication as he or she nurtures the goodwill of others.

Action-centered skills are no less critical in the informational and decision making roles. While top managers receive, through formal channels, a great deal of information that he or she must analyze and consider, the real work of monitoring the organization depends upon current information culled from personal contact, both face-to-face interactions and telephone conversations. Top managers rely on gossip, hearsay, and speculation gathered from these informal oral exchanges. Moreover, top managers were found to prefer what Mintzberg calls "trigger information"—concrete stimuli including specific events, conversations, and problems.[19] The personal, idiosyncratic, and oral nature of top managers' most important information presents a problem when it comes to dissemination. The kind of information that derives from personal contact can be communicated only through personal contact, thus limiting most top managers' efficiency as disseminators of important organizational data. Success in the informational role depends upon the quality of the top manager's social, nonverbal, and oral conduct.

In the decision-making role, Mintzberg found that top managers rely on "tangible information in the form of stimuli—specific events and ad hoc data—rather than the gradual trends displayed in routine reports."[20] The organizational disturbances that the top manager is required to handle typically arise in an unpredictable, ad hoc manner and are reacted to quickly with methods that frequently involve immediate oral exchange, discussion, persuasion, and negotiation. Mintzberg stresses that a top manager's plans tend to be flexible and largely implicit, in order to allow room for a dynamic response to the immediate environment: "My own impression is that the manager's plans are not explicit, documented in detail in the organization's files for all to see. Rather, crude plans seem to exist in the manager's mind in the form of a set of improvement projects that he would one day like to initiate."[21]

Mintzberg summarizes the characteristics of managerial activity that run through each role domain. There is, he notes, a strong preference for live action: "The job breeds adaptive information-manipulators who prefer the live concrete situation. The manager works in an environment of stimulus-response, and he develops in his work a clear preference for live action."[22] Another general trait is the attraction to oral, as opposed to written, communication. Mintzberg concurs with several other studies of managerial behavior in his finding that most of the top manager's time is spent in face-to-face communication, the telephone being the second preferred mode of interaction:[23] "Documented communication requires the use of a formal subset of language, and involves long feedback delays. All verbal media can transmit, in addition to the messages contained in the words used, messages sent by voice inflection and by delays in reaction. In addition, face-to-face media carry information transmitted by facial expression and by gesture. . . . The manager's productive output can be measured primarily in terms of verbally transmitted information."[24]

Top management activity is also relationship-intensive. Direct contact with subordinates and with actors external to the organization each require one-third to one-half of the top manager's time. Finally, Mintzberg, like others who have studied the management function, concludes that the job is physically taxing. Top managers' days and nights are filled to the breaking point with a myriad of activities, contacts, events, discussions, and meetings, which tend to be brief, rapid, and fragmented. Many students of managerial activity have proposed ways in which top managers could limit the demands on their time from the constant flow of interruptions. Mintzberg, however, takes another tack, pointing out that most top managers prefer to have their time organized this way, precisely because it keeps them in touch with the live action context of the organization. "They frequently interrupted their desk work to place telephone calls or to request that subordinates come by. One chief executive located his desk so that he could look down a long hallway. The door was usually open, and his subordinates were continually coming into his office."[25]

Though the top manager's work certainly has its intellective challenges, action-centered skill defines the core of each role domain. The same characteristics of action-centered skill as those encountered in craft work can be identified here:

1. *Sentience*. Top managers rely on seeing and hearing the people who constitute their relationship network. They seek ways to develop a "feel" for situations and actors.
2. *Action-dependence*. Top managers' skills are developed and conveyed in action. Their most critical activities demand bodily presence. Their experience tends to be organized into brief but intense action episodes. Learning and influence occurs primarily through action.
3. *Context-dependence*. Nonverbal communication is an important communication medium and is inherently context-dependent. Top managers require trigger information—concrete stimuli, rooted in an action context, which convey problems and issues. Personal knowledge is most efficiently communicated in face-to-face settings, where individuals share contextual meanings.
4. *Personalism*. Most of what the manager knows remains implicit and thus personal. The top manager's responses are of necessity filtered through his or her personality and style. Personal charisma and sociability are likely to be an important influence on the quality of the top manager's relationship network.

The skills of the top manager are not explicitly taught or explicitly learned; rather, they are assimilated through years of experience in the action context of the organization. As Mintzberg summarizes, "Today managing is an art, not a science. Most of the methods managers use are not properly understood; hence they are not taught or analyzed in any formal sense."[26] Minztberg laments the fact that management science has shed relatively little analytical light on top management activities. As a result, professional education does a better job of training specialists and middle managers whose work involves a greater degree of explicit knowledge than it does in teaching these skills associated with the executive process. As Barnard had concluded, "We know very little about how to do it."[27] The key obstacle facing the management scientist who would seek to analyze and then rationalize top management work lies in the implicit, embodied nature of executive knowhow: "The manager is the nerve center of his organization, with unique access to a wide variety of internal and external contacts that provide privileged information. But most of this information is not documented, and much of it is unsubstantiated and nonquantitative. As a result, the manager lacks a systematic method for passing it on to the management scientist, and most of it never reaches him. . . . Today the manager is the real data bank. . . . Unfortunately he is a walking and a talking data bank, but not a writing one. When he is busy, information ceases to flow. When he departs, so does the data bank."[28] Lodged in the body and dependent upon presence and active display, the implicit heart of the executive's special genius appears to evade rationalization.

HOW EXECUTIVE WORK WAS RATIONALIZED

This evasion has left many observers, including Mintzberg, quite frustrated. Reflecting on his findings concerning the implicit quality of top management know-how, Mintzberg hypothesized that management science would eventually arrive at the door of these managers, ready to apply the same principles of "scientific research" that Taylor's disciples had applied to the shop floor. It was just a matter of time before rational analysis would decompose managerial work and "reprogram" that work more efficiently. In this Mintzberg concurs with other scholars who have used the deskilling of craft work as the paradigmatic illustration of the rationalization of work.[29]

My own interpretation of the relationship between top management work and the process of rationalization is a different one. Top management work has now undergone almost a century of rationalization— and in a manner that is the precise opposite of the craft-work experience. In the case of executive activity, those elements most accessible to explication, and therefore rationalization, were carved out of the executive's immediate domain of concern. These more analytical or routine activities were projected into the functions of middle management, just as those functions were also absorbing new responsibilities for planning and coordination that had resulted from systematic analysis of the production process. Thus, the activities that made the executive most special, based on action-centered skill, were left intact, while the more explicit and even routine aspects of executive responsibilities were pushed downward and materialized in a variety of middle-management functions. This contrasts with the case of craft workers, in which the action-centered skills that had made them so special were researched, systematized, and expropriated upward. To put it bluntly, workers lost what was best in their jobs, the body as skill in the service of *acting-on*, while executives lost what was worst in their jobs, retaining full enjoyment of the skilled body as an instrument of *acting-with*.

To say that executive work can be rationalized is thus misleading. It may be that the future holds an increasingly diminished core of top management activity, but the work of the executive has been, by definition, work that is not subject to rationalization. Once managerial activity became subject to that procedure, it was no longer considered executive work. In fact, the more executive activity was projected downward and materialized in more rationalized processes, the more the executive was freed to indulge in the essence of his or her craft— the artful expression of knowledge in action. Executive power has been, among other things, a means by which to preserve the ultimate ineffability of this inner core of implicit knowledge—a power that most skilled workers did not enjoy.

This process of carving out and rationalizing aspects of executive activity underlies the structural articulation of the modern organization. For example, in his discussion of the bureaucratization of the economic enterprise, Reinhard Bendix observes that "seen historically, bureaucratization may be interpreted as the increasing subdivision of the functions which the owner-managers of the early enterprises had performed personally in the course of their daily routine. These functions may be divided into labor management, technical staff work, administrative management and mercantile functions of purchasing, sales, and finance. As the work involved became more extensive and complex . . . it came to be delegated to subordinates."[30]

The theme is sounded again in Chandler's discussion of the emergence of middle management in the American corporate enterprise. He notes that while owner-managers were reluctant to become more systematic about their own activities, they eventually hired salaried executives who "pioneered" the development of middle-management functions.[31] These new managers provided the infrastructure of their firms as they literally invented the methods and systems of administrative coordination and, in the process, gave definition to a wide range of functions such as finance, collection, service, marketing, distribution, purchasing, inventory control, transportation, production, accounting, pricing, sales, training, and labor management. Peter Drucker has railed against owner-managers like Henry Ford and Werner von Siemens precisely because they refused to recognize the necessity of middle-management functions, insisting instead on surrounding themselves with "helpers" who were dependent upon the boss's implicit knowledge, directives, and whims.[32]

During the 1920s and 1930s, there were earnest interpreters of business practice who, flushed with the success and rational appeal of scientific management, argued strenuously that executive activity should be subjected to the analytic rigors of Taylor's principles. One of these was Mary Parker Follett. In 1925 she told a conference of personnel administrators in New York City that "the next step business management should take is to organize the body of knowledge on which it should rest. . . . The recording of executive experience . . . should have . . . our immediate attention. . . . We need executive conferences with carefully worked out methods for comparing experience which has been scientifically recorded, analyzed, and organized. . . . From such experimenting and from the comparison of experience, I think certain standards would emerge.[33]

Mary Parker Follett deplored the idea that executive leadership involved an "intangible capacity" or that executives relied on "hunches" in making decisions. She praised the still-youthful trend toward functional management based upon expert knowledge. Ten years later a prominent management consultant, Harry Hopf, presented a paper to the Sixth International Congress for Scientific Management, in which he proposed that the next great step in developing a science of management was the practice of "optimology"—the science of the optimum. In certain respects his notions foreshadowed the field of operations research. He complained that executives tend to be circumscribed in their thinking because they are limited to the concrete and contextual. "They could readily interpret their relations with others in terms of working understandings which had grown up among them and their immediate associates; but to project their minds beyond was difficult."[34] He criticized executives who were guided primarily by "a strong speculative instinct" and insisted that successful management depended upon good planning: "Entering into the major aspects of planning and intimately associated with its manifestations, are the processes of analysis, simplification, and standardization. The ultimate realization of optimal conditions in a business enterprise is predicated upon adequate employment of these processes."[35]

If we accept the portraits of executive activity that emerge from the work of Barnard, Kotter, Isenberg, Kanter, and Mintzberg, then we are led to the conclusion that these earlier criticisms of the implicit action-oriented quality of top management work did not succeed in eliminating its artful core. Rather, these critiques were part of a larger movement toward the development of a new stratum of managerial functions that systematized important aspects of executive activity and, in so doing, extended its reach.

MIDDLE MANAGEMENT AND THE DEMANDS
OF *ACTING-WITH*

The case should not be drawn too starkly. The executive role involves its share of intellective endeavor that demands explicit, data-based, conceptual reasoning. Conversely, the middle-management role, with regard to both line and staff positions, retains much of the political and interpersonal activity associated with the requirements of general management. The world of the middle manager is unrelenting in its demand for skill in *acting-with*. Success and mobility depend upon working through one's subordinates and working well with one's peers. Like their superiors, middle managers must communicate, influence, motivate, persuade, and confront. The necessity for these fundamental encounters with others has been a critical part of all but the most specialized and technical managerial roles.

Moreover, middle management is the primary training ground for future executives. Since executive skill is experience-based, it follows that those middle managers who excel in *acting-with* are likely to be considered as executive material and their years in the ranks of middle management provide the opportunity to develop those skills. Throughout the century young managers have been advised to perfect their bodies as instruments in the subtleties of interpersonal influence. As early as 1902, a "how-to" book written for young aspirants to business success warned, "Be manly, and look it. Appear the gentleman, and be the gentleman. What's the good of unknown good? Negotiable intrinsic value must have the appearance of intrinsic worth."[36]

Objective criteria for judging the future potential of managers were virtually nonexistent. One study of the emergence of the white-collar occupational category in the Krupp Steel Casting Works before 1900 found that there was a great deal of upward mobility from the lower ranks of white-collar employment to the highest management level. However, advancement tended to occur within areas of functional exposure, highlighting experience as a qualification for managerial work, which was still relatively uncodified. Advancement also depended less upon formal criteria than upon such factors as "the impressions of an official, private connections, or kinship."[37] Another recent study, exploring the emergence of business schools at the turn of the century and how they attempted to meet the needs of the emerging class of middle managers, explained that "while the earlier version of the success theme had set forth ownership of large enterprises as the ultimate goal, now the focus was on rising into the managerial elite. Schooling took on new value, and the more one could obtain the better. Less emphasis was put on improving 'character' and more on improving on 'personality'; to get ahead, one had to get along with others, conquer self-created fear, and develop personal efficiency."[38]

The classic text among the success literature of the period was written by Dale Carnegie. Originally published in 1926 as *Public Speaking and Influencing Men in Business*, the now familiar title, *How to Win Friends and Influence People*, appeared on a new edition brought out ten years later. The book was used as the official textbook for training aspiring management recruits in a variety of major organizations, such as the New York Telephone Company and the American Institute of Banking. Carnegie told his readers that their success or failure depended upon the impressions they made in the four kinds of contacts that people have: "We are evaluated and classified by four things: by what we do, by how we look, by what we say, and how we say it."[39]

By 1938 Chester Barnard was telling his readers that "learning the organization ropes" was a matter of learning the "who's who, what's what, why's why, of its informal society."[40] Nor has the importance of this knowledge diminished in the fifty years since Barnard's observation. In Kanter's study of corporate men and women, she observed that it is generally the individual with the most intense aspiration for mobility who devotes the greatest share of his or her energy for learning to master organizational politics.[41] In the context of the interpersonal demands of the modern organization, this is a rational investment. Like the court societies of preindustrial Europe, bureaucratic leaders "often rely on outward manifestations to determine who is the 'right sort of person.' "[42] It is worth reviewing Kanter's description of this situation:

> There were other examples of the difficulty in pinning down what made a good manager. . . . The traits were so vague as to be almost meaningless, and they included a large number of elements subject to social interpretation: "empathy; integrity; acceptance of accountability; ambition; makes decisions; intelligent; takes appropriate risks; smart; uses the organization through trust and delegation; a good communicator; a good track record." A group of junior managers also made a list. . . . If anything the young managers' list increased the judgmental, interpretive social components: "good communicator; well organized; good interpersonal skills; a successful performer; high peer acceptance; a risk taker; highly visible to other managers; able to recognize opportunities; results oriented; and possessing the requisite amount of prior experience in the company and in the function."[43]

The emphasis in middle management on action-centered skill in the arena of *acting-with* has been both a rehearsal for a more comprehensive executive role and a measure of the integration between middle-management and executive functions. Though middle management developed as an exteriorization of those aspects of executive activity most accessible to rationalization, it was also necessary for a certain amount of the implicit action-centered skill characteristic of the executive process to be subsumed by successively lower ranks of management. Complex organizations are composed of complicated webs of relationships, and management requires motivation and coordination within this system of interdependencies. Management is fundamentally something that occurs between human beings and, as such, has employed all of the most artful methods that humans have devised for dealing with one another in order to get something done. In this way, every manager of subordinates must, to some extent, enact the executive role. Even managers in more specialized staff positions must know how to communicate and influence if their point of view is to be heard or their recommendations are to be implemented.

Again, the issue is a matter of emphasis. The research on executive activity cited earlier suggests that the core of that function involves the action-centered skills associated with *acting-with*. High-ranking middle-management functions are likely to involve considerably more extensive intellective work as well as action-centered skill. At successively lower management levels, the intellective component tends to become more routinized—standard reports, collection of daily operating data, and so forth—but some degree of action-centered skill remains crucial. Indeed, many studies have found that the position of foreman or first line supervisor is one of the most interpersonally demanding jobs in an organization.[44] Thus, while the bulk of rigorous intellective activity has tended to be concentrated in the middle ranks of the management organization, in varying degrees in line and staff positions, the requirements for action-centered skills related to the interpersonal world of the organization have also filtered down from the executive role.

The precipitation or diffusion of the executive process has tended to be a source of social cohesion among the various levels of management. It has provided a basis upon which these various groups could generate a rationale for a coincidence of interests between them, even where there is a considerable disparity in wages between the upper and lower levels of the managerial hierarchy. At every level, managers are united in their assumption of accountability for the organization's performance. Because organizations are, above all, configurations of persons, this accountability has inevitably required some immersion in the methods and manners of interpersonal presence and action.

THE ORIGINS OF CLERICAL WORK

The process by which activities subject to rationalization are projected downward and materialized in new functions, and the parallel, though more restricted, precipitation of interpersonal aspects of the executive process also account for the origin of clerical employment. The rationalization of office work during the course of this century has been viewed as another version of the deskilling process that transformed industrial work. Instead, the routinization of clerical work can be viewed as the result of a continual extrusion of middle-management activities as they became subject to further rationalization through the introduction of new technology and new techniques. These extrusions were the occasion for the creation of new organizational functions and strata, in much the same way that middle management first emerged as a rationalization of activities that were once integrated in the executive process.

This interpretation helps to explain why the activities of today's high-status clerical workers tend to have a great deal in common with those of an earlier generation. In both cases, these positions are close enough to the management domain to have absorbed some measure of the executive process as it trickled down the corporate hierarchy. It also helps explain why the rationalization of office work has resulted less in the displacement of old functions than in the creation of a vast number of new, highly differentiated low-status clerical positions.

David Lockwood used nineteenth-century pamphlets and periodicals to construct a description of the early British office. According to his study, *The Black-Coated Worker*, the first clerks were men, and their positions often served as entry points into management careers. The distinction between clerical and managerial functions was not rigidly drawn, and bookkeepers frequently were required to assume responsibilities that would now be considered managerial. In 1871 an observer described clerical work as requiring "knowledge of languages, skills in accounts, familiarity with even minute details of business, energy, promptitude, tact, delicacy of perception."[45] Pollard has noted that in those industrial enterprises where craft know-how was not considered crucial to the tasks of management, the position of accounting clerk was an important route for promotion into management. "The forte of such men would be their business and financial acumen and their relationship of trust to the employer, leaving technical know-how to be acquired later, as the less important consideration."[46]

In Toni Pierenkemper's study of the internal differentiation of employment at the Krupp Steel Casting Works during the late nineteenth century, he found four status groupings of white-collar employees marked by the system of payment (monthly versus biweekly) and by the budget from which their salaries were drawn (top management budget versus shop management budget). The status gradations roughly corresponded to the degree of executive process that their positions had absorbed. Pierenkemper compares his own data to that of several other studies of white-collar employment at that time and concludes that "the evidence suggests that industrial white collar employees in the late nineteenth century were a distinct but heterogeneous group. They performed a broad range of tasks—at one extreme close to those of management, at the other difficult to distinguish from those of the blue collar work force."[47]

Another study documented the experiences of female clerks in the federal government during the later part of the nineteenth century. The testimony of one woman who worked as a clerk examining the accounts of Indian agents, reveals the range of her accountability: For years I worked faithfully . . . the work being brain work of a character that requires a knowledge not only of the rulings of this Department, but also those of the Treasury, Second Auditor, Second Comptroller, and Revised Statutes; demanding the closest and most critical attention, together with a great deal of legal and business knowledge."[48] The experiences of another clerk, Jane Seavey, have survived in her correspondence. As a clerk in the Internal Revenue Bureau, she was put in charge of the recording room, where she was credited with introducing "a new system of organizing work in her section, a method of filing adopted throughout the Treasury Department and used as a model for other agencies as well."[49]

As the size of enterprises grew, it became increasingly difficult to operate by word of mouth. Written communication was required in order to ensure clarity in both lateral and subordinate relationships. There was a growing need for internal documentation, record keeping, and external correspondence. People and systems were needed to produce, maintain, and access the burgeoning load of written information.

More than any other single factor, the introduction of office machinery made it possible to relieve the pressure on the traditional office organization by carving out those functions subject to routinization from the more integrated activities of the early clerk. The most significant mechanical intervention was the typewriter, which was first introduced in the American market in the mid-1870s and was selling at rate of 60,000 per year by 1893. In 1919 the editors of the journal *Modern Business* published a list of thirty machines then commonly found in the office, ranging from the ubiquitous typewriter to mechanical messengers, envelope feeders, and statistical machines that punched and read cards.[50] The introduction of typewriters, the bookkeeping machine, and other forms of office equipment made it possible to extract from the clerk's job the laborious manual tasks associated with copying, preparing and checking data, printing, preparing mail and internal correspondence, billing, timekeeping, and routine arithmetical calculations. These machines could be operated by individuals with far less training than the years of experience, general education, and business knowledge that had characterized the clerk. A vast number of women were employed to fill the new positions.

Several studies have documented the spread of office machinery and its impact on the routinization, fragmentation, and feminization of clerical work.[51] I will not repeat the entirety of those findings here, but I will point to a few highlights. For example, the years from 1880 to 1890, when the typewriter was introduced to most American offices, saw the greatest increase of female clerical workers of any decade—a more than tenfold increase from 7,000 to 76,000. During the same year, the enrollment of women in commercial schools jumped from 2,770 to 23,040, an increase of 732 percent, compared with an increase of only 140 percent for male students during that decade. In 1890, 64 percent of all stenographers and typists were women; by 1920, the figure had risen to 92 percent.[52]

As portions of the clerical function were carved out and routinized with a combination of lower-paid labor and mechanical support, the clerks who had functioned with quasi-managerial responsibilities typically were not displaced. Just as executives were freed to become more artful when middle managers absorbed a portion of their activities, so these traditional clerks were pushed further toward the managerial arena, often assimilating even more of the executive process as they now supervised the new, lower-status clerical workers. During the forty years from 1890 to 1930, typists and stenographers had grown to constitute 22 percent of the clerical labor force, but there was also an impressive growth in the numbers of bookkeepers, cashiers, and accountants, all high-status (and male) clerical positions. What changed was the proportion of these positions as a percentage of the total clerical population—it declined. These employees typically inherited supervisory responsibility over entire offices of clerks who performed some fragment of the earlier, more comprehensive clerical task, such as bookkeeping. Routinization created a vast new array of clerical employment opportunities, absorbing functions that had once been integrated at a higher status level but, largely because of the achievements of technology, had become accessible to rationalization.[53] The zest for rationalization was also expressed in the development of new office systems and methods. Joanne Yates, in her historical account of the vertical filing system, found that by 1918, a twenty-seven-page bibliography of materials on office methods, primarily concerning filing systems, had appeared. In the list of general works on filing, the author listed forty-four sources, and an additional twenty-eight were listed as relevant to the specific task of filing correspondence.[54] The French sociologist Michel Crozier summed up this historical transformation in the following way:

> This transformation has profound consequences, since the arrival of women, coinciding as it did with very great expansion, was superimposed on a process of mechanization and automation, whose effects upon males were therefore diminished. The latter were pushed toward more skilled occupations and toward executive positions, so that the general proletarianization of the white-collar group—which seems quite clear if one analyzes its composition, its remunerations, and its tasks in the abstract—was not experienced as such by those directly involved. To the old white-collar group which had pretty much retained its social status—when it had not improved it by technical and hierarchical promotions—was added a new group consisting in part of females with a distinctly inferior social status. To be sure, many white-collar employees were personally victims of these transformations, but many among them were, on the other hand, beneficiaries.[55]

In 1925, the same year that Mary Parker Follett made her speech exhorting managers to become more scientific, William Henry Leffingwell published his well-known text, *Office Management: Principles and Practice*, which he dedicated to the Taylor Society in appreciation of its "inspirational and educational influence." Leffingwell presented a copy of his book to Carl Barth, one of Taylor's best-known disciples. That copy bore the following inscription: "It is with deep appreciation of the honor of knowing one of management's greatest minds that I sit at your feet and sign my name." Leffingwell was obsessed with the notion of bringing rational discipline to the office in much the same way that Taylor and his men were attempting to transform the shop floor. Though his was not the only treatise on the subject, it quickly became one of the most influential.[56] In an earlier work, published in 1917, Leffingwell had discussed "mechanical applications of the principles of scientific management to the office." His new text was written to address the need for "original thought" concerning the fundamental principles of his discipline and their relationship to office management. Leffingwell summed up the message of his book with one sentence: "In a word, the aim of this new conception of office management is simplification."

Leffingwell recognized that clerical work had its origins in and derived its purposes from the managerial function. In an early chapter of his text, he set out to define "the elusive character of office work." He concluded that the purpose of clerical activity was "the facilitation of any business function." It was to this facilitative endeavor, which aptly characterized the comprehensive activities of the traditional clerk, that he applied his principle of simplification.

Leffingwell wrote in detail about his work in the Curtis Publishing Company, which included a large mail-order operation. He had reorganized the flow of work so that five hundred pieces of mail could be handled each hour by one clerk, as compared to an earlier standard of one hundred. He used the same methods, with comparable results, in over five hundred other clerical operations. There was no aspect of the office that was too trivial for Leffingwell's attention. He not only addressed major functions like correspondence, record keeping, and communication but also applied his logic to the subjects of light, heat, ventilation, desks, chairs, tables, filing cabinets, forms, office supplies, mail, and office machinery of every variety. He considered work flow, measurement, standards, planning, and control for every aspect of the clerical day, hour, and minute.

The overwhelming purpose of Leffingwell's approach to simplification was to fill the clerical workday with activities that were linked to a concrete task and to eliminate time spent on coordination and communication. This concern runs through almost every chapter of his 850-page text; it is revealed most prominently in his minutely detailed discussions of the physical arrangement of the office and in his views on the organization, flow, planning, measurement, and control of office work.

Leffingwell advocated what he called "the straight-line flow of work" as the chief method by which to eliminate any requirement for communication or coordination. The ideal condition, he said, was that desks should be so arranged that work could be passed from one to the other "without the necessity of the clerk even rising from his seat . . . for where the work does not flow in this manner there is a constant tendency for clerks to do their own messenger work. . . . It should not be overlooked that while a clerk is not at his desk he may be working, but he is not doing clerical work effectively."[57]

Leffingwell recognized that the growth in the size of the office was a major force that would increase the coordinative demands on the office worker, and he saw his own principles of organization, together with the appropriate use of mechanical devices, as the chief bulwark

against the threat of inefficiency and chaos: "A larger volume of business requires a large force of clerks to handle it; . . . this . . . makes the
necessary communication between them more difficult, and there will
be much walking back and forth between them for this purpose, unless
some means is adopted to prevent it and save the time thereby
expended. . . . Routine . . . tends to reduce communication."[58] Layout,
standardization of methods, a well-organized messenger service, desk
correspondence distributors, reliance on written instructions, delivery
bags, pneumatic tubes, elevators, automatic conveyors, belt conveyors,
cables, telautographs, telephones, phonographs, buzzers, bells, and
horns—these were just some of the means Leffingwell advocated in
order to insulate the clerk from extensive communicative demands.

These efforts illustrate how scientific management in the office tried
to provoke a discontinuity between the new clerical activity and the traditional clerical work that had preceded it. Scientific management sought
to reorient the office on a new axis, so that clerical jobs would no longer
be able to absorb even vestigial elements of the executive process, with
its requirements for action-centered skills in the service of interpersonal
coordination. Before this reorganization, the functions of supervisors and
their clerks had been ambiguously defined. Procedures were determined
loosely enough that coordinative responsibility had to be shared, if only
informally. The application of scientific management to the office sought
to redefine clerical work and to set clear boundaries on the downward
diffusion of coordinative responsibility. The new concept of clerical work
tried to eliminate the remaining elements of action-centered skill related
to *acting-with* (that is, interpersonal coordination and communication) in
favor of tasks that were wholly devoted to *acting-on* (that is, direct action
on materials and equipment).

The requirements of *acting-on* associated with these new clerical jobs
demanded more from the body as a source of effort than from skilled
action or intellective competence. It is only at this stage, and in the
context of this discontinuity, that the fate of the clerical job can be
fruitfully compared to that of skilled work in industry. Yet even such a
comparison has its limits, as the distinct history of clerical work is
charged with a peculiar set of tensions and biases. When the clerical
job is enriched, it tends to resume its traditional position in a direct
line of descent from the executive function. In such cases, clerks are
reintegrated into the sphere of coordinative responsibility, with all of
its implications for skilled *acting-with*.[59]

The application of scientific management to the office, particularly as it combined with mechanization, had a far-reaching impact on clerical work in the industrial enterprise as well as in the service organizations that grew to support both industry and the economic power of its growing labor force. Frequently, the jobs that were created had the effect of driving office workers into the role of laboring bodies, engulfing them in the private sentience of physical effort. Complaints about these jobs became complaints about bodies in pain. In 1960 the International Labour Organization published a lengthy study of mechanization and automation in the office. The study documented changes in the physical environment of the clerical employee and the working conditions associated with these new environments. While acknowledging that in some cases the introduction of expensive equipment had motivated employers to improve the office environment, the report concluded: "Of far greater importance, however, were the negative effects of mechanization. . . . Machinery in offices created an entirely different atmosphere from that which had prevailed before. . . . In contrast to the mechanization of production processes, which often relieved workers of physically tiring jobs, mechanization introduced work of this nature into offices where it had not existed before. . . . Clerical workers often complained of muscular fatigue, backache, and other such ills as a result of the unaccustomed strain of operating machines. . . . Machine operation is still more tiring for many workers than straightforward manual methods of copying or calculating, and can in some cases be a serious drain of their physical resources."[60]

The study identified the chief sources of physical complaints as follows: fatigue induced by the increased speed of output, heavy lifting, standing, bending, the intensity of work measurement made possible by mechanization, the noise level of machines, and eyestrain. Moreover, it found that the nervous tension generated by the new forms of office work were an even greater threat than the physical exertion. Clerks complained of being "treated like trained animals" because of the "uniformity and excessive simplification of the work of many machine operators." It also noted that these clerical jobs were peculiar in requiring a high degree of monotonous and repetitive activity coupled with the demand for continual attentiveness to the work at hand: "Tabulating machine operators, for instance, even when the controls are set for them and an automatic device stops the machine when something goes wrong, cannot let their attention flag. . . . The strain of this kind of close attentiveness to a repetitive operation has resulted in a rising number of cases of mental and nervous disorders among clerical workers . . . physical and intellectual debility; disturbances of an emotional nature such as irritability, nervousness, hypersensitivity; insomnia; various functional disturbances—headaches, digestive and heart troubles; state of depression, etc."[61]

As widespread as these new forms of clerical work had become, the reach of scientific management and mechanization was still far from complete. Throughout the late 1960s and the 1970s, management periodicals continued to devote considerable attention to the urgent need for an engineering approach to office work. Productivity, they cautioned, would never increase in the service sector unless the techniques of industrial engineering were applied to the tasks of the clerk. One such periodical, *The Office*, featured an article in 1969 by the director of a New Jersey industrial engineering firm who said: "We know from our company's studies that manpower utilization in most offices—even those that are subject to work measurement controls—rarely exceeds 60%. In some operations the percentage of utilization may fall below 40%. At least 17% of the time, employees are literally doing nothing except walking around or talking. . . . While many companies have squeezed out much of the excess labor costs in their production operations, only a few have given serious attention to the so called indirect labor or service operations."[62]

In 1970, *Business Week* reported that companies were reducing their payroll costs by millions, using factory techniques to measure "how office workers work." One industrial engineer quoted in the article indicated that 75 percent of his firm's work measurement jobs were in the office, as compared to 25 percent just five years earlier: "Clerical jobs are measured just like factory jobs. The analysts add together scientifically predetermined time standards for human motions to find the time standard for a specific job—the standard by which worker's efficiency then is measured."[63] The progress of these efforts, however, continued to be confounded by the persistence of elements in the diverse repertoire of clerical work that could not be rationalized. Measurement efforts overwhelmed the lowest paid and most routinized clerical jobs, while it tended to bypass higher-paid jobs entirely—jobs that continued to absorb, however weakly, both interpersonal and intellective aspects of the managerial function. As *Business Week* put it, "The trouble is that, with higher pay, routine lessens, and there is more decision-making of increasing complexity. The MTM [Methods, Time, Measurement] Assn . . . is sponsoring research on decision times at the University of Michigan. But data now available are primitive, and those who seek a time fix on the work of, say, a loan processor, will for some time to come have to accept far less precision than for a keypuncher. . . . The developing discipline of work measurement does not face its only challenge from creative jobs. . . . Statistical clerks, mail girls, and expediters are tough . . . and the job of a secretary is considered "unmeasurable."[64]

The problem was that jobs could only be measured successfully once they were converted to the dimension of *acting-on* and insulated from activities related either to *acting-with* or to more complex intellective effort. In 1972 General Electric published its "Program for Clerical Cost Control" and implicitly acknowledged this problem: "The program is based wholly upon the use of time values . . . selected from scientifically prepared tables of the Motion Time Studies (MTS), which provide proven time values for each physical motion likely to be used in performing any operation. . . . Clerical costs can be controlled on any routine, i.e., repetitive or semi-repetitive work. Non-repetitive tasks, such as research and development, cannot be economically measured. Similarly, jobs such as receptionists, confidential secretaries, etc., do not lend themselves to control."[65]

Kanter's description of the secretarial function also illustrates the difference between clerical jobs as *acting-on* and clerical jobs as *acting-with*. She found two broad groupings of secretaries—those who worked in a "pool" and those who were assigned to a particular boss. Secretaries disliked working in the pool arrangement, where jobs could be measured by the amount of typed output. Managers tended to avoid interaction with these typists, treating them instead with a purely "utilitarian" attitude, like input-output devices. In contrast, secretaries who worked for a single boss were required to absorb many subtle responsibilities associated with coordination and communication. They "could stop worrying about their own skills and work on their relationship with the boss. They could orient their work life around their connection with this one person. Some executive secretaries acquired their own corps of typists to do routine work, devoting their time to the social and interpersonal aspects of their jobs. . . . They participated in the behind-the-scenes transformation of chaos into order, or rough ideas into polished, business-like letters and documents. . . . They set the stage for an atmosphere that was designed to awe or impress visitors. They served as a buffer between the boss and the rest of the world, controlling access and protecting him from callers. And on occasion, they were asked to collude in lies on behalf of this front.[66] For secretaries, much like their bosses, the salience of these implicit, action-centered skills of *acting-with* also put a premium on the body as an expressive instrument of interpersonal politics. Personal secretaries were supposed to look and behave in a certain manner; dress, posture, and physical attractiveness were each considered significant.

Thus, clerical work entered the decade of the 1980s still marked by considerable diversity and internal contradiction. Some clerical jobs continued to represent the furthest reach of the executive process. Despite efforts at simplification, they continued to absorb elements of responsibility for coordination and communication that precipitated from the managerial function and can be traced to the executive role. In these cases, the "elusive character of office work" persists in requiring clerks to engage in activities related to *acting-with*—sharing the communicative and problem-solving burden of "facilitating business functions" with their supervisors and managers. However, the combination of scientific management and mechanization did succeed in creating a new sphere of clerical work discontinuous with this historical trajectory. These jobs reflect those aspects of middle management's coordinative responsibilities that were most readily rationalized. In this new scenario, office workers were decisively driven into the demands of *acting-on*, engulfed in the rhythms and exertions of the laboring body.

How will the application of information technology further transform white-collar activities? Will it enlarge the sphere of "industrialized" clerical positions, or will it be a force to reintegrate clerical work with its managerial past? If so, what implication might this have for our current conceptions of the middle-management function? The first step in answering these questions turns upon the issue of skill. In the case of industrial workers, we saw the informating power of information technology driving out opportunities for action-centered skill in favor of intellective skill demands. As clerks and their managers are required to work through the computer medium, what kind of knowledge will they need? Will the demands for action-centered skills related to communication and coordination be reinvigorated? Will office workers or their managers face accelerated demands for intellective competence? Will clerks be pushed further into the sentient but mute terrain of fatigue and nervous exhaustion?

CHAPTER FOUR

Office Technology

as Exile and Integration

I always deemed him the victim of two evil powers—ambition and indigestion. The ambition was evinced by a certain impatience of the duties of a mere copyist, an unwarrantable usurpation of strictly professional affairs. . . . The indigestion seemed betokened . . . especially by a continual discontent with the height of the table where he worked. . . . He put chips under it, blocks of various sorts, bits of pasteboard, and at last went so far as to attempt an exquisite adjustment, by final pieces of folded blotting-paper. . . . If, for the sake of easing his back, he brought the table-lid at a sharp angle well up toward his chin, and wrote there like a man using the steep roof of a Dutch house for his desk, then he declared that it stopped the circulation in his arms. If now he lowered the table to his waistbands, and stooped over it in writing, then there was a sore aching in his back. . . . If he wanted anything, it was to be rid of a scrivener's table altogether.

—Herman Melville
Bartleby the Scrivener

AUTOMATING AND INFORMATING THE
WHITE-COLLAR WORKPLACE

For the millions of people who work in or have occasion to visit corporate facilities, the on-line office has become a familiar, even a clichéd, image. There are the clusters of desks, usually separated by partitions, and each is home to a video display terminal. The office may be softly lit; some even have a smattering of potted palms or rubber plants. A quick glance can give the impression that the women and men who work in these offices have been mesmerized by the green or amber glow of their video screens, as they spend the better part of each day with attention fixed on luminous electronic numbers and letters.

In 1982 I began a series of visits to one such office. After a strenuous and sometimes chaotic conversion from "paper-and-pencil" processing to an on-line computer system, production had just begun to reach the level expected from the investment in new technology. The rows of desks and paper clutter had given way to clean surfaces and desktop terminals. The work stations were separated by tall partitions, which created a cubicle effect around the work space of each clerk.

One afternoon, after several weeks of participant observation and discussions with clerks and supervisors, I was returning to the office from a lunch with a group of employees when two of them beckoned me over to their desks, indicating that they had something to show me. They seated themselves at their workstations on either side of a tall gray partition. Then they pointed out a small rupture in the orderly, high-tech appearance of their work space: the metal seam in the partition that separated their desks had been pried open.

With the look of mischievous co-conspirators, they confided that they had inflicted this surgery upon the wall between them. Why? The small opening now made it possible to peek through and see if the other worker was at her seat, without having to stand up and peer over or around the wall. Through that aperture questions could be asked, advice could be given, and dinner menus could be planned. At the time I took this to be the effort of two women to humanize their surroundings. While I still believe that is true, the weeks, months, and years that followed led me to a fuller appreciation of the significance of their action.

Installing those partitions was the final step that completed the clerks' relegation to the realm of the machine. Exiled from the interpersonal world of office routines, each clerk became isolated and solitary. That interpersonal world involves the work of managing; it is the domain in which coordination and communication occur. These clerks not only had been denied benign forms of social intercourse but also had been expelled from the managerial world of *acting-with* that had formerly required them to accept, in some small degree, responsibility for the coordination of their office. Installing the partitions was one concrete technique, among others, designed to create the discontinuity needed to achieve Leffingwell's goal: to convert the clerk from an interpersonal operator to a laboring body, substituting communicative and coordinative responsibilities with the physical demands of continuous production.

The first sections of this chapter will describe how information technology is being used in the service of Leffingwell's goals and the consequences that the simplification, isolation, and computer-mediation of clerical work has had for the psychological experience of office work and the forms of knowledge that it implies. The era of computerization has already produced several compelling studies of the industrialization of office work and its effects on clerical workers.[1] It is necessary to understand these effects in the context of the historical trajectory of clerical work (that is, its managerial heritage, the transition from an emphasis on *acting-with* to *acting-on*) and in relation to the managerial choices that will determine the future configuration of the clerical occupation.

The story of automation in the office does not end with Leffingwell's vision. Because information technology has a voice; because it has the power to convert events and processes to a symbolic medium and make them visible in a new way; because, in a word, this technology informates as well as automates, its consequences for the office are more complex than the principles of scientific management can account for. The second half of this chapter will explore how the informating power of the technology may increase the intellective demands of work, not only for clerks, but for managers and professionals as well, even as it encroaches upon the traditional action-centered skills that have undergirded the managerial process. In many cases, organizational functions, events, and processes have been so extensively informated—converted into and displayed as information—that the technology can be said to have "textualized" the organizational environment. In this context, the electronic text becomes a new medium in which events are both observed and enacted. As an automating technology, computerization can intensify the clerk's exile from the coordinative sphere of the managerial process. As an informating technology, on the other hand, it can provide the occasion for a reintegration of the clerical role with its managerial past and for a reinvigoration of the knowledge demands associated with the middle-management function.

Information Technology in Two Offices

For many office organizations, the first years of the 1980s were a time of transition from the assembly-line paper factories of earlier decades to computer systems that allow clerks to accomplish all aspects of a transaction in an "on-line" mode. This means that when a transaction is completed, the clerk presses the key marked ENTER, the transaction is recorded instantly in the central computer, and appropriate follow-up functions (for example, checks mailed, accounts debited or credited, et cetera) are set into motion.

The dental claims operation in Consolidated Underwriters Insurance's suburban Massachusetts office represents its most ambitious effort to convert from a paper-based to a computer-based office environment. According to senior executives, costly automation projects in the 1970s had generated a new determination to use advanced information technology to achieve "a more attractive price/value relationship in customer services." Claim service was a top priority. The new automated claims system was designed in-house during 1980 and installed in one suburban claim office in 1981. The office was composed of sixty-five benefits analysts who were predominantly young women earning a second income for their families. The conversion process occurred over an eight-month period in 1981. By 1982, when I first visited this office, productivity increases of 30 to 40 percent already had been achieved.[2]

In the old environment, a benefits analyst began the day by collecting claims in the mail room. She next went to the file area to pull the ledgers corresponding to each account and then to check the customer data in the files against the data on the claim forms. Taking the claims and ledgers to her desk, the benefits analyst checked contract limitations and any other arrangements pertinent to the account, completed the necessary paperwork, updated the ledger, and then finished the day by refiling ledgers, after having sent the claim to a check-processing unit. During the course of completing a claim, a benefits analyst might consult with her supervisor or with other benefits analysts for opinions about different dental procedures, how to handle a specific set of arrangements, or where to find necessary documentation. Benefits analysts were often hired on the basis of prior knowledge of dental procedures, as such information proved to be a useful resource for the judgments required by the claims process.

With the new on-line system, the procedure changed significantly. Benefits analysts still began their day in the mail room rounding up claims for processing, but the ledgers had disappeared. Instead, the analysts logged onto their computer terminals, called up the account in question, and processed the claim by entering data into the machine. Once the ENTER key was pressed at the completion of the claim, a check would be issued to the customer.

Several hundred miles away in suburban Pennsylvania, the corporate offices of Universal Technology housed a back office operation called Stock and Bond Transfer. The office was composed of approximately seventy transfer assistants and data-entry clerks, predominantly middle-aged women, who completed the transactions associated with the transfer of shareholder stock certificates. Such transfers might be initiated because of marriage, death, gift-giving, or a variety of other reasons.

In the old environment, the transaction had been shared by two different employees. First, the transfer assistant received the paperwork associated with a transfer. She checked to see if transfer requirements, which included the shareholder's endorsement, guarantees, and legal documentation, were fulfilled. When the transfer assistant had completed the necessary paperwork, she delivered her cases to a data-entry clerk, who inputted the transfer data into the computer system. The transfers were processed in batches by the system at the close of the day. In this office, the position of the transfer assistant was considered part of management, albeit at the lowest stratum in the managerial pyramid, while the data-entry position was nonmanagement and explicitly referred to as "clerical."

A new system that made it possible to process an entire transfer on-line was installed in 1981. The transfer assistants absorbed the data-entry function, although their positions retained the formal designation as "managerial." The data-entry clerks were upgraded to become full-fledged transfer assistants. With the new computer system, work was automatically routed to a transfer assistant, though she would still receive print copies of the legal documents associated with the transfer case. The system was carefully formatted, so that each stage of the transfer procedure was accomplished in interaction with the machine. The input procedure was preformatted and simplified. The system would not proceed to the next stage of the transaction if it detected errors in the information already entered. With the installation of the new system, the transfer assistants spent approximately 70 percent of their time interacting with their machines, while the remainder of their time was spent reading procedural revisions, references, and incoming investor-generated material; talking to shareholders over the telephone; or preparing written forms and letters in response to shareholder inquiries. The goals of the conversion were to create "a continuous production environment," to achieve standards of 98 percent accuracy, and to increase productivity. Most managers agreed that these goals generally had been met. One-and-a-half years after the conversion, the work force had been reduced by almost 20 percent. (Those employees had been transferred to another part of the back office.)

The responses of these two groups to computerization was remarkably similar, as were the dilemmas associated with the changing skill demands in each office. There were also some important differences. The sections that follow will show how the automation of dental claims pushed the job of the benefits analyst more decisively into the domain of *acting-on*. In the case of the transfer assistants, however, on-line automation allowed them to "reabsorb" a data-entry function that had already been exteriorized and routinized. The data-entry clerks' function was reintegrated upwards; however, for the transfer assistants, like the benefits analysts, the new configuration of their task further distanced them from involvement in the managerial process.

AUTOMATING THE OFFICE

The Computer-Mediation of Clerical Work

The work of office clerks has always been more abstract than, say, that of a pulp mill operator or machinist. Clerks typically spend much of their time recording and processing papers full of written symbols that represent objects and events at some remove from their immediate environment. Despite this, the transition to computer mediation was experienced as a significant break with what they called the "manual" work of the traditional office. Though their feelings were not as intense as those of the pulp mill operators, the clerks at both Consolidated Underwriters Insurance and Universal Technology frequently felt off-balance and discomforted by the new computer-mediated task relationship. They viewed the old environment as "manual" work—pulling and filing ledgers, writing, and handling papers. Each of these activities was physically engaging in an immediate, concrete way. "The other way was much more physical," one woman said. "Now your fingers do the walking—your fingers and your brain."

While most of the clerks in each office appreciated the ease with which a transaction now could be completed, many were also frustrated by the loss of the concreteness that had provided for them a sense of certainty and control. They wondered where the material on the screens "came from" and where it "went." Because the machine's operations were invisible, intangible, and largely inscrutable, learning to trust the computer system was initially an emotionally exhausting process. One transfer assistant tried to explain these uncertainties:

> It has been hard for many of us to accept that the machine is really going to do this for you. It's almost like you don't want to believe that the system is really doing that because it was never like that before. And we even ask ourselves, "O.K., is it really debiting the account out? How can I really be sure that these things are happening?"

In the first months after the conversion to an on-line system, many experienced the inclination to reach for the old aids, which could be touched and which provided a greater feeling of certainty. Managers tended to discourage this dependency on the concrete, however. They wanted the clerks weaned away from the old objects as quickly as possible. One benefits analyst described an experience shortly after the technological conversion:

> It was hard not to fall back to looking at the ledgers. One day, when we were still getting used to the new system, I got a call and I started to turn to get the ledger, and my supervisor saw me and she slapped my hand. She told me not to touch the ledger but to do the claim in the system. She said we cannot depend on the ledgers or check the ledgers.

Why was it felt to be important and natural to check the ledgers? Many of the clerks experienced a loss of certainty similar to that of the pulp mill operators when they were deprived of concrete referents. In the office the referent function operated at a higher level of abstraction than in the mills. For these clerks, written words on pieces of paper had become a concrete and credible medium—for several reasons. First, paper is a three-dimensional object that carries sensory weight— it can be touched; carried; folded; in short, dominated. Secondly, writing is a physical activity. The pen gives voice to the hand. Each written word is connected to the writer both through the intellectual relationship of authorship and through the immediate physical relationship of fingers and pen. In the act of writing there is a part of the self that is invested in and so identified with the thing written. It comes to be experienced as an extension of the self rather than an "otherness." This identification occurs so subtly, that it is rarely noticed until it has been taken away. Electronic text confronts the clerk with a stark sense of otherness. Text is impersonal; letters and numbers seem to appear without having been derived from an embodied process of authorship. They stand autonomously over and against the clerk who engages with them. A benefits analyst described the sensation:

> You can't justify anything now; you can't be sure of it or prove it because you have nothing down in writing. Without writing, you can't remember things, you can't keep track of things, there's no reasoning without writing. What we have now—you don't know where it comes from. It just comes at you.

The "hands-on" paper environment also made it possible to leave a trail of "trigger" stimuli, which provided the clerk with more information about the work than was required by the formal system of documentation. For example, benefits analysts would note on their ledgers various irregular contractual arrangements, customers' special problems, or unique agreements that they had worked out with a client. The customers' handwriting was sometimes the trigger that evoked memories of prior conversations and the particular issues associated with that account. The benefits analysts would make special notations on ledgers of the VIPs who were to be paid most promptly. The ledger thus provided not only a concrete referent in the transaction process but also a personal record of their own initiatives and judgments in dealing with an account. The computer system seemed, by comparison, to be impervious to their special knowledge. It had become impossible to put their personal stamp on their relationship with the customer.

Under these conditions, the sense of a concrete reality became vested in one source—the telephone. This remote and faceless medium came to represent a source of confirmation and certainty that to some degree compensated for the impersonality and abstractness of the computer system, simply because it afforded an opportunity to hear a real voice. A benefits analyst said:

> Now we have numbers without names—no ledgers, no writing, no history, no paper. The only reality we have left is when we get to talk to a customer.

The feeling of being out of control was both epitomized and confounded by the ENTER key. In an on-line system, pressing the ENTER
key causes the transaction to be accomplished in the organization's
central computer. Once taken, this action cannot easily be reversed. In
both offices, clerks noted that it could take days or weeks for an error
to be corrected, even though it was known seconds after the ENTER
key was pressed. The immediacy and significance of the ENTER key
often engendered anxiety. A benefits analyst explained:

> Now, once you hit that ENTER button, there is no way to check it,
> no way to stop it. It's gone and that's scary. Sometimes you hit the
> buttons, and then it stares you in the face for ten seconds and you
> suddenly say, "Oh no, what did I do?" but it's too late.

At the same time, the knowledge that one was actually accomplishing the transaction—not just completing paperwork—entailed a sense
of control, responsibility, and seriousness. A transfer assistant put it
this way:

> We have so much responsibility now because we not only approve
> the transfer but it takes place by the time it leaves our desks. Once
> you hit that button, it's gone; and you feel a lot of pressure to make
> sure you did it right.

The loss of concrete stimuli to trigger memory and the responsibility
associated with the on-line system combined to increase the intensity
of concentration and the continuity of attention that individuals must
bring to their tasks. As routine as the transaction process might become,
clerks in both offices widely agreed that the work requires a continual,
conscious engagement. Most agreed that it has become easier to maintain this level of concentration, but few thought that it was possible
for the execution of the work to become as routine as the content of
the work. This is how a transfer assistant put it:

> We really did not have a need for such intensive concentration be-
> fore. There are times when you are looking at the screen but you
> are not seeing what is there. That is a disaster. Even when you get
> comfortable with the system, you still have to concentrate; it's just
> that you are not concentrating on concentrating. You learn how to
> do it, but the need doesn't go away.

The need for concentration is not necessarily linked to the complexity of work content. In both offices, clerks perceived that the knowl-

edge demands of their tasks had been diminished (there were also some significant differences in the degree to which each job had been simplified—an issue to be visited later in the discussion), but attentional requirements and responsibility had increased.[3]

The Diminished Importance of Substantive Knowledge

The managers with executive responsibility for each of these offices had clearly defined intentions. In each case, cost reduction and increased productivity were preeminent goals, which required systems that would simplify transaction processing while substantially increasing the volume of work that could be completed by one clerk. In the case of Consolidated Underwriter Insurance's dental claims operation, this meant reducing the knowledge demands of the task in order to increase the speed with which claims could be processed. The product manager for dental claims described the purpose of the new system:

> We were always a production environment, but now, with the computer system, it's more so. A lot of the quality issues are now built into the machine. It requires less thought, judgment, and manual interventions. It's designed to let you pump claims out the door.

The project manager with overall responsibility for seeing that the new system not only fulfilled its purpose but also could be used as a model for back office automation throughout the corporation expanded on this theme:

> We rely on the notion that the system does things better than humans do. It is amazing how people were able to remember rules and exceptions. When you give them the system, they stop remembering and rely on the system. We debriefed all the special deals and arrangements that applied to each account and programmed it right into the system to maintain existing situations. We cracked down on idiosyncratic options. All options are now built right into the system.

Consultants advising the company on the design of the new system advocated that all tasks involving elements of interpersonal coordination, such as collecting mail or answering the telephone, be eliminated from the benefits analyst's job in order to maximize productivity. With the benefits analysts focusing only on claims processing, the consultants predicted a 70 percent productivity increase; however, they forecast only a 60 percent increase if the job was allowed to remain "enriched." The project manager dissented from the consultants' recommendations and chose to retain these vestiges of diversity, believing that "there's a limit to how boring you can make a job if you want even reasonably capable people." Despite his decision, by the end of 1983, two years after the system's implementation, productivity had increased by 105 percent and continued to climb. Even this manager felt somewhat appalled at the nature of the job he had helped to create:

> It's reached a point where the benefits analysts can't move their fingers any faster. There is nowhere to go anymore if you don't want to sit in front of a terminal. The quantity of pressure may be the only difference. Labor will sooner or later get smart and see that unions are their only answer.

In the case of the Stock and Bond Transfer operation in Universal Technology, the goals were somewhat more complex. There was a driving commitment to reduce labor costs and increase productivity. The regulatory environment also had a role to play: the Securities and Exchange Commission now required that such transfers be accomplished within seventy-two hours. This made it important to have a system in which transfers could be tracked easily and supervisors could identify processing bottlenecks. The company was also committed to improving its service to shareholders by providing more information, more functions, and improved response times. Finally, Universal Technology's managers were explicitly concerned with what they called "creating meaningful jobs." A senior manager described their intentions this way:

> We insisted that the new system take into consideration human needs. We wanted the computer to do as much record keeping as possible, but we don't want to make the job worse. We wanted to make it easier for them to judge whether they had entered data correctly, where the case stands in the process, and to take responsibility for a real-time update. We wanted to avoid overspecialization— denuding the job or whatever you want to call it.

Line managers with responsibility for the transfer operation believed that although the new system had simplified the work, the complexity of the task itself imposed a limit on just how much could be routinized and, therefore, programmed. Transfer assistants remained responsible for reviewing the legal documentation associated with a transaction and

making sure that they had all the material required for executing the
transfer. The system broke down each step of the transfer process and
required the transfer assistant to move logically through the series of
machine interactions. The program would not allow an operation to
continue until all logic requirements had been satisfied. Still, the system could not account for those materials handled by the transfer assistant but not entered into the data base, thus leaving an additional measure of responsibility and judgment in the hands of the transfer
assistants. There remained enough exceptional and unusual transfer
procedures that, unlike the dental claims operations, all contingencies
could not be accounted for in the system.

Employees in each office had strong feelings about the simplification
of their jobs. They recognized that the computer system now contained
much of the knowledge upon which they had once prided themselves.
In the dental claims operation, benefits analysts were accustomed to
memorizing a great deal of information associated with each account.
Some could recite complicated arrangements, triggered only by seeing
a customer's signature or hearing the customer's voice. In the new environment, the combination of several factors—the increased volume of
transactions required to be processed each hour, the loss of written
records, the impersonalization that resulted from feeding the machine
numbers (for example, social security numbers) rather than words (for
example, the customer's name), and the fact that all arrangements were
now stored in the system—caused a shift in the benefits analysts' relationship to the substance of their task.

> The computer system is supposed to know all the limitations, which
> is great because I no longer know them. I used to, but now I don't
> know half the things I used to. I feel that I have lost it—the computer
> knows more. I am pushing buttons. I'm not on top of things as I used
> to be.

In each office the clerks believed that they were overqualified for
the tasks as they were now organized. The knowledge they had acquired was now less important than typing skills and the sheer stamina
needed to meet daily production quotas. As their bodily presence became more important than their knowledge, the women began to see
these jobs as circumscribed by the animal body, barely requiring dis-
tinctly human forms of intelligence. Compare the lament of a benefits
analyst:

> You don't have to think that much because the system is doing the thinking for you. You don't have to be concerned with what is on that claim. People here have begun to feel like monkeys.

with that of a transfer assistant:

> You don't have to remember things, because the system does. You could get a monkey to do this job. You just follow the keys.

If in the cases of the benefits analysts and transfer assistants the primary effect of computerization was a reduction in opportunities for the exercise of already acquired know-how, then these cases would indeed conform to the typical pattern of craft deskilling as a result of automation. This component of deskilling does indeed appear to be amply accounted for both in the observations of the clerks and in the explicit intentions of their managers. However, computerization has transfigured these jobs in yet another way. These parallel effects illustrate the discontinuity between clerical jobs that have retained some vestige of the managerial process, as reflected in the ongoing necessity for interpersonal coordination and communication, and clerical jobs that have been pushed more fully into the domain of *acting-on*, which demands little in the way of skill but makes considerable demands upon stamina. In this process, the white-collar body is detached from its skillfulness as a medium of communication and social action, and re-emerges in its availability for effort and sustained attention.

The Clerk as a Laboring Body

The knowledge traditionally associated with clerical work is not limited to the substantive knowledge of the methods by which a task should be executed. Such substantive understanding has been embedded in a much wider, richer, more detailed, and largely unspecified interpersonal reality. It is through "informal" contact with peers and supervisors that appropriate courses of action generally are determined. Office work is chatty, but that chattiness is more than a social perquisite of the job. It is the ether that transmits collaborative impulses, as people help each other form judgments and make choices about the work at hand. As we saw in the previous chapter, office functions have always had a "soft" character. They have been sufficiently unspecified so that clerks, in collaboration with their supervisors, must take on a certain amount of coordinative and communicative responsibility if the work is to be accomplished in a way that can be held accountable to generally recognized criteria of orderliness and rationality. In other words, despite recurrent efforts to rationalize clerical work, clerks must retain at least a slender hold on the managerial process if things are to run smoothly. Their knowledge is reflected in the collaborative problem-solving abilities related to *acting-with* as much as in technical mastery of their administrative functions.[4]

The office has been the action context in which clerical know-how is embedded. Its social and material aspects provide the clerk with the concrete cues necessary for the development of competence. The social dimension is crucial because the interactions with others who are facing or have faced similar contingencies inform judgments about what to do. The material dimension provides a context for unspecified informal collaboration, based upon the proximity of individuals and their accessibility in face-to-face communication.

Despite the degree to which the jobs of the benefits analysts and the transfer assistants had been rationalized prior to computerization, each had retained much of the character of traditional office work; each had been infused with the practical necessities of interpersonal coordination and communication in order to accomplish "smooth" operations. While my own data do not include first-hand documentation of these earlier activities, the accounts of the clerks and their supervisors in each of these offices attest to the transformational effect of the computer system (and of the choices about how it would be managed) on those practical *acting-with* functions once associated with clerical work.

A key aspect of system design in both cases was to locate the resources for accomplishing a transaction within the computer system to the maximum extent possible. This meant that a clerk could accomplish most of what was needed without ever rising from her chair. Either the necessary information was available through the terminal or the system's procedural organization had reduced problem-solving requirements by eliminating the need to make choices about technical aspects of the transaction process. The abstraction of the computer medium imposed new attentional demands, and the production pressures were derived from managers' beliefs about how to fully exploit this new form of technological support. These additional elements, when combined with the notion of the machine as a unitary resource, had a withering effect on the sociality of the office environment. The elimination of social exchange not only diminished the quality of the work environment but also demonstrated the elimination of precisely those aspects of the clerk's work that had derived from the managerial function.

In some cases, the reduction of social exchange resulted from the way managers chose to interpret the new work arrangements and from the behavioral norms they sought to enforce. In both offices, managers wanted the clerks to realize that social engagement was no longer a legitimate dimension of work behavior.

> The computer system is giving you a message. It's saying, "You don't have to be on top of it anymore." The thing is, we make a lot of mistakes, and the less you encourage people to know things, the less anybody is ever likely to notice all these errors.

At Universal Technology, most transfer assistants agreed that the immediate impact of the system on their jobs was one of reducing the need for task-related knowledge and judgment. Because the system had been designed to break down the transaction into a series of simple steps, and because there were built-in safeguards to prevent errors, many transfer assistants saw that there was little possibility of mistakes. As long as one followed the prompts at each step, the process required minimal thought.

> The way I do my work now is by pushing buttons. We have all had formal training to tell us what buttons to push to get the information that we want.
>
> I have no decision making on that computer. It's been programmed to do this, and this, and this, and we are programmed to do the same thing. I don't want to be programmed. It does things automatically, and if you feel it's wrong, you really have no choice but to let it go that way on this formatted screen.

Some transfer assistants wondered how the company could afford to be so entirely dependent on its computer systems. Like the workers in Cedar Bluff, they found that when the computer went down, there was nothing to do but sit and stare.

> If the system doesn't work, nothing gets done. We sit there all day and smoke—there is nothing you can do. Everything is at a standstill.

One powerful means that managers used to communicate and enforce new patterns of conduct was the material organization of the office—

the placement of people and furniture. A benefits analyst told the following story:

> We used to be able to see each other and talk. Sure, sometimes we just talked about what we were going to make for dinner, but we always worked while we talked. Most of the time, we talked about something related to a claim. Then with the new system, they put in two filing cabinets between us, because we weren't supposed to see each other anymore. But there was a small space between the two cabinets, so she could still turn around and look at me, and we would talk across to one another. Well, one day a manager walked by, and I was asked who left this space there. I said that was how they left it when they put the cabinets in. The manager had them move the cabinets together because they don't want us talking.

The Stock and Bond Transfer operation reflected the same tensions. The line manager with direct responsibility for the office discussed the use of furniture to shape new behaviors:

> There's not a whole lot of need for people to interact with one another anymore. The system allows you to be really very private between you and the system. Now with the furniture we've chosen, that's another reinforcement of the message, "Here you are, doing your own job." It's designed for increased productivity because it puts everyone in their own little cubicle. Some people can work well that way, but others cannot. Some supervisors are noticing that people are asking questions of one another even though the system tells you just about everything you need to know. I have wondered about this—do people really have questions or do they just want to talk? Maybe they just want to hear someone's voice talking to them.

Opportunities for social exchange were also diminished as a result of the organization of the work itself. Since the computer system contained most of the resources a clerk needed to complete the transactions, even as it simplified the required procedures, it tended to obviate any need for collaboration or inquiry. One result was to isolate individuals at their workstations, with the exception of breaks for coffee or lunch. Again, the benefits analysts comment:

> I think we're all more separate now. Before, there was more that I could help someone out with. There's not really that much I can do now. You just don't seem to get to know people the way you did when you were paying manually, because you don't interact.

> The office has become much more impersonal now, because we don't talk to each other. The girl who pays the Consolidated Underwriters' claims sits right in front of me. There was a question on my claim form. She didn't turn around and ask me. She sent me a letter. She didn't realize it was me. I said, "Cindy, do you know that you sent me a letter?" She said, "Did I really?"

In the Stock and Bond Transfer office, the manager with direct responsibility for the transfer operation reflected on the relationship between the design of the system and the changing behavioral requirements of the work:

> The system controls the transfer assistants in some ways because it ties them to the desk. It forces them to do the input and to really be tied to the machine. That forces control in terms of physically having to just be there.

A transfer assistant remarked:

> When we were just working at our regular desks, you could see an individual face to face, and you had a lot more tendency to say, "Hey, I don't remember such and such. What's the answer?" rather than looking in your reference material. Now everyone's partitioned off from each other. People are less likely to get up out of their desks and come over and ask you a question. I think it has a lot to do with the simple fact that we just don't see each other's faces anymore.

A supervisor noted that because the system eliminated the need for social exchange, instances of interaction had become easy indicators that a clerk was encountering problems in doing her job.

> Now if I repeatedly see somebody at another person's desk, I'm going to go over and see what the problem is. It becomes obvious when they don't know how to do something.

As a result of the computerization process, the jobs of the benefits analyst and the transfer assistant were removed from the evolutionary path that had characterized traditional clerical work. A discontinuity had been created, and these new jobs could no longer be counted as descendants of the managerial process. Being "tied to the machine," as so many had described their jobs, was understood to be an inferior status, severed from the managerial function. As one transfer assistant put it, "Working with the CRT [video screen] is doing the dirty work."

It is small wonder, then, that so many of these clerks' complaints about the work became complaints about bodily suffering. The clerks in both offices repeatedly spoke of eye strain, nervous exhaustion, physical strain, irritability, enervation, sedentariness, back pain, short tempers and intolerance, and a host of other concerns—from visual distortion to fears about microwaves. Automation meant that jobs which had once allowed them to use their bodily presence in the service of interpersonal exchange and collaboration now required their bodily presence in the service of routine interaction with a machine. Jobs that had once required their voices now insisted they be mute. Jobs that had been able to utilize at least some small measure of their personhood now emphasized their least individually differentiated and most starkly animal capacities. They had been disinherited from the management process and driven into the confines of their individual body space. As a result, the employees in each office became increasingly engulfed in the immediate sensations of physical discomfort.[5]

During my discussions with these office workers, I sometimes asked them to draw pictures that represented their "felt sense" of their job experience before and after the conversion to the new computer system. Frequently these pictures functioned as a catalyst, helping them to articulate feelings that had been implicit and hard to define. I invited them to use pictures, diagrams, symbols, or any means that helped them express their sense of their situation. No particular themes were singled out for illustration; rather, I stressed the importance of expressing whatever they felt but found difficult to convey in words.

Perhaps the most striking feature of the clerks' pictures is their similarity. Though the pictures were drawn in private sessions, the images used by individuals both within each office and across the two offices were quite consistent. Moreover, the pictures from the two offices, taken as one set, can be grouped into distinct categories. One group of pictures (the largest) illustrated a single theme: the various forms of bodily alteration resulting from the new conditions of work, including hair loss; impaired eyesight; contortion of facial muscles; radical decrease in bodily dimensions; rigidification of the torso, arms, and faces; inability to speak or hear; immobility; headaches; and enforced isolation. The clerks portrayed themselves as chained to desks, surrounded by bottles of aspirin, dressed in prison stripes, outfitted with blinders, closely observed by their supervisors, surrounded by walls, enclosed without sunlight or food, bleary-eyed with fatigue, solitary, frowning,

Figure 4.1   Transfer assistant

Before

Figure 4.2   Transfer assistant

After
"The after picture is only the back of my head because it is a nonperson."

and blank—without a face. Figures 4.1 through 4.16 show a representative sample of these illustrations.

These simple drawings convey feelings that often elude verbal expression. The condition of being "tied to the machine" represents a new kind of confinement, not just the spatial confinement of having to sit in one place for long stretches, but an interior confinement. These clerks, driven into the confines of the laboring body, have seen their

Figure 4.3   Transfer assistant

Before

Figure 4.4   Transfer assistant

After

"There's a lot of tension now, and that makes people get mean. We had more control before and less confusion. You could get things done. Every once and a while my head starts to throb. I can't take it."

Figure 4.5 Benefits analyst

Before

Figure 4.6 Benefits analyst

After

"I used to have someone behind me in case I needed to tell them about this irate phone call. But now there isn't anybody there. Now she is stiff. She is all by herself. You feel stiff. You're just out there."

Figure 4.7 Benefits analyst

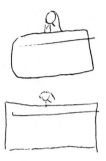

Before

Figure 4.8 Benefits analyst

After

"No talking, no looking, no walking. I have a cork in my mouth, blinders for my eyes, chains on my arms. With the radiation I have lost my hair. The only way you can make your production goals is give up your freedom."

Figure 4.9   Transfer assistant

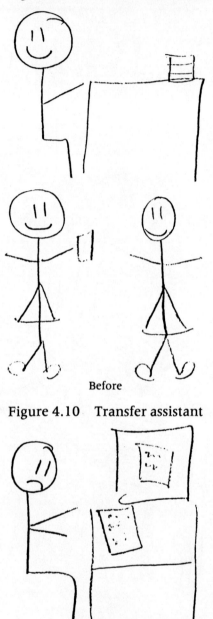

Before

Figure 4.10   Transfer assistant

After

"Before I was able to get up and hand things to people without having someone say, what are you doing? Now, I feel like I am with my head down, doing my work."

Figure 4.11   Benefits analyst

Before

Figure 4.12   Benefits analyst

After

"My supervisor is frowning because we shouldn't be talking. I have on the stripes of a convict. It's all true. It feels like a prison in here."

Figure 4.13   Benefits analyst

Before

Figure 4.14   Benefits analyst

After

Figure 4.15   Transfer assistant

Before

Figure 4.16   Transfer assistant

After

tasks shorn of opportunities for using interpersonal and substantive skills. The principal challenge of their current jobs is an effort of endurance. It is a sullen effort, subtly corrosive, felt in diffuse interior discomforts, rarely dramatic, but persistent and inescapable.

The Clerk in Exile

Another measure of the alteration in these jobs was the perception that a new gulf had opened up between the clerks and their supervisors. Their relationship had been one of the most important arenas for mutual collaboration in problem solving and information sharing. As coordinative and communicative opportunities were eliminated from the office worker's domain, the clerks felt a new distance from their supervisors, a feeling that was acknowledged by the supervisors as well. Previously, the unspecific nature of their office tasks had required that clerks and supervisors collaborate on a myriad of practical but underdetermined discursive activities. As clerical work was reduced to the terms of machine interaction, the need to collaborate with supervisors became as infrequent as the need to collaborate with peers. The supervisors found themselves in much the same position as did bookkeepers earlier in this century. The clerks' enforced self-sufficiency did not displace the supervisory function; rather, it appeared to draw the supervisors away from a direct involvement with the execution of clerical transactions toward an increased emphasis on coordination.

Benefits analysts described these changes in the clerk-supervisor relationship:

> Before, the analyst worked directly with their supervisor. Now we are looking into these electronic boxes. The supervisors are totally separate, even farther away than we are from each other. The supervisors used to sit down and do a difficult claim with you, and now they don't. We're closed in now, and we don't have any communications anymore.

These changes were also apparent to the supervisors:

> Our relationship with the analysts is more distant now. We are able to supervise more people because they are so much more independent. The system now calculates the benefits for the analysts, so they do not seek us out as much. So you do not have as much of a personal relationship with them as you might have had in the past. We tend

to get more involved in writing letters and corresponding in problem cases, or helping out the assistant manager on projects. We have more of a focus on looking at the big picture of how the work is flowing, how best to organize it and try to keep things moving.

A similar redefinition of the supervisor-clerk relationship was evident in the experiences of transfer assistants and supervisors in the Stock and Bond Transfer office. One transfer assistant summarized this change:

> Most of the communications between transfer assistants and the supervisors has been lost. All the data that the supervisors need they can get right from the machine. Before, they would just walk around and ask each one of us. We still have communication with them about career development, feedback, appraisals, if you're a bad girl, if you're a good girl. It's like your supervisor doesn't need you as much anymore.

A second group of pictures drawn by the clerks and their supervisors illustrate both the isolation of the individual office worker and this new sense of distance between the clerical function and those who supervise it. Figures 4.17 through 4.24 include four sets of these before and after drawings.

In the offices of Consolidated Underwriters Insurance and Universal Technology, the transformation of clerical work has extended Leffingwell's dearly held principles concerning the application of scientific management to the elusive tasks associated with administrative support. Leffingwell idealized the image of a job that was pure labor—continual production uninterrupted by the coordinative and communicative demands of administration. The new forms of clerical work that he and other practitioners of scientific management created shared an emphasis on the bodily effort of the office worker. For the first time, the "desk" job began to closely parallel the logic of unskilled factory work. In the case of the benefits analysts and transfer assistants, the technology had been used to automate: it was treated as a highly sophisticated form of office machinery. Automation had pushed the clerks into activities that concern *acting-on*, removing the social and material dimensions of office life that once provided the context for the action-centered skills associated with the ordinary but vital activities of social problem solving. It entailed a more complete form of exile from the

Figure 4.17   Dental claims supervisor

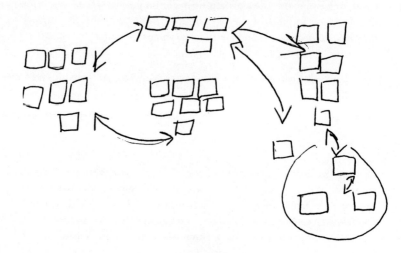

Before

Figure 4.18   Dental claims supervisor

After

"Under the old system, people interacted more with each other. I think that now the supervisors interact more with each other and not as much with their units. We are not as dependent on them or them on us as we were under the other system. The supervisors are involved in the office as a whole rather than their own unit."

Figure 4.19   Dental claims supervisor

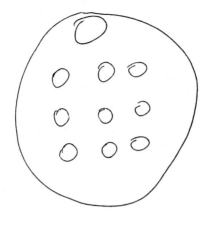

Before

Figure 4.20   Dental claims supervisor

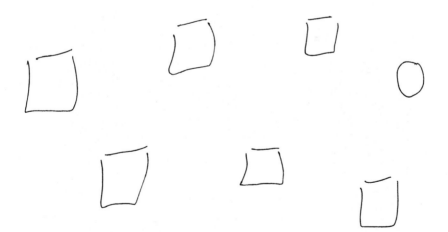

After

"Before, we were all pulling files. You knew everyone. And now it is, like, every-body has their own desk and they do not really need me. They kind of do their job. They need me for questions they cannot handle, but for the most part, a girl can come in all day and not ask me anything and go home at night. I do not feel they are as close to me as we were before, and they are not as close with each other. Not that the office should be like a party, but before we were more of a family."

Figure 4.21   Transfer assistant

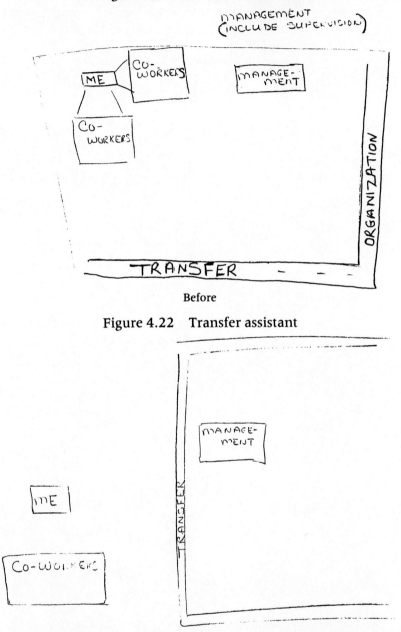

Before

Figure 4.22   Transfer assistant

After

"Before, I felt part of my co-workers. I felt we had some kind of camaraderie. I still felt management was separate, but we were all part of Transfer. We were an organization with everyone inside it. We seemed to be working for the same thing. Now I think management has become much more distant. They are so hung up over figures and commitments and this whole change that computerization has brought. They have just taken Transfer and put it around them and forgot about us. I feel as though I am much more alone now."

Figure 4.23 Transfer assistant

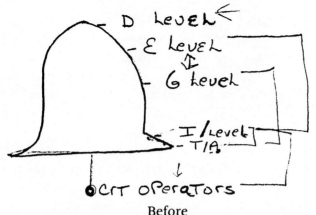

Before

Key

D-level	Upper managers	I-level	Supervisors
E-level	Middle managers	T/A	Transfer assistant
G level	Assistant managers	CRT	Data-entry clerk

Figure 4.24 Transfer assistant

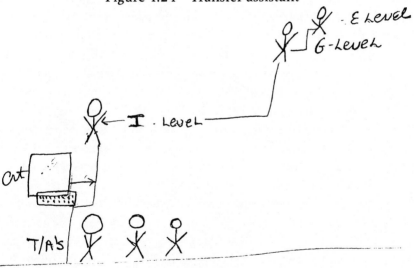

After

"Before, your nonmanagement CRT operator hung at the bottom of the pyramid. No communication; they are down there by themselves. But you have a lot of communication between your transfer assistants and your supervisors. The other levels—I guess they communicated but we never saw them, except your E and G levels, they communicated a lot. We could not do anything without involving the supervisors. They would ask for input from us, but they never dealt directly with the poor CRT operators. Now we have their little nowhere job. Now the supervisors have a closer relationship to the machine than they do to us. There are things that they used to have to depend on us to find out. Now they can go right in the machine and find out anything they want. They don't have to communicate as often. The communication has been lost. They look at reports and spend all their time with numbers."

managerial process, creating a new felt distance between the clerk and the managerial organization. It also allowed first-line supervision to become more thoroughly integrated with the management function, which, paradoxically, brings into focus the otherwise-neglected informating power of the very same technology.

Informated Elements in the Automated Office

Describing the effect of office technology as an occasion for exile still falls short of fully describing the emerging nature of office work. There remains a missing element, and it is one that provides a clue to an alternative conception of information technology and office work.

In both the offices of Consolidated Underwriters Insurance and Universal Technology, the new information systems provided a rationalized, public, independently authored electronic text that was treated as a complete account of the information necessary for smooth operations. This text relied upon an objective (thus, in theory, universally accessible) language thick with codes and numbers, as compared with the personal language each clerk had invented to both trigger and convey a wealth of implicit knowledge. The inherent abstractness of this text, constituted by the invisible procedures of its authorship; the impersonality of its language; the intangibility of its content, and the autonomous electronic "other" character of its enduring presence, placed unique mental demands upon the clerks. They experienced a need for vigilance and sustained concentration. Knowing that their input would be inscribed immediately onto a permanent record and would, without further intervention, initiate a series of interdependent organizational operations (for example, checks mailed, accounts credited) imposed an additional measure of tension and purpose upon this attentional effort. Clerks needed skills in procedural reasoning in order to successfully navigate the programmed logic that controlled their interaction with the text.

While the informating power of the technology resulted in a more comprehensive textualization of office work, it did not lead to an increase in the intellectual content of clerical tasks. Instead, these tasks embodied the uneasy requirement of sustained concentration and procedural reasoning without offering substantive content to naturally anchor the clerk's attention. This is because, in both cases, managers and designers chose to emphasize the automating rather than the informating capacity of the new technology. The technology's informating power was not seen as an occasion for creating new sources of value in customer service. To paraphrase the dental claims product manager, the idea was to pump more work out the door. For these managers, volume had overtaken service as the key to profits.

There are, however, some indications in the data from the Stock and Bond Transfer operation that the informating consequences of the technology were not lost on employees. Though their managers had not yet achieved a conception of the work that really would have exploited these consequences, the observations of supervisors and transfer assistants at least are suggestive of an alternative approach.

It was the supervisors in Stock and Bond Transfer who benefited most from the informating power of the new technology. The textualization of the operations that they supervised provided them with a wider, more accurate, timely, and accessible record of work. They were able to use this text to augment and enhance their supervisory function. As one of them explained:

> The best part about having this new system is knowing what is in the unit and being able to feel like I have control over the work. That is one of my responsibilities, but I never felt like I had that control before. We were constantly chewed out by management—"You should have done this or that." If I had known what was going on, if I had had a clear picture of it, I might have been able to do the right thing. Now that I can see the total functioning of the office, I feel more ownership towards all of the units, not just my own. I do more coordination of the work flow with my peers. I finally feel like I am really doing my job. I am not just a record keeper, but I can really use my brain.

In this situation, supervisors are informed on the basis of, and at the expense of, their subordinates who are automated. While this contributed to the perceived distance between the clerks and the supervisors, the transfer assistants did experience at least some positive effects of the technology's informating power. For example, many felt they were able to provide better service to the shareholders with whom they frequently had telephone contact:

> Having everything on-line is fantastic. Now as soon as a transfer is completed, it's there! You can really look up what you need. If someone calls, you know exactly what's going on. Sometimes you are looking for a part of a case that someone else has. You used to have to go looking around for it, and maybe you wouldn't find it. Now

you can see where it is without ever getting up from your seat. It's all right there at my fingertips.

The benefits analysts at Consolidated Underwriters Insurance had little to say about the informating effects of the technology. However, discussions with the senior managers revealed a vision of their technological future (at least as it applied to operations like claims service) that differed dramatically from the current narrow emphasis on automation. This vision gave primary importance to the informating power of computer systems, based upon a more efficient automated infrastructure. They planned to use a combination of interorganizational information systems (for example, systems that could provide data directly from the health care providers, eliminating routine in-house data-entry functions such as dental claims), optical character recognition devices, and high-speed communications networks, in addition to the current emphasis upon on-line transaction processing, in order to create a comprehensive, highly automated, data base that would provide a continually updated portrait of the organization's business.[6] This kind of integrated data base increases the visibility of a firm's productive and administrative activities. It provides a powerful means with which to gain new insight into and control over business functions. The integration of text and data processing can create informated environments in which organization members can "see" and understand the business in new ways.

Earlier, I suggested that the automated dental claims and transfer systems had begun to textualize the work of the office. An integrated organizational data base is a more ambitious effort, as it attempts to textualize the work of an entire organization. It constitutes a new technological infrastructure, a new medium in which the business of the organization is observed and enacted. According to a recent study of technology in the insurance industry, many leading companies, like Consolidated Underwriters Insurance, are exploring this approach as an initial step in the next major phase of technological development. The study concludes that "the next stage of office automation is integrated information processing." The strategic goal is to develop a technological infrastructure whose informating capacity can be used to support both "clerical and decision-making functions."[7]

Indeed, the managers at Consolidated Underwriters Insurance believed that this data-base environment would create a new kind of office job. Employees would be needed to work with the data base, manage exceptional cases, and use the information for improvements in customer service. The managers believed such jobs would require skills related to information management as well as technical knowledge of insurance products. In other words, these new positions would exploit the informating capacity of the new infrastructure and would demand intellective skills. In this way, the automated office, which had intensified the industrialization of the clerical worker and completed her or his exile from the managerial process, was seen as a transitional solution to the relentless pressures of volume and cost. The new vision was one of fewer clerks but better jobs—jobs that at every level would be enriched by an informating technology.

INFORMATING THE OFFICE: WORK AS ELECTRONIC TEXT

Global Bank Brazil provided the opportunity to explore the development of just such an integrated data-base environment. During the period of my research visits, that organization was involved in the planning and initial implementation of what they called "a new phase of technological development" in banking. Although the full range of the project would take several more years to complete, the early data suggest how an informated environment might reconfigure patterns of conduct, sensibility, and skill within the various levels of a white-collar organization. In particular, they indicate how the traditional skills related to *acting-with* may be eroded and the new qualities of knowledge that are likely to substitute for, or complement, that action-centered know-how.

The point here is not to set up a direct comparison between the two clerical operations we have discussed and Global Bank Brazil. These organizations were in distinct phases of technological evolution, and the systems under consideration were designed to address different problems. What the Global Bank Brazil case does provide, however, is a better understanding of the choices that may eventually face the managers at Consolidated Underwriters Insurance and Universal Technology. As they accomplish a more efficient and complete textualization of office work, what kinds of opportunities for creating value will they perceive? What kinds of jobs will they create? Will the technology finally become the occasion for a reintegration of clerical and managerial occupations? In short, what might it mean to move from an automated to an informated office?

In Global Bank Brazil, the impetus toward data-base technology development came from the need to improve internal operating efficiencies as well as from a commitment to building a data infrastructure that banking professionals could exploit in order to create new value-added, information-based products and services. For Global Bank Brazil, the data-base environment concept represented a technological strategy in direct support of its competitive strategy. Because this case represents an opportunity to investigate the linkages between competitive strategy in a service enterprise, technological development, and organizational transformation, it is worthwhile to trace briefly the business context that provided the drive for Global Bank Brazil's approach to the technology.

During the late 1970s and early 1980s, international banking experienced wrenching changes. Revenues from traditional sources, such as lending, decreased, and banks became more dependent on fees generated from new products and services. Deregulation meant that banks also faced increased competition from nontraditional banking sources, particularly other financial services companies. Finally, the Latin American debt crisis had caused the major institutions to reexamine their lending and marketing strategies.[8] As a result, many banks were racing to develop their capacity to utilize computer technology, both for productivity and for the development of information-related products and services.[9]

Global Bank had become a leader in high-tech banking. Global Bank International (the division that serviced corporate clients around the world) led the way with technological applications (telecommunications networks, automated delivery vehicles, on-line cash management, data-base services, electronic funds transfer, and letter of credit and foreign exchange services) that between 1979 and 1984 represented investments in technology of $1.5 billion, almost half of what the entire bank had allocated for expenditures on technology during that period.

The international division's leadership saw the technological infrastructure as vital to achieving its strategic objectives, which included an emphasis on product expansion, differentiation, and cost allocation, coupled with continued market penetration in key countries and the customization of services for local clients. The development of value-added products and services was considered the most important factor in accelerating the pace of revenue growth.

Global Bank Brazil was one of the largest and most profitable U.S.-based banks in Brazil. In 1984 the revenues from the Brazilian operations represented almost 20 percent of the parent corporation's total profits. Global Bank Brazil was growing rapidly, but the debt crisis had given particular urgency to the new business strategy. Dollar loans, which had been a principal source of revenue, had been eliminated. New fee-based revenues, many of which would be generated from information-intensive products and services, were crucial for Global Bank Brazil's continued growth and financial success.

During 1984 many discussions at the bank focused on the difficulty of defining banking products and the challenge of creating what they called a "product-oriented culture." It was clear that the bank's expertise with information technology would play a crucial role, both in the content of new products and in the processes used to develop them. While there was no single definition of new products, there was a consensus about three important requirements: quick response to a rapidly changing financial environment, flexibility to customize products, and high information content as a means of adding value. Diverse ideas were being generated:

> We could buy information and build integration of information from several sources and give it to the client. We could find out how they dream. Give them information about real estate to buy a house . . . and then tell them we'll provide the loan for the house, too . . . and insurance . . . then we've got him hooked.

> With the right data-base technology it becomes cost-effective for us to provide our clients with a continual and accurate picture of their cash position. We can manage their accounts payable and accounts receivable through our system. We can advise them when they need a loan or when they have an excess of funds they should invest.

> With a data-base environment, we can see that Company A needs money and Company B has money to loan. We can broker that loan for them, analyze the credit risk, and charge a fee for undertaking that risk. The data base allows a broad integration of data from many companies so you can really find opportunities. This kind of data used to be in one broker's head. Now it can be in a data base with a vast memory.

Each of these products depended on a sophisticated technological infrastructure that could integrate data from the bank's internal functions, as well as from its clients and other external data bases, while providing opportunities for flexible access to information, data manipulation, and analysis. The existing technological infrastructure did not fulfill these criteria. It had been built to "automate the factory," with an exclusive focus on internal operations, high-volume transactions processing, and cost reduction. The systems were designed in separate modules representing different functions, and they did not "talk" to one another. Changes in the regulatory environment necessitated different calculations and required that each module be updated separately. Depending on when the system was accessed, reports could show different numbers, and the awkward updating procedures created a constant stream of errors. Some managers estimated that only 20 percent of the standardized reports available from the systems were ever utilized, mainly because they provided what managers referred to as "an autopsy of the corpse"; that is, data about events that had already occurred rather than data about processes under way. Moreover, it was impossible to access these various systems according to one's own immediate and specific analytical needs.

The leaders of both the operations and the financial control divisions in Global Bank Brazil, which had primary responsibility for technology and financial data, saw the need for a new technological infrastructure. They believed that it should provide a data base in which numbers were accurate and consistent, and that it should integrate data from the various functional areas for easy use in the creation of new products and services. In other words, the bank had used its massive investment in technology almost exclusively as a means to automate its transaction base. Now the time had come to build on that base and finally exploit the technology's unique informating capacity. They made a commitment to a new project, one that would develop and implement a database environment in Global Bank Brazil. Though such an undertaking was ambitious and costly, they, together with other senior managers, believed that Global Bank Brazil's experience would provide a model for other Global Bank operations around the world.[10]

For the Global Bank Brazil managers and technologists who became involved in the conception, planning, and implementation of the database environment, it represented "a new direction for the bank . . . the infrastructure for the new business plan . . . a big piece of the overall

strategy." These managers explained the data-base concept as "a library
. . . a place where I can do research," "experiment with any idea," and
"implement ideas immediately." One project member explained:

> We'll be able to see what's happening. Not only will we have num-
> bers, but we'll be able to see the dynamics for yesterday, today, and
> tomorrow. Using the projection capability, you can see immediately
> the impact on earnings or the portfolio. We'll be able to see the
> business through the terminal.

As the business became available for more rigorous analysis, project
members believed that bankers (that is, middle- and senior-level professionals with client responsibilities) would be able to "manage the
business instead of just reacting to individual client situations." They
saw the data-base environment as the infrastructure needed to create
new value-added information products and anticipated new product
discoveries based on the ability to explore a variety of financial configurations. Another banker explained:

> Eighty percent of the bank's products can be produced with 150
> procedures. The other 20 percent of the products require at least
> that many procedures. It's like a production line. We want a data
> base that will give us the pieces to assemble. If you use the same
> procedure in a different order, you would get a different product; or
> you could eliminate one procedure, and you'd get a different prod-
> uct. When data is independent from the function, you create an infi-
> nite number of products. Data and procedures—that's the concep-
> tual thinking that's required.

Many people also saw the data-base environment as a way to consolidate and formalize information currently existing in a variety of informal media. The data base could transpose data from people's heads or
personal files into a unified, visible, accessible medium.

> Today I have to work hard to get information from folders, letters,
> scraps of paper, conversations. It's very confusing. Now I'll get infor-
> mation easily.

The project team worked over a two-year period on the planning
and initial stages of implementing the data-base environment. As their
activities intensified, bankers and clerks alike began to consider the
likely implications of the new technology for their tasks, especially

concerning the nature of the skills they would need. They anticipated two ways in which current patterns of skill were likely to be challenged and potentially transformed. First, many managers identified the current importance of action-centered skills to the professional activities of the banker as well as the clerical work force. They feared that the new environment would encroach upon, displace, or transform the traditional importance of such implicit know-how.

A crucial arena in which action-centered skills had contributed to a banker's success was that of managing the relationship with the customer and assessing credit risk (account officers were referred to as "relationship managers"). They described the "art" of banking as "the ability to develop a gut feel of the client" based on business discussions as well as social activities like luncheons, golf games, and cocktail parties. These activities were not considered frivolous but were seen as vitally important sources of data. The relationship between banker and customer was an example of action-centered skill related to *acting-with*; it demanded the bodily presence (gut) and personal sensibility of the banker in a face-to-face action context:

> Our credit decisions have been more related to feeling than to technical skill. For big loans, the officer knows the client and the client's environment. He spends time with that person. They dine together, play golf together. That is why we specialize by industry and company size. This is why the officer comes to know things that are not written. Credit is given by the feeling in one's stomach. Technological development and the more challenging demands of our marketplace will change this. The objective component of the decision will be increased as we have data visible to all. You can make the terms of lending so secure that the gut-feel credit judgment becomes secondary.

Many others agreed that the growing information presence and the availability of flexible analytical software was turning this "art" of banking into a science. They claimed that decisions "will be on more solid ground, not just based on feelings."

> Now managers are seat-of-the-pants people wearing goggles and white scarves. But we're moving too fast, too high, and too quick, and we can't fly by the seat of our pants now. The new technology provides a sophisticated means of navigating in the business environment. Holding your finger up to the wind won't be acceptable anymore.

> A banker used to be a salesman—a lot of interaction and personality involved. Now people who are good will manage and use information to be better . . . on a more objective and scientific basis. They'll be more analytical, and make more use of computing and statistical management tools.

Action-centered skill had another role to play. Despite the bank's huge investment in technology, the rapid growth of Global Bank Brazil had made it difficult to keep up with the demand for automation. There were many back office processes that continued to rely, either in part or entirely, on manual means. Many professionals and clerks were accustomed to dealing with paper and pencil, with the same hands-on, personally developed know-how that had characterized the dental claims clerks' interactions with their ledgers. One manager described the operations of the bank as full of "artisans who make information by hand."

The central liabilities operation was one of the first slated to go on-line with the new data base.[11] The current procedures in that area still depended upon a great deal of written documentation, ledger cards, and personal files. The senior operations manager in charge of the largest branch office in Brazil was concerned about the implications of the technological change for the kind of knowledge upon which his office and others like it had depended:

> Today, my people do notations in a ledger with pens. They write down rules in the ledger about how we will do a given type of transaction. Some ledgers have ten years of written history in them. The knowledge that people have is very personal. It is connected to their own thinking, their own writing. It's my writing, my data; I do it, I make it. I am concerned that we will lose contact with the data, which is after all the original data base. Man needs to feel, to touch the data. With the new technology, the contact with the data is impersonal.

The concerns about loss of contact with the actual dynamics of the business due to this impersonal quality of the new data environment was also voiced by professionals in relation to their own work:

> The old banker is a bloodhound—he sniffs out deviations. The auditor is a bloodhound, too. You learn to recognize when something is wrong. With the manual system, we had a smell for errors. You could pick up the ledger, scan it. The sense is formed by years of experi-

ence. Now the bloodhounds are disappearing. You can't sniff the new technology.

There was a second way in which people expected the data-base environment to affect the nature and distribution of skill. The growing consensus was that a depth of intellective skill would be required at each level of the organization. Through the first half of the 1980s, technological development had automated processes in a way that eliminated, minimized, or simplified human intervention. To the extent that technology had penetrated the work of professionals and clerks, many believed that it had not only encroached on action-centered skills but also failed to replace those skills with new forms of knowledge that could become the basis for new competencies. The computer system had become a black box into which a great deal of intelligence about banking procedures had been loaded. People at all levels had become dependent on that box and were poorly acquainted with much of the financial logic that was fundamental to the banking business.

Some managers reflected on what had happened to the clerical and lower-management work force. In their view, this group once contained the "knowledge of the bank"—an understanding of how the transaction base operated. With the automation of the 1970s and 1980s, as we also saw in Consolidated Underwriters Insurance and Universal Technology, much of that knowledge had been stored in the machine.

> With our automated systems, the clerk's tool became a terminal. . . . You don't need to think, because the machine makes the calculations and performs the control. People don't understand the meaning of their jobs. It's a void. A clerk goes in and out of a task, but whoever made the system is the only one who knows what is in the box.
>
> As we have more and more processing in the black box, fewer people know what a bank is really like. Some guys now are walking encyclopedias of banking information, but they are a dying breed. Do we need people who really know all the processes? Is there a risk?

Others pointed out that these growing knowledge deficiencies and machine dependency were not restricted to the lower levels of the organization. Bankers had lost much of their technical knowledge of the business. The head of the technology division explained the history of automation in the bank this way:

> The technologists have concentrated intelligence in the machine. The user pushes the button, and it's done for them. You don't have to know bookkeeping or understand the general ledger. In the old days, people had that intelligence. When you make loans manually, you have to understand the dynamics of the loans you are making. With automation, you just fill out the forms. People stop using their skills, and pretty soon they don't know the business very well.

Another banker explained:

> Now the banker loses knowledge when he uses reports produced by the system. They don't know how to do it manually anymore. The machine calculates, and people see reports with figures that they themselves could not produce. They are unfamiliar with the basic concepts of the business, the basic accounting principles.

These dynamics can be recast in the historical perspective developed in chapter 3. The work of the banker had entailed considerable technical and action-centered knowledge. The technical aspects were most subject to rationalization and so could be carved out and repositioned in lower-level management or even clerical routines. With the growth of automated systems, this knowledge increasingly came to be lodged in software, further reducing the skill requirements of those lower-echelon jobs, transforming them into machine-oriented procedures. As this process continues, the organization arrives at a point where most of its technical knowledge is embodied in software, and very little of it is developed or required in the course of ordinary professional or clerical activities.

The liveliest debate in the bank centered on whether the data-base environment would exacerbate this trend or reverse the downward spiral of banking skills. Some were beginning to realize that a data-base environment, without a knowledgeable work force to utilize it, would be of little value:

> If people aren't aware of the opportunities in the data-base environment to use the integrated information it can make available, then they will only be terminal operators. They will be filling in the blanks on the screen rather than thinking.

The senior technology planners agreed that the data-base environment required an entirely new logic of skill development:

> The data-base environment means a concentration on data, not on procedures. You have to choose which procedures you want to impose on which data. This means that using the technology becomes a very creative process. It will push people's intelligence. Everyone will be a systems analyst, using their business expertise. We will have to think before pushing buttons.

Many managers agreed that a serious training investment would be required if organizational members were to have the skills necessary to exploit the informating power of a data-base environment. But what might be the kinds of skills that would be necessary?

In a series of discussions with managers who were informed about the new technology, their reflections as to the nature of the new skill demands began to take shape. They anticipated a kind of knowledge that closely paralleled the intellective skill profile that we have already seen in the informated plant environment discussed in chapter 2. First, they widely agreed on the problem of meaning as a central challenge in the informated organization.

> There is a big difference between the person who knows and the person who just looks at the screen. You must know your business to use the data base. You find yourself asking, "What does it mean?" "What am I looking at?" There need to be many mechanisms available for answering that question.

Second, they believed that people would need to be more oriented toward abstract thinking. People were accustomed to thinking of products as material things. Now they would have to think of products as conceptual innovations. "We need to have some people with a new frame of mind," said one banker. "Bankers tend to have very square minds. They think concretely. We will need people who are conceptualizers, who are not afraid to think in abstractions and to learn through analysis." One manager, who had spent his early career in the navy, provided the following analogy as a way of illustrating the implications of the change:

> I spent years and years on the bridge of a ship looking for the horizon, and gave orders based on the information my eyes gave me. With computer technology, the commander of a ship is no longer on the bridge. He is in a room filled with computers. Now he looks at the screen with a lot of information and makes decisions. He must have new ways of making sense. He must feel the numbers, trends, and

plots, and relate it to the outside, to what really happens. He must reconstruct the scenario from the information on the screen. I believe the same thing is happening in the bank—bankers will have the same problem.

Some bankers had already begun to recognize that data-based inferential reasoning would be a crucial aspect of these new skills. They believed that a more theoretical understanding of the business would provide the means by which people would "navigate" in the information-rich environment.

> The banker needs to know the structure of the data and associations, relationships, and links within the data. To navigate in the data base, you need a conceptual model of the business, the data, the logic. Users have to define their conceptual model of the bank . . . to make the model in their heads explicit. For the first time they will need to know the meaning of their work.

As in the mills, the ability to handle the comprehensive array of data would depend in part on "top-down" processing, which, in the absence of an immediate action context, is in turn dependent upon theoretical understanding.

Finally, managers repeatedly identified the need for procedural reasoning based upon a comprehensive grasp of the information system. People would have to know what data are available, how they are accessed and analyzed, and how they might relate to other sectors of data. Information would no longer be organized according to separate bank operations:

> The new technology makes you look at the whole. Tasks become more comprehensive as a result. You need to know where to look for what you need and how to get it. You need to see patterns in relation to the whole.

Some managers felt strongly that the clerical positions created during the past decades of mechanization would become obsolete. The jobs, like the ones at Consolidated Underwriters Insurance and Universal Technology, had become increasingly mechanized and specialized. The new technological infrastructure would integrate many disparate functions and eliminate the need for a great many of the simple procedures that still required repetitive clerk-machine interaction. Just as the insurance executives envisioned future changes in the clerical function that would make the job more comprehensive and intellectually demanding, these bank managers foresaw a new semiprofessional role that would replace the current clerical job. As in most organizations, clerical work had proliferated as a means of isolating and efficiently dispatching the most routine aspects of the organization's work. The new phase of technological development would begin to reverse this process. Routine tasks would be either subsumed by automatic processes or subcontracted out to a processing organization external to the bank.

Activities that had once been extracted from the professional domain and rationalized in lower-level jobs could now be reintegrated with those higher-level positions. For example, bankers could interact directly with the data base, perform analyses, and develop ideas. The remaining clerical positions would take on a quasi-professional status, requiring information management and business knowledge.

> The information will be available to everyone. We are "killing" the clerks as we know them now. The new clerk must be trained to make decisions, to deal with the information relevant to that function. It will mean a need for more educated people. You can't just type in information and not know what it means. At the same time we will need far fewer clerks. Data will be entered and accessed by the people who have it and use it. The vice-president will learn to use a keyboard, and eventually he will become a pianist.

The clerks in the central liabilities area also realized that management had some clear choices to make. In the past, they had received minimal training in operating computer technology. Like the other clerks we have heard from, they were taught to push buttons and little else. Would implementation of the data-base environment really represent a new approach? Would they be trained to handle information and perform their jobs in a new way? Would they be given the skills to make a more valuable contribution? The clerks expressed their concerns, but the answers to their questions were still unclear.

> We need a more global view so we can solve our problems when we have them. When you just push buttons and don't have a general idea of what it is . . . that's not much of a job. The most important thing is to know my job in the context of all the tasks of the bank. How else can I exercise any judgment?

I wish senior management would think about how to give information to the people. Give more training and information about the bank and the technology and the business. They take a person and say, "Sit here and do this and do that." If I have no opportunity to learn, I have no value. Will things be any different now?

WILL THINGS BE ANY DIFFERENT NOW?

The history of the white-collar body has led to a series of questions regarding the application of information technology in the office. Would the technology be used, like the office machinery of earlier decades, to further disinherit the clerical position from its managerial legacy? Might it be the occasion for a reintegration of clerical work with the managerial function? How would either of these scenarios affect the managerial role? How might the increased textualization of work affect the knowledge that managers, as well as clerks, would require? Would the presence of technology increase the rationalized content of the middle-management job and encroach on those skills related to *acting-with*? Would the intellective component of the manager's function be enlarged?

The evidence presented in this chapter suggests the dynamic interplay between intrinsic and contingent aspects of information technology and illustrates some of the ways in which these questions might be answered. At Consolidated Underwriters Insurance and, in a more qualified way, at Universal Technology, we saw information technology applied in ways that resembled Leffingwell's goals for office machinery, with an almost exclusive emphasis on the technology's automating capacity. In these settings, the clerk was absorbed into the machine system, and the managerial process became anchored in the supervisory role. In the context of managerial choices that emphasize cost reduction, productivity, and increased volume, the clerical experience became one of laboring bodies engrossed in the demands for ongoing physical and attentional stamina, and removed from the forms of social exchange that once signified their integration with the managerial hierarchy.

However, these two cases also reveal a crucial distinction between computer systems and the office machines that preceded them. The further development of office machinery begets only new and more specialized office machinery. Typewriters, adding machines, filing systems—equipment may become more sophisticated, but its function does not change. In contrast, the further development of computer systems unleashes their informating potential. As time frames become more immediate, as more sectors of data can be integrated, as software helps limit inaccuracies, as data entry and access become more widely distributed, and as programmed logic becomes more comprehensible and flexible, the surrounding life-world of the organization comes to be more comprehensively reflected in a dynamic, fluid electronic text. New methods of automating this textualization process, such as building it into organizational members' natural activities (for example, account officers enter their own data), sharing it among several organizations through interorganizational systems, and relying on increasingly sophisticated automated data-entry devices based on optical character recognition and high-speed communications, mean that fewer people will be needed to accomplish routine transactions in conjunction with the machine system.

This new scenario calls into question both the forms of knowledge that people need and the way in which that knowledge should be distributed. New intellective skills are required, but the mere fact of this requirement does not imply that it will be fulfilled. As some members of Global Bank Brazil feared, institutions may be unable to respond to the technological presence other than as an occasion for decreasing their dependence on human talent, ignoring the opportunities to gain value from the technology in a qualitatively different way. However, one thing seems clear—the informating potential of the technology cannot be exploited without human skills in ways of thinking that are conceptual, inferential, procedural, and systemic.

When the clerk at Global Bank Brazil asks, "Will things be any different now?" one wants to answer, "Yes!" Rational analysis suggests that things indeed should be different now. However, rational analysis neglects some of the most trenchant features of organizational experience—realities that cut to the quick of managerial power as it is conceived and displayed in everyday life at work.

Before we can determine whether things will be different, what may drive them to be so, and what may impede change, chapter 5 will consolidate the evidence from the mills and the white-collar settings in order to better define the qualities of knowledge associated with an informated organization. With that in hand, we will move on to confront these dilemmas of power and see if, and how, that crucial question—Will things be any different now?—might be answered.

CHAPTER FIVE

MASTERING THE

ELECTRONIC TEXT

"I will sing to cheer you and to make you
thoughtful too," said the nightingale. "But if
I am to sing, I must be free to fly about the
kindom."

—HANS CHRISTIAN ANDERSEN
The Nightingale

ACTION-CENTERED SKILL AND ORAL CULTURE

Piney Wood's operators, Global Bank Brazil's account officers, and Consolidated Underwriters Insurance's benefits analysts share more than any objective analysis of their work will tell. They have all been described as "manual workers," or "concrete thinkers" by co-workers or superiors, with barely concealed disparagement. They also have been referred to as "artists", evoking admiration and amazement with the amount of highly detailed know-how they keep "in their heads" and display in their activities.

The know-how of each group exemplifies what I have called action-centered skill. For the pulp mill operators, these skills were organized in the mode of *acting-on*: their active bodies were oriented toward producing effects on material and equipment. For managers and clerical employees, the mode of their knowledge was that of *acting-with*: they used their active presence as a medium for learning, coordinating, and communicating within a web of complex human relationships. The special know-how of each group developed from physical cues (feeling a roll of paper, seeing a face); it was learned and displayed in action (kicking the boiler, conversing in the corridor, interpersonal office routines); it was triggered by a shared context (the presence of equipment, gestures and tones in a meeting, open office space); and it was highly personal (subject to sensibility and style, known implicitly, lodged in the "interior," felt experience of the individual).

When it comes to action-centered skills, the crucial know-how that distinguishes skillful from mediocre performance eludes formal codification. People learn by experience—imitating and attempting. They certainly may discuss their performance with each other and try to learn more about what to do and how to do it, but these are action-centered skills because the things that must be learned and done have, in the final analysis, the character of events. The manager who skillfully leads a meeting uses language, gestures, and deeds to shape the quality of an interpersonal event—an event that passes out of existence when the meeting comes to a close. The bleach operator who controls chemical flows on the basis of sniffing and squeezing a fistful of pulp has participated in a sentient event. The office workers who confer over the processing of an account have engaged in a conversational event. In each case, knowledge is embedded in practical action that is evanescent. The knowledge that underlies action-centered skill is not recorded; rather, it is constituted as the action is executed. It does not enjoy an independent life, outside of those practical activities in which it can be learned and displayed. The knowledge associated with doing cannot be reduced to talking or writing about doing. Action-centered skill can be lived and it can be witnessed, but it vanishes into mere potential when the action is completed. It leaves no trace, except for the know-how acquired by its practitioners and the effects it has produced.

Action-centered skills thus are limited to the time frame of events and the presence of actors in the context where those events can occur. In other words, action-centered skills are part of oral culture. They demand present-tense engagement in the immediate world of objects and people. Oral culture can be distinguished from other cultural forms in which knowledge mainly derives from and is conveyed by the written word. Primary oral cultures, those untouched by writing, are practically extinct. However, literate societies continue to preserve, within their

various subcultures, patterns of thought and feeling that bear the markings of oral culture. A brief comparison of oral and written culture
provides a vantage point from which to regard the transformation in
the quality of knowledge engendered by computer-mediated work.

The work of Milman Parry and his son Adam Parry, as well as the
work of Eric Havelock, Harold Innis, Marshall McLuhan, and Walter
Ong, has been a source of powerful new insights into the fundamental
characteristics that distinguish oral culture from the orientation toward
the written word that thoroughly imbues literate societies.[1] In his recent work, *Orality and Literacy*, Walter Ong reviews several features of
what he calls the "psychodynamics of orality," which help illuminate
the action contexts I have described.

Ong emphasizes the physicality of the sounded word. In the context
of oral culture, the word is a sounded event. Because words depend
upon the physical power of the speaker for their existence, they can
be thought of as bodily actions. Spoken words are events in time that
leave no record of themselves. We can see the interplay of orality and
written culture in the convention of speaking "for the record" or "off
the record." When words vanish with speech, speakers can risk expressing themselves in ways that might evoke conflict if listeners had the
opportunity to appraise the words in their written form.

In an oral culture, one knows what one can recall. Conversation and
personal notes are important stimuli for memory; rhythmic speech patterns, metaphors, and syntactic formulas each aid recollection. In previous chapters, we saw that operators, managers, and clerical workers
relied on "trigger" information to help them store and later recall
knowledge relevant to a particular action context. In each case, observers remarked upon the quantity of knowledge that skilled individuals
had stored "in their heads."

Orality tends to be redundant. Because words vanish, repetition
keeps both the speaker and the listener on track. Knowledge must be
repeated to be preserved. Individuals with lengthy experience tend to
be the most highly valued because their past experience makes them
vessels of knowledge. They become less important when that knowledge can be codified independently and carried away in written words
(or computer programs).

The written word can abstract from the human experience, but orality relies upon situational and operational frames of reference that remain close to real human activity. Ong notes that learning a craft, even

in modern societies depends upon immediate shared action, rather than abstraction: "Trades were learned by apprenticeship (as they still largely are even in high-technology cultures), which means from observation and practice with only minimal verbalized explanation."[2]

The nature of learning in an oral culture depends upon achieving a close empathic identification with what is known. In contrast, writing sets up the conditions of objectivity, creating a new distance between the knower and the known. An intense identification with the objects of knowledge was evident among pulp mill operators who relied upon seeing, touching, and hearing their equipment and products, among those managers who must engage with their subordinates in hallways and corridors in order to feel they "know" what is going on; among account officers who feel they must interact with the client in order to make a credit decision; and among the clerical employees who used signatures, voices, and other situational features as a way of developing personal knowledge about a particular account.

In this way, oral discourse is oriented toward the present tense, because word meanings are shaped in the present by the influence of the shared action context—"the always insistent actual habitat, which is not, as in a dictionary, simply other words, but includes also gestures, vocal inflections, facial expression, and the entire human, existential setting in which the real, spoken word always occurs."[3] That the action context supplies meaning was evident for each group. Operators felt disoriented when distanced from the production floor; managers and office workers required face-to-face interaction in order "to know." Oral communication tends to be more highly charged, emotional, and potentially conflictful. When communication must be face-to-face, interpersonal attractions and antagonisms are kept high. This emotional charge was evident in bankers' relations with their clients as well as in those of mill operators and their managers or clerks and their co-workers and supervisors.

Finally, orality is always externalized and public. The emphasis on a shared action context tends to unite people in groups, while writing and reading create the possibility of solitude and introspection. We see evidence of this in the quality of knowing reported by the mill operators and those executives studied by Mintzberg, Kotter, and others. In each case, individuals tended not to think about what they knew; rather, they acted it out in their daily lives. People tend to be less reflective when they are immersed in the present-tense dynamism of utterance and action.

To the extent that skilled practice eludes codification, it provides a living resource for the preservation of oral culture. In each of the workplaces I have discussed, significant dimensions of oral culture have been sustained, drawing their strength in part from the production and reproduction of action-centered skills. In this way, the degree of orality that surrounds a set of practices is also related to the degree of power and autonomy that can be enjoyed by its practitioners. The explication of skilled practice characteristic of scientific management is an example of how codification erodes a group's power as it increases the transparency of their know-how and detaches that knowledge from the requirements of an action context. Senior executives, because of the authority they enjoy, have been able to preserve the orality of their culture, perhaps more successfully than any other group. This serves to maintain the conditions that support their authority, as it protects the opacity of their know-how.

COMPETENCE AND PERFORMANCE WHEN WORK IS TEXTUALIZED

The skilled workers, office employees, and managers discussed in the previous chapters each took part in many of these features of oral culture. This is not to say that their world had not been penetrated by the written word. In the mills, there were log books, charts, and memos. In the offices, there were reports, memos, and reams of paper documentation. Nevertheless, the extent of this written culture was limited enough to permit, and to actually require, the present-tense know-how that can competently shape events and processes.

With the advent of computer mediation, the process of codification has been radically extended. In its more advanced forms (illustrated in the mills and anticipated in Global Bank Brazil's data-base environment), the technology moves beyond codifying discrete activities or procedures to a more comprehensive textualization of work content. In the mills, we saw once-mute material processes now translated and displayed as data. In the bank, the structure and content of the data base was intended to include judgments, heuristics, processes, and informal knowledge—all of which formerly escaped codification. In each case, the informating capacity of the technology produced a new medium of electronic text through which organizational events, objects, transactions, functions, activities, and know-how could be enacted or observed.

What is the character of the text that is created, and how might it differ from that of paper-based documentation? First, the electronic text of an organization, at least at the level of sophistication exemplified in the mills or anticipated in the data-base environment, is not discrete but comprehensive and systemic. It is a question, not of individual events converted to text, but of systems of events that are revealed comprehensively. In the mills, the data interface provided a view, not only of one piece of equipment but also of the process in an entire production module; not only of one module but also of the production process across the mill; and not only of the production process but also of management information, expert models with which to calculate optimization parameters, and other data related to personnel, markets, sales, and much more. Thus, access to the electronic text meant access to far more than discrete memos or reports could ever provide: the organization's work is made visible in a new way.

Second, programmed logic means that procedures and informal knowledge can be codified and built into the structure of an information system, thus increasing the depth of the text. For example, the benefits analysts were debriefed, and their knowledge was built into the design of the system; the skilled operators were debriefed, and their knowledge contributed to the programs that automated aspects of the production process; and managers were debriefed and their methods of utilizing information were designed into the structure of the data base. The structure of the text, as well as its content, reflects material that had been private and implicit. When the computer medium is used for communication, as in the case of electronic messaging or computer conferencing, informal discourse is also absorbed by the textualization process (a case which will be examined in more detail in chapter 10).

The electronic text exists independently of space and time. When text is confined to concrete objects, such as books or pieces of paper, it generates pressures for centralization (you must go to the text if you want to read it) or for possession (you can own the book or maintain your own files). The electronic text is the result of an even more radical centralization: a wide range of information can be gathered and codified in a single computer system. However, this radical centralization enables an equally radical decentralization: in principle, the text can be constituted at any time from any place. The contents of the electronic text can infuse an entire organization, instead of being bundled in discrete objects, like books or pieces of paper.

Finally, the electronic text does not have an author in the conventional sense. It may be produced from many individual acts of "authorship" (for example, account officers enter their own data, managers send messages, customers provide data through automated teller machines), or it may result from impersonal and autonomous processes (for example, microprocessors register data from the production process, optical scanners read and input data).[4] The text that is produced can be more immediate and raw than, for example, written reports that are heavily edited and otherwise shaped to conform to local standards. As in the case of the office employees, the impersonality and obscurity of authorship can elicit a sense of otherness in the reader. The text can seem more definitive and less vulnerable to criticism than a written document whose human authorship is clear.

The textualization of work-related processes can destroy the sense of meaning inherent in action-centered skills and the oral culture in which they are embedded. This was evidenced among both the mill operators and the bankers, who felt that their "art" was made obsolete by the new computer systems and who found it difficult to let go of the action context that had corresponded to that art. In a more limited context, the office employees of Consolidated Underwriters Insurance and Universal Technology suffered a similar loss of meaning and context.

Textualization can also be the occasion for the construction of new meaning. The symbolic medium provides a new distance from experience, and this can be felt as a "thinning" of meaning, a deprivation. When that medium becomes the basis for constructing a more comprehensive and explicit understanding, however, it can also be experienced as a source of instruction and empowerment. Knowledge is freed from the temporal and physical constraints of action; it can be appropriated and carried beyond the moment.[5]

When meaning is uncoupled from its action context and carried away in symbols, a new playfulness becomes possible. Events and the relationships among events can be illuminated and combined in new ways. As surrounding events and processes become the objects of a disengaged awareness, they become susceptible to examination, comparison, and innovation. For example, operators at Piney Wood and Tiger Creek became acquainted with a now explicit version of their formerly tacit practices as they confronted and manipulated newly defined and quantified variables made visible in the electronic text. They were able to "play" with the variables and so discover new potential in the production process for cheaper and more efficient processing. (One such case will be illustrated in detail in chapter 7.)

These liberating aspects of symbolization have long been recognized by historians of written culture. Eric Havelock has extensively discussed the role of written language in freeing the human mind from the tremendous burden of memorization that was required to preserve knowledge in an oral culture.[6] "Extramental" forms of information storage accelerated the growth of knowledge, as it no longer depended upon what could be remembered. The human mind became capable of creating and manipulating theoretic, logical, ideational statements, as opposed to being limited to the interpersonal, the particular, and the concrete.[7]

The computerization of productive and administrative processes in an organization reproduces some of these effects of the written word, but it does a great deal more as well. The technology takes over for a certain amount of human activity, even as it renders that activity in text. Action-centered skills (*acting-on* and *acting-with*) are built into the technology as it substitutes for bodily presence—that is automation. At the same time, activities are made transparent. They are exposed in detail as they are textualized in the conversion to explicit information—that is informating. In principle, the technological substitution for bodily presence frees the human being from having to participate in the immediate demands of action (and the lengthy investment in the associated skills). However, the technology not only frees individuals "from" but also frees them "to." The automating capacity of the technology can free the human being for a more comprehensive, explicit, systemic, and abstract knowledge of his or her work made possible by the technology's ability to informate.

Whether or not this new knowledge is achieved depends upon two crucial conditions: the presence of individual competence and the opportunity to express that competence. First, organization members cannot construct meaning from the abstract cues of the electronic text without mastering intellective skills. The computer-mediated jobs that I have discussed each bear a different relationship to the text and so have varied in their emphasis on intellective skill development. In the case of the professional and managerial staff in Global Bank Brazil, it was clear that they will have to know how to create value based on their engagement with the data-base environment. Intellective mastery will allow them to become interpreters of the text and so to add value to its contents. This relationship can also be viewed in terms of the technical distinction often drawn between data, information and knowledge: intellective skill is the basis upon which data are translated into meaningful information, and finally into knowledge.

The benefits analysts and transfer assistants can be described as functionaries of the text. They were treated like mechanical devices in the textualization process, and were not encouraged to utilize the text to create value. As a result, their training was mechanistic and superficial. The mill operators' positions were ambiguous. Early on, managers believed that the operators merely provided backup and monitoring capabilities. In time it became obvious that the opportunities offered by an informating technology could not be exploited without new intellective skills in the operating work force. As we shall see more clearly in later chapters, the managers in these mills also found themselves faced with the challenge of utilizing the electronic text as a basis for adding value to the business.

A second condition for fulfilling the knowledge-generating potential of an informating technology involves performance (the opportunity to express competence), which is determined in part by the manner in which the technology is both designed and deployed. Technological design embodies assumptions that can either invite or extinguish a human contribution. By incorporating one form of knowledge into the technology, human beings, in principle, are freed to develop new forms of knowledge. However, the process of skill incorporation can also proceed to an extent that completely obviates the necessity of human skills.

A dramatic example of this process is evident in the technological history of weaponry. Consider the skill of the swordsman, who had to devote many years to attaining the skill level necessary to use a sword competently. The introduction of the gun enabled someone with far less preparation to kill even more effectively. The gun required less participation in skill development and less direct physical participation in the act of injuring. Whole classes of specialists were eliminated as a result of such innovations: the gun destroyed the special role of the samurai warriors, the introduction of the crossbow eliminated the need for a class of knights. With each successive technical innovation in weaponry, more of the skill required to use an older weapon was built into the new weapon. This has tended to free populations from the most burdensome requirements of war. Rather than spend an entire lifetime developing the skills for battle, it became possible to partici-pate in war-related activities only when a moment of national crisis made it necessary. In principle, this liberation from the lifetime de-mands of war also freed people to participate in other, more construc-tive, forms of activity. Yet when the moment of war arrives, despite the technological advances of weapons, skillful human participation has continued to be necessary. This necessity represents one way for populations to register their consent to the waging of war. This histori-cal process was fundamentally altered with the advent of nuclear weap-ons, a form of weaponry which has so completely embodied the human skills associated with battle that it has eliminated requirements for both human skill *and* human presence in the conduct of battle. "The building-in of skill thus becomes, in its most triumphant form, the building-out of consent."[8]

The history of weaponry contains a lesson for the progress of infor-mation technology in the service of production. Design advances in the field of automation require less participation of the laboring body in terms of both skill and effort. The informating capacity of the technol-ogy, however, does provide for a new form of participation in produc-tive activity. Such participation, based in part upon the contribution of intellective skills, represents an opportunity for humans to influence the nature of a productive organization, to add value to its processes, and to develop their own capacities. If automation were to go the route of nuclear weapons—obviating the need for human skill and human presence—then it would be clear that managers and technologists had come to believe that it was both possible and preferable to design hu-man beings "out of the loop," despite the potential costs of suboptimi-zation, inflexibility, and lost opportunities for adding value through insight and innovation.

The way in which the technology is deployed is crucial in determin-ing whether intellective skill, once developed, can be utilized. There is a need to create organizational environments that support the quality of effort and the kinds of relationships in which intellective competence can be demonstrated. As we shall see later in this chapter, the characteristics of such environments need to be better understood if they are to be consciously planned and nurtured.

The likelihood of achieving these two interdependent conditions for the fulfillment of the technology's informating potential as the basis for new knowledge—the development of competence and the opportunity to demonstrate it—will vary in distinct businesses, at distinct levels of the organization, and during distinct phases of the evolutionary path toward an informated organization. The issue is also confounded by the difficulty of assigning a narrow time frame to this process. For example, what appear to be changes in job content in the short run, such as the new intellective demands of operators' work, may lead, in a longer time frame, to occupational shifts that fundamentally reconceptualize the roles appropriate to a manufacturing organization. In a similar vein, the automation process that turns one group of employees into mechanical variables in the production process (for example, the operators in Piney Wood's digester area and the benefits analysts in the dental claims operation at Consolidated Underwriters Insurance) may give way to a new scenario in which primary tasks are completely automated and a new class of employees is required to manage and add value to information. This scenario was anticipated by the managers in Piney Wood as well as by executives in Consolidated Underwriters Insurance and Global Bank Brazil.

It is likely that most organizations will need to make a certain amount of progress in constructing an automated base before they can turn their attention to exploiting the technology's informating capacity. However, the way in which automation is accomplished can either impede or facilitate later efforts to apply an informating strategy. A narrow approach to automation may fail to select or develop a work force that is prepared for the later challenges of informating. It may also incorporate forms of technological design and implementation that create barriers to further development by "building-out" most requirements for intelligent human participation or failing to develop those aspects of organizational culture that would be resources in an informating approach. Technological applications limited to automation may be appropriate for certain tasks (for example, a discrete assembly process) in particular business contexts (for example, where success depends on volume, not quality). In those cases where success requires extracting value from information (for example, innovation in products and services), however, such a limited approach can become an impediment to later efforts to utilize the technology's informating capacity.

Despite these complexities, if and when an organization chooses to exploit the technology's informating power, it will have to ensure the conditions for competence as well as for performance. Before we can explore the likelihood that organizations will move in this direction, and examine the forces that will constrain or facilitate their efforts, we need to improve our understanding of each of these conditions. What is actually involved in intellective skill development? What cognitive patterns distinguish intellective from action-centered skills and so define competence? What are the social-psychological dynamics associated with the expression of intellective competence in the workplace?

PATTERNS OF COGNITION IN ACTION-CENTERED AND INTELLECTIVE SKILLS

We have seen pulp mill operators, bankers, and clerical employees in a transition that they frequently describe in the same words: "It's a thinking job now"; "You must use your brain, not your hands"; "The job is more mental, it takes place in your head." In each case, the means with which to accomplish one's task have become more abstract relative to the precomputerized environment. Particularly in the cases of the mill operators and the bankers, we have seen new skill demands that involve constructing meaning from the dynamic flow of electronic text.

The felt difference that these individuals experience toward their jobs before and after computerization is puzzling. After all, can it be so different to engage with a computer screen rather than with a piece of equipment, paper documentation, or a face-to-face meeting? Yet their sense of difference is stubborn; it is voiced repeatedly and in remarkably similar terms. How can it be explained?

In part, we can explain this felt difference by the disruptions of identity that such change provokes. The operators identified themselves with their hands-on mastery of equipment; the bankers knew themselves as masters of the interpersonal parley, whether on a golf course or in the executive suite; the clerks knew themselves as quasimanagerial coordinators of office procedures. Another equally important set of considerations helps explain the felt difference between action-centered and intellective skills: the patterns of cognition that are associated with each skill domain.

Though I have emphasized the bodily involvement associated with action-centered skill and the mental effort associated with intellective skill, it must be clearly stated that all skillful human activity depends upon the brain and so involves cognition. What is less clear is precisely how cognition operates to support what appear to be very different forms of skill. Are the cognitive processes that underlie the mill worker's hands-on know-how the same as those related to his or her work in a computer control room? Is the cognitive activity of "psyching out" a client identical to that of analyzing spread sheets? Questions like these are the subject of considerable debate within the field of cognitive psychology, and it is beyond the scope of my ambitions here either to trace this debate comprehensively or to attempt my own resolution of its many complexities. There remains, however, the startling regularity of the felt difference between these two skill domains, and the solution to this puzzle requires at least some further exploration of recent developments in cognitive science. These materials, while not definitive, suggest the distinguishing characteristics of each skill domain and provide a basis for additional speculation, discussion, and research.

First, what is the quality of knowledge associated with action-centered skill? According to the scientist and philosopher Michael Polanyi, know-how that cannot be verbalized is possible in part because of what he called "tacit knowledge." He began with the need to explain how it is that humans know more than they can say: "This fact seems obvious enough; but it is not easy to say exactly what it means. . . . We know a person's face, and can recognize it among a thousand, indeed among a million. Yet we usually cannot tell how we recognize a face we know. So most of this knowledge cannot be put into words."[9] Polanyi contrasted this implicit way of knowing the world to the more explicit forms of knowledge characteristic of science. He argued that some forms of meaning are comprehensible only as a whole and can be destroyed when objectified and analyzed: "We can see how an unbridled lucidity can destroy our understanding of complex matters. Scrutinize closely the particulars of a comprehensive entity and their meaning is effaced, our conception of the entity is destroyed. . . . By concentrating attention on his fingers, a pianist can temporarily paralyze his movement. We can make ourselves lose sight of a pattern of physiognomy by examining its several parts under sufficient magnification."[10] Action-centered skill, like all purposeful human activity, requires the intelligent participation of the human brain, but it is an intelligence that tends to be blended with the body's responsiveness and capacity to act. Thinking rarely has to stand alone, explicit and abstracted from this flow of action. The body is an instrument, actively registering information and, in turn, expressing what it learns in action. Inferential linkages between actions and their consequences need not be made explicit in order for skill to be learned or enacted. Action-centered skills are so called in part because their development, execution, and memory can remain confined to the sphere of tacit knowledge.

Ulric Neisser's discussion of skill development supports the notion of a linkage between action-centered skill and tacit knowledge.[11] According to Neisser, action skills depend upon a detailed understanding of the physical medium to which the skills are applied. These properties of a medium have been called "affordances"—the physical properties of the local environment that make a difference by shaping or constraining what an organism can do.[12] In Neisser's view, action skills develop based upon an increasing knowledge of the "affordances" of the medium to which one's skills apply. At the same time, this knowledge remains largely tacit—the fabric of affordances is too subtle and complex to be made explicit easily, and the display of skill does not require such explication: "The skilled carpenter knows just how a given variety of wood must be handled, or what type of joint will best serve his purpose at a particular edge. To say that he 'knows' these things is not to claim that he could put his knowledge into words. That is never entirely possible. The affordances of a real medium are too rich, too deeply embedded in crisscrossing relationships, and too continuous to be captured in a verbal description. The practitioner's knowledge of the medium is tacit. It is essential to skilled practice: the carpenter uses what he knows with every stroke of his tool."[13]

It would seem from this description that explicit awareness has a relatively minor role in the performance of action-centered skills. We might imagine that such awareness could be invoked in order to communicate or teach skills, or when a particularly problematic situation arises. It is likely, though, that attempts at explication of such tacit knowledge must always be incomplete. The knowledge is too layered and subtle to be fully articulated. That is why action-centered skill has always been learned through experience (on-the-job-training, apprenticeships, sports practice, and so forth). Actions work better than words when it comes to learning and communicating these skills.

Consider the experiences of the operators in Piney Wood and Cedar Bluff, which illustrate most clearly the felt experience of difference between the two skill domains. In the conventional plant environment, workers were engaged with the production process through action and proximity. The senses at the surface of their bodies were available to respond to a variety of concrete cues—noises, sights, and smells. With computerization, they found themselves surrounded by electronic data and a different kind of engagement was required.

Many operators experienced the computerized environment as demanding a new kind of deliberate cognitive commitment to their work. It has long been accepted in industrial administration that technological change necessitates a reevaluation of the effort bargain between management and the worker. A new technical means for accomplishing a task requires each side to reassess the acceptable level of effort that the worker must give and the appropriate means through which managers can control the stability and intensity of that effort. In each of the plants, the new technology's informating capacity had done more than simply reduce or increase the worker's effort. Effort itself had undergone an essential redefinition: the terrain of effort had shifted, not from muscles to brain, but from the complete sensual involvement of the worker's physical presence to an involvement that depended more exclusively upon the worker's quality of mind.

For those who have never worked with their bodies, such a change might seem an invitation to a better world. But for the worker whose skill has been inextricably bound up with physical activity, intellective effort does not necessarily feel better or easier. Operators frequently articulated their sense of this difference in terms of the amount of attention that the new work required:

> With the computer controlling the process, it has cut out the manual labor. You don't have to work as hard; you don't have to be out there in the hot, smelly, dirty environment. But it also means that your mind is working twice as hard. Production has increased by about 40

percent. More is being processed and much more quickly. There is a greater flow of data, and so you have to be continuously monitoring and paying attention in order to stay on top of it.

When operators discussed these attentional demands, they often acted out their feelings by gripping their foreheads and feigning sudden pain:

At least in the manual operation there are no headaches. It is hard to pay attention for such a long time.

Maintaining an attentional commitment to the data interface can be a difficult prospect, and the operators repeatedly described the ease with which their attention could lapse:

It's a problem keeping up your attention, particularly when things are running smoothly. You have a tendency to be looking at something and at some point you realize that you are staring and you don't know what you are seeing. . . . You are staring at something when you thought you were looking at something.

This worker has identified the interior structure of attentional commitment. It is not sufficient to look; one must see. Attention implies intention, without which it is merely a superficial activity, the appearance of engagement without proactive deliberation.

Managers in each plant found themselves having to invent ploys to engage operators' attention. When they supervised a worker's physical activity, having to foster attentional commitment was not perceived as a problem. The physical engagement necessitated by the work activity ensured an organic involvement in the work at hand. As the mode of effort changes, however, how does a manager keep others mentally engaged?

The problem was most pronounced in Cedar Bluff, where information systems dominated the environment and operators had no history of manual involvement with the pulping process. As much as five years after the plant's founding, some managers insisted that operators keep written logs of their activities. Though there was little data an operator could record that was not already available through an information system, these managers saw the physical requirement of recording data as one way to ensure attentiveness. One manager explained:

With our information systems we don't need the operators to keep logs, but we have them do it anyway, because we think the activity of logging in will force them to pay attention to certain parameters. Physically writing down certain numbers is thought to maintain some kind of involvement. As a manager, I have to think of ways to keep people consciously involved, rather than just staring at the screen.

While this manager had the right concerns—how to avoid habituation to the data display—his method for addressing them was greeted cynically by the operators. They knew that there was little they could record in a log book that would not be redundant with the computer's data, and they resented the useless activity.

In the case of the office workers, we saw that their perception of increased attentional requirements were partly explained by the abstract quality of the task medium and the responsibility associated with on-line operations. It is likely that these features also help to explain the reactions of the pulp mill workers. Their responses suggest still another explanation, however, concerning the role of tacit knowledge in intellective skill development. My hypothesis is that the knowledge associated with action-centered skill could remain largely tacit throughout the course of learning and execution, but the knowledge relevant to intellective skill development must be made explicit in the learning process and can only become tacit when an individual has attained a high level of expertise. Even then, it is likely that this form of knowledge can become only partially tacit and is readily accessible to explication. Recent work in cognitive psychology lends some support to this view.

Historically, cognitive scientists have treated attentiveness as the psychological opposite of automatic behavior, but current research indicates that this formulation masks a greater complexity.[14] First, there are distinct interpretations of automatic behavior. Is such behavior to be considered involuntary and thus similar to the functioning of the autonomic nervous system, which operates free of conscious control? Alternatively, should automaticity be understood as a kind of preattentive behavior in which the sensory-based perceptual systems notice and respond to stimuli in a way that bypasses explicit consciousness? To what extent is automaticity simply a result of already having learned a procedure, like driving a car, so thoroughly that it no longer requires a significant drain on finite attentional resources? Even in the context of studying automatic behavior, psychologists have found that attention is required to initiate or terminate activities, especially when they are ill determined, poorly learned, or particularly complex. In the course of automatic behavior, the unfamiliar or the unexpected can also provoke a sudden demand for conscious attention.[15] There are, then, real questions as to whether any behavior can be considered entirely automatic. Even so, if attentiveness were primarily a function of one's position on a learning curve, then we might reasonably suppose that the operators' responses to the new technological environment simply indicate the unfamiliarity of the situation, and in time, the perceived attentional demands will decline.

This explanation still falls short of accounting for the frequency of similar responses over a period of several years. Might it be that certain kinds of tasks—those that are intrinsically symbolic and abstract—require more attentiveness (that is, deliberate cognitive effort) than tasks that are more concrete and sensory? Several studies do in fact suggest that higher-order cognitive processes involving symbolic manipulation and deliberation—such as strategy formulation, problem-solving, and planning—do not lend themselves to automaticity. Researchers are also discovering that in those tasks that require an ability to generate multiple interpretations, automatic cognitive processing, though fast and efficient, tends to be inflexible and thus less effective. Automatic processing may preclude access to the underlying details and components of a situation or information set, and so it may inhibit the development of alternative interpretations of the information at hand.[16] Other studies have shown that automatic processing can give way to more controlled, aware, and flexible cognitive strategies when people are motivated and involved with their tasks.[17] When people are highly involved, they expend a great deal of effort in elaborating the content of a message and bring extensive prior knowledge to bear upon its interpretation.[18]

These findings suggest an additional explanation for the operators' responses to their informated task environment. The construction of meaning from the electronic text that now represents the production process is likely to require more deliberate, controlled, aware, cognitive effort than earlier action-centered, context-dependent routines. The reason involves the nature of the inference process that links environmental cues with a meaningful response. When those cues are primarily concrete, the inference process can remain relatively implicit or tacit. When those cues are primarily abstract, meaning must be constructed through an explication process that assigns referents and analyzes relationships. This suggests that intellective skill development depends upon explicit understanding in a way that feels like heightened mental effort. When individuals are motivated to do well, when they care about their work, those feelings are likely to be intensified.

This does not imply that tacit knowledge has no role to play in intellective skill development. Attention is a finite mental resource, and even a highly motivated individual can maintain only a limited amount of explicit material within the bounds of attention, especially when the breadth of data at the information interface requires understanding of a range of events, choices, and possibilities.

Many cognitive psychologists have concluded that long-term memory is based on the apprehension of meaning rather than on precise verbal or visual content.[19] For example, when people were asked to recall pictures or sentences as part of a psychological experiment, it was discovered that what they had stored in their memory was really an abstract representation that captured its meaning, rather than the actual details of how the picture or sentence was constructed.[20] Newell and Simon discovered a similar pattern when they studied chess masters.[21] They found that what made these people so skillful was that they had learned the array of action possibilities associated with distinct patterns of chess pieces. These patterns were stored in memory as "chunks" that defined "meaningful game relations among the pieces." In other words, the pattern, once understood, could become part of a tacit store of knowledge. When the chess master recognized the pattern on the chessboard, it triggered an immediate knowledge of the relevant action possibilities. While other players have to consciously think through the available courses of action, the chess master's attention is freed to deal with the more sophisticated problem of overall game strategy.

What might this imply for the human being at the data interface? Over the long term, intellective mastery will depend upon being able to develop a tacit knowledge that facilitates the recognition of decision alternatives and frees the mind for the kind of insight that could result in innovation and improvement. Such tacit recognition depends upon first being able to explicitly construct the significance of patterns and relationships in the data. Such meanings cannot be achieved without a level of intellective skill development that allows the worker to solve the problem of reference, engage in reasoning that is both inductive and deductive, and apply a conceptual framework to the information at hand. Meaning must be constructed explicitly in order to become implicit later. Intellective skill is necessary for the creation of meaning, and real mastery begins to emerge when such meanings are consolidated in tacit knowledge. While the development of mastery in the action medium does not require extensive explication, mastery in the symbolic medium depends upon explicitly constructed meaning, and intellective skill is the means by which this is achieved. While this does not solve the problem of attentional commitment, it does imply that attention can be freed for increasingly comprehensive tasks, invention, and experimentation as intellective skill allows the consolidation of lower-order information in the form of tacit knowledge.

If the learning processes associated with action-centered and intellective skills are fundamentally distinct, then we can better understand why the individuals whose voices we have heard consistently expressed a felt difference between what appeared to them to be two distinct modes of effort. Until recently, cognitive psychology had been dominated by theories of behaviorism that tended to treat learning as a simple, unitary process derived from the stimulus-response relationship.[22] Now, cognitive scientists are turning to a reexamination of these assumptions, and many have concluded that the acquisition and execution of action-centered skills are inherently distinct from those processes associated with the development of intellective skills.[23]

One cognitive psychologist, Howard Gardner, has synthesized these developments and offered his own formulation, which he calls a "theory of multiple intelligences": "There is persuasive evidence for the existence of several relatively autonomous human intellectual competences. . . . The exact nature and breadth of each intellectual 'frame' has not so far been satisfactorily established, nor has the precise number of intelligences been fixed. But the conviction that there exist at least some intelligences, that these are relatively independent of one another, and that they can be fashioned and combined in a multiplicity of adaptive ways by individuals and cultures, seems to be increasingly difficult to deny."[24]

In his book, *Frames of Mind*, Gardner identifies the following six intelligences: linguistic, musical, logical-mathematical, spatial, bodily-kinesthetic, and personal. According to his elaboration of these domains of human competence, spatial and bodily-kinesthetic intelligences have a great deal to do with action-centered skill in the mode of *acting-on*:

> In my own view, fine motor bodily intelligence, in combination with spatial capacities, is most strongly entailed in the use of objects and

tools. Particularly during the initial use of an object or a tool, the individual should carefully coordinate the information that he can assimilate through his spatial intelligence, with the capacities that he has elaborated through his bodily intelligence. Confined to spatial intelligence, he may understand a mechanism reasonably well and yet have no idea of how actually to manipulate or operate the object. . . . Restricted to bodily intelligence, he may be able to execute the appropriate motions yet fail to appreciate the way in which the apparatus or the procedure works and therefore be stymied should he encounter it in a somewhat different setting.[25]

However, when it comes to the capacity to view material in an innovative way—to see choices and alternatives and to be able to abstract its underlying principles—then what Gardner calls logical-mathematical reasoning (more closely related to intellective skill) becomes necessary:

When it comes not merely to understanding complex tools or machinery but also to the devising of new inventions, a combination of several intelligences is clearly desirable. In addition to that fusion of bodily and spatial intelligences which may suffice for understanding a common apparatus, the individual will have to use as well his logical-mathematical capacities in order to figure out the precise demands of the task, the procedures that could in principle work, and the necessary and sufficient conditions for the desired product. To the extent that the individual relies on trial and error or approaches the task as an improvising handyman, or to use Levi-Strauss's term, *bricoleur*, the use of logical-mathematical reasoning will be less crucial.[26]

Extrapolating from this formulation, we can imagine that in a computer-mediated environment, where the opportunities for learning and displaying bodily and spatial intelligence are reduced or sometimes eliminated, the necessity of this logical-mathematical competence becomes all the more urgent. Gardner believes that formal education has been the primary vehicle for developing this form of intelligence. That logical-mathematical competency is highly related to the intellective skill domain, which has been described on the basis of the field data, is evident from the following characterization:

One learns in school to deal with information outside of the context in which it is generally encountered; to entertain abstract positions and to explore the relations among them on a hypothetical basis; to make sense of a set of ideas, independent of who says them or of the tone of voice in which they are said; to criticize, to detect contradic-

tions, and to try to resolve them. . . . This valuing of abstract concerns, which relate to reality only by a lengthy chain of inference, and
a growing familiarity with "objective" writing, reading, and testing,
eventually spawns a person at home with the principles of science
and mathematics.[27]

The skills necessary for competent operation in an informated environment appear to be related to the kind of explicit, inferential, scientific reasoning traditionally associated with formal education.[28] Yet
there is no simple one-to-one correspondence between the intelligences Gardner has identified and the patterns inferred from the evidence in the workplace; within each skill domain, several of his "frames
of mind" can be detected. For example, the ability to draw a mental
image of the production process was an aid to intellective competence
in the control rooms and probably involved what Gardner calls "spatial"
intelligence. The know-how relevant to action-centered skill in the
mode of *acting-on* entails Gardner's "personal" intelligence in addition
to bodily skill. Gardner's observations also lend support to the notion
that the body is an instrument for accomplishing the crucial interpersonal activities associated with communication and coordination that
we have identified as *acting-with*. He notes that the expression of interpersonal insight depends upon bodily intelligence: "mastery of such
symbolic functions as . . . expression (communicating a mood, like
gaiety or tragedy) provides individuals with the option of mobilizing
bodily capacities in order to communicate diverse messages."[29]

These patterns of cognition are lodged in the activities of individuals
who engage not only with their tasks but also with one another. How
might the interpersonal patterns associated with the development, execution, and communication of intellective skills differ from those typically engendered in a world of action-centered skills? What are the
social-psychological conditions under which intellective skills are best
developed and expressed?

THE SOCIAL-PSYCHOLOGICAL SIGNIFICANCE
OF INTELLECTIVE SKILLS

About one year after the Cedar Bluff start-up, I listened to a group of
corporate senior managers describe the differences between Piney
Wood, with its tradition of hands-on know-how, and the new highly

automated Cedar Bluff plant. After swapping anecdotes and data, one man summed up the gist of the comparison when he said, "When there is a problem at Piney Wood, someone goes out and kicks something; when there is a problem at Cedar Bluff, the operators have a meeting."

This comment reflects the fact that action-centered skill, in principle, can be learned and exhibited without extensive verbal communication. Action-centered skill is a constituent of oral culture, in which communication depends upon a shared context. Knowledge is typically implicit; therefore, individuals who share a similar context can communicate a great deal of meaning with minimally elaborated speech. The operators in Piney Wood communicated in a way that did not differ greatly from the executives whom Rosabeth Kantor studied (referred to in chapter 3). When human beings are engaged in doing what they know, and when what they know is largely tacit, then it is unlikely that they will spend much time talking to one another about what they have done or why. As in Piney Wood, or among the executives in Daniel Isenberg's study (discussed in chapter 4), most of the time these skilled individuals are unable to articulate the content or rationale of their actions.

The demands of constructing meaning from a symbolic medium diminish the salience, or even the possibility, of a shared action context. Without a context in which meanings can be assumed, people have to articulate their own rendering of meaning and communicate it to others. Indeed, the very activity of constructing meaning often necessitates a pooling of intellective skill in order to achieve the most compelling interpretation of the text. For action-centered skills, this pooling of expertise depends on actions taken jointly, probably with minimal explicit discussion. Pooling intellective know-how, however depends in large measure upon language—not as a minimalist vehicle in the consolidation of face-to-face interaction, but as a precise vehicle for conveying explicit reasoning, often in the absence of action. When people confront the electronic text and ask the questions, "What is happening? What does this mean?" the answers, whether in the form of an interior dialogue or in a conversation with others, will be in the medium of language. The insight that motivates action-centered skill can be physically displayed, but the explication of meaning created with the application of intellective skill to a symbolic medium requires a different kind of vehicle through which meaning can be articulated, appropriated, and so made public. In the workplace, this medium is typically that of language.

The frequent necessity of pooling intellective insight in order to achieve the best possible interpretation of the text, and the requirements of explicit communication to match explicit thought, were each in evidence in the control rooms at Piney Wood and Cedar Bluff. Though managers often envisioned the ideal control room as staffed by one operator supported by centralized data displays, the realities of sense-making and problem-solving at the data interface appeared to call for something quite different.

The proper interpretation of data as they appear on a video screen is rarely self-evident. In my observations, the interpretations developed by operators and managers were actively constructed in dialogue and joint hypothesis testing. I observed that from two to eight people typically participated in such dialogues. As the operators described it:

> If there is a problem, everyone gets together and figures it out. There might be umpteen dozen things it could be.
>
> I can tell the computer what to do, but it still may go off and do something else. You cannot take a book and find out exactly how this computer works. It is not like that. It is the sort of thing where we have to put our knowledge together in order to understand what it is doing, and what it should be doing.

During my visits to control rooms, situations periodically arose in which someone believed that data on the screen was incorrect or inconsistent. For example, one afternoon in Piney Wood's bleach control room, an operator was monitoring a screen when an alarm went off, indicating that a vat of pulp was overflowing. He began to check other data and determined that the vat was, in fact, empty. However, he could not shut off the alarm and did not know why it continued to sound. After approximately five minutes of attempting to cut the alarm off, he asked another operator for his opinion.

The two men stood in front of the screen and discussed what the problem might be. They generated several hypotheses, moved through data on various screens, and determined that none of these explanations was satisfactory. Soon, three operators and one manager were gathered around the screen. One of them noticed a reading that had abruptly dropped to zero. They talked quietly; the discussion was highly participative, with no obvious indications of deference or superiority. Throughout the discussion, hypotheses were generated and the means for testing these hypotheses were discussed. Sometimes it was possible to reject an hypothesis by screening data. Periodically, it required that one of them go out into the process to physically check something.

The men discussed whether the problem might be an overload on the alarm for the scanner system, an overloaded circuit due to a backup in the central fuse system, a short circuit, or faulty wiring. Each hypothesis required calling up new screens and scanning data. One by one, each hypothesis was checked and discarded. From time to time they referred to a set of thick manuals, which gave descriptions and graphic representations of the various instruments and electrical systems. The manuals seemed to jog their minds and spur new ideas, rather than to serve as a reference for actually determining answers. An hypothesis emerged: perhaps there was a short circuit. The manager left the group in order to check out this possibility. Some ten minutes later, he returned to the control room, where the other three were still gathered, and announced that he had indeed found a broken circuit on another floor of the plant. The problem was resolved, and life in the control room returned to normal. The entire episode had taken about thirty-five minutes.

On another occasion in Cedar Bluff, two members of the maintenance crew approached two operators at one of the terminal screens in the control room. They had just finished adjusting a CO_2 analyzer and wanted the operator to check his data to determine if the analyzer had been set properly, since the reliability of the computer analysis depended upon this reading. In order to check the reliability of the analyzer, one operator left the screen to collect a sample of white liquor from the bleaching process. If his lab analysis corresponded with the computer analysis, then they could accept the reliability of the data.

In the absence of this operator, the second operator, who had continued to monitor the screen, spotted an acid-flow reading that she believed was too high. She asked a third operator to go out into the process and shut a valve. As he was leaving, two other operators sitting at separate screens but overhearing the interaction began to suggest other possibilities for that operator to check as he went out to close the valve. Once the valve had been shut, the third operator out in the production area began communicating by walkie-talkie with the operator at the screen. Had the acid flow leveled out? The answer was no.

In ones and twos, seven other operators and managers gathered around the woman monitoring the screen who had first noticed the problematic reading. They spoke rapidly but quietly. The discussion was participative, though somewhat dominated by the managers, whose age and experience put them ahead of the still-inexperienced work force. Together they generated a list of possible sources of the problem and checked each one by scanning data or by asking the third operator (still out in the process) to do something to the equipment. Thirty minutes of scanning data yielded a new hypothesis: perhaps a filter was clogged. An other operator was sent to look at the filter and found that it was indeed clogged. The filter was changed, and the acid level returned to normal. Slowly, the seven individuals drifted away from the screen, returning to their other duties. The event had lasted forty minutes.

I personally observed a dozen such incidents, each requiring thirty minutes or more to resolve, and many more episodes that involved fewer people for a briefer time. Abstracting from these occasions, the following pattern seems to hold. First, an operator notices a something that strikes him or her as unconsistent or troubling. The operator will do some immediate checking and scanning to determine if there is a problem. If it can be determined that there is no problem, he or she quickly returns to routine tasks. If it cannot be determined that there is no problem, then questions arise: what is the problem, what are the potential solutions, and can it be corrected? If the operator cannot answer these questions alone, he or she must include other individuals in defining the problem by generating and testing hypotheses: data are scanned, connections and linkages are explored, and sometimes physical equipment is checked.[30]

These procedures continue, sometimes with a growing number of people involved, until the problem is defined, the solution is identified, and the problem is resolved. Most often, the lone operator cannot determine whether or not the original discrepancy actually constitutes a problem. As long as there is uncertainty, others will be pulled into the deliberations. Only when the original discrepancy has been defined as a problem, typically through collective hypothesis generation and testing, can the search for solutions and resolution begin. An operator at Cedar Bluff described this process in his own words:

No one person ever makes a decision to do something; it's at least two to three people. We all get involved in the problem, so we all know what happens. A couple of people stay at the terminal, and a couple of people go out and check things. First, we look it all over on the computer. Then, you see what you need to do outside. Or, if there's little time, someone runs to the door, and the person at the terminal will yell "Check this and that" while you're running out the door.

A certain amount of this kind of troubleshooting activity will occur in any complex process, even without the salience of information technology. These scenarios suggest, however, that the abstract quality of the data that surround people in an informated environment places a greater and more widely shared premium on such activity, precisely because of the problematics of meaning associated with the symbolic electronic medium. In contrast to the offices of Consolidated Underwriters Insurance and Universal Technology, where clerks were meant to create the text rather than to understand it, the informated control rooms required people who could competently engage with the data interface. To do this, they needed the communicative skills related to joint data-based problem solving.

In addition to problem solving, Cedar Bluff's operators described their efforts to experiment with production variables in order to discover improved methods of operation or to test the limits of equipment. These operators discussed the collaboration and dialogue from which experimentation emerges:

> George and I work closely together. We discuss problems. We'll play around with variables every day. We experiment with BTU values and with different air flows.

> My team has been experimenting with a piece of equipment rated at 260 tons per day. We watch all the checkpoints in the data and generate ideas for how to push it up. One day we got it up to 288 per day. It was a careful controlled experiment—other teams and management gave us flack, but we didn't tear anything up. In two months, the managers put pressure on the other teams to work their rate up, too!

Data represented on a screen do not announce their meaning, nor is their meaning buried. Instead, meaning must be actively constructed. What contributes to this process of construction? First, individual critical judgment brought to bear at the interface allows a "sense of a problem" to take shape. The knowledge and imagination that one brings to this sense, in combination with the complexity of the candidate "problem," determines how much uncertainty will persist and, thus, the degree to which collaborators will be necessary. As the systems become more reliable in executing routine functions, it follows that problems, when they occur, will be more complex. The complexity may result from a combination of routine breakdowns, as was the case in the accident at the Three Mile Island nuclear power plant, or from the magnitude and uniqueness of the problem conditions.[31] In either case, complexity means greater uncertainty. Thus, a more automated future would seem to increase the importance of this kind of collaboration.

In addition to the quality of skills, the fruitfulness of such collaboration will depend largely upon the grace and enthusiasm that individuals bring to the participative process. Managers who place a premium on control and workers who feel disaffected do not made good colleagues, for the spirit of hypothesis generation and testing is above all a collegial one. One operator sums up the importance of sociality in the new technical environment:

> The new technology really brings people together. You need people who can understand electronics, programming, and the complexity of the information. It requires teamwork because you need to have different specialties and understanding to work together. This type of computer system will always bring people together because you have to discuss what you see, what you understand, what you know, and what should be done.

For many managers in the mills, it was difficult to accept that this kind of communication now constituted an important part of the operator's work. Their model continued to be one of individual accountability, as if the single laboring body could still be measured as it performed an isolated physical task. Dialogue was treated as an absence of work rather than as the very heart of work. An operator at Cedar Bluff explained:

> We get hypothetical things on the screen and go through the groups to learn. But we can only play on night shift. On the day shift, they don't like to see more than one person at the terminal. It really annoys them to see three people at the terminal. The managers will go out and check to find stuff for us to do then.

In Global Bank Brazil, there was also a growing recognition that as the new technology integrated data from across all banking functions, a new quality of communication and collaboration would become necessary. Many managers questioned the current functional organization of the bank, which separated people into areas of special expertise with little cross-fertilization.

> Because everyone will be looking at the same data, and everyone will be selling products, is there any reason to continue to organize ourselves as we currently do? Our current delineations between operations, credit, marketing—maybe that is obsolete or even counterproductive. How far can we integrate our activities to complement the integration of our information?

These managers believed that the range, visibility, and integration of the data-base environment would require collaboration among the various functions, simply in order to properly leverage data in the pursuit of new products and services. How could the business goals for innovative, information-intensive, technology-based products be fulfilled without combining the knowledge of marketing, credit, and operations? As one manager said, "People will need to put their knowledges together." Another commented, "A variety of people will need to be involved in discussion. The issue is to generate new ideas on how to make money, and for this, we will need collaboration." Functionally segregated expertise would be less important than the ability to generate comprehensive interpretations based on public data.

> Now we have lots of specialists with in-depth knowledge in one area. Everyone has their own information system—usually in a drawer or written on small note cards. With the data-base environment, there is one information system for all to see. Tasks become more comprehensive. You can see the whole, not just the part. People will need a broader skill base to take more of a helicopter view.

Their vision was one of a group of people with various competencies brought together around the data base in order to collaborate in the construction of meaning that would lead to the identification of opportunities for innovation. One manager described the data base as the new "vault" that contained the bank's real assets. Intellective mastery and teamwork could provide the keys to the vault. Yet the pre-data-base environment in Global Bank was quite different. Not unlike the management systems in the pulp mills, which assumed individual accountability and individual rewards for individual performance, Global Bank Brazil's personnel systems and corporate culture rewarded highly individualistic and competitive behavior. Managers at each organizational level were ranked against one another (10 percent excellent, 20 percent above average, 60 percent average, and 10 percent low), and compensation was directly linked to one's performance category. As a result, it was difficult to create a positive approach to teamwork. Ambitious managers believed that their individual knowledge had to remain private in a world where excellence was a strictly enforced zero-sum game.

> We work against each other. Five people can sit at a table working on a project, but they are all working against each other because one of them will have to be in the 10% category and another in the 20 percent. All the energy is directed toward individual goals and performance. There is no mechanism to address team spirit, collaborative product development, innovation, or risk taking.

This individualistic orientation extended to the organization's procedures for recruitment and selection. The bank would send scouts each year to the best universities to look for the most "aggressive" people. A group of twelve applicants would be put together around a table "to discuss issues and fight." The idea was that whoever "wins the fight" was hired from that group. This culture of individual competition also was evident in the way that information was used. In one area that was heavily dependent on management information systems, an executive observed:

> As we introduce a computerized information base into this environment, we get a lot of people using it as an electronic game to compete with each other.

These dynamics illustrate some of the crucial social-psychological challenges associated with intellective skill development and execution. From a cognitive point of view, these skills may be thought of in terms of individual competence. In an organizational setting, however, their social-psychological significance introduces another level of complexity. The informating process creates a symbolic medium, an electronic text, that renders the organization more visible as it reveals a wide range of data to provide an integrated portrait of organizational functioning. Because textualization entails the need to construct meaning, and because the text can integrate data, it implies a natural advantage for collaboration across conventional boundaries. Collaboration over the text requires joint problem solving in which interpretations are explicated, tested, and improved. Meaning cannot be tacitly assumed nor remain implicit in action. Instead, people have to talk about what they think and why. This kind of interaction introduces new psychological demands and implications for social relationships. These social-psychological stakes are further clarified when we look through the lens of a theory known as sociolinguistics, which was developed by the British linguist, Basil Bernstein.

Bernstein studied language in a variety of natural settings, particularly among working-class children and adults. He discovered the existence of distinct linguistic codes, and his signal contribution has been to link his understanding of these codes to the structures of authority and social identity in which speakers function. The two linguistic codes he describes are labeled *restricted* and *elaborated*. Communication in a restricted code assumes a shared context with the listener. As a result, the speaker relies upon shared meaning and shared intent. Meanings are not explicitly articulated in a way that would allow them to stand independent of the action context. They are likely to be concrete, descriptive, or narrative, rather than analytical or abstract. In the elaborated code, however, "meanings are expanded and raised to the level of verbal explicitness."[32]

Even from this brief characterization, we can see that in a restricted code, speech is consistent with our understanding of action-centered skill and the oral culture in which it is typically embedded. In an elaborated code, speech does not depend upon an action context and, thus, is related to conditions in which reality is more symbolically mediated.[33] Bernstein's analysis of the psychology of communication in each code supports this view. He notes that when speakers rely on a shared context, they do not create individualized interpretations; rather, they refer to or comment upon the situation at hand. In this sense, speech becomes another form of action embedded in a physical setting. Recall the example provided by the pulp mill operator, Gregory, in chapter 2. Removed from the production process and surrounded by electronic text, he appeared unable to produce speech capable of communicating meaning independent of the concrete situation he wanted to describe. He had turned the screen itself into an action context and could communicate about the data it displayed only by pointing to symbols and their spatial relationships on the screen. Psychologically, restricted-code speech subsumes the speaker in the context; its effectiveness depends upon consensual understanding of shared contextual elements.

When context is not shared, effective communication carries a very different burden. The speaker must be able to offer an individually elaborated interpretation that conveys what he or she believes to be significant. Thus, the speaker takes on an authoritative role with respect to the listener as he or she makes choices about what will be conveyed. The speaker also becomes more vulnerable, as communication exposes the quality of his or her effort to make sense of the data. In the elaborated code, the speaker faces the need for argumentation, explanation, and analysis in ways that are not required when it is possible to assume shared meanings.

> Elaborated variants of this kind involve the speakers in particular role relationships, and if you cannot manage the role, you can't produce the appropriate speech. For as the speaker proceeds to individualize his meanings, he is differentiated from others like a figure from its ground. . . . The insides of the speaker have become psychologically active through the verbal aspect of communication.[34]

An individual's readiness to take on the risks and rewards of creating and communicating explicit meaning is likely to be related to the character of his or her other social experiences, the psychological and communicative competencies that have been regularly emphasized, and the structure of the current social context as regards its capacity to invite or inhibit the individual effort to create meaning. For example, Bernstein directly links linguistic performance and occupational experience, observing that where work offers little variety of participation in decision making and requires primarily physical, rather than symbolic, manipulation and control, the linguistic codes that are developed will emphasize the concrete over the abstract, substance over the elaboration of processes, and the here and now over any exploration of motives and intentions.[35]

Historically, the great majority of working men and women have been required to give of their bodies and so have been rooted in the physical demands of their tasks. Given our current understanding of action-centered and intellective skills, and the distinct qualities of knowledge associated with each, we can postulate the consequences that this historical division of labor has had for the distribution of elaborated communicative competence. The great weight of occupational history has skewed the access to precisely those forms of intellective skill that permit the individual to appropriate experience, to examine its grounds, and to put it back together in new and different ways.[36]

The social psychology of group life in a world of action-centered skills is likely to differ from collective activity in an informated environment that places a premium on the exercise of intellective skill. In the first case, the context is more likely to be accepted as a given, and action know-how is displayed within that context. Communicative competence tends to involve questions of how to do things, rather than what to do or why. Private knowledge is the basis for interdependence within a group, but private knowledge is also an important source of individual power and, thus, must be judiciously guarded.

In an informated environment, the electronic text displays the organization's work in a new way. Much of the information and know-how that was private becomes public. Personal sources of advantage depend less upon maintaining earlier forms of private knowledge than upon developing mastery in the interpretation and utilization of the public, dynamic electronic text. This kind of mastery benefits from real collaboration. Communicative competence requires psychological individuation, which introduces a new sense of mutuality and equality into group life. Hierarchical or other status-based distinctions hold less power in a group of individuated and competent interpreters, each with access to the metalanguages of choice and innovation.

IMPEDIMENTS TO COMPETENCE AND PERFORMANCE IN INTELLECTIVE SKILL DEVELOPMENT

These forays into the cognitive underpinnings of action-centered and intellective skills and the social-psychological conditions of their expression help to delineate the range of impediments to intellective skill development. At the individual level, these impediments are both cognitive and characterological. If intellective skill depends upon certain intelligences (in Gardner's sense of the term), then it is probable that such intelligences are not equally distributed. Some people will excel more than others. If the expression of explicitly constructed meaning requires a considerable degree of psychological individuation, as Bernstein suggests, then despite sufficient talent, individuals can also confront psychological barriers to voicing what they think.

The social system can also impose limitations on the development and expression of intellective competence. First, role requirements engender particular patterns of experience and, therefore, shape opportunities for practice. For example, in the case of the bankers, the traditional demands of their roles encouraged their reliance on action-centered skills, despite high educational levels that, in a general way, have been associated with the competencies related to intellective skills.

Social systems are more than objective constellations of roles. They express complex relationships of authority that reflect a particular distribution of power and, thus, of opportunity. The boundaries between roles are charged with the claims of authority. Such authority may be hierarchical or functional. Where hierarchical authority helps maintain strong boundaries between the roles of superior and subordinate, then subordinates' performance opportunities can be limited. Where functional authority helps maintain boundaries, as in the case of the marketing, credit, and operations managers at Global Bank Brazil, then specialized roles are enforced, cross-functional collaboration is minimized, and performance opportunities are restricted.

Competence and performance are not static attributes, however; they are dynamically related experiences. Intellective ability is only partially limited by an individual's capacity; competence grows under conditions in which it is required, invited, and nurtured. In the absence of changing role requirements and flexible social boundaries, opportunities to develop competence are reduced. Performance not only displays competence but also contributes to the development of competence. When roles are fluid, those who can learn are more likely to do so, because their daily experience provokes development.

The differential effects of hierarchical and functional boundaries illuminate potential dissimilarities in the situations faced by workers and managers as they each confront new intellective skill demands. Hierarchical boundaries, as we shall see in the following chapters, tend to maintain the more intellectually substantive tasks within managerial ranks. As a result, these role boundaries are more likely to have a chilling effect on opportunities to develop intellective competence than boundaries that reflect functional territoriality within management. For example, the bankers at Global Bank Brazil found opportunities to develop intellective skills within a variety of functions but faced obstacles to performing (and thus improving these skills) because of the rigidities of their functional roles. Thus, of these two forms of authority, each of which can contribute to rigid social boundaries, hierarchical authority is likely to present the more imposing barrier to an organizationally comprehensive informating strategy, with its constituent requirements for broad-based intellective mastery.

The systemic nature of these impediments to competence and performance indicates a logically integrated order of barriers to intellective skill development. Individual potential is a necessary but not sufficient condition for intellective skill development. However, the way in which roles are conceived, and the rigidity or permeability of those roles, are likely to be more definitive indicators of the possibility for a serious commitment to intellective skill development and, thus, to the opportunities for insight and business innovation that such skills afford in an informated organization.

WHAT HAPPENED IN GLOBAL BANK BRAZIL?

Global Bank Brazil's experience during the initial phases of implementing the data-base environment illustrates the tensions that can exist between the need to create opportunities that develop intellective skills and role boundaries, the claims to authority that support them, and the emotions that animate them. The context for the implementation process was shaped early in the life of the project, when the head of operations and the head of financial control appeared before a meeting of their executive colleagues—the senior managers who set policy for the bank and approved all major expenditures—with a proposal to secure funding for the work. Though the two managers were convinced that the project represented the "future of the bank" and that it would entail broad organizational changes in addition to introducing the new technology, they presented their plans in terms of the narrower focus of improving back office processing:

> We sensed there would be enormous secondary consequences of the data-base environment, but we decided to be very low-key. We chose to call it the "Back End" rather than the "Data-Base Environment" project. We didn't think that the policy committee would have understood or believed the real business benefits of the project. Keeping the existing factory alive was enough to justify the expenditure.

Another financial control manager, who would later be assigned as the project manager, described the strategy as "keep our heads down and avoid consciousness-raising to minimize the political games we have to play."

Four pilot sites had been identified for implementating and testing the data-base technology. The first of these was the central liabilities department, where implementation was accomplished during the period of my research, thus providing an opportunity to see how the implementation approach would complement the ambitious business goals and innovative technological design.

The project team's implementation plan outlined three phases: eight days of "user training," conversion (entering manual data into the system), and parallel (manual and automated) operations as the new system was thoroughly tested. However, there was little evidence that people at the pilot site were being prepared to "make the leap." As one manager protested:

> Central liabilities is the oldest part of the bank; the project will be like going from a horse to a jumbo jet. These people aren't prepared. They'll just give them the terminal and say, "Do it." They won't get the proper training to understand where we're going. It will be like riding with blinders on in a car that someone else is driving. They'll be taking the risk, but they're not driving the car. They'll just pray . . . some clerks will take to it, but others won't. The excuse will be, "They're too old, they're just resisting." But the real reason is they weren't prepared well. . . . Someone should have responsibility for the human resources involved in this project!

Although there were no specific provisions in the budget for "user training," a clerk from a small branch was assigned full-time to the project. For the first two weeks of her new assignment, she felt "lost . . . just floating" and continued her struggle to learn the new system with little help from the project team. She was responsible for training two clerks from the pilot site. They spent three days learning to operate the system and five days inputting credit approvals. When this was com-

pleted the clerks referred to their eight-day experience as "input training," but they still had such basic questions as, "What does 'data-base
environment' mean?" No further training was planned. A project team
member explained their philosophy:

> We just teach them the actions they need to know to perform their
> work on the terminal. It's too difficult to teach algorithms to clerks—
> so we don't.

The two clerks were uncomfortable about returning to the branch to
continue entering data while training their co-workers, because they
felt insecure about their own level of comprehension.

Discussions with the project team revealed that they had focused on
building the technical model of the data base and that there had been
little consideration of the details of implementation. Project team
members admitted that training had been "unstructured." They had
underestimated the effort required for conversion and were considering hiring temporary data-entry operators to lighten the load. The was
also no clear assignment of responsibility for the third phase of implementation. One manager suggested that these "oversights" were part
of an even bigger problem: "Implementation planning was not our
strength."

Further conversations with these and other managers suggested that
poor implementation planning was only a small part of the problem. In
fact, the "low-key" approach had entailed a series of crucial choices
that handicapped the project's ability to deliver on its ambitious promises. For example, project team members had a vision of the new technology and how it would support the business strategy through innovation, improved decision making, and product development, but they
had chosen a pilot site that represented back-office processing—
"control oriented, not product oriented."

> The central liabilities pilot will change people's work, but it will only
> do it in relation to production. We're still automating; the focus is
> not on creating new products, creativity, or innovation.

In light of the strategic potential of the data-base environment, why
was central liabilities chosen as the first pilot site? A project team member explained that while the central liabilities pilot did not fulfill the
strategic promise, it offered little risk to the business:

> Central liabilities is a good automation project. It was fully manual, so we can run in parallel without risk. We're not dealing with money directly, so there's less risk. This enables us to play around with the data base without hurting the customers; the only impact is internal.

In retrospect, some of the project team members questioned their implementation strategy. One reflected:

> We went on the safe side with the central liabilities pilot. The drive was cost reduction, big volumes, and control. We should have at least studied the marketing needs. In the business analysis, we didn't ask what they needed for selling, for the creation of new products. "What information do you need to determine potential clients?" We didn't ask this. We asked accounting-driven questions, not business-driven questions.

Another project team member went further and questioned the business value of all four pilots:

> All the pilots focus on reducing processing costs and increasing internal control. But in terms of the business—what are we doing to support product development? Could we create a data base for potential clients?

The people closest to the project believed in its strategic potential, yet they chose central liabilities as the first pilot site. They were convinced that skills, roles, and organizational structures would need to change in order for data administration to fulfill its strategic potential, yet there was no training program and no mechanism for dialogue about organizational issues and opportunities. How are these contradictions explained? What were the "enormous secondary consequences" that were deemed so threatening?

As project team members and other managers close to the project discussed the organizational issues raised by a data-base environment, their thoughts and concerns continually returned to one theme—how would the new technology challenge the banker's role and undermine the sources of authority upon which his or her influence depended? In their view, the account officer's role had evolved in such a way as to have exteriorized routine functions and preserved those activities involving the banker's art—credit judgments in the context of personal contact with customers.

Today account officers are the masters of ceremonies, the prima don-
nas. They are pampered. They make one call and everyone runs. They
need to know what the customer's credit limit is, the outstanding,
et cetera. They pick up the phone and wait four hours to get the
information. They're used to having babysitters; they have support
for all their dirty work.

In the context of the data-base environment, the project team anticipated important changes in the structure of the banker's role, in addition
to the new skill demands that were implied. Much of the activity that
had been exteriorized in clerical support functions could be reintegrated:

The account officers will be able to go to the terminal and call up
the customer information on the screen. They won't have to ask the
clerk. The account officers can enter the credit approval at the point
of sale, and it won't have to be done in the credit department. It
might mean a little more work for them, but they'll be able to get
the information quickly and it would simplify their lives.

Not everyone believed that this reintegration of the banker's activities would be met with enthusiasm. The historical evolution of their
roles had allowed them to shed the most routine activities, and the
dependence upon others that this created was an important source of
self-protection. The head of human resources believed that managers
had good reason to oppose any reintegration of their roles:

It's like making managers naked—taking their clothes off. You feel
you're now on your own and have to take the initiative to do your own
thing. Managers are normally protected by walls of people and paper.
You can pretend you're doing something relevant, but the only things
that are really relevant are analyzing and deciding. It's a strange feeling
for line managers; they'll resist. It's not a mere resistance to innovation
and technology; it's something more complex. The feeling of being
alone; I'm relying on myself to do things. I can't blame the "bloody
staffers" that didn't deliver on time or blame it on the mistakes they
made. It means more responsibility for senior managers.

A second issue concerned the new technology's implications for how
bankers were evaluated and rewarded. A widely shared perception was
that sales traditionally were "personality driven" and that performance
measures were very subjective. The data-base environment was perceived by some as a welcome source of objective data for performance
evaluations. As one senior manager described it:

I was an account officer for a long time. Telling if an account officer is good or bad . . . it's not possible to quantify. It's totally subjective. It has a lot to do with how lucky you are—if you have the right customers. I was judged on how many assets I had, not on how much profit I made. I was never judged on how much my processing costs were—only how much I sold. There was no ability to really see where the profits were made. It would have been much more challenging to be evaluated more objectively.

Again, others were less sanguine about how such developments would be greeted. Some managers close to the project believed that this provided account officers with a compelling reason to resist the notion of a data-base environment:

With all the financial numbers in the data base, it will show that the account officers have been doing sloppy work over the years—that clients have been mismanaged and allowed to exceed their credit limits. Individuals may have their power reduced and be judged for the first time.

Finally, the data base would provide wide access to information that had been fragmented and private:

Now a banker is "good" because he owns the most data on his area. But with the data-base environment, he'll have to be able to play different games with the data because everyone will have access. He won't be the owner of the data anymore. Influence will be more abstract—"What is my degree of control over the infrastructure?" Before, he had control over the data because his people collected it, but with the data-base environment, it will automatically flow from a number of business transactions. Then his influence will come from knowledge about the data, not ownership. People might react to this access with anything from passive aggression to real anger.

The project team concluded that the new public quality of an integrated data base would challenge the preeminence of upper-level managers in their role as the organization's thinkers. They believed that inaccessibility of data, rather than such factors as cognitive ability, education, or motivation, traditionally had prevented people from making thoughtful contributions.

People can think no matter where they are in the hierarchy, and with access to all this information, we'll have a lot more thinking going on in this organization.

Despite their judgments about these "enormous secondary consequences," the project managers' implementation strategy did not provide any mechanisms for open dialogue or experimentation—let alone
for planned organizational change. Project team members and their
superiors had remained faithful to the "low-key approach," because
they believed that surfacing organizational issues would evoke destruc-
tive, recalcitrant responses from other managers, particularly the marketing hierarchy.

One project team member said that a discussion of the organizational
choices offered by the new technology would "blow the minds" of
senior management. Concerns and questions were voiced behind closed
doors, but the team believed that most managers did not consider organizational issues to be legitimate topics for discussion.

> Most senior people in the bank don't perceive the organizational
> issues. They have a gut feel that something big is coming, but they
> block. It's like Orwell's *1984*—you are not allowed, and you have
> never been allowed, to think about these things.

In the absence of senior management's leadership and vision, project
team members had subscribed to a theory of technology-driven change.
They saw technology as an autonomous force that, once unleashed,
would necessitate new organizational forms. In their view, the technology would foster an awareness of organizational inadequacies and require managers to consider changes that they would not have embraced, or even discussed, of their own volition.

> Service, excellence, and innovation are only buzzwords right now. As
> we push the technology, people will realize that they have a really
> valuable tool on their hands. Then they'll be forced to use it. Then we
> can change the way they think and do their work. First you have to use
> the technology to prove that the current organization is inadequate.

> We're on a learning curve now, trying to understand the technology.
> But at some point we'll have a revolution. The technology will prove
> that the current organization is inadequate. Some people will accom-
> modate to the new environment, and some won't. In every revolution
> a lot of people are killed. And some people will be dead at the end
> of this project, too.

Still, as the project team members surveyed the results of their initial
implementation efforts, some began to question the wisdom of their

strategy. The implementation had imposed certain limitations on the way the technology was perceived and used. The unique opportunities for innovative thinking that had seemed so promising now appeared to be just out of reach. Given the organizational realities of Global Bank Brazil, however, was there any choice? Was it so unreasonable to rely on the technology to force changes that would otherwise, they believed, meet resistance?

> Right now, we have a locomotive that can only go up to the point where the tracks end. The competitive advantage is *after* the tracks end! But we can't formulate the questions we need to be asking. I guess the biggest question is how to really manage, not just react to, the organizational changes that will come with the new technology. But is that possible?

TECHNOLOGY AND THE BURDEN OF CHANGE

The autonomous informating power of computer technology created a similar effect in the pulp mills, in the back offices, and in the bank. In each case, oral culture and the associated action-centered skills were eroded as the organization's work—objects, events, and processes—was translated into explicit data and displayed in the medium of an electronic text. This is not the first time that technology has displaced oral culture and the know-how associated with action-centered skill. The mechanization of work drained the craft worker of his or her skills and altered the traditions of group life in which craft knowledge had once thrived. Work was made more explicit but not in a way that enriched the worker. In the office, mechanization provided the occasion for the creation of a new stratum of routine clerical tasks. Office work, at least at its lowest level, finally could be subjected to the explicating rigors of scientific management. Again, the clerk's work became available for rational control and analysis but not in a way that enriched the clerk.

The computerization of the back offices in Consolidated Underwriters Insurance and Universal Technology repeats this history. Oral culture and action-centered know-how give way to increasingly explicit and visible routines, but their heightened textualization does not enrich the clerical employee (though some positive effects were apparent among the transfer assistants and their supervisors). As noted earlier, these jobs can be seen as mechanisms in the textualization process (data entry), so little emphasis was placed upon the clerks' abilities to exploit the text for more complex value-adding activities.

The textualization process that was well under way in the mills, and that had begun to unfold in Global Bank Brazil, represents a stark contrast to the experience of these clerks. In the bank, insightful, informed, and inventive utilization of the text was coming to be seen as the core of the banker's work. In the mills, there was a growing recognition that operators had to do more than simply bear witness to the text: they, too, would have to use it to manage and add value to their operations. In these cases, explication encroaches on the implicit knowledge that undergirds oral culture, but it does so in a way that can be enriching. It provides the basis for a more comprehensive understanding of one's own work in an elaborated language that introduces the possibilities of questions, choice, and innovation.

Under these conditions, the textualization of work places a premium on intellective mastery. The development of such mastery depends upon two interdependent conditions: competence and performance. Individuals need to develop those intelligences associated with intellective skill, which may differ from the intelligences they have had to emphasize in their traditional roles. The development of competence is not sufficient, however. Organizations must provide performance opportunities; that is, conditions must exist that require, invite, and nurture these new skills. Such conditions are likely to involve relationships of collaboration and mutuality, where the emphasis is on achieving the best interpretation of shared information rather than on gaining personal advantage on the basis of private knowledge. The interdependence of these two conditions can not be overemphasized. Opportunities for performance are themselves developmental, and they increase the probability of the kind of learning that is necessary for developing intellective competence.

What, then, is entailed in creating the conditions for the development and expression of intellective skill, with all of its implications for a broadly distributed communicative competence in the metalanguages of questions, choice, and innovation? Clearly, the solution is not a mechanistic one. Job descriptions can always be rewritten to define new role requirements, but these are mere formalities. They mask deeply rooted conceptions of authority that heighten the boundaries between organizational roles, particularly those roles that define hierarchical relationships.

The cognitive demands of intellective skill suggest that computerization should be accompanied by a serious educational effort, if the informating capacity of the technology is to be exploited. However, as we have seen in the case of Global Bank Brazil, the claims of authority can overwhelm the rational goals of implementation. Indeed, they can so inhibit thoughtful discussion and observation as to make it difficult to even recognize the technology's informating capacity and its related skill requirements. It was such a scenario in Global Bank Brazil that drove its visionary project team members to put their faith in the technology itself. They hoped that the technology would carry the burden of strategic change, that it would initiate a process of natural selection from which new organizational forms would finally emerge.

Their experience leaves us with two immediate problems to address. First, we need to understand why managerial authority, as it has developed over the past two centuries, appears to be inimical to the quality of organizational change implied by the cognitive and social-psychological conditions of wide-spread intellective skill development. The claims of authority that infuse role boundaries can impose limitations upon the development and expression of intellective competence. Only an analysis of the sources of those claims and the ways in which they are manifested can provide a context in which to address the second problem: Can the technology carry the burden of strategic change? If we unleash the autonomous informating effects of this new technology, can it transform the conception of managerial authority and, thus, the social structures that are sustained by that conception? Will new organizational forms consistent with the social-psychological demands of an informated environment inevitably occur?

With these questions, our exploration of the first dilemma of transformation draws to a close. We have seen that the informating power of information technology creates an epistemological crisis, altering the grounds of task-related knowledge and the basis for competent participation in the life of the organization. If the informating process is to be exploited for its competitive opportunities, then widely distributed mastery over the new intellective grounds of knowledge becomes an acute demand. For this to occur, organizational innovation is required.

With this, we turn to a second dilemma of transformation, one that concerns authority. The task now is to determine the likelihood of such organizational innovations. It means exploring the relationship between managerial authority and the autonomous informating power of the technology. Can the technology transform authority? Or will authority impose restrictions on the informating process?

PART TWO

AUTHORITY:
THE SPIRITUAL DIMENSION
OF POWER

AUTHORITY IS THE SPIRITUAL DIMENSION OF POWER

Knowledge and power. Power and knowledge. They circle one another like figures on a Greek vase. Now knowledge overtakes and transforms power. Now power gains momentum, engulfing knowledge. In prior chapters we saw the alteration in the grounds of knowledge implied by the autonomous informating capacity of computer technology. The questions before us now are these: To what extent will the changing requirements of knowledge transform the conception and conduct of power relations in the informated organization? Or, will the deeply etched patterns of belief, behavior, and feeling associated with these power relations ultimately subvert the distribution of new knowledge?

Part 2 explores that aspect of power called "authority." In organizational life, power is widely expressed through a framework of what Max Weber called "imperative control," in which commands yield a high probability of obedience. Weber defined authority as the legitimate exercise of imperative control.[1] Since authority presupposes the unity of command and obedience, the use of coercive power implies that, to some degree, authority has failed. Similarly, authority can be defined in contradistinction to persuasion and dialogue, since obedience to authority is achieved through a belief in a hierarchical order that creates the mutuality of command and obedience. Legitimate authority need not depend on either violence or reasoned argument to elicit the desired action.[2]

Authority depends upon legitimacy, not as a goal of persuasion, but as a moral fact assumed by those united in the hierarchy. In her discussion of the history of authority, Hannah Arendt argued that legitimacy can be "proven" only by an invocation of a source above or beyond the authorities themselves. Such a source might be the law of nature; the word of God; a coherent body of philosophy, such as the work of Karl Marx or Adam Smith; ancient customs sanctified by tradition; or one great event in the past, such as the foundation of the body politic. "In all these cases, legitimacy derives from something outside the range of human deeds; it is either not man-made at all, like natural or divine law, or has at least not been made by those who happen to be in power."[3]

The legitimating idea forms a religious context capable of infusing all members of a hierarchical organization with a sustaining belief in the appropriateness of the ranking rules with which their roles are determined.[4] The hierarchical order is meaningful and acceptable as long as people believe that such ranking rules reflect a higher order of moral necessity. This impersonal transcendent order is equally binding upon each member of the hierarchy and delimits the ways in which they can execute their respective roles. Those whom the hierarchy has rewarded with power must be circumspect in the ways they choose to exercise that power, just as those with less status must be careful not to exceed the boundaries of their roles.[5]

Authority is the spiritual dimension of power because it depends upon faith in a system of meaning that decrees the necessity of the hierarchical order and so provides for the unity of imperative control. Authority requires collective participation in a system of meaning that extends beyond the immediate context, beyond those who command or obey, and reaches into the domain of transcendent values. Members of a hierarchical order are linked together through allegiance to or faith in a common belief system, and every action that ensures the smooth exercise of imperative control refers back to, and expresses the bonds one has with, some fundamental source of meaning. Such meanings may be held implicitly, barely conscious and rarely articulated. They may vary somewhat from member to member. Nonetheless, they are consistent and forceful enough to allow authority to sustain itself through the exercise of imperative control, because they command the faith of enough people, enough of the time.

In part 2 we shall see how authority is used to shape conduct and sensibility in ways that contribute to the maintenance of current configurations of power. We shall also see how manifestations of managerial authority in the informated environment can disrupt the very sources of legitimacy from which it has traditionally derived its strength.

The dilemmas associated with managerial authority are addressed in chapters 6, 7, and 8. Chapter 6 traces the belief systems that have legitimated managerial authority in order to understand how the manager's role came to be identified with the guardianship of the organization's explicit knowledge base. It is this identification of management with codified "scientific" understanding that presents one of the most significant impediments to intellective skill development within the work force and, ultimately, to an informating strategy of technological deployment.

In chapters 7 and 8, the discussion turns again to the living detail of the pulp mills—Piney Wood, Tiger Creek, and Cedar Bluff. These environments were the most extensively automated and informated of the organizations I have described. In each mill, the informating process had unfolded over several years, providing an ample time frame in which to view the interplay between conceptions of managerial authority, role boundaries, and the informating process. The feelings and patterns of conduct that took shape in each mill can help illuminate how even an autonomous and undermanaged informating process can provide the impetus for new models of organization and management.

CHAPTER SIX

WHAT WAS MANAGERIAL
AUTHORITY?

In aristocratic societies the poor man is
familiarized from his childhood with the
notion of being commanded. To whichever
side he turns his eyes the image of hierarchy
and obedience meet his view. Hence in those
countries the master readily obtains prompt,
complete, respectful, and easy obedience
from his servants, because they revere in him
not only their master but the class of
masters. . . . In democracies servants are not
only equals amongst themselves, but it may
be said that they are in a way the equals of
their masters. . . . At any moment a servant
may become a master, and he aspires to rise
to that condition. . . . Why then has the
former a right to command, and what
compels the latter to obey?

—ALEXIS DE TOCQUEVILLE
Democracy in America

EARLY SOURCES OF MANAGERIAL AUTHORITY

In the workplace, managerial authority has been the tie that binds
members together in productive activity. In order to establish the unity
of imperative control, employers and, later, managers have had to develop a context of belief that could legitimate and sustain their right

to command. This right was not tacitly granted by those called upon to obey but represents a hard-won historical achievement.

The first generations of managers in most Western industrial countries drew their authority from the concept of ownership. Many of the early British managers were recruited from the families of partners in the firm. However, the mere fact of ownership did not compel the depth of obedience necessary for an industrial work force. Labor could be recruited only with great difficulty and, even then, its staying power was limited. Elaborate systems of fines and work rules as well as frequent use of corporeal punishment and dismissal all speak to the fragility of authority. Some employers consciously used machine design or piecework systems to extract the sort of behavioral discipline needed for productive operations. So frustrated were these employers that they regularly sought out laborers who could be counted upon for extraordinary docility and obedience, either because they were not free (paupers, convicts) or because they were exceptionally vulnerable (young, female). Ownership had to be amplified with transcendent meaning if it was to be powerful enough to unite workers and their managers in a communal belief system capable of sustaining imperative control.

Throughout the eighteenth century, the emerging class of employer-managers cast about for the ideological formulation that could be invoked to legitimate their authority. As Weber has amply documented, the beliefs associated with Protestant asceticism provided the employers with a crucial source of support.

> The religious valuation of restless, continuous, systematic work in a worldly calling, as the highest means to asceticism, and at the same time the surest and most evident proof of rebirth and genuine faith, must have been the most powerful conceivable lever for the expansion of the attitude toward life which we have here called the spirit of capitalism.[1]

If success was a sign of virtue, then the employer and those closest to him could invoke divinity in their claim to authority. The philosophical and economic treatises of John Locke and, later, Adam Smith explicitly fused transcendent values with the concepts of ownership, a hierarchical division of labor, and the competitive individualism of the free market. These were each considered to be part of God's natural order. Businesses operating according to these principles of economic organization were thus conforming to a divine plan. As a result, it could be argued that the interests of employers and their right to command were inseparable from the interests of workers and society as a whole. In 1870 a British employer spoke out against trade unions, arguing that they ran counter to the transcendent truth of a free market. The correct wage, he reasoned, was that of a competitive market, which worked according to that "grand law, which we all believe to be of divine origin, by which everyone who promotes his own true interest necessarily promotes, at the same time, the interests of society at large."[2]

The Lockean virtues later expanded upon by Adam Smith's *The Wealth of Nations* were absorbed in the United States as political gospel. According to George Lodge, the formative impact of this fusion of political, economic, and theological thought upon early American entrepreneurs cannot be overestimated: "Much of the power of Locke derived from the contention that the rights he asserted were in and of the nature of things. They were in fact God's Law. . . . In America they were energized by the Calvinist notion that hard work represented the holy life. . . . Traditional American ideology was thus fused with religion. It constituted a single, integrated, and synthetic body of belief."[3]

The explicit linkage between the natural rights of ownership and divine grace had faded. Property rights began to develop their own independent validity. Thorstein Veblen described this shift in his discussion of nineteenth-century business principles. In an analysis of the natural rights doctrine, he concludes that its "central tenet, that ownership is a natural right resting on the productive work and the discretionary choice of the owner, gradually rises superior to criticism and gathers axiomatic certitude. The Creator . . . drops out of the theory of ownership."[4]

Popular appeals now focused on individual self-help, duty, and character. The emerging creed suggested that not only had the entrepreneur worked hard and been rewarded with success but also the means by which he had achieved grace were available to anyone willing to exert the requisite amount of disciplined effort. The attraction, and indeed the progressiveness, of this ideology was that it bound workers and managers to the same rules of life, the same necessities, and the same possibilities.[5]

With the increasing secularization of American society in the nineteenth century, the moralists and reformers preached the importance of socially useful work, and the property-owning middle class embraced the dignity of work as a means of achieving upward mobility.[6] The image of the self-made man working his way to fortune and respectability from lowly beginnings through tireless effort, discipline, ambition, self control, and persistence expressed the seductive power of the work ethic. These beliefs could legitimate managerial authority as long as workers' real life experiences lent some degree of credibility to their claims. Pollard's analysis of early British industrialization notes the acute shortage of technically competent managers in all of the rapidly growing industries, including textiles, mining, engineering, and pottery. This meant that the skilled worker who was able to exert some discipline over his fellows enjoyed considerable opportunity for promotion into the ranks of management. Men from the lower classes could be tapped for supervisory positions, if they had accumulated the right mix of technical skill and business sense. It was a period of considerable social mobility within the industrial enterprise.[7]

The moral vision of U.S. society had been based upon the mythic image of the independent self-employed man. Home and workshop continued to be the principal centers of production as late as 1850. Under these circumstances, supervision was either nonexistent or informal, and a considerable degree of independence could be assumed.[8] In the workshops and small industrial enterprises, social mobility was relatively fluid. Inventiveness was frequently the most important advantage for men striving to better their position.[9]

But the fluid boundaries between managers and workers, whether imagined or real, did not last. By the late eighteenth century in Britain, there was already a growing dissatisfaction with the reliance on managers drawn from the ranks of craftsmen without formal educational preparation. The employer-managers became a potent influence on the educational system as they attempted to create programs of formal instruction that would prepare their sons and nephews for the responsibilities of presiding over an expanding industrial enterprise. As the need for managers grew, and their social status was enhanced, the expectations regarding a manager's background and talents began to change as well. Though formal management training was rare, a prospective steward of the enterprise was expected to have studied a range of commercial subjects such as accounting, modern languages, geography, metallurgy, and so forth, in addition to, or in some cases as a substitute for, technical know-how in a particular industry.[10]

Education became one of the primary factors that served to rigidify class boundaries within the enterprise. British schools and colleges for middle-class children improved their curricula, orienting the course of study toward creating captains of industry, while the schools of the poor deteriorated.[11] Downward social differentiation became more pronounced than upward, as reflected in rising salaries for managers, which sharply distinguished them from both workers and foremen. "As the manager rose frequently to become a partner, and the boundaries between the two groups tended to be blurred, new ones were being created, between them and the men they had left behind them."[12]

A growing consensus about the importance of formal educational preparation for the manager was beginning to drive a wedge between the emerging class of salaried managers and their subordinates in the United States as well. Of the prominent businessmen born in the United States between 1831 and 1875, about two-thirds had attained only a high school education, while the remaining third had some formal higher education. For those born between 1875 and 1920, the picture changed dramatically. Two-thirds of these managers had attended college, which distinguished them from the owner-entrepreneurs, whose educational preparation remained minimal. Access to the ranks of those who command had narrowed and was coming to depend, at least in part, upon the credential of a formal education.[13]

By the 1890s, the conditions of work had engendered a new sense of labor militancy, leading to efforts to organize workers on a mass basis. It was in this context that the earlier equation of hard work, success, and divine favor began to take on an important new dimension. A new source of legitimacy was found in Darwin's concept of natural selection and its translation into sociological terms by the English philosopher Herbert Spencer. The characterological virtues that had been widely accepted as crucial for success were imbued with the weight of inescapable biological truth. "The employer's authority was justified by oft-repeated references to his success, which was a sign both of his virtue and of his superior abilities. Those who failed were believed to lack the requisite qualities, and they were enjoined to obey the men whose success entitled them to command."[14]

Social Darwinism fueled a new emphasis on the material basis of character. Psychologists and criminologists began to develop standards of physical measurements, which they claimed predicted character traits, intelligence, and psychological tendencies. They formed part of an intellectual movement that sought to identify individuals for purposes of placing them in the appropriate occupation and hierarchical position.[15]

Journalists and academics of the period defended these doctrines as providing the scientific rationale for the facts of economic life. They did not simply extol the traditional virtues of the successful businessmen but saw characteristics such as aggressiveness, materialism, and even selfishness as necessary requirements in the struggle for existence. One academic, writing in the *American Journal of Sociology* in 1896, reasoned: "It would be strange if the 'captain of the industry' did not sometimes manifest a militant spirit, for he has risen from the ranks largely because he was a better fighter than most of us.[16] The well-known Gilded Age journalist E. L. Godkin, founder of *The Nation* and editor in chief of the *New York Post*, frequently called upon Darwinism to justify the importance of the businessman to society. They were "explorers of the race" who undertook huge risks. "The great capitalist," he wrote, "is generally a man who has been appointed by natural selection."[17]

Over the course of the nineteenth century, the rationale used to invoke faith in the necessity of managerial control underwent considerable change. The claims of divine election softened, giving way to the traditional values of the work ethic—unstinting effort, persistence, discipline. An emphasis on the divine origins of property rights slowly gave way to more secular assumptions about the natural rights of ownership. In the early stages of industrial bureaucratization, the boundaries between management and labor began to harden and the claims of the work ethic showed signs of strain. Social Darwinism gave a new boost to managerial authority. Fortified with scientific reasoning, Spencer's popularizers could provide the society with a new rationale. Those who were in control were naturally superior, and so it was incumbent upon everyone to show their respect for the truth and power of biological destiny with deference to their superiors.

THE MANAGER AS SCIENTIST

The period from 1890 to 1920 has been called the Progressive Era precisely because of the belief that progress was itself a natural law. The progress of an individual through the jungles of capitalistic competition reflected an underlying biological truth as surely as the progress of technology reflected new discoveries in engineering, physics, and chemistry. It was into this context, characterized by a new romance with science, a profound belief in progress, an urgent demand for coordination and efficiency in increasingly complex and large-scale organizations, and a growing professionalization of the managerial class, that Frederick Taylor's scientific management approach was born.

Though firms varied widely in the degree to which they adapted to Taylor's complete program of change, the essence of his philosophy had a transformative effect upon American managers and their claims to authority. They learned from Taylor and others like him that the interior of the labor process had to be penetrated, explicated, and rationalized. Buried in the detail and habit of each task was a hidden truth—the "one best way" to accomplish the work according to criteria of efficiency. Workers left to perform on their own would never achieve a "scientifically" rigorous organization of their tasks. No matter how diligently workers might apply themselves, they simply did not understand their work well enough to optimize their effort.

Systematic analyses of production tasks were developed, and this information was expropriated to the ranks of management. Together with the rationalized activities passed down from the executive role, this information provided the occasion for a considerable expansion in the numbers of middle managers and the scope of their functions. Managing this explicit knowledge base became an important part of the middle manager's role. Scientific management argued that rigorous understanding, the stuff of formal education and specialized training, had to be applied to the action-centered know-how of the worker if production was to become maximally efficient and, therefore, maximally profitable. It fell to the growing managerial class to dominate the new knowledge that resulted from this conjunction of science and skill and to turn it into the basis from which rational planning, organization, and coordination could proceed.

Scientific management appeared to provide the ultimate rationale for managerial authority. Taylor believed that scientific truth would replace divinity, "character," or biology as the arbiter of commands; and he boasted that his approach substituted "joint obedience to fact and laws for obedience to personal authority."[18] Fundamental to this theme was the notion that only a special class of men—formally educated, specially trained, able to reason scientifically—was fit to control this knowledge and administer the organization on the basis of the insight it made possible. As Taylor put it, "I can say without the slightest hesitation that the science of handling pig-iron is so great that the man who is fit to handle pig-iron and is sufficiently phlegmatic and stupid to choose this for his occupation is rarely able to comprehend the science of handling pig-iron."[19]

In the emerging rationale for managerial authority, "college-bred men" and scientific experts would impose technical standards on production for the good of all organizational members.[20] The emphasis on the professional and scientific orientation of the manager lent force to the growing conviction, informed by social Darwinism, that managers and workers were intrinsically different—each with their own psychology and social orientation. One historian of scientific management, Samuel Haber, observed that in the early years of the movement, Taylor saw middle-class values among the workers whose effort he sought to rationalize. By the 1920s, however, the concept of the worker had changed dramatically. "The worker has a psychology all his own," insisted one of Taylor's followers. "We are absolutely wrong in judging the psychology of the worker from ours."[21] Haber summarizes this new perception: "The worker was no longer to be thought an individualist. He was most comfortable, and could be dealt with most productively, in a group. He usually had little desire to rise or to increase his income by very much. What he did want was security and enough pay to satisfy his comparatively limited wants."[22]

The emphasis on authority as derived from formal preparation and the ability to master systematic knowledge served the growing class of managers, who were increasingly differentiated from the firm's owners. Their derivative relationship to ownership became more acute as ownership itself became diffused among wider and more anonymous groups of shareholders. There were traditionalist employers and top executives who resented Taylor's system as an "impetuous abstraction of their prerogatives," because it "transferred initiative away from them and questioned their natural superiority."[23]

One well-known academic who wrote an influential 1920 business text argued that success in business depended upon formal training and a scientific attitude. The entrepreneurial tradition was no longer a match for the challenges of business administration:

The first thing required for success in business is accurate knowledge. . . . The old-time businessman learned all that he knew about business by "doing." . . . Only recently have the schools and universities in the U.S. undertaken to teach the essentials of business. . . . The need for better trained men and women in business has become daily more and more apparent to the businessman. . . . Every lack of knowledge means lessened efficiency, high cost, smaller profits, and possible failure. . . . The impression that prevails in many places that "nerve" will make one's way is entirely erroneous.[24]

The professionalization of the managerial class was well under way by the turn of the century (as evidenced by the establishment of professional societies, journals, and graduate schools of business administration), and scientific management lent a new vibrancy and purpose to these efforts. Colleges and professional schools were to be the new crucibles from which the talent to manage the complex industrial enterprise would emerge. Taylor's system occupied a prominent place in the curricula of the new schools of business administration at Harvard, Dartmouth, and the University of Pennsylvania, and it was eventually absorbed into British management curricula as well.[25]

Middle management thus became the repository for the explicit knowledge of the organization. This was in part due to the downward precipitation of executive activities and in part due to the expropriation and rationalization of knowledge about the production process. Rationalized knowledge was the occasion for the expansion of middle management and became the basis for its legitimation. Middle managers could not claim the authority of ownership, but they could claim authority derived from their domination of information, as they controlled its interpretation and communication. That authority was accepted in large measure because enough people believed that those who had made it to the managerial ranks were smarter, a "superior class of people," for whom it was most natural to deal in the coin of knowledge.[26]

Managerial authority also rested upon the correlative conviction that all interests would be best served if the most capable people were in charge. The exoticism of industrial work—its pace, discipline, regularity, and uniformity—seemed to require specialists to direct, control, and coordinate these increasingly complex activities. What elicited faith under these conditions was the belief that the industrial formula for efficient production would create the greatest possible wealth for a nation. Given the complexity and vastness of the undertaking, necessity required that those who had the knowledge and preparation (and thus who could be considered most competent) exercise command. More than ever, the worker was confined to the exertions of the laboring body, and managers were increasingly defined in terms of their distance from, and administration of, physical effort.

The progressive consolidation of the industrial bureaucracy and the increasing rigidification of the boundaries that separated managers from workers thus required a continual reformation of the "religious" framework called upon to legitimate managerial authority. That is not to say that the beliefs associated with Protestant asceticism disappeared—their force and utility remain undeniable. The evolution of the religious context of managerial authority is best rendered with a geological metaphor. Each period leaves a layer of sedimented beliefs. Any attempt at exploring the veins of meaning that bind members to an organizational hierarchy is likely to encounter traces and deposits from several layers. Contemporary events (an oil crisis, flagging American competitiveness) can reanimate meanings normally associated with an earlier historical milieu.

By the 1940s, managers faced a public whose belief in their right to command had been sorely shaken by the Great Depression and the significant progress of the trade union movement. Historian Alan Fox has pointed out that although the claims based on the transcendent character of property rights may not have been sufficient to motivate labor's compliance with management's direction, they did continue to animate managers' faith, loyalty, and sense of sacred purpose: "Businessmen were not given to much disagreement about the justification for *their* control over *their* enterprises. On this matter, more than most, they spoke with one firm voice. It expressed their timeless faith that their power was founded essentially on property right, and that their chief responsibility was to maximize profitable production in the interests of shareholders before anybody else."[27]

The pragmatic claim to managerial authority was most often articulated publicly. Large industrial organizations were so complex, the reasoning went, that efficient operations required managerial control. "Technical necessity denied the possibility of any nonhierarchical power structure in industry. There had to be a single source of authority, a single line of command, with no confusion."[28] The objective character of industrial enterprise, the "machine process" to use Veblen's term, had itself become a kind of transcendent object. Fulfilling its requirements was intrinsically right and good. Efficiency was invested with a moral power that implied social well-being, not just profits. For many managers, the naked functional requirements of the machine were all that was needed to justify their prerogatives.[29]

Historian Reinhard Bendix has credited the pioneering industrial psychologist Elton Mayo with providing the synthesis that rejuvenated managers' claims to authority during this crucial period. Mayo developed a new language of cooperation and consensus to express the problem of imperative control. He agreed with the classical thinkers of earlier decades who stressed the necessity of unity of purpose and central authority. However, he argued that obedience could not be achieved solely by pragmatic claims that appealed to the individual worker's rational self-interest. The worker was instead recast as a psychological self who was likely to submit to authority to the degree that his or her feelings, needs, and motives had been properly understood and responded to. Unity and consensus were crucial ingredients for organizational success, but they would be achieved only if methods were designed with which to satisfy workers' desires "for meaningful activity and for prestige among their fellows."[30]

Mayo insisted that both workers and managers could be understood in terms of the same kinds of psychological constructs, but he also argued that managers had to be scientifically trained to understand these constructs and to put them to use. An understanding of human relations could be transmitted in codified technical language and as such should become an important part of business education, along with other technical matters like finance and production. "The administrator of the future must be able to understand the human-social facts for what they actually are, unfettered by his own emotions or prejudice. He cannot achieve this ability except by careful training—a training that must include knowledge of relevant technical skills, of the systematic ordering of operations, and of the organization of cooperation."[31]

Managers and workers both may operate as psychological creatures, driven by "sentiments" and "needs" more than by logic, but Mayo expected those in administrative positions to be able to free themselves from emotional involvement. Only cool, rational, logical thought would enable them to "assess and handle the concrete difficulties of human collaboration." The implication was that managers could understand workers' nonlogic (or psycho-logic) in a way that workers themselves could not. The implicit structure of the task had been explicated, systematized, and expropriated. Now the implicit emotional structure of the worker could undergo the same codification and absorption into the managerial knowledge base.

THE NEW EQUATION: STATUS, ABILITY, AND THE RIGHT TO COMMAND

These perspectives marked a confluence of earlier appeals to social Darwinism and the newer emphasis on management as the guardian of special knowledge. Managers were still seen as different from workers, but not because managers were better fighters in a savage struggle for existence. Now their distinctiveness was defined by their ability to master intellectually substantive work—to understand information and its implications for coordination, administration, and, finally, profitability. Managers in the 1940s "still felt themselves to be the other side of wide cultural divide from their workers."[32]

As managers attempted to adapt and apply the lessons of Mayo and his followers, the theme most frequently sounded was that of "communication." If management did a better job of listening to workers' perspectives and, in turn, provided them with more "facts" about the enterprise, then the possibilities of unified command would be enhanced.[33] Academics pleaded the case that a policy of improving communication and sharing information was the cornerstone of industrial harmony. One such business-oriented academic attempted to catch the conscience of his executive readers by chiding them about their feelings of superiority and "difference": "In spite of the fact that most executives in American enterprise have risen from the ranks, many of them secretly believe that there is a difference between their own mentalities and those of the men of today who are in the ranks. They feel vaguely, and sometimes say definitely, that the rank and file cannot understand the information which management can give them. This belief can neither be ignored or denied."[34]

In recent decades, the educational distinctions between middle managers and their subordinates have been thoroughly inscribed into institutional life. As a society we have accepted the idea that formal preparation is a necessary, if not sufficient, requirement for managerial responsibility, which incorporates the many tasks associated with administering the organization's knowledge base.

The belief that one's position in the organizational hierarchy actually does connote intelligence and ability has been sustained well enough to preserve the claims of imperative control, though they have been intermittently battered by militant workers, trade unions, and poor economic performance. Many objective and subjective features of this phenomenon have been illuminated in diverse social science research efforts since the 1950s. In 1952 the sociologists W. Lloyd Warner and James Abegglen conducted a comprehensive study of 8,300 "big businessmen." Seventy-six percent of the men had attended college, 57 percent had graduated, and 19 percent had advanced degrees. Not surprisingly, they concluded, "Education is now one of the principal avenues to business leadership. The mobile men use it in greatly increased numbers in their drive to places of leadership and power."[35] In 1979 Eli Ginzberg published a demographic analysis of the U.S. labor force, in which he found that managers and professionals accounted for 25 percent of the entire working population and that membership in these groups was closely associated with educational attainment.[36] In 1982, two University of California sociologists published a study of "person-machine" relations in the workplace based on 525 cases. Their findings, at least with respect to the role of education, did not differ substantially from those of Warner and Abegglen thirty years earlier. Formal education allocated people to high-status occupations marked by more interdependence and diversity. It functioned "as a filter or credential for entering a specific line of work or kind of firm."[37] In another tradition, the social philosopher Nicos Poulantzas placed educational legitimation at the heart of the social division of labor. Expertise, according to Poulantzas, is used to justify the exclusion of workers from knowledge of the production process.[38] A similar point is made by the sociologist Claus Offe in his analysis of the "achievement principle" as providing the criteria according to which life chances are distributed.[39]

The use of formal education to legitimate the managerial role as guardian of the organization's explicit knowledge base does not imply how that guardianship is actually practiced. We can imagine managers with an interest in helping subordinates learn from that knowledge, even as they retain ultimate control of its administration and distribution. Maximizing the opportunities for all organizational members to learn would seem consistent with the pragmatic claims that are used to justify the managerial role. If more people knew more, wouldn't things run better?

One explanation for managers' tendency to maintain more or less exclusive access to the knowledge base concerns their feelings of "difference"—the underlying conviction that subordinates could not understand the kind of information that managers administer. Another explanation involves the values of property rights that continue to haunt modern labor law and, as we shall see in the following chapters, the attitudes of many contemporary managers. These values have operated to intensify the demands for in-group loyalty among managers and, as a consequence, to exclude workers from information and decisions.

In a recent study of U.S. labor law, James Atelson provides a lucid analysis of the implicit and unstated but "deeply held" values and assumptions that underlie the language of legal statutes and the judicial and administrative decisions that derive from them. He identifies five assumptions common to most labor statutes: (1) continuity of production must be maintained; (2) employees, if not controlled, will act irresponsibly; (3) employees owe a measure of respect and deference to their employers; (4) management can exert unilateral control; and (5) critical decisions about the enterprise should be made exclusively by management. Atelson concludes that the status assumptions buried within these legal statutes combine an earlier belief in the sanctity of the master-servant relationship (with its emphasis upon loyalty and subservience and the image of a society in which "subordination to legitimate authority was thought to be a natural, inevitable, even welcome accompaniment of moral grace and practical virtue") with the post-Lockean conception of managers as the representatives of ownership wherein property rights, buttressed by claims of technical necessity, legitimate their exclusive control.[40]

Managers are thus united in their responsibility toward the rights of ownership and by the weight of their own pragmatic claims. Workers whose roles do not carry the same obligations cannot be trusted to operate in ways that serve these ends and so must be excluded from access to knowledge that might give them an opportunity to undermine the well-being of the firm. Imperative control functions to maintain this exclusivity by creating a division of labor that loads explicit knowledge into managerial roles and limits its seepage into nonmanagement roles. The courts have further solidified the assumption of a difference

between managers and the managed by their assertion that some functions are inherently managerial and others are not. Judicial rulings have
maintained that employees protected by the National Labor Relations
Act (that is, nonmanagers) are those "who have some conflict of interest
with management," even though the law also requires those employees
to act in ways that benefit their employer.[41]

These currents of feudal piety, Lockean individualism, Social Darwinism, and economic pragmatism animate U.S. labor law even as they
inform the daily experiences of managers and workers. Managers confront the heavy premium placed upon their loyalty to the hierarchy.
Chester Barnard vividly described the ways in which a manager's success
can depend upon exhibiting such loyalty. He recognized that such loyalty constituted a kind of faith—a practicable belief in the values that
undergird managerial authority. "The most important single contribution required of the executive . . . is loyalty, domination by the organization personality. This is the first necessity because the lines of communication cannot function at all unless the personal contributions of
executives will be present at the required positions, at the times necessary, without default for ordinary personal reasons. This, as a personal
qualification, is known in secular organizations as the quality of 'responsibility'; in political organizations as 'regularity'; in governmental
organizations as fealty or loyalty, in religious organizations as 'complete
submission' to the faith and to the hierarchy of objective religious
authority."[42]

The demand for loyalty combines with the manager's role as guardian
of the organization's knowledge base to heighten the importance of
exclusivity, not just in terms of rights of decision making, but in relation to access to information. From the perspective of the judiciary,
the prospect of shared access to information threatens the fundamental
distinction between managers and the managed.[43] For many managers,
sharing information and maximizing opportunities for all members to
become more knowledgeable is felt to be a kind of treason.

These dynamics can also influence workers' self-understanding. For
example, the sociologist of the workplace Robert Schrank recounts an
incident during a meeting he held with a group of autoworkers. He had
described to them some innovations in automobile assembly that had
been pioneered by Volvo in Sweden. He hoped for a discussion of the
merits of these innovations and their viability in Detroit. He found that
while the autoworkers may have known a great deal about their own

discrete tasks, they had little systematic or comprehensive sense of the production process. Their ignorance undermined their confidence in their ability to envision an alternative method of organizing the work. He frankly admitted his disappointment when the only response he was able to evoke was "that's ridiculous. I mean, the company knows more about this stuff than we do, and if this was a good way of doing things, wouldn't they do it that way? . . . If there is a better way of running a plant, the companies know how to do it."[44]

The sociological literature of the past thirty years is studded with other examples of workers whose beliefs about the relationship between status and ability spilled over into similar forms of self doubt. In Ely Chinoy's 1955 study of autoworkers in the ABC corporation, he found that few men in the hourly ranks harbored ambitions of upward mobility. "There isn't much chance of going up there in the company," one said. "The ones with specialized training get the jobs now; they all have degrees. . . ."[45] Despite the corporation's continued rhetoric about promotion from within, college education had become a prerequisite for a managerial position. This equation had psychological consequences as well: "Linked to the lack of education may be the insecurity and self-consciousness of men whose lives have been spent in overalls or workpants."[46]

Richard Sennett and Jonathan Cobb's psychological portrait of blue-collar men, The Hidden Injuries of Class, depicts a similar phenomenon. They describe the attitudes and feelings of one man, described as a "meat-cutter turned bank clerk," toward his educated "superiors." While he rejects the idea that his managers are innately more able, he does not dispute the notion that the educated have the power to judge him and to rule. "He accepts as legitimate what he believes is undignified in itself, and in accepting the power of educated people he feels more inadequate, vulnerable, and undignified."[47]

In summary, the strategies chosen by employers and managers to achieve efficient coordination of the industrial apparatus appropriated the knowledge of craft work in order to make it the basis for rationalized bureaucratic control. Gradually, educational preparation came to be seen as the prerequisite for membership in the managerial bureaucracy, further separating workers from their managers. For most of this century, the arrangements of industrial organization have reinforced common experiences within each class and the divergence of experiences between classes. It was the consistency of such experiences that made the necessity of industrial organization believable. Each day workers and managers could see and feel those things that make them different from one another. This lived experience helped to sustain the credibility of beliefs about who should command and who should obey and why this must be so. Within this technological and social context, the rules of efficiency that create the industrial division of labor seemed to have the power of a natural phenomenon, of necessity itself. Hard pressed to envision any "realistic" alternative, most people accepted these rules and the hierarchical distinctions they entailed. In this way managers and workers, fitfully, kept the faith.

RECENT CHALLENGES TO MANAGERIAL AUTHORITY

These conceptions of the rights and obligations of workers and their managers remained relatively stable throughout the 1950s and 1960s. The trade union movement had significantly improved the economic well-being of the worker and helped to buffer the impact of managerial decision making. Yet the basic thrust of collective bargaining continued to reflect the spirit of New Deal legislation: management manages while workers and their unions protest unsatisfactory managerial decisions or attempt to negotiate their impacts.

The late 1960s and the 1970s saw the beginning of a new kind of challenge to the old faith in the necessity and legitimacy of manager's exclusive right to command. Fundamental changes in U.S. society had already begun to erode once-reliable class distinctions.[48] When the Lynds wrote their classic ethnography of a typical American city in 1929, they documented the acutely different values and ways of life that separated "business class" and "working class" families. In 1977, a comprehensive updating of the Middletown study found that these families were barely distinguishable from one another. "Working class people play golf and tennis, travel in Europe for pleasure, and send their children to college. Business class people do their own laundry and mow their own lawns." Educational opportunities had multiplied throughout the working population, and by 1976, one of every four persons between the ages of twenty-five and twenty-nine had received a bachelor's degrees, as compared with one in twenty in 1940.[49]

During this period, the psychological interpretation of work behavior spread its roots and took firmer hold of the popular, as well as the managerial, imagination. Fueled by postwar existential philosophies and their various reiterations in the popular psychologies of the day, a new generation of better-educated professionals and workers began to demand greater responsiveness from their political, economic, and educational institutions.[50] Self-fulfillment and satisfaction became values that bore a self-evident validity.[51] Unrest within private enterprise grew. Autoworkers in Lordstown, Ohio staged a strike that became a national symbol of workers' absorption of countercultural values, once associated with the children of the middle class. High levels of absenteeism, turnover, and walkouts were considered to be evidence of a sharp increase in blue-collar dissatisfaction. *Work in America*, a study published by the U.S. Department of Health, Education, and Welfare in 1973, became an immediate cultural artifact when it declared that significant numbers of men and women in virtually every occupational category were alienated from their work.[52]

By the mid-1970s, there was a new appreciation among many management leaders of the challenges associated with successfully harnessing the aspirations of the new worker to the goals of private enterprise.[53] At an increasing rate, social scientists were invited to design and evaluate new work arrangements meant to provide psychologically more enhancing, and economically more productive, work experiences. These efforts, which came to be known as the "Quality of Work Life" movement, stressed the value of individual participation, cooperation, problem solving, and trust, in contrast to collective bargaining's emphasis on the management of conflict, due process, and contractual work practices. This approach questioned the image of the manager as the only one who knows and the one who always knows best.[54] The Quality of Work Life movement resulted in a wide range of innovations of varying degrees of comprehensiveness. In a recent study of unionized industries, labor-relations experts Thomas Kochan, Harry Katz, and Robert McKersie have grouped these reforms into three categories— innovations with a focus limited to the workplace (quality circles in which workers and managers collaborate on ways to improve production, or improvements in worker-supervisor communication); innovations with extensive linkages to traditional collective bargaining issues (pay-for-knowledge systems, self-managing work teams, or increased sharing of business information); and innovations that link work reforms to the business strategy (union board representation, profit sharing, or employment security policies).[55]

The movement that began in the 1970s as a response to social discontent and failing productivity took on a new urgency in the 1980s, with the competitive decline of many key U.S. industries. The pragmatic claims of earlier decades lost much of their force as a growing number of industries found it impossible to retain the preeminence they once took for granted. As a result, the economic crisis of the 1980s finally compelled many managers to embrace changes in the substance and style of work organization.

To what extent do work-reform efforts represent a significant shift in the nature of managerial authority? There are those who claim that these activities are merely a temporary distraction from the real trends in the modern workplace, such as increased bureaucratization and more restrictive supervision. Other critics insist that work reforms, undertaken to "avoid the costs of class struggle," do little to alter the basic claims of managerial prerogatives.[56] Even at their most ambitious, work reforms have tended to focus on the reorganization of shop floor activity and managerial practices that affect hourly workers in the manufacturing sector. They have rarely introduced changes of similar magnitude within the management hierarchy or among white-collar employees.

Within the context of these limitations, however, there is evidence to suggest that work-reform initiatives can offer a substantial challenge to managerial authority, particularly on the factory floor. In his evaluation of the workplace changes in General Foods' Topeka, Kansas, dog food plant, one of the chief architects of the Quality of Work Life movement, Richard Walton, argued that such team-based, self-managing systems are causing "a revision in assumptions about what actions management may take unilaterally and what actions should be open to influence by other stakeholders."[57] He calculates that thousands of firms have undertaken similar reform efforts.[58]

In their appraisal of the Quality of Work Life movement, Kochan, Katz, and McKersie cite its potential impact as well as the impediments to change. They conclude that when work-reform efforts are comprehensive—integrating shop floor initiatives with those linked to business strategy—the potential for a fundamental shift in the nature of authority is indeed high. However, they also note the difficulty of mounting such a comprehensive approach. "Management," they remind us, "tends to closely guard control over issues that have traditionally been viewed as its prerogatives."[59]

The current technological transformation creates a new context for these centuries-old dilemmas. To the extent that technology is used only to intensify the automaticity of work, it can reduce skill levels and dampen the urge toward more participatory and decentralized forms of management. As earlier chapters have suggested, however, this approach cannot exploit the unique power of an informating technology.

In contrast, an approach to technology deployment that emphasizes its informating capacity uses technology to do far more than routinize, fragment, or eliminate jobs. It uses the new technology to increase the intellectual content of work at virtually every organizational level, as the ability to decipher explicit information and make decisions informed by that understanding becomes broadly distributed among organizational members. The informating consequences of computer technology challenge the distinction between manual and mental work as it has evolved in the industrial bureaucracy. An informating technology can intensify the knowledge-management demands within the managerial ranks by increasing the complexity and visibility of information. It can simultaneously disperse those demands throughout the organization. When this occurs, the experiential divergence that has defined the boundaries between managers and the managed is diminished. Under these conditions, what is "managerial" work? What are the values that animate the daily pieties of deference and command? Are these pieties themselves made dysfunctional and obsolete? In this way, an informating approach not only lends new force and urgency to the trends toward work reform, but implies the need for even more comprehensive and systemic organizational innovation.

In chapter 5 we concluded with a recognition that the way in which organizations respond to the changing substance of work is likely to be a function of the tenacity with which they attempt to maintain the hierarchical distinctions that are at once the sign and source of managerial authority. Chapters 7 and 8 will explore the dynamics associated with this collision between the transformation of the substance of work, managerial authority, and the division of labor that it has created and upon which it depends. The dilemmas of knowledge and computer-mediated work made people ask, "How do I know the world?" These dilemmas of authority carry that inquiry forward, raising new questions: "Who will know?" "Who will decide who knows?" "What will be the criteria for such decisions?"

CHAPTER SEVEN

The Dominion of
the Smart Machine

Of every fairly stable elite group, caste, or
social stratum that is exposed to pressure
from below and often from above as well, it
can be said . . . that, to the people
comprising it, their mere existence as
members of an elite social unit is . . . a value
and end in itself. The maintenance of
distance thus becomes a decisive motor or
matrix of their behavior.

—Norbert Elias
The Court Society

THE MANAGERIAL MEANING OF AUTOMATION

In a heated discussion with his top management group, Piney Wood's plant manager asked, "Are we all going to be working for a smart machine, or will we have smart people around the machine?" Building the smart machine preserves the boundaries between those who command and those who obey. Surrounding the machine with smart people can undermine those boundaries and introduce a new ambiguity into the rationale for managerial authority.

Many of Piney Wood's managers believed that the question posed by the plant manager had been answered four years earlier when the conversion to a microprocessor-based control system was begun. At that time, the guiding vision was one that minimized the amount of human involvement in operating decisions. During the first year of my visits, a former plant manager discussed the advantages of digital process control for the plant's technological future:

> The new base of instrumentation makes a hierarchical control system possible. These data summaries made available by the microprocessors can be fed into second-level controls that can actually substitute for operator monitoring and intervention. These data can be fed to a third-level that summarizes the entire plant and becomes the basis for management control, analysis, and planning. This gives us the maximum opportunity to link the instrumentation directly with the computer and take the human interface out of the process.

The technical vision was one of increased automatic control made possible by a combination of intelligent sensors to replace the worker's body and intelligent systems whose algorithms replace the worker's tacit knowledge. Under such conditions, it becomes feasible to reduce human intervention and to increase the possibilities for centralized control and coordination. One manager had spent most of his career as a process engineer but had recently taken on a high-level staff function as director of training. In a discussion of the objectives that guided the technological conversion, he said:

> Management's goal in all of this new technology is to upgrade process control, but the covert motive is to centralize all the controls from a monitoring standpoint, tie all the modules into one data system, and manage the entire mill from one central location, eliminating the need for people as much as possible. However, as the computer system does more operating and makes more decisions, it will free up more of the operator's time for problem solving.

As more control rooms were converted to microprocessor-based instrumentation, the principle centralized control was the major focus of planning. The head of operations had devoted considerable resources to designing a central coordination center that would integrate operating data from all of the modules. This broad perspective had always been difficult to achieve; it could only be approximated by functions such as production coordinator—a manager who toured each module, facilitating communication and integration among the units during each shift. The head of operations made no secret of his enthusiasm for the computer's ability to provide more comprehensive knowledge of "what is really happening":

> I have modeled the whole mill well enough to predict from a central-ized basis where we will be in hours. The computer system will allow us to replace assumptions with what is really happening. That beast will do more thinking than we have time to do. In the long term, we may have all the people we need to run the place in the same room. But the machine won't make decisions for you—it will guide you. It will free up more of the operator's time for problem solving.

One notices a curious twist in these enthusiastic visions of automatic-ity and centralized control. No matter how extreme the vision, many of Piney Wood's managers seemed at the last moment to feel compelled to qualify their statements with references to the primacy of the human being. There is a decidedly ritualistic quality to these statements, like a tail dutifully pinned to a long body of discourse that focuses exclu-sively on the technology. These statements are rarely accompanied by any sign that consideration has been given to just what kind of "problem solving" operators will do, how they will develop such problem-solving skills, or how the organization will afford the time for skill develop-ment as centralized control reduces staffing levels. In fact, training had never been explicitly regarded as a budget item in any of Piney Wood's $200 million conversion plans.

Of course, these managers knew of my research and could have framed their responses to suit their perception of my interests. How-ever, the pattern of these juxtapositions has been so regular in my interviews at Piney Wood and other organizations that I am led to speculate further about its origins. One important clue is provided in the work of the historian of religion, Jonathan Z. Smith. In his essay "The Bare Facts of Ritual," Smith offers a compelling explanation of ritualistic utterances, particularly those that obviously contradict the contexts in which they are embedded.[1] Smith compares reports of the hunting practices of groups as disparate as the Yakuts of Siberia, who hunt bear, and the elephant-hunting Pygmies of equatorial Africa. In each case, he studied the ritual practices associated with the kill. These practices display an elaborate etiquette that must be followed if the animal is to be sanctified for consumption. In some groups, the animal may be killed only when facing or running toward the hunter. Some require the animal's wound to be bloodless or prohibit wounding the animal in other than specifically designated parts of its body. In many groups, the hunter must recite a disclaimer of responsibility for the kill either immediately before or after the animal is wounded.

Smith points out that, in actuality, a hunting people that depends upon fresh game for its survival could hardly afford to leave behind a corpse because it was killed "impolitely" or to pause before the kill in order to recite a love song to the onrushing beast. Such accounts are not plausible, but their regularity suggests a deeper significance. The existence of such rituals indicate the groups' awareness of "the way things ought to be" in a perfect, well-ordered world. The demands of everyday action rarely permit us to act in accordance with what we know is best, but the presence of ritual is a way of overcoming this discrepancy between values and actions.[2]

So it is among many of Piney Wood's managers. In their visions, plans, budgets, and practices, they are actors in a tight web of economic and organizational logic that is difficult to question. Yet something makes these individuals believe that what they are doing is not quite "all right." It is as though they believe that in the best of all worlds, machines would serve people, but in the real world, it cannot always be so. Their statements betray both what they believe *ought* to be, according to some larger human etiquette or sense of responsibility, and what they know *is* the case. In ritualistic phrases, such as "more time for problem solving" or "the machine won't make decisions," they have achieved psychologically what they cannot achieve in fact—a world where their values are upheld and tough choices or contradictory commitments quietly fade away. If Smith's hunting peoples can teach us something, it is that the need for such ritualistic statements will grow in proportion to the remoteness of values from actual practice. As George Bernard Shaw put it, "I may be doing wrong, but I'm doing it in the proper and customary manner."

Perhaps the most compelling reality that drives managers to a narrowly conceived emphasis on automation is the web of economic logic in which they must operate. Frequently, new expenditures for technology can be justified only as a capital substitution for labor. It is often assumed that whatever was provided by the human contributor can be transferred to the automatic functioning of the machine system. A top manager at Piney Wood explained:

The signal to the organization is, "reduce the number of people." The traditional logic here is that if you begin with one hundred positions and bring in new technology, you should end up with seventy-five positions. The technology is used as a lever to reduce staffing.

Other managers agreed that the general orientation at the plant had been, "To justify a computer, we have to show job eliminations."

Upper management has looked at modernization as a way to eliminate jobs. The reduction of the work force has been a key element in the justification for all our new computer technology. Reducing head count has been the focus of managerial rewards. We have simply looked at bodies rather than price per ton. We never asked the question, "Can I keep this person and get more tons?"

These lines of economic force cut a deep path and carry certain inevitable implications. For example, organizational resources are channeled in ways that support the fundamental technological strategy. Investment dollars and staff know-how are dedicated to enhancing automaticity. It is a simple and obvious fact that in a world of finite resources, the choice of investments will have long-term consequences for which organizational potentialities become robust, will atrophy, or are stillborn. One manager remarked:

We have just finished a big report on how do we make sure these damn computers will talk to each other. I say, "Who gives a shit!" What about the operators? It's too bad we don't have the same number of people working the other interfaces. All our resources go into making machines talk to each other, not people!

These economic concerns are bolstered by the hierarchical pressures that middle managers must face as they are held accountable for results. For example, managers were under pressure to reduce production costs, and labor was considered a prominent cost variable. Most importantly, the traditional conception of the manager as a surrogate for the owners or shareholders continues to carry considerable force. Many managers believe that only the managerial group can be counted on for the loyalty and dedication that this conception implies. A top executive at American Paper Company, the parent company of the three pulp mills, reflected on what he perceived to be the challenge that new information and control technology would offer to this conception of the managerial role:

The classic managerial role has been that of the handler, manipulator, dealer, and withholder of information. An issue that the technology is forcing us to face involves the loss of managerial control. That has a lot to do with the assumption of what the hell managers are. There is a legal definition that management is the steward for the owners of the enterprise. They are expected to not let the situation ever get out of control to the extent that things aren't going to happen the way the owners might want them to happen.

There are many situations in which we keep the management group unnecessarily large because we want to know that in case we have to, those managers can run the operation themselves. This means you never become overly dependent on those hourly folks who can be disloyal and walk out. There is a whole element here of control that we don't talk about.

The new technology introduces some very new problems. Suddenly you are vesting in folks at the control station, folks who are interfacing with a tremendous technology power—power to see all the functions of the operation. That is kind of scary to some managers.

Many managers have tended to experience their own worth in relation to their ability to carry out this charge as the surrogate for the owners. They frequently take it to mean that they must exert unilateral control, maximize the certainty of outcomes, and retain the authority to select appropriate objectives. Often they feel that they must be the ones who "already know," in order to justify their superior position. In this view, workers do not need to know, they merely need to obey. When these complimentary roles are enacted, faith in the hierarchy can be preserved.

For managers who participate in this psychological context, it is difficult to share knowledge or to be concerned with helping their subordinates to learn. First, this implies that workers can learn what managers know, thus calling into question the necessity of managerial authority. Second, it implies that workers need to understand in order to execute, which is an affront to the collective faith that keeps a hierarchy afloat. Persuasion, influence, education—these are not easily compatible with the beliefs necessary to maintain imperative control. Finally, managers acting as teachers creates the possibility of their own vulnerability. Teaching and learning lead to insights, doubts, and questions. There are likely to be questions that managers cannot answer. If that is the case, what gives them the right to manage?

Considered within this framework, the choice to create "smart people" can be experienced by some as a threat to managerial authority. A manager at Piney Wood voiced his fear that they were creating an organization in which "nobody knows if the computer is doing the right thing." He explained the reason this way:

> We have not given the operators the skills they need to exercise this kind of judgment because we don't trust them. We bypass all our other concerns about the future of the plant—our long-range strategy, our need to optimize, our desire for organizational change—and we put all the knowledge in a black box that no one understands and kid ourselves that we will come back later and explain it.

Managers throughout the plant admitted the degree to which their need for certainty and control determined their approach to deploying technology:

> We are afraid that if we quit controlling things, the organization will fall apart.

> Managers here prefer closed-loop control because they do not trust operators to respond properly to the computer. We want to know that it will get done. We must have certainty around that.

Nor were these attitudes lost on the operators:

> It seems management is afraid to let us learn too much about how this system operates. The more we know, the more we could sabotage it.

> They think we're kids and they know what's best. There's no trust, no respect.

Though many managers reluctantly acknowledged the limitations of their strategy and wondered if it would be possible to operate the plant successfully without a strong intellective skill base at the point of production, they continued to cling to their traditional roles. People at every organizational level—managers, engineers, and operators—each spent a good deal of time speculating on the sources of this dynamic and its ultimate consequences. One top manager maintained that the core of the problem was the lack of an alternative to the traditional managerial function.

> The problem is that managers don't have skills and knowledge or a vision of their new role. They are asking, "What is going to happen to me?" And so they are in a panic.

The plant manager agreed:

> As we face change, the big issue is, "What's in it for me?" If I can
> keep the box narrowly defined, then I know my strength as a man-
> ager. I don't know what my new skills will need to be, so that makes
> me uncomfortable. Managers say, "You want me to build skills in
> others that I'm not sure I have myself, and my future is uncertain to
> boot!"

One line manager described the problem this way:

> Managers perceive workers who have information as a threat. They
> are afraid of not being the "expert." They are used to having every-
> one come to them and ask what to do.

An engineer who had been closely involved with the technological
conversions in the mill's bleach plant and powerhouse complained
about the indignities and inefficiencies of the managers' withholding
attitude. Shortly after the conversion of the bleach plant, operators on
the night shift, working without managers, would be faced with repeated system failures. If the system went down, it halted bleaching
operations and threatened production millwide. Operators had no idea
how to bring the system back up once it crashed, and because there
were no managers on the night shift, they had no one to turn to.

> We don't know anything about the software, and the managers don't
> want us messing around with it. But if we are on the night shift and
> the computer goes down, there is a real problem. The process is
> entirely dependent upon the computer system.
>
> They don't want us to know very much, and the more they keep us
> in the dark, the more they can order us around. Therefore, they
> haven't really told us what we need to know.

The engineer agreed:

> Many managers are not clear about what their new role should be.
> They tend to try and keep the operators in the dark as a form of job
> security.

Though he had no direct line of authority to train the operators, this
engineer finally succumbed to his own frustration and anger. He explained to the operators the technical basics regarding how to bring the

system back up when it failed. He then scribbled these instructions on the cover of an old phone directory in the control room.

In Piney Wood's powerhouse, managers talked about the operators' position becoming more of a thinking job, as their responsibility for data broadened and routine functions were placed on closed-loop control. However, the level of automatic control that places the worker in the role of observer at the data interface will create a thinking job only if operators are given the encouragement, latitude, and skills with which to think. Three years into the conversion, there were already examples throughout the plant of complete closed-loop control, where operators had little idea of how to influence the system and, therefore, little idea of what to think about. A closed-loop computer system in the powerhouse was programmed to control the boilers and determine where in the plant to shed power in the face of an energy reduction or generator problems. One engineer described the system:

> It takes the decision out of the operator's hands. It takes a load off the operator. He doesn't set priorities. This is done by management, and if it doesn't work, it is management's fault.

Later, a cost-monitoring system was installed that was to allow operators to use data from the control system for the purpose of finding ways to operate more economically. The operators were stymied by this so-called thinking job.

> What leeway is there for us to figure out how to do things better? Besides, we have no idea how this new system works. It was brought down here, but no one ever showed us what it does or how to use it.

Intellective skill becomes a determinative factor in whether or not a worker is able to exert influence and thus fulfill the potential of a thinking job. The powerhouse operators lamented:

> If my job was open now, no one would bid on it. No one understands what the job is supposed to be. No one seems to be able to teach me or anyone what this job should be. If the company doesn't grab the ball to train people, I am not going to stay here.

Piney Wood's managers admitted that training had been ignored in the technological conversion. For example, when the computerized interface was first introduced into the powerhouse, the line manager

wondered whether there might not be a need for some training. He
called the director of training, who in turn called the vendor. An instructor was sent to conduct a seminar, which was to meet each morning for two weeks. The training director attended the sessions and,
after two days, decided that they were so costly and superficial that he
would dismiss the instructor and do the job himself. His assessment of
the training?

> It doesn't really amount to much. We set up menus and teach them
> to press buttons, but we don't expect them to understand what they
> are doing.

The situation in the bleach plant was not much better. One manager
described the conversion process:

> We had all the wires bunched up in the corner of the room, and when
> we could get everything wired up, we switched over. Our goal was
> to avoid any downtime. The training budget was ridiculously small.
> Almost nothing, really. No one had training numbers in their bud-
> gets. When hardware training is done, we don't ever explain how
> things work. The operators don't believe in the technology and can-
> not do anything with the calculations and decisions the computer
> makes. We have not shared with them the logic behind the informa-
> tion systems.

How do we explain this poverty of training in the face of a massive
technological expenditure? In part, it reflects a profound underestima-
tion of the skill demands associated with a technology that informates.
Most managers approached the technological conversion with the belief that the technology would eliminate, not exacerbate, the need for
operator understanding. The lack of emphasis on training also reflects
some deeply held assumptions about the distribution of knowledge in
the organization. For many managers at Piney Wood, substantial investment in developing critical understanding at the data interface symbolized a threat to their authority. It is almost as if these managers preferred to deal with chronic dysfunctions and suboptimal performance,
rather than challenge the faith that held organization managers together in the covenant of imperative control.

THE CASE OF TIGER CREEK MILL

Tiger Creek's Expense Tracking System (ETS) illustrates the dilemmas of authority that can be engendered by an informating technology. Before the implementation of the ETS, cost data for operating the paper machine were relatively sketchy and cost-improvement plans depended on time-consuming managerial analyses. Microprocessor-based sensors and control technology had increased the amount of information operators had about the paper machine. This made it possible to run the machine at higher speeds, but it also increased the complexities of operation, which required tracking and monitoring hundreds of variables as well as sixty-five control loops. Costs were also becoming a more important competitive variable in the marketing of finished paper products.

Harvey DeWitt, a process engineer assigned to paper making, and Bob Phillips, the department manager in the paper-making group, believed that the most effective way to reduce costs was to put accurate, detailed real-time information on operating expenses into the hands of the operators who actually made the minute-by-minute decisions that could significantly influence cost swings.

DeWitt and Phillips knew that the process for getting such a system funded by corporate management and embraced by plant management would not be easy. Their approach to expense tracking represented a significant break with typical process-control applications. John Loveman, the operations manager in the paper-making area, explained:

> It means a subtle power shift. Taking the decision making out of some people's hands and giving it to others. There were difficulties in getting the appropriation because it was new and different in three important ways. The technology was going to make accurate information available. The system would give full license to operators to manage the business on a cost basis. They would have cost data that managers never had. And, finally, it would be a system that did not help the machine. Instead, it would be strictly for using information from the machines to make better decisions.

DeWitt and Phillips were counting on the commitment of the parent company, American Paper Company (APC), to innovative plant organizations like Cedar Bluff, which gave workers considerable responsibility and encouraged them to "contribute to the business." Such organizations were considered more flexible and better able to achieve cost reductions. APC's successful experiences in manufacturing plants with innovative designs based on such an approach had convinced its leadership that these "high commitment" work systems made an important contribution to competitive advantage. Though a unionized plant, Tiger Creek's top managers had been working with the union to bring about changes consistent with such principles. Severe competitive pressures on Tiger Creek had increased the managers' convictions that a more cooperative and flexible organization attuned to cost reductions was essential.

DeWitt and Phillips believed that operator ownership of the new system was crucial for its success. They involved two operators from the targeted paper machines, Lee Deutsch, a third hand, and Guy Needham, a machine tender, in a special task force and gave them responsibility for workers' participation in the selling, design, and implementation of the system.[3]

Deutsch and Needham received special training in how to run meetings and acted as the liaisons between the operators on the paper machines and the process/software engineers working on the ETS. They helped define cost variables, build the data base, and design the screens. David Oswegan, the process control engineer in the department, described the operators' contribution:

> The operators contributed things no one else even conceived of. They decided what information they needed and how to display it.

The implementation of the ETS covered a fourteen-month period. Finally, the system was installed and put into use. Though specific changes in the tasks for which operators and managers were accountable had not been made explicit, those close to the project noticed that the opportunity to utilize the information from the ETS was causing a redistribution of functions.

Before, the ETS operators had no data on costs, only summaries of data from the previous shift. Each operator would align the key operating variables on the paper machine (a procedure known as centerlining) based on his or her judgment as to how it ran best.[4] This meant that cost levels could vary widely with each shift. In this environment, managers made all the cost decisions. Each weekday morning, they received a "key factors" report based on the operators' logs. They would calculate costs and post the results on the bulletin board in the control room—a "report card" of the previous day's performance. When it came to specific issues related to costs per machine or troubleshooting, managers had responsibility for communicating with other shifts. The conventional division of labor was neatly preserved, with workers exercising their know-how and managers in charge of the data that allowed them to make sense of the operation.

After the implementation of the ETS, workers had increasing responsibility for costs, process stability, and troubleshooting, because they had immediate data and the ability to influence the process. The quality of data meant that operators could make the decisions that were once the exclusive domain of managers and engineers. They no longer resorted to their idiosyncratic methods for determinating centerlines, because they had objective data on which to base their choices. Information was automatically passed between shifts, as the data base was accessible to everyone. The system also created a powerful correlational capability that allowed operators to relate their decisions to the quality of paper coming off the machine. If a particularly bad grade of paper was produced, it was possible to use the data base to determine the precise factors that contributed to poor quality and to correct negative trends more quickly.

With respect to decisions bearing on costs, operators' rules of thumb and personal preferences for machine operation were no longer the only, or even the most important, grounds upon which to base their choices. A hole had been poked in the knowledge dam. The objective information that had been preserved for managerial use and that had bolstered the necessity of imperative control was seeping out.

One year later, the initial results of the ETS were in. While savings of $370,000 had been predicted for the first year, actual savings were $456,000. Operators were now managing their paper machines to achieve lower costs, and the savings had surpassed everyone's expectations. The most significant gains, however, had been made during the first eight months and seemed to have reached a plateau after one year. There was a decrease in the number of dramatic new insights, and the system began to be used less for making discoveries than for more routine monitoring.

There were varied opinions as to why savings had leveled off. Bob Phillips believed that the problem was ultimately an organizational one.

Since managers remained formally accountable for costs, it had been difficult for operators to sustain a feeling of responsibility of cost-related problems and for managers to encourage them in that sense of responsibility. John Loveman seemed to accept the plateau as a natural development and talked about using the system to enhance paper machine stability and equipment reliability. Harvey DeWitt strongly disagreed, however. He believed that only 30 percent of the system's potential had really been exploited.

> In order to get the other 70 percent, we would need a positive and active program in management or the union. They would have to really support the operators using the ETS.

Lee Deutsch agreed:

> We haven't even come close to using this system's potential. We've just tackled the things we already knew.

Had the system reached a real ceiling on the degree of cost savings that were possible? Were there other explanations for the dwindling insights from the cost data? David Oswegan, a young line manager in the paper-making area, issued a list of problems with the ETS, in which he outlined four sets of concerns identified as "barriers that are keeping the module from utilizing the ETS to its fullest potential": data problems, outages in user skills, user/computer interface problems, and implementation problems.

In his analysis of operator skills, he found that "people do not have sufficient skills to be able to incorporate the ETS into their daily job" and cited three causes: performance-based qualifications had not been completed, additional training material was needed, and operators did not understand how the ETS calculated most of its key variables.

The list of problems did not identify what kinds of skills were actually needed by operators or what it would take to develop those skills, but a lack of operator understanding was evident in each of the major problem categories. For example, the list of data problems noted that "people are unsure of what to do when they suspect the ETS has inaccurate data, because there is an inadequate understanding of how it calculates its key variables." The discussion of interface problems noted that operators did not have sufficient skills to be able to identify trends in the data. In listing implementation problems, the report concluded that savings documentation occurs infrequently because "operators don't have a clear understanding of the intent or procedures for documenting any tests."

The superficiality of operators' skills seemed to haunt the ETS project. The training program Deutsch and Needham had devised had been aborted before completion. They had planned two levels of training. The first level was directed at reducing "computer phobia" and teaching keyboard skills. The second level was to have addressed the intellective challenges of working with the ETS. Deutsch explained:

> It is important to understand the interrelationships between different parts of the process. If you do something to one part of the equipment, you can see the cost effects in another part of the equipment, so you really have to understand the interdependencies. You have to work experimentally to see what affects what, under what conditions, and how. This computer won't lie. You look at it, and you instantly know if you have saved money or not. But maybe we raised electric costs when we tried to save money on something else—so you have to make a trade-off. That is how people have to be taught to understand the dynamics between different parts of the process.

Deutsch developed and intended to use an "experimental approach" to achieve the second level of operator training.

> We're always running experiments on the machines, and my intent was to show them what a resource the ETS was. I would have them make changes in the paper machines and then come and see what it did to the other variables in the system.

Needham and Deutsch discovered that their students learned in different ways and at different rates. Some needed more time than others to get beyond basic operating skills and into the real potential of the system. One process engineer close to the project estimated that about 20 percent of the operators developed an in-depth proficiency very rapidly; another 50 percent learned more slowly but were capable of reasonable proficiency, if properly trained and motivated; and a final 30 percent were relatively indifferent toward the system. He believed that some of these were capable of learning but simply were not interested. For others, mastering the skills required to really utilize the system would be difficult.

The first level of training was accomplished, but in spite of Deutsch's enthusiasm, the second level was abandoned when his assignment to the task force ended. His explanation was as follows:

> The managers came in and started taking over. . . . They would come in and create new frames and not tell us what they had done, so we couldn't use them. . . . They discouraged us from exploring more aspects of the data to try new things. The managers were all over us, formalizing things right away, giving us rules, telling us how we had to use it, second-guessing us, wanting to get their names on every report.

As a result of the limited training, operators were left to their own devices when it came to figuring out how to use the system more creatively. The qualifications procedures reflected the simplicity of the training and tended to test for only the superficial skills involved with basic keyboard operation. As Bob Phillips described it, "We didn't ever take skills training to the point of telling them how to use the system to impact business."

Despite these training problems, some operators had made a significant effort to learn about the system, to take risks, to experiment, and to use it in an imaginative and productive way. Given the minimal levels of encouragement and the failure to develop a comprehensive educational program, what explains their extra effort?

One of the themes most frequently repeated in conversations with the operators concerned how the ETS permitted them to enhance their expert authority. Many felt that they had long known how to improve the operation, but as long as their knowledge was relatively restricted to the qualitative, the sentient, the intuitive, and the experiential, no one in management would listen to them. The system had provided them with a means to translate their hands-on knowledge into the precise quantitative terms that managers believed in. For the first time, they were able to prove that they "knew better." The system had given them information that even managers never had available. Those who had developed the skills to really use the system had gained access to more than information: they had encountered a new, more universal language that took them to the heart of the managerial arena. They had stumbled upon an important source of legitimation.

> The Expense Tracking System is a vehicle for us to talk to our managers. Managers only believe quantitative data. If our managers read the printout and it says that snow is black, they will believe it.

All along, we have known the best way to run this process, but we couldn't prove it to them. Now we have a common ground for talking to them.

Nevertheless, the paper machine operators believed that their ability to contribute had been severely curtailed by their managers. When asked what accounted for the plateau in cost savings, the operators who had been most involved with and proficient in the use of the system were in unanimous agreement. The managers felt threatened, they resisted, and finally they had tried to "steal the thunder" from the operators. As a result, the operators began to withdraw their care and concern. They were not prepared to fight; they were not sure how.

The control rooms at Tiger Creek, where the paper machine operators spend much of their time, share the same design aesthetic that graces elementary schools, prisons, and community centers built in the late 1950s. Green cinder block, brown linoleum, white formica—these are the materials that define the work environment. One windowed wall looks out on the paper machines and the plant beyond. There are five terminal screens—one for the Expense Tracking System, two related to a closed-loop system for controlling moisture in the paper, and two for monitoring process data—along with several keyboards and printers. One wall is covered with large sheets of paper that display shift change data, special notes for the maintenance crew, and instructions for the electronics and instrumentation crews. Another sheet of paper lists operating problems and summaries of yesterday's quality figures. The cabinets and a long formica table along one wall are crammed with gear—"Little Playmate" lunchboxes, reports, magazines, oil tins, old clothes, coffee cans, notebooks, paper towels, work gloves, hardhats, a coffee maker, printouts, plastic straws, tool belts, spools of wire, newspapers, coffee cups, tool boxes, instruments for lab testing, a telephone book densely covered with graffiti, and a large looseleaf binder with the words "STOP INJURIES NOW" printed across the front. On two of the three shifts, there are no managers. The operators monitor the terminal screens; check printouts; and frequently move out into the plant to cut a spool of paper, adjust the machine, or perform any of a score of other tasks. Sometimes there are stretches of time with nothing pressing to do. It is from this vantage point, in the comfortable clutter of the small room in which they pass much of their work lives, that the operators observe the managers' behavior, and it is here that they think about and discuss what went wrong with ETS.

Guy Needham's reputation was consistent throughout the hierarchy. Managers and workers alike referred to him as a "straightshooter," articulate and honest, a man who could always be counted on to speak his mind. He talked about the view from the control room—how to explain the sudden plateau in gains from the ETS.

> What happened with the Expense Tracking System? Everything was great until management took it over. It was our system, and they got their paws on it. We said, Fine. You want it? It's yours. You do it. That is when we washed our hands of it.

Other operators complained that management had begun prematurely to formalize new procedures. Management had brought a new emphasis to using the ETS data for identifying centerlines and then required the operators to hold to those parameters. Many operators believed that the abrupt turn to a rigid centerline program was evidence of management's resentment of the ETS. They questioned how managers could be committed to the principle of ETS as an operator's tool if they were going to use the data to impose centerlines and thus minimize the operator's discretion in optimizing the process. As a result they found that

> it was no longer possible to play around with the thing, to experiment. But that is how you have to use the system if you are going to get at its potential.

To combat this situation, operators designed their experiments to be conducted on the graveyard shift, from midnight to 6:00 A.M. This way, they were free to "play" and learn, without managerial pressure. Later, they could present the results of their experiments to managers on the day shift, and they would be well equipped with the documentation to back up their arguments.

Operators perceived managers as trying to make the system their "plaything" and to take credit for all of the savings achievements.

> The managers are real ambivalent about these changes. They want to give us responsibility, but as soon as we hit on something that is really good, they jerk it back and start writing reports about how well *they* have done.

They saw managers developing new data frames and not telling the operators about them. Further, they came to believe that intensive scrutiny had become the method by which managers used the system to track individual performance and to "check up" on people.

> The ETS has become a vehicle for management to check up on us. They can pick up any changes on a minute-by-minute basis if they want to. A report was issued a couple of months ago. It emphasized being able to track what the operators do. When we saw that thing, we decided to call the system the electronic tattletale. As long as things are going well, they don't care about tracking performance. But if it is not running well, they start digging around the data looking for someone to blame.

The operators noticed what they believed was an abrupt escalation in the degree of bureaucracy that surrounded the ETS. They dug into cabinets and produced dozens of memos sent by their managers. Though many of the memos had nothing to do with the ETS, the operators pointed out the tone in which they were written—"petty . . . arrogant . . . hot air . . . three pages to say nothing." Another event outside the unit had contributed to these perceptions of bureaucratization. Several operators on another special task force had abused their position. Management had identified them as "late for work . . . not working very hard . . . goofing off." As a result, managers in the papermaking department wrote a memo stating new rules for operators assigned to special task forces. These rules outlined when and where to report to work, areas of the plant that were off limits, when to take lunch breaks (a half hour only, when special task force operators had been able to take longer), whom to report to, whom to notify when they leave their work area, et cetera. The memo was signed "Crew Management Group," an entity the operators had never heard of. The paper machine operators were furious, as they believed the managers were "too chicken . . . too cowardly" to sign their names to the memo.

The operators had not only noticed their managers' behavior but also interpreted it. First, they believed that managers in the paper-making area had never really bought the concept of the ETS but had "jumped on the bandwagon" when the project appeared successful and began to receive senior management attention. The operators explained their managers' behavior as a result of insecurity and dependence on hierarchical recognition.

> All that managers care about is exposure. They want to do things so
> that other people up in the hierarchy will see what they are doing,
> will know that they are doing "good work." For managers, exposure
> is their bread and butter. Once they found out that this expense
> tracking thing was going to be really looked at by corporate manage-
> ment, they started to latch onto that thing and they wouldn't let it
> go. They are looking for the glory from the system.

Operators believed that each manager was mortally afraid of being seen
as nonessential and, therefore, expendable.

> The managers have a bigger job security problem than the operators.
> We have a union; they don't. It's a big fear, so they have to ask them-
> selves, What am I contributing? And they have to be able to show
> something, so they take over what we do on the ETS.

The operators also revealed a capacity for philosophical speculation
as to the psychological sources of managerial behavior. Many of my days
and nights with them in the control room culminated in discussions of
the nature of management and what it does to the people who manage.

> Managers need to believe that hourly people are dumb. They come
> out of school and have to show that they are smarter than the people
> who have been working here for so long. They can't share informa-
> tion with us, because only by holding onto knowledge that we don't
> have can they maintain their superiority and their ability to order us
> around.

In their ruminations the operators would ask, Why do managers need
to feel power over others? Why the need to dominate? What is the
terrible threat?

As far as the operators were concerned, their success with the ETS
had created an environment in which an old question, "What do we
need middle managers for?" had taken on a new urgency. It was a
question the operators were asking themselves, but unknown to them,
many managers at the plant, divisional, and corporate levels were asking
the same question. The information systems, both for expense tracking
and for process control, had given the operators tremendous amounts
of data with which to control and optimize the production process.
Much of the data had never before existed with this degree of accuracy
or detail.

Many operators saw a connection between the information system's power that had been made available to them and the growing confusion as to the purpose and function of the middle manager. Even the degree of organizational integration made possible by the presence of net-worked real-time systems seemed to obviate the role of the manager as someone who supervised others, gathered information, and controlled communications. Here is how one operator summarized the problem:

> With this new technology it is easier for operators to take on a mana-gerial role because we have more data. There is data every few sec-onds on everything that is going on. Plus, managers don't have to be standing guard over you to find out what is happening. They can come back in ten days, and from the computer, they can see everything that happened. This eliminates the middleman. It is like going right to the farm to buy your eggs.

Outside the control room, the same events were interpreted very differently. Managers were well aware that "cost responsibility still re-sides high in the management organization." They continued to be held accountable for costs; it was one important criteria in terms of which they were evaluated. This accountability made them highly sensitive to division and corporate management's interest in the ETS. They knew that the attention drawn to this system had made it a symbol of Tiger Creek's ability to adapt to its new competitive environment.

> ETS was the first savings project for passive information utilized by operators. Division management was out on a limb, and they had high expectations. Their message to us was, "It will not fail!" ETS became a symbol of success or failure in looking at our plant, at our ability to adapt. We made a presentation to divisional senior management, and they said, "Make it successful—or else."

Since the funding appropriation had gone through, division manage-ment sent frequent notes asking, "How's ETS coming?" There had been several visits by managers from other divisions to learn about the ETS.

Some managers conceded that the new emphasis on centerlines con-tradicted the notion of creating opportunities for operators to influence the business. Phillips described the centerline program as "a knee-jerk reaction of managers to get the operators to behave the way they want them to behave." Other managers maintained that their concerns were legitimate. They sincerely doubted the operators' ability to handle the increased responsibility. They also feared giving cost information to a unionized work force. Furthermore, giving the operators free reign to influence cost decisions might mean that they would lose money, and managers would ultimately be held accountable. One manager admitted, "Under these conditions, it is hard to get the leeway for experimentation to generate data that might persuade us to do things differently." Phillips summarized the quandary as he saw it:

> A vacuum is created in this process. When managers impose center-lines of great detail, operators lose discretion. This means that managers have to step in to do analysis. Managers don't feel that operators are mature enough to have such discretion. Operators pull away, because they feel they don't have enough discretion.

Knowledge and power are like two lines looping through history. Typically, they converge, but sometimes they do not. When they converge, hierarchies both create knowledge and use it to reproduce the status quo. When they diverge, the consequences can be volatile. The managers at Tiger Creek who resisted operator responsibility for the ETS were acting in a manner consistent with their spiritual allegiances. In order to sustain faith in the logic of the hierarchy and the appropriateness of their authority, it would be necessary to continually reaffirm the difference between subordinate and superior. Since that difference rests largely on the control over and skillful handling of information, a leak in the knowledge dam is cause for concern. If managers and workers alike have shared this faith, albeit imperfectly, then it is rational for managers to doubt the capacities of workers to be successful in the realm of information. After all, these are the very people who are supposed to be different from managers. How can they be trusted to perform managerial work?

The operators' success with the ETS begins to challenge this perceived difference. One response leads to a crisis of faith—as when the operators asked, "What are managers for?" Another response leads to a reaffirmation of the status quo, a denial of the threatening evidence. The fresh emphasis on centerlines is a rational response to quell the threat, particularly as these managers continued to be held accountable for the control and analysis of cost information. The hierarchy they were struggling to affirm did not invite them to relinquish that control, even it if did, somewhat unwittingly, allow a Trojan horse to enter the kingdom. As one manager reflected:

Traditionally, managers bring discipline to their organizations around centerlines, documentation, sharing information. The computer means that can done without a manager. If we combine the computer with comments from operators, most of these things can be accomplished. We are all struggling for our turf. The technology will mean change in our social systems, but so far, this social change in management is not orchestrated.

THE TERROR OF COMMAND AND THE REVENGE OF SUBMISSION

When we ask why managers choose to emphasize the smart machine, we find ourselves examining the convergence of many streams of meaning, each of which may exist with a different degree of explicit awareness. Economic exigencies can serve as a rationalization for almost any capital investment, but the implications of the ideology of ownership are less explicitly articulated. Very often, the sense of threat to managerial authority, purpose, and meaning are latent, more embedded in practice than expressed in public discourse.

Enthusiasm for the smart machine can also serve as a summary of a hundred daily frustrations in which managers feel thwarted in their attempts to direct and control subordinates. Process engineers tell of the thousands of hours spent writing codes for automating control procedures that operators refused to enforce. One engineer complained that he could not get the operators to control a particular piece of equipment cost effectively, so he programmed the computer to do it without operator intervention. Another manager gave the following example:

> One problem we have had in the powerhouse is how the operators run the boilers. We have explained to them that if you give more air to a boiler, you will lose heat. But they compare it to their fireplaces, and don't believe us. I keep explaining, but their experience tells them different. So we have programmed the computer to do this, instead of trying to get them to do it. We are trying to keep the process on the computer—keep it closed loop instead of having them take it over manually.

In traditional process-control environments, the high level of responsibility accorded to the operator represented management's dependence on the worker's action-centered skills. In the emerging environment, automatic control provides management with a route by which to escape this dependency. Two of Piney Wood's managers put it bluntly:

> If we can build intelligence into our controls, we will not be as dependent on the special knowledge of our crew leaders.

> The more we can control with the computer, the less dependence we will have on operators with in-depth knowledge. When there is a problem, we will have computer programs, logic, electronic sensors. We will be able to understand the problems.

Some managers experience a sense of relief at the prospect of being freed from this dependency. Their enthusiasm reveals an underlying but potent fantasy, one in which perfect control through total automaticity allows them to avoid the messiness and potential conflict of real human interaction. Many of the practices associated with the deployment of technology communicate this fantasy to the men and women on the production floor. There are also many casual interactions that drive this sharp point home more intimately. An operator at Piney Wood told the following story:

> One of the higher-ups brought some customers in here for a tour. He showed them one of the new computers we have controlling the process. The man came in here and stood in front of the machine. He rubbed it back and forth. It was like he was lusting after it. He just kept stroking it, and we were all in here, and he said to these customers, "This is a marvelous machine. It is a wonderful piece of equipment. It doesn't take coffee breaks or come in with a hangover. And it does a better job than a man can do." He said all this to them just like we were not there, like we were not human or something.

When managers express a preference for computers over people, the effects find their way into every corner of the worker's mind. One day, an operator in the bleach plant took me to see the area built above the control room where the computers are housed. "Here's where all the brains are," he said. He pointed out two air-conditioning units, one for the control room, and one, significantly larger, for the computer room. "See, the unit for the computers is four times bigger than the one for us. Try and tell me that management cares about the people here!"

Another operator responded this way when asked about his vision of Piney Wood's future:

> They want to have a computer run twenty-four hours a day. No one
> will touch anything. The computer will completely control every-
> thing, and you will need one man pushing a broom somewhere. . . .
> Managers here think that computers are the most important things
> in the plant. With all these managers running around trying to prove
> things with their computers, it's like one big anthill with all those
> little ants ringing and twisting and buzzing.

As managers use computerization to escape their dependency on
workers' unique skills, both managers and workers alike become more
dependent upon the computer system. The feelings of dependency
among the operators, at first fiercely resisted, take over slowly, like a
creeping vine that can eventually strangle any sense of personal investment in and accountability for their work. The computer system becomes a presence to which workers attribute human characteristics.
Sometimes the system is seen as omnipotent, with a power of intelligence so close to perfection as to diminish any value of human involvement. This perception can shape the vision of the future for the plant,
as articulated by a group of operators:

> Twenty years out, you just need a computer operator to run the mill.
> They will put the process in memory banks and program it for every
> conceivable thing that can go wrong. Operators will be out, and the
> computer will make the decisions.

Sometimes the computer is treated with contempt, an expression of
the operator's hostility at being shunted aside in favor of the machine.
In one area of Piney Wood, where a computer system automatically
controlled the pulp-drying process, operators had taken to calling the
computer Otto (for automatic). They spoke about Otto according to
their mood and estimation of its current level of performance. "Otto
is the person who does all the thinking." "Otto won't speed up fast
enough." "Otto just isn't making any sense." In another control room,
a large axe was mounted on a wall, and underneath it was a sign that
read, "IN CASE OF COMPUTER FAILURE, USE FIRE AXE." The
crew leader told me that the axe had been presented to him by his co-
workers—a sympathetic gesture toward his frequent frustration with
the automatic controls.

Frequently, the operators' attitude toward the computer presence is
simply cunning. When perceived as an extension of management, as
management's effort to circumvent the worker, the computer becomes

the perfect foil for every latent inclination to ease the burdens of work. If managers choose to set so much store by the computer, then they must absorb accountability for performance. The worker becomes an extension of the computer system but reciprocates this loss of centrality to the task by putting the work at the margins of his or her own concerns.

Nowhere was this dynamic more starkly illustrated than in Piney Wood's digesting module, the part of the pulping process where wood chips are cooked and turned into the dirty brown pulp that is later bleached white, dried, and rolled into flat sheets. Piney Wood's batch digesting process consisted of nineteen vats into which wood chips and chemicals would be loaded and heated according to a careful formula that optimizes time and temperature. Traditionally, each operator, or "cook," had responsibility for a number of vats. The operator continually checked circle graphs and strip charts in order to determine the optimal time to empty, or "blow," each vat. Operators described running from one vat to another, checking readings, writing down figures, and mentally calculating the right time to release the pulp from the vat.

Because of the relatively few variables involved in this process, computerization created the opportunity for an almost completely automated control loop. The computer now records the volume of wood chips fed into each vat and controls the cooking process. It also tracks the dirt buildup in each vat, indicating when it needs cleaning. As each digester may be in a different stage of the cooking process, the computer schedules cooking time so that the vats may be emptied at appropriate intervals in relation to one another.

The digester control room is the oldest and grimiest in the plant. Rectangular in shape, its two long walls are covered with the gauges and graphs once used for manual cooking but now ignored. The dingy yellow paint is cracked and peeling. Along one long wall are a low wooden bench and four rickety metal-frame chairs placed around an old linoleum-topped table. High on the wall opposite the bench are two video display screens. Each of the nineteen vats is listed on the screens, along with readings that represent the cooking time, vat temperature, and the precise minute at which the vat is to be emptied or "blown." The operators in the control room (the number varied from three to six on my visits) sit on the bench or lean back in their chairs around the wobbly table. They look like birds on a wire, their necks perpetually stretched at an upward angle to stare at the video screens.

One operator walks outside periodically to blow another vat—a routine that consists of opening a valve on the vat to release the cooked pulp into a surge tank. The operators chew tobacco and spit into a large metal bucket that sits on the floor between them. They seem bored, and a continual stream of small talk drifts from their lips, while their eyes rarely stray from the screens on the wall.

Piney Wood's plant manager depicts the computer control of the digesting module as having turned the operator into "simply another variable in the process that we manage the way we manage all of the mechanical variables." The production manager for the digesting module describes the changes wrought by computerization:

> The computer schedules the blow; we get a lot more production this way. Before, the operator went out there and had to think about when to blow each vat. Now, we basically take them by the hand and lead them through it. . . . We let the computer do the habitual things, and this frees them to do things that really take thought, such as problem solving, troubleshooting, and managing their time better.

Again, this manager's statements reflect a reluctance to admit the full implications of the authority lodged in the computer system. The notion of "freeing the operator's time" to do more interesting things is a kind of code phrase used to soften the fact that the worker has been reduced to "simply another mechanical variable." When questioned at length, this manager could not provide an example of the troubleshooting or problem-solving activities that were presumably taking up more of the operators' time, nor was there any indication from the operators that their jobs had become more complex.

On the contrary, the most striking feature of the operators' behavior was the dependency they had developed on the computer system. Because of the relative simplicity of automating this part of the pulping process, the digesting module was the first in the plant to have a high level of computer control in the early 1970s. By 1982, there was wide agreement that it had become impossible to achieve a high-quality cook without the computer system. Management purchased an expensive backup computer when a systems failure revealed that the operators had lost their manual cooking skills. The operators freely admitted their dependency:

> We would be lost without the screen. Sometimes when it goes down, we sit and stare at it; we don't know what to do, we just sit and stare. Our job now really is to observe the screen. You may not be thinking exactly, but you sure have to pay attention.

> Before I started working in the control room, I would walk through here and think that everyone was crazy because they were just sitting in here and all day long staring up at the screen. Now I do the same.

With this new dependency, the operators discovered some new rewards. They learned that they could relinquish responsibility for the quality of the product they make. The old-timers recalled their skepticism when computer control was first introduced:

> At first we didn't like the computer because we could do the same thing off the charts and didn't think the computer could do it right. We didn't want to have to sit in here and look up at that screen all the time.

By the time my study began, twelve years after the module had first been placed under computer control, it appeared that the predominant sentiments had changed. Realizing that there was no way back from computer control, the operators finally gave up their attachment to personal control. As management had devalued the operators' contribution to the process, the workers found that they could respond by withdrawing their care—the sense of commitment to and responsibility for their tasks. If management wanted to put the decision-making responsibility into the computer, the operators would not allow themselves to be held accountable for what occurred. The digesting module crew leader had thirty years' experience and was considered the most knowledgeable of all the cooks. He voiced a sentiment that brought agreement from the other operators in the room:

> If I do what the computer tells me to do, then the computer is responsible, not me. This takes a big burden off me. It is a relief. I don't have as much responsibility on my shoulders; therefore, that makes my job easier. I am responsible to do what the computer says I should do, or it is going to tell on me. This simplifies what my responsibility actually is.

I asked another old-timer what would happen if the numbers displayed on the video screen were inaccurate.

I never trouble myself about the accuracy of the numbers. That's management's problem. These are the aids they give us to do the job, and I use them.

One operator with more than twenty years of experience in the digesting module discovered that cooking with the computer meant less "aggravation and effort." His evaluation revealed the mix of fatalism, cynicism, and, finally, self-protection that characterizes forced dependency. The following is an excerpt from our discussion:

Now the computer does the analysis. If we think it needs more steam, we can't do anything about it. But they must have their reasons for doing it this way. Maybe the computer knows more than we do. Maybe it does a better job.

(Q) Do you think it does a better job?

No, I don't, but that is the way it is. It is less aggravation for us anyway. . . . It frees you from some worry. . . . It's less aggravation and . . . individual effort.

When observed from another angle, it is possible to see these operators' attitudes mirroring their managers'. Management used the computer system to extend its control, and the workers responded by intensifying their obedience. What is lost in this process is the degree of integration and mutuality that existed when managers needed the skills that operators took pleasure in developing. The prediction with which chapter 1 concluded—that the social integration of Blauner's continuous-process environment would diminish as the action-centered skills of workers were deemphasized—appears to have been realized in Piney Wood's digesting module. There, obedience fed by cynicism became a form of revenge for the indignities imposed by obsolescence.

As the intrinsic meaning of the work dries up, its only source of motivation resides in extrinsic rewards. The operators have slowly learned to withdraw any investment of self in their work. What remains is a good paycheck, tasty tobacco, and, if one is lucky, some decent chums with whom to while away the hours of staring at the screen.

The best thing about this job is the pay. The computer system is great because we have an easier job and less responsibility. We still make more money than most college graduates in this state.

The plant manager at Piney Wood acknowledged that soon even the perfunctory role of the operator in the digesting process would be automated. He envisioned many fewer operators, perhaps even a single operator, who would monitor data, observe, and troubleshoot. He then sounded what had become a relentless refrain: "It would then become more a thinking job as opposed to a dumb job." The future seemed a more congenial time to resolve troubling contradictions.

AUTHORITY MAINTAINS ITS DISTANCE

At Cedar Bluff, the technological vision evolved differently from Piney Wood or Tiger Creek. The plant was intended to be one of the most sophisticated of its kind, relying on a complete microprocessor base of instrumentation. The process-control system, together with an information system known as the Overview System (which recorded and displayed real-time information from 2,500 key pieces of operating equipment every five seconds), had created an operating environment saturated with information.

An early awareness of the data-intensiveness of the operator's job had shaped the recruitment process. There was a widespread belief that this new plant would require a qualitatively different kind of work force:

> Computers have changed the type of people that we hire. The more remote the technology makes you from the process, the tighter we screen the people that we hire. We looked for youngsters who would bring complete awareness and flexibility without the fear. They are less shocked than experienced people. Persons with a high level of education and more recent schooling are more likely to be successful with data. We look for mental discipline.

Operators and managers had access to information from the Overview System and used it to track specific data as well as to keep informed of trends in the total overall production process. A slowdown or problem in one module was an indication that it would be necessary to signal people that they needed to reformulate production plans. An important feature of the Overview System was its "calculator models," which were based upon an exhaustive debriefing of experienced managers, vendor experts, and other technical resources within the parent company. These models depicted optimal relationships among operating variables and could simulate distinct sets of plant-operating conditions.

To use a calculator model, an operator would plug in data representing current operating conditions, and the model would compute those values in light of the optimal relationships among the variables. The operator could then use those calculations to make appropriate changes in the process, bringing it into a closer alignment with optimal performance. For example, if pulp was not being adequately bleached, a calculator model could be used to help the operator isolate the changes that needed to be made in order to increase bleaching with a minimal increase in chemical usage. The calculator models could also be used to test strategies before putting them into operation or to predict likely consequences of current operating conditions.

By the third year after start-up, another system that would integrate all existing plant data was being designed. This system, known as the Data Access System (DAS), contained an integrated plant data base that could be accessed by personal computers placed throughout the plant. The data base would include all current and historical data from the Overview System and the process-control systems as well as business data such as costs, inventories, sales, market data, personnel records, et cetera. The data base could be accessed with software that enabled the analysis and manipulation of raw data.

During the first year after start-up, it became apparent to the plant leadership that if the mill was to be a success, the young, relatively well-educated, but completely inexperienced work force would need to become competent at turning data into intelligent information. The plant manager believed that operators would need critical judgment based on a solid conceptual grasp of the operation:

> The operators are in a position to monitor, judge, and analyze data. Sure, we will need to close loops where we can, but we need people who can make sure that loop makes sense and who can put it into manual if it doesn't look right. We usually automate something according to the way we have always done it, without questioning it. We need people who can bring intelligence to this process. Otherwise, we will suboptimize.

Cedar Bluff's leadership had made a commitment to a team-based organizational structure in large measure because they believed the "group dynamics effects" of peer interaction and discussion would induce people to become more thoughtful and expressive about their work. One top manager explained:

> We need people with an analytical understanding, and we pay for that depth of understanding. At Piney Wood, you never have to express your understanding; you just go out and do what you have to do, and you are judged on your actions. Here, we have to judge people on their understanding. The team approach makes it necessary to express your understanding.

Another manager, who had spent several years in Piney Wood and had been transferred to a top operating position at Cedar Bluff, compared the two environments:

> I can tell you there is a world of difference. In Cedar Bluff, when you have a problem, you think, sit down and have a meeting, then think again. The computer allows people to work on bigger problems— things you couldn't tackle without it. It gives us the capacity to do things and use data that we couldn't otherwise have done. It facilitates seeing new things. What has happened at Cedar Bluff is that we have both given people the tools and expected them to use them. This is what makes Cedar Bluff a thought-oriented place, in contrast to Piney Wood, which is environment-oriented. There they solve problems by asking, how did we do it last time? Thinking is a last resort.

This commitment to developing operator intelligence was exemplified in an unprecedented training investment. The work force was hired before the plant went into production and spent several weeks in classrooms learning the basics of math, physics, and chemistry in addition to specific material on the pulping process. Mock terminals simulated fragments of the production process. The first thirty people to be hired were trained to serve as "operator trainers" so that each control room would have a designated resource for education and guidance.

During the first three years of operation, the work force did indeed learn a great deal about how to run a highly automated pulp mill, yet it was apparent by the fourth year that for all of its commitment, the plant leadership had underestimated the persistent features of organizational life that would inhibit a full exploitation of their technological investment. Cedar Bluff had not escaped the very dynamics that were driving Piney Wood headlong toward its emphasis on the smart ma-

chine. When considered in a relative framework, Cedar Bluff's operators had done remarkably well in developing their intellective proficiency. When considered in the light of the plant's ambitions or in
relation to the full potential of an informating technology, it had fallen
short of its goals. Why?

First, the plant had difficulty finding an alternative to the conventional economic justifications for new technology. All computer-
related purchases were justified on a productivity basis, usually requiring documentation of a 20 percent rate of return. One of the designers
of the new DAS saw the way in which the insistence on proof of such
savings hampered the diffusion of new technology:

> You can't say, "If I had it I could be doing X, Y, or Z that I am not
> able to do now." You can only justify technology in terms of what
> you do today.

The technology itself presented another set of complications. Consider the calculator models available through the Overview System. The
models, it would seem, both call upon and help to develop intellective
skill. They require an understanding of the production process complex
enough to perceive when an operation is suboptimal and might be improved. The calculator models also enhance an operator's awareness of
the interdependencies among variables and the values associated with
optimality. It is also easy for the models to remain opaque: if an operator does not have access to the assumptions that are the basis for a
model's calculations, then it is difficult to critically judge its output.
Cedar Bluff's top staff person for information systems was doubtful as
to how much judgment an operator could really exercise in using the
calculator models:

> There are at least a dozen different models that we have built. We
> wanted to use the expertise of the people who are not available, but
> who add expertise to the model. People don't understand everything
> that goes into the model, and they need to. But we are saving millions
> of dollars a year with these models. I am not sure how much judg-
> ment you can exercise in using one of these models, but if it has
> substantiated itself, you just do what it says.

An operator who worked regularly with the calculator models described his frustration at not having access to their underlying assumptions and algorithms, which he called "fudge factors":

The models use equations, fudge factors, put in there to make sure you make quality pulp. If you don't know these fudge factors, they can work against you. I had to talk the engineers into explaining the fudge factors to me. The assumptions of the designers are never explained to us. You cannot really be controlling the process if you don't understand these things. As long as it's a black box to me, all I can do is babysit the computer.

While this operator had been successful in persuading an engineer to instruct him on some of the more sophisticated issues involved in a model's calculations, most operators had become somewhat embittered about the prospects of extracting from their managers the kind of education they needed to really feel empowered at the data interface.

They involve us in training, but it's not the right training. They tell us what the new equipment is and what to do to run it. But the most important part is the theory, things they have worked on for months. The whys, the formulas, the equations, and assumptions—they don't tell us about that. So when a problem occurs, we have to call them because we can't explain why.

The technology lets us know a lot, but we need to know more. As a manager, you should teach everybody what you know—keep passing the knowledge on. But they do not give us the knowledge to think for ourselves. I think it's because it would do away with their jobs, or they would look stupid if we had that knowledge.

What made it so difficult for managers to pass on their knowledge? The answer takes us back to the faith experience that undergirds imperative control. Despite the team organization among the hourly workers, the skill-based compensation, and a widely shared sense of commitment and responsibility, the management system was quite traditional. In addition to the predictable tensions, the informated environment had intensified the rate at which operators learned and gave many of them a thirst for knowing more. However, too many of their managers could not wrest themselves from deep-seated images of managerial command.

Indeed, as the technology increased the ambiguity of the middle manager's role, many felt an increasingly acute need to assert themselves as different from and better than their subordinates. "The biggest problem we have," lamented the plant manager, "is ourselves." One young manager recalled a meeting he had attended in which the head of employee relations had made a presentation on managing in the Cedar Bluff work system:

> When it got to the pay and responsibility issues, it was like a whirl-wind went through the audience. Everyone forgot about the subject at hand and just got fixated on questions like, what is my role? what is my power? Fear and jealousy is a big issue among managers. Everyone agreed that the technology is driving this issue harder than it has ever been driven. The technology is making the worker more and more like an operational manager.

Many of Cedar Bluff's middle managers found it difficult to "pass the knowledge down," because this would only increase the ambiguity and tenuousness of their roles. Furthermore, abandoning their right to command would force them to call into question their own faith in the hierarchy that surrounded them, its features preserved in the systems by which they were evaluated and the terms according to which they continued to be held accountable. Operators sensed that the ultimate barriers to their skill development involved their managers' need to revive an already tenuous sense of authority by affirming the inherent difference between manager and subordinate.

> Managers are in a hell of a position. They have to appear to be under control all the time. They all have college degrees, and they start talking all kinds of terminology. They get an idea and then tell you to do it.

> Managers are supposed to be superior. They have all the outward trappings, like an office, no time clock, no shift work, and they can be transferred. Being an operator doesn't have prestige because you can get dirty. When you've gone to college, you don't wear jeans. Managers are supposed to be better, and their work is cleaner.

> Management is in a yacht, and we are in a rowboat. We're raised different. Education is a big thing—we didn't go to a formal college and get degrees. We've got different personalities and interests. We like to fish and drink beer, and they. . . . I'm not sure what they do. All I know is you never see them humble down. Their minds are set and they won't change.

> You see a lot more uppity behavior between managers and operators compared to just between operators. Being in a management role, you don't want your friends who graduated from college to think you're like a worker.

It seemed clear that many of Cedar Bluff's managers felt a need to distance themselves from the operators in order to sustain a belief in the legitimacy of their command. They chose to do this by identifying the operators with the work of the animal body while claiming for themselves another territory—of clean clothes, "mental" work, college education, and controlled emotions.

When operators were asked to describe the characteristics of the ideal manager in the new technological environment, there was unanimous agreement. One man expressed it this way:

> In a traditional system, managers are drivers of people. You focus on driving people to work as hard as possible. With our new technology environment, managers should be drivers of learning. They should be driving everyone to use technology for better understanding and ways to expand the business.

Recall the early twentieth century steel mill foreman described in chapter 1, whose talent was to drive men's bodies, to goad them into physically spending themselves. To be a "driver of learning" requires a vastly different talent.

There were two managers in the plant who were universally adored by the operators. They exemplified the notion of a "driver of learning." The evaluations of these two managers were extraordinarily consistent.

> If they know you are interested, Henry and Kurt will pump you full of everything they know.

> Henry wrote a report, and he gave it to us in handwriting because otherwise it would take two or three weeks. He made sure every operator got a copy, not just one copy floating around. He covers everyone, not just the ones who will make him shine in the hierarchy. He doesn't try to impress anybody.

> Henry and Kurt are the best managers in the plant. They will tell you just like it is. They are great teachers. They treat everyone the same. They will document what they know and share it with you.

Most middle managers sensed the threat concealed in the learning relationship. They shared the psychological burden of feeling that they must be people who already know, not people who learn. They felt their position required that they elicit obedience, not doubt and questioning.

> As a manager, it is not okay to admit you don't understand or that
> you have a problem. Those above you in the organization will make
> you feel like they are "with it" and you are not.

> I am not willing to break things down real simply to explain some-
> thing to the operators. I won't give up my terms that I learned as an
> engineer. The concepts are hard to understand. I am not here to
> teach those concepts. I went to college to learn these things, and so
> it proves I have a right to tell people what to do.

> I'm not willing to share all the information I have with my people.
> After all, there are things that I don't have a full picture of, but I can
> take things on faith.

The plant leadership remained relatively well insulated from threats
to their roles and viewed the middle managers with frustration. Many
believed that middle management's ability to develop the knowledge
base in the hourly work force was critical to the plant's long-term success. They were irritated and somewhat stymied by what they saw as
an unnecessary imperiousness among the middle managers. The plant
manager characterized the problem as follows:

> The middle managers are afraid that operators might make a mistake,
> but it never occurs to them that they might make a mistake. Our
> managers are not teachers. We don't recruit for that or base pay or
> promotion on that. It is difficult for some managers to believe it's
> possible for some "uneducated" operators to do something that an
> "educated" manager cannot understand.

Other top managers agreed:

> Our managers thought there was something magical in the manager's
> role. They were looking forward to authority, respect, and power.
> They came in with traditional expectations while we are struggling
> to create a new image of the manager.

In Cedar Bluff, the systems designers also had contributed to the
difficulty of using the technology to facilitate learning for either managers or operators. Systems like the Overview System and the Data
Access System were considered unfriendly, even byzantine. Those who
had learned to use them found that these systems had tremendous po-
tency, but the road to proficiency was strewn with cut glass. More than
three years after the Cedar Bluff start-up, a manager who had been
transferred to the plant six months earlier said:

> I use the Overview System damned little. It's the most user-unfriendly system I know of in my life. It is an aggravating beast. Folks who really know their way around it have a tremendous tool, but I'm not there yet. It's not humane. You can't find an instruction manual. . . . I dare you! You have to punch buttons and find out what happens. It does nasty things like lets you go down a path and won't let you branch or turn around. My frustration is my lack of knowledge about the system. It's all trial and error. If someone pulls up something that looks neat, you have to ask, "Hey, how did you get that?!"

Others voiced agreement:

> There's thirty colored keys—no numbers, no words on the keyboard, no codes to get anything. It's not even menu-driven. There are no options listed. The menu is buried in the device. Access is poor, and you don't know how to get it.

> There must be 300 applications, and you only learn to use it one at a time. You find out by accident, by seeing someone else do something interesting. I memorize keystrokes.

While the technical designers admitted that many of the systems were difficult to use, they also complained that "people are barely scratching the surface" in terms of using available data in ways that would enhance the business.

> Getting the data is one thing, but using it is another. In order to use the data, not just read the data, people need huge amounts of education. Systems people can't tell them all the ways they can use the data. We don't know what all their potential uses are. It comes from understanding your business.

The designers complained that as systems use became more central to task performance, managers and operators would need a more analytic understanding of their work in order to determine their information requirements. They would also need a deeper level of insight into the systems themselves (procedural reasoning) that would allow them to go beyond simple information retrieval to actually becoming familiar with data and generating new insights.

> People don't know enough about what goes into making up their job. Time hasn't been spent with them to tell them why. They've just been told, "Here's the system and here's how to use it." But they have to learn more about their job and more about the systems if

they are going to figure out not only how to get data but what data they need.

And so the tiger chases its tail.

There is ample evidence to suggest that these plants are highly representative among manufacturing organizations in the manner in which they have chosen to interpret new information technology. One Honeywell Corporation survey, which probed human resource planning instituted by major corporations in conjunction with factory automation, found that only one company out of fifteen had a recognized method for assessing the human resource impact of factory automation. Not a single firm had a process for actually addressing impacts, from educational needs to work force reduction issues.[5] Another survey of plant managers conducted by Honeywell Corporation among its major customers for integrated information and control technology found that, almost without exception, the "technology ideal" reported by plant managers was having one screen in their office from which they could operate the entire plant.[6] Ramchandran Jaikumar studied installations of flexible manufacturing systems and concluded that U.S. managers tend to use these systems in ways that rigidify the production process and increase central control, thus missing the real opportunities for adaptibility and customization such systems can provide.[7]

In a detailed study of the history of numerical control machine tools, David Noble documents the series of technological choices that favored forms of automation which concentrated knowledge and control in the managerial domain. In Noble's view, management's preoccupation with control over the physical and human contingencies of production reflects an ongoing class struggle in which technology is used as another means of enlarging authority and securing the prerogatives of power.[8] In a similar vein, Harley Shaiken has argued that "an obsession with total managerial control" is guiding the way in which computer technology is being used to restructure the production process.[9] Another recent study of computer technology in the workplace by Robert Howard concludes that information systems are indeed being used to reproduce the logic of scientific management—top-down control, centralization of knowledge, deskilling—more comprehensively than ever before.[10]

Earlier in this chapter, we asked the question, what drives managers toward an emphasis on the smart machine? The answers have taken us on a journey through the heart of managerial authority. The choices that managers and workers have made would seem to imply certain irreversible consequences, at least in the near future. A technology that informates injects a new ambiguity into the rationale for imperative control. Many managers, particularly those in the most vulnerable middle ranks, seek ways to eliminate that ambiguity and, instead, use technology to reproduce those experiences that help justify unilateral authority. In so doing, they must highlight the differences between themselves and those whom they would command. Driven by this need, they attempt to use the technology to reproduce experiences that force the worker into the mute role of a laboring body, while providing themselves with exclusive access to and control of the organization's knowledge base. The less attention that is paid to enabling workers to make a contribution at the data interface, the less they will be capable of contributing, and the more automatic control will necessary. This dynamic finally results in the kind of absurdity that is well expressed by this Cedar Bluff manager:

> The manager has the responsibility to make people understand what they just saw. But it's hard to teach them what is happening when they don't understand.

In the center of all this activity is the "vacuum" that one manager had described at Tiger Creek: managers limit their subordinates' discretion because they don't trust them to be smart enough; workers withdraw because they feel they have no discretion . . . and so it goes, a full-blown Laingian knot.[11]

Despite this apparent compulsion to repeat history, it would be a mistake to assume that the future can be extrapolated, logically and neatly, from the dynamics that I have described. The most interesting aspects of these organizations are not the ways in which they repeat the past but the ways in which those traditional behaviors fail to meet the challenges of an informating technology. It is necessary to examine those interstices where the scenario of the smart machine already shows traces of fragility, where the fabric has already begun to unravel. It is from these crevices of uncertainty, dysfunction, discord, confusion, incongruence, and nonsense that another branch of the dialectic is beginning to emerge.

CHAPTER EIGHT

THE LIMITS OF HIERARCHY

IN AN

INFORMATED ORGANIZATION

Much madness is divinest sense
To a discerning eye,
Much sense the starkest madness.

—EMILY DICKINSON

WHO WILL HARVEST?

In chapter 7, we saw the vigor with which authority will attempt to use technology as an opportunity to reproduce itself. We also began to glimpse the peculiar challenges to authority that derive from the informating process. A technology that informates can have a corrosive effect on the hierarchical organization of work, but its transformative power finally depends upon a series of crucial managerial choices. When the plant manager asks, "Are we all going to be working for a smart machine, or will we have smart people around the machine?" he portrays two divergent scenarios. In the former, the line that separates workers from managers is sharply drawn. Workers are treated as laboring bodies, though in fact there is less that their bodies can contribute in effort or skill. As workers become more resentful and dependent, managers react by sinking more resources into automation. In the alternative scenario, both groups work together to forge the terms of a new covenant, one that recasts the sources and purposes of managerial authority. The choice to automate will strike many as the easier and more expedient of the two. There are, however, fresh complexities that muddle and confound the seductive elegance of that solution.

Three years into the Cedar Bluff start-up, and three years after the first wave of major technological conversions at Piney Wood, a growing number of managers in each mill had tasted enough of the dynamics of machine dependency to identify a potential future that was all the more frightening for the way in which it no longer seemed outlandish. A top manager at Piney Wood described it this way:

> The fear is that people will become an extension of a machine, and in this way of someone else's logic process. I would just as soon throw some of these new systems away and invest our money in training people how to think. The operator has to understand the logic patterns. We need to equip machines to help us, not to replace us. Individuals literally become an extension of the tool. I have asked our other top managers, where does the computer fit in the hierarchy? Will we end up with thinkers at the top, the computer at the next level down, and then the masses who if it says jump, they jump? It's downright scary.

In Piney Wood, where an adversarial culture created a natural setting for the logic of automatic control, many managers were finally forced to acknowledge the way in which the lack of intellective skill development ultimately limited operational competence and prevented the organization from exploiting the opportunities created by so much new data. One manager framed the problem this way:

> As the plant becomes unified under a computer system, if the master computer screws up, no one else will know about it until there is actual physical evidence. Using computers to handle unmanageable amounts of information is necessary, but who will manage the computer? What will be the skills necessary to do that? What kind of training will people need?

Other managers voiced similar concerns. They spoke of the importance of troubleshooting and problem-solving skills at the data interface, in addition to a solid understanding of the process. There was a growing perception that instead of a gut feel, operators would be required to have a level of technical competence that would even exceed the current expectations for intellective skill within management. In short, intellective skill would become the new grounds for "knowing better" than the systems one operated. Intellective skill would be necessary if those closest to the point of production were to know when to say no.

> We need more understanding of the theory of the process, a higher level of knowledge of the equipment and process operations. You can't afford to build in everything into the computer. And you don't want to have to back up everything. You need people to understand what they're looking at and know that when this says this and that says that, it's got to be a lie.

Most of Piney Wood's operators had arrived at a similar conclusion as they thought about what would constitute the basis of their expertise. Some insisted that only the hands-on knowledge honed by years of experience would provide an operator with enough judgment to be able to be critical of what the computer presented to him or her. Over the three-year period, however, I began to hear a new point of view, one that reflected a growing awareness of the profound and irreversible nature of the changes that were occurring. The operators seemed to feel that they faced a choice of either taking direction from the computer system in a kind of stupefied fog or developing a sophisticated understanding of the computer system that they could then use to express their in-depth knowledge of the production process.

A new sensibility was reflected in the belief that superior process skills would no longer have value if they could not be expressed in the terms of the computer system. Operators saw that if they did not make a serious attempt to develop intellective skill, any possibility of judgment and accountability would be lost to the systems that claimed to supplant human direction.

> I am used to using my own techniques and systems for how I run my job. Now they have put my hands into the computer, and I am just a puppet, a common laborer. Therefore, if I want to have value in this new environment, I have no choice but to learn the computer.

Management's growing recognition of the need for critical judgment at the information interface was accompanied by the realization that the emphasis on the smart machine prevented the organization from exploiting the vast quantity of new information for fundamental business improvement. One line manager complained:

> We have cut out so many people there is no one to do the neat things
> we could use the information for. It's like a vast crop and no one to
> harvest it.

Other managers agreed:

> We have concentrated exclusively on job elimination. But we are not
> dealing with the people we have left. We need to look at added value
> and we don't know how. Unfortunately, no one is considering the
> trade-offs.

The ill-considered trade-offs involve the special characteristics of a technology that informates. As more and more managers throughout the three plants gained experience with advanced information technology, they began to see that dealing with the tidal wave of increased information in a timely and insightful way was likely to provide their most crucial source of comparative advantage in the emerging economic environment of global markets and cost-conscious consumers. Many managers had begun to sense that technology alone would not provide an enduring competitive edge, as it would become widely available and quickly equalize competition within the marketplace. If the full power of the data interface were to be exploited, then the organization would need people at each level who could analyze and respond to the data most relevant to their functional responsibilities. This implied a new vision of the organization and a strategy of technological deployment that gave preeminence to the informating capacities of the technology.

At American Paper Company, many of the senior managers who had observed and considered the progress of advanced information and control technology at the three plants had come to question the conventional wisdom about applications of computer technology. It was fine to read about the information explosion in the popular press, but it was another matter to observe the manufacturing sites caught in a deluge of data. Tiger Creek's experience with the Expense Tracking System had demonstrated the potential benefits of developing intellective skills at the data interface. There was a growing sense that the unique capabilities of the technology for generating more, better, and different data than had ever been available would require organizations to invent an entirely new logic for deploying the technology. Some believed that organizations in the future would achieve competitive advantage based on their ability to better understand their own businesses and apply imagination to newly available data in order to generate higher levels of innovation. A corporate vice president, reflecting on the emerging manufacturing environment, struggled to formulate such an alternative:

> What has been managerial access to information is not as comfortable a notion as it may seem. There has been a fear of letting it out of our hands—that is why information is so carefully guarded. It could be misused or misinterpreted in a way that cannot be managed. Traditionally, we have thought that such data can only be managed by certain people with certain accountabilities and, I hesitate to say, endowed with certain skills or capabilities. But with the new technology it seems there is an almost inevitable kind of development if you have as a goal maximizing all business variables and maximizing the entire organization's ability to contribute to that effort. I don't think you can choose not to distribute information and authority in a new way if you want to achieve that. If you do, you will give up an important component of being competitive.

Critical judgment means the capacity to ask questions, to say no when things are not right. It also creates the possibility of asking "why?" or "why not?" One of the Cedar Bluff managers most respected for his willingness to "pass the knowledge down," described what he called "the developmental learning process" that operators must go through if they are to become critically competent at the data interface. He recognized its implications for managerial authority.

> At the first level, of course, people need to know how to keep the equipment running. But the next step is to ask, "Why am I doing what I am doing?" Only if people understand why, will they be able to make sense of the unknowns. The third step is process optimization and diagnostic problem solving. At that point, they can hone in on the real issues. Once this happens, the need for management goes down the drain and my job is over.

Some managers continued to struggle with their own sense of vulnerability; they recognized that subordinates' questions could all too easily unravel the painstakingly constructed facade of infallibility to which many still clung.

> Every day I go up and look at the screens, and I ask questions, and my questions generate questions. I do lots of probing, and often I

> don't know the answers. Asking questions puts me in a vulnerable position. I show more ignorance than I like to show. When I get conflicting answers, I pursue that, and usually I find that they don't know why they are doing something that way. I am learning as much as they are with the questions I ask.

Others had begun to discover new mechanisms of influence associated with this learning process, even as their conventional sources of influence were in decline. They had begun to see that the interpretive process itself could be a powerful vehicle for extending one's influence while encouraging learning.

> In this environment, the key to influence is not telling people what to do but in helping to shape the way they interpret data. For example, in our unit, information is available to everyone, but I am the only one who can interpret it. I can either give them the result of my interpretations, or I can show them how to interpret it. If I choose the latter, I increase my influence. Now there are fifteen people who think like I do. And it is not just data. It is the priorities and philosophies that I bring to the analysis.

Questions, in a fundamental way, are inimical to authority. The question values change over tradition, doubt over reverence, fact over faith. The question responds to knowledge and creates new knowledge. The question initiates and reflects learning. The question is incompatible with the unity of imperative control. Yet the question is essential if information is to yield its full value. Obedience will not lead to and does not require a depth of understanding. But in a world where value is created through understanding, obedience no longer fulfills the demands of production. An operator at Cedar Bluff reflected:

> We need to know the whys of this process. I can't just punch this button because I was told to. I have to do it because I know why and what happens. That's the only way I can run it better.

LIFE AT THE DATA INTERFACE

Work Is Invisible

An informating technology challenges the organization to recognize the skill demands associated with computer mediation and the redistribution of knowledge that intellective skill development implies. Yet the intricacies of life at the data interface can confound managerial assumptions in still other ways. Obedience has been the axial principle of task execution in the traditional environment of imperative control. The logic of that environment is reproduced when technology is used only to automate. When tasks require intellective effort, however, obedience can be dysfunctional and can impede the exploitation of information. Under such conditions, internal commitment and motivation replace obedience as the primary bond between the individual and the task.

As the work that people do becomes more abstract, the need for positive motivation and internal commitment becomes all the more crucial. It is far easier for a manager to determine that a worker has not properly repaired a boiler (it continues to malfunction) or has failed to adequately monitor the levels of a surge chest (it overflows). What will ensure that when an operator is face-to-face with a real-time array of relevant operating information, he or she will actually be responsive to it and will exert the intellective effort that is necessary to go beyond the surface of the data and learn from it? How does the manager evaluate the possibility of missed opportunities to learn more about the production process and to improve operations? In the world of industry, where workers' bodies have been the target for precise performance measures from time-and-motion studies to piecework rates, how does a manager measure the ability to solve problems, to analyze, or to think critically at the data interface?

The shortcomings of a traditional approach to supervision and evaluation were evident at both Piney Wood and Cedar Bluff, where computer mediation had altered the appearance of work. Even as managers exhorted operators to trust the computer system, they had difficulty accepting that when the worker finally did so, he or she was still "working." The complaints voiced by many managers revealed their conventional assumptions about the nature of effort. Work and skill were almost exclusively associated with those activities that require the active engagement of the worker's body.

As operators learned to rely on the computer systems, many managers saw them as having succumbed to a self-indulgent laziness. Some managers at Piney Wood complained:

> One of our problems now is that we have created a lazier operator. There is less to do physically, less physical involvement. It requires more and more prodding to get him out of the control room and do

detailed jobs. Now they sit with their feet propped up, waiting for an alarm bell to go off.

A number of managers at Cedar Bluff voiced the same complaints:

> Because so much information is available, you have a tendency to sit down and look at eight or nine key variables and let the rest go unless there is some kind of an alarm to alert you that something is off. You sit and stare at something instead of walking around looking at things.

It is true that some operators experienced the computer as an excuse to escape tasks that were unpleasant and physically depleting. But many of them believed that they were simply beginning to accept the implications of the transformation of their work. The terrain of effort had shifted to what they could do with their minds, but it was difficult to fully comprehend that one could be working while sitting still. The trade-offs were perplexing, even for the operators themselves.

> I have thirty-six main screens to watch, and fifteen are really critical. I need to be mentally alert. On a bad day, I can look at the screen and ask myself, "Why am I looking at this?" If you want to get into it and do everything right, it takes a lot out of you. If I am in a bad mood, I would rather be out in the process. If I screw something up out there, no one will see it. But it is so much easier to be in here; it is hard to give that up. Why should I kill myself?

On the one hand, this operator recognized the pressure of the intellective demands he confronted in the control room. The consequences of "screwing up" can be far greater if one makes a mistake through the system than if one makes an error on a discrete piece of equipment. It is easier to be doing something physical when the stress begins to eat at you. Finally, it is hard to give up the gracefulness of work that does not use the body up. Like the ancient Siren, freedom from physical effort is almost impossible to resist.

Many operators felt confined by this paradox. They had been required to devalue their action-centered skills and the activities in which those skills were displayed. They had been pressured into trusting a medium that initially evoked suspicion, doubt, and frustration. Some came to embrace the new circumstances as an opportunity to escape from physical effort. Others took pride in discovering the new modalities through which they could have effects, and they found that the reduced physical requirements of the computer control room provided an extra measure of pleasure. Under these circumstances, are workers lazy, or are they simply living out the implications of the technological transformation that has rendered work abstract? Have they lost the motivation to make a contribution, or is that contribution now dependent upon one's quality of mind and intellective effort? Should we conclude that these operators had given up on work or that the very nature of life at the data interface had now come to define work? Operators at Piney Wood said:

> The managers see us sitting, and they think we are not doing anything. If I am not moving, they think I am lazy. If I am sitting, that means I have my mind on something out there in the process. Before, you had to walk around to see what was happening. Now we can see it from in here on the computer.

> My managers think I should wear my britches out all the time. But when I am watching the computer, I am working. They think I am goofing off, so I am afraid of being caught in the control room. Here in Piney Wood, people think that the only real work is physical work. But the key man at the computer has the most responsibility.

These complaints were not exclusive to Piney Wood, where the psychological impact of technological change was most extreme. At Cedar Bluff, most operators had been "raised" with the new technology, but the majority of their managers had enjoyed careers in more traditional plant environments. They responded to production pressures in the only way they knew—they wanted to see the operators "working hard," and this meant bodies in motion:

> Managers come in here, and they think we're not working if you've got your chair kicked back and you are watching a screen. They can't see you thinking. They can't look inside your head. What is work now, anyway? It seems to me that our work has really changed, and our work is now a lot of sitting, and watching, and thinking. You try to anticipate problems and concentrate on the process, even if you are having a conversation. Your mind never leaves the information.

> My manager wanted the other managers in the area to believe I am a good worker. So when they were nearby, he told me to go out into the process and clean up a pile of wood chips so they could see me working.

> Our manager tells us to sit up straight so he can see that we are paying attention.

There were at least some managers in Cedar Bluff who realized that the abstraction of work necessitated a fundamental reappraisal of their methods of supervision and evaluation. They had begun to grapple with the notion of supervising what people were doing "in their heads," but the first step was to invent a way to make that activity more "visible." The plant manager regarded this as an issue of real importance, insisting that some of the most vital questions confronting him concerned how to effectively manage the operators' cognitive life.

> What are the operators really doing at the screens? What is actually going on in their heads? How are they reacting to the information they see? Where are their skills leveling out? What is the degree of concentration and full use of the individual that we are achieving? We need to know these things so that we can figure out how we structure their minds so that they are consistently aware of what is going on.

Cedar Bluff developed an elaborate "qualifications procedure," which required each hourly worker to appear before a panel of process experts drawn from the plant and from the wider company. The panel would pose a variety of open-ended questions designed to elicit the depth of the operator's process knowledge and problem-solving skills. People would be asked both what they would do under a particular set of operating conditions and why they would choose that course of action. The goal was "to understand how an operator sees the process, what is in their heads, their level of conceptual skills. The procedure asks them to say how they think."

Such a procedure puts a premium on an individual's capacity for verbal explication. It is unlikely that one would be seen as very proficient without a well-developed ability to articulate one's thoughts in what Bernstein called an "elaborated" linguistic code. Speech had become an important vehicle for making visible what was "in people's heads."

> In my first evaluation, I got dropped down a curve because I wouldn't talk. I like to take it all in and figure out my evaluation of the situation. But I knew my stuff and surprised them about their initial evaluation of me. The second time around, I was able to tell them what I thought.

The qualifications sessions were charged with so much tension that on at least one occasion, a manager's office was burglarized. The notebooks containing questions for the qualifications examination in his area had been stolen in the night.

There were some managers and operators, however, who believed that the inability to "see" what was taking place inside someone's head encouraged managers to use more subjective, trivial, and even irrelevant criteria for judging an operator's competence.[1] Many workers complained:

> The people who get the highest rankings do the most talking, but it can be a real snow job. The managers can't see the work, but they can hear you talk, so that is what they pay attention to.

> Managers can't tell if you are operating the system right or wrong. They just see people with long hair or a beard, and they evaluate you on perceptions, not on actual fact.

Many managers were in agreement:

> Since it's hard to see what people do, you tend to get rewarded if you are a neat dresser or if you make it sound like you did great.

> It's not easy to tell if people are working, so you tend to fall back on appearances or personal liking. We respond more than we should to the management of appearances.

At the same time, more managers were beginning to discuss the need to manage the psychological relationship between the worker and the data interface. They had come to the conclusion that, in the final analysis, only the strength of an operator's commitment and motivation would ensure high-quality performance. This commitment would be developed as operators felt they had a real share in the business, an opportunity to learn, and the freedom to inquire without confronting arbitrary barriers of managerial authority. As one operator put it:

> The money for this job is very good, but that won't keep your enthusiasm high all the time. Around here, you get enthusiastic when you can talk about reoccurring problems with other people. When managers share information and help us track results that we would not normally have access to, that kind of information peaks enthusiasm.

A few managers had begun to see the implications of intellective work for their supervisory approach:

There is just so much going on here that we call "work" but that you can't see. You can look busy and not be doing a damn thing. If someone is productive, they are asking questions, interested, and inquisitive.

As action becomes secondary to intellective effort, our images of work continue to draw upon a set of experiences that are as old as our species. It is the body that works, and until quite recently, no amount of mechanical assistance has overcome the central fact of bodily involvement. As long as the body defined the scene of work, face-to-face supervision had real meaning. When work is abstract, direct supervisory observation is not well equipped to discern the quality of performance. This quality is itself now an abstraction that must be deduced from more subtle behavioral cues, such as inquisitiveness, or from the objective record of operating results.

Work Is Responsibility

Another aspect of the transformation of work at the data interface concerns the heightened responsibility of jobs that demand continual responsiveness to a flow of data. In a traditional work system, job descriptions carefully define the range of a worker's responsibility and, together with considerations of seniority, are used as the index for decisions regarding promotions and compensation. The logic is such that increments in years of experience imply eligibility for increments in responsibility, which in turn imply increments of pay. Narrow definitions of occupational functions are feasible in a world of action, because events have observable boundaries. In a traditional manufacturing environment, machinery makes it possible to locate work, and to a large extent, responsibility could be defined concretely in terms of where one stood and the equipment with which one engaged. Actions make it possible to see work, so performance can be evaluated based on observation as well as output.

As work becomes computer mediated, it is difficult to distinguish responsibility from the work itself. Much of what now constitutes "work" involves the mindfulness and intellective effort necessary for continual responsiveness at the interface. What, finally, is the difference between being responsive and being responsible? *Webster's* defines *responsive* as "answering" and *responsible* as "liable to be called upon to answer." Looked at this way, responsibility implicates the worker as the one to respond: the capacity to comprehend and react to data becomes the essence of work. The limits of responsibility thus would be determined by the limits of what an individual could appropriately be expected to be responsive to. How should limits be drawn, when the obvious limitations of geography and action no longer apply?

The entire technological apparatus of the mills, hardware and software, was oriented toward broadening the domain of potential responsiveness. Alarms, closed loops, centralized data displays, data summaries, graphics—these are all mechanisms that serve to increase the amount of data for which an individual can be responsible, as they augment and stretch the capacity for responsiveness. A senior technologist involved in the design of integrated information and control technology wondered how reasonable limits on the breadth of job responsibility should be set:

> How much data can one person actually control? When you can centralize information in space and time, you are only limited by intellectual capacity.

The objective integration of the production process created by the new information and control systems creates jobs that take an integrated view of operations, and such jobs are intrinsically more responsible. The message underlying the emerging job structure is that being exposed to data implies that a person sees, comprehends, and is appropriately responsive. For example, in Piney Wood's bleach plant and powerhouse, operators found that instead of having data from local instrumentation regarding the discrete pieces of equipment for which they were responsible, they now routinely saw data that corresponded to many aspects of their unit's operations as well as data on operations in other parts of the plant. The assumption here, only occasionally made explicit, is that such newly visible data becomes the responsibility of those who see it. It is further assumed that the individual who views the data actually sees the data and assumes responsibility for what is seen.

A manager at Piney Wood, who has worked closely with his operators in the conversion to the new microprocessor-based control system, explains:

> In computerizing the controls, we exposed people to data that had nothing to do with their jobs, but they couldn't ignore the data once they identified it. So they are taking the responsibility without being

formally assigned the responsibility. Before, they were not allowed to touch the instrumentation and did not cross the borders between jobs.

Cedar Bluff's managers also admitted that there had been a tacit transfer of responsibility to the worker at the data interface:

> If you see the data, even if it's not about your own area, it's your responsibility to bring it to someone's attention. It's a blanket responsibility. Everyone is responsible if you see something that doesn't look right.

However, in a traditional workplace like Piney Wood, where even small increments of responsibility are treated in terms of their dollar value and seen as a reward for seniority, identifying the new work as "more responsible" meant that managers risked calling into question some fundamental tenets of the union contract. In Piney Wood's bleach plant, where the integration process was well under way and operators perceived the responsibility in their jobs as having dramatically increased, a grievance was filed and brought before the plant manager. The operators argued that more responsibility should translate into more pay. They also wanted the task of working at the interface to be confined to one or two control room positions, which would be assigned a pay rate at the upper end of the scale and opened to bidding by operators with the most seniority. The plant manager took as his primary objective maintaining the current pay levels and job definitions. He told the operators who brought the grievance:

> We have not increased your job responsibilities, and you are being paid for job responsibility. You do not have additional responsibilities; you simply have new equipment. You have new equipment, and you are required to do your same job, simply with new equipment.

Maintaining this narrow objective meant that the plant manager was not free to concede publicly the demands associated with the new technology nor to explore ways to exploit its potential. In private discussions, however, he acknowledged that the new technology provided an opportunity to fulfill a general goal of American Paper Company's approach to manufacturing management—making the worker a part of the business. He viewed the technology as particularly well suited to "integrating the worker in the business," because exposure to data "increases the operator's responsibility" and ultimately his or her ability to make a contribution.

> Our desire is to make people part of the business. The technology helps that happen because it gives them the data, and this means responsibility. With this system, you push one button and it gives you all the data—trends, averages, comparisons. We choose to expose them to this integrative data because we think it will make them part of the business. . . . Let's get the responsibility more personalized so an operator can say, "On my shift, here is what I accomplished."

The problem wouldn't go away, largely because the operators in the control rooms believed that their jobs had changed fundamentally, not superficially.

> The computer is more responsibility because you've got to watch many pieces of equipment instead of just the one piece that you were assigned before. You have all the data in front of you, and you've got to be able to understand that data, to find things in it, to make sense of it, to know what to look for. You're the one with all the data, and you're the one who has to decide what to do.

They felt the weight of the demands of intellective effort and responsiveness, and wondered how the plant manager defined responsibility.

> We resent the fact that the computer has added something to our jobs. There are more things that we have to think about, know about, worry about. They add something to your job, and they don't pay you more for taking that responsibility and learning new skills. . . . We cannot get management to concede that the jobs have changed. They never will concede because it will cost them more, but most of us agreed that the computer has increased our responsibilities. My question is, what is the difference between responsibility and work? We have got more work to do. What does it mean to say that we are not more responsible?

Two years later, the issue was still a lively one in Piney Wood's bleach plant and had spread to the powerhouse as well. Workers across the plant were disgruntled. In part, their grievance focused on pay: they argued that their wages should be increased in proportion to the increase in responsibility. The unifying theme in their comments was one of a contract violated. Their "sense of contract" could not be reduced to the formal document signed by management and the union; rather, it reflected something deeper and more enduring—a coherent body of shared assumptions that seemed to be eroding rapidly without anyone ever having agreed to let them go.

This sense of contract played an important role in the operator's most intimate self-evaluation. Having a clear notion of what is expected of you on the job helps shape the personal criteria against which you inwardly assess your performance. It is as if a private competition against these standards provides the measure of one's competence. Some of the criteria that are applied in this judgment of the self come from the work group, from the collective sense of what constitutes being skillful. Other criteria, the promotions and wage increases that allow an operator to take on more comprehensive, responsible, and well-paying positions, are supplied by the formal organization.

The critical point is that the workers who draw sustenance from developing their competence seek measures that they believe will reflect their skills. These are the measures against which they want to be judged, and the reflections of competence provided by such judgments are critical to their own feelings of value. Throughout Piney Wood, operators complained, "They are not letting me do my job." For them, their jobs had been related specifically to pieces of equipment; since they no longer were able to use familiar skills, they had lost the certainty that "I can do a good job."

The sense of contract performs another psychological function: it sustains a belief in justice and fairness, allowing the worker to feel like an actor, not a victim. Under these conditions, one feels that "I know what I am getting into, I know what is expected of me, I know what I can expect in return. I have made a choice. It is fair."

The ambiguity that results from an erosion of this contractual equilibrium can evoke feelings of incompetence and victimization. When it does, reactions are hostile. In this situation, some workers focus on realigning structural elements in order to recreate a psychological equilibrium and a renewed feeling of control.

> We are a ship adrift at sea. We know where we want to be, but we don't know how to get there. Most of us are high school graduates, and we have been in the service. We are used to structures that let you know where you stand. The way we expect to get rewarded is by moving up one grade at a time in the mill. With all the changes that are taking place in my job, it's not fair, not just. It's like I hired you to rake my yard, and now I say I won't pay unless you also clean

up the garage. They keep putting off addressing the tough issues: What is my pay? What is my responsibility? How will we be trained? They should not have implemented the new technology without taking care of these things, too. If it had been fair, there would not be trouble.

In the area of the mill where operators experienced the greatest sense of ambiguity and victimization, they fashioned their own methods of reestablishing order. These workers believed that their jobs had been unfairly expanded, that they were not being empowered with the skills they needed to cope with computerization, and that their managers had abdicated their leadership roles for a kind of technological fatalism. One solution was to redefine their own jobs in terms that they believed represented a fair work load. They simply stopped performing some of the tasks for which they had formal responsibility.

> They keep giving us more responsibility, and they don't pay us more. So what we are doing is just chopping off some of the duties at the bottom of the job. This has meant that things are getting more sloppy around here. People are just not doing part of their jobs.

A second adaptation was to challenge the notion that exposure to data demands responsiveness. Piney Wood's managers began to notice that in the most adversarial areas of the plant, operators had developed a new method of expressing their discontent. Why resort to the machine-breaking tactics of an earlier century when it was so much more elegant to simply ignore data?

> We are exposing them to all this data now, which means more responsibility because you can't ignore it. But in one module, the operators are digging their heels in. They want more pay and they are mad. So they are ignoring the data they see.

INFORMATING: AUTONOMOUS PROCESS OR CONSCIOUS STRATEGY?

Life at the data interface invites the worker into the abstract precincts of managerial work. It provides access to a broader view of the business as well as a deepened understanding of one's tasks and their role in the

wider sphere of organizational functions. When work becomes synonymous with responsiveness to data, it engenders inquiry and dialogue,
thus opening the way for workers to envision new possibilities and
fresh alternatives to the reigning definitions of process, product, and
organization.

The autonomous power of the informating process was clearly felt
in each of the three pulp and paper plants by workers who frequently
found themselves generating the kinds of data-based insights that their
organizations had always expected from managers and engineers.

> It is a different kind of decision making now. The computer is already
> making the smaller process decisions that I used to make. So that
> means I have to make the larger decisions and I have to have the
> information to make those decisions.
>
> Having access to so much information makes you think ahead. There
> are always some problems that you have no control over, but many
> problems can be avoided if you are just monitoring the information,
> concentrating on it, thinking about it, understanding what it means,
> seeing the patterns in it, and being alert to the things it is showing
> you. Once you gain confidence with the new technology, you have
> time to think about how to do the job better and how things could
> be done differently. That is the real potential of this equipment.
> That would never have occurred if we had just stayed with the old
> technology.

Thinking about "how things could be done differently" has not been
part of the worker's function, at least not since the advances of Taylor's
logic helped to build the management superstructures of the modern
organization, nor has the worker had access to the kind of data that
would facilitate such insight. In many industries, management itself has
had to apply enormous diligence in order to compile the kind of data
that could be subject to systematic analysis and to yield new insights
into process or product improvements.

The significance of the new opportunity open to operators can be
appraised only in light of the legacy of scientific management, which
dramatically limited the worker's legitimate contribution to the production process. Consider again the logic of Taylorism: (1) the worker's
implicit know-how is analyzed in order to generate data that contribute
to (2) the development of a series of management functions that enable
(3) management to take on responsibility for coordination and control
of the production process.

The process of automation in these plants follows precisely the same course. Just as Taylor wanted to systematize the know-how that was "in the worker's head," so process engineers and managers discuss establishing the basic algorithms to duplicate "what an operator does in his head." Automation also shares the same goal as Taylorism—to establish managerial control over a knowledge domain that serves as the basis for a division of labor that is minimally dependent upon the skills or disposition of a (shrinking) work force.

Like scientific management, computer-based automation provides a means for the managerial hierarchy to reproduce itself, because it can concentrate knowledge in the managerial domain and so be used to renew belief in the necessity of imperative control. It must be an unwritten law of social life that hierarchies will utilize any means available as a potential method for reproducing, extending, and heightening those experiences through which elite groups win legitimation. In this sense, computer-based technologies represent merely one more episode in a two-century-long effort to define, consolidate, and reproduce managerial authority.

When automation is the exclusive end of computerization, it not only repeats the structure and objectives of Taylorism but also replicates its inherent antagonisms. In one area of Piney Wood where automatic control and manning reductions were emphasized, the technology already had become the target of adversarial feelings. Operators there complained:

> They need the operators to help them figure out what the computer should do. But why should you tell a man all your knowledge about how this place runs so he can put it into a machine and then it's going to take your job away?

> It robs my dignity; it robs my dignity of what I know how to do. They are removing my job, the job that lets me use my judgment. Now if you work on any one piece of the process, you have access to information about the entire bleach plant; you have access at your fingertips. That means that my knowledge—which used to be special knowledge—becomes open and available to a lot of people.

When the application of computer-based technology informates the task environment, the results can be dramatically different. Intelligent technology textualizes the production process. When that text is made accessible to operators, the essential logic of Taylorism is undermined.

For the first time, technology returns to workers what it once took away—but with a crucial difference. The worker's knowledge had been implicit in action. The informating process makes that knowledge explicit: it holds a mirror up to the worker, reflecting what was known but now in a precise and detailed form. In order to reappropriate that reflection, the worker must be able to grapple with a kind of knowledge that now stands outside the self, externalized and public. Intellective skill becomes the means to interact competently with this now-objectified text, to reappropriate it as one's own, and to engage in the kind of learning process that can transform data into meaningful information and, finally, into insight.

> Before, we did not have any way to know what we were learning or to understand the effects of our actions. Now we have so much information and feedback—not to be able to conceptualize it is the real crime.

Tiger Creek's Expense Tracking System reveals the impact that such reappropriated knowledge can have. The operators' knowledge had been action-centered. They had no public language with which to articulate their know-how, so their influence was limited to the direct machine control changes they could make as they came on shift. An automation strategy would have meant extracting as much of that implicit knowledge as possible and building it into a closed-loop system to minimize costs. Instead, the ETS provided operators with a mirror in which to see the effects of their actions and learn the meaning of their choices. An automation strategy would have consigned such explicated material to the managerial domain, depleting the skill base and authority of the worker. In Tiger Creek, an informating technology design returned that explicit knowledge to the operators, allowing them to learn and to use that learning in the service of real improvements to the production process. The essential features of this dynamic were repeated in many examples throughout each of the three plants. Workers' influence had been severely constrained by a lack of explicit knowledge or the inability to translate know-how into the objective terms of managerial discourse. As the informating process textualized their work and task execution came increasingly to depend upon witnessing and responding to data, the boundaries that once defined the domain of managerial knowledge began to blur.

The activities associated with both automating and informating represent intellectual effort; but their objectives, assumptions, and the nature of the organizational processes they entail are different. In the case of automation, intellectual effort is a fait accompli. Learning about the processes in question has already been completed by the time automation begins. Automation thus preserves what is already known and assumes that it knows best. It treats as negligible the potential value to be added from learning that occurs in the living situation. Automation reproduces the status quo and consolidates the managerial hierarchy's monopoly over knowledge.

The informating process takes learning as its pivotal experience. Its objective is to achieve the value that can be added from learning in the situation. Informating assumes that making the organization more transparent will evoke valuable communal insight. From this perspective, learning is never complete, as new data, new events, or new contexts create opportunities for additional insight, improvement, and innovation.

The value of an informating strategy varies in relation to the degree of necessity associated with learning and innovation—necessity that may derive from market conditions, the nature of the production process, or other organizational considerations. For example, rapidly changing markets that put a premium on flexibility and responsiveness, competitive conditions that offer opportunities for value-added products or services, substantial variation in customer needs, short production cycles or variability in raw materials, interdependence among production operations or between production and other business functions, the persistence of "unknowns" in the core production process, opportunities for increased quality or decreased costs of products or services, the need to avoid the high levels of cost and risk associated with error when computer systems are broadly integrated, and the perceived need to develop and maintain a motivated and committed work force—these are factors that contribute to the appropriateness of an informating strategy. Where these factors are *not* present to any significant degree, an automating strategy is likely to be most feasible.

In the case of the pulp and paper mills, most managers recognized the presence of several of these factors and believed that an alternative to conventional automation was required. One of the easiest factors to agree upon was the presence of many "unknowns" in the core production process. Pulp and paper making remains an imperfect science; there is as yet no complete explication of the entire production process. Managers and operators alike live with a certain awe for the terrifically complex process that refuses to yield much of its essence. "We can't measure most of the things that need to be measured on a piece of equipment," they say. Operational unknowns and variability in raw materials mean that it is impossible to put an entire operation on automatic control.

There were also many managers who believed that product and service innovations would become an increasingly crucial competitive variable. Pulp makers facing increased competition from a variety of synthetic products would need to discover new ways of combining materials or of utilizing less costly combinations of materials while maintaining similar levels of quality. They believed that pressures for more customized and flexible manufacturing were likely to develop, coupled with a greater emphasis on customer integration in production and distribution processes. Many managers at the corporate level in the American Paper Company, and a significant number within each plant, believed that these current and anticipated demands put a premium on information technology as a primary means by which to learn more and to do more with the manufacturing process. Further, they had compelling evidence to suggest that each level of the organization could make an important contribution to these objectives.

I approached the dilemmas associated with managerial authority with a question to answer: would the informating capacity of the new technology be able to carry the burden of strategic change as the Global Bank Brazil visionaries had hoped, or would its effects be thwarted by the system of power relations into which it must unfold? The evidence indicates that informating typically unfolds as an objective, unplanned, autonomous process. Though a technology that informates invites learning, organizational members can find themselves confronting a system of imperative control that is inimical to learning. Under these conditions, intellective skill development occurs only haltingly, as it battles wide-scale efforts to reproduce those everyday experiences that legitimate managerial authority. Operators at Tiger Creek sought to develop their intellective skill during the graveyard shift, because it provided some of the essential characteristics of a learning environment—freedom to play, experiment, and enter into dialogue. A manager at Cedar Bluff responsible for developing the strategic plan for the new technology offered an observation. The following set of curves illustrates how he drew the distribution of what he called "intellectual, knowledge-based skills."

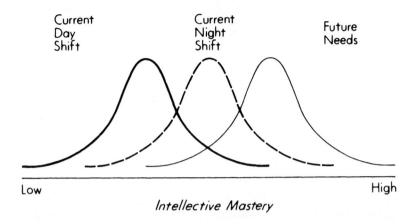

The first curve represented the distribution of operating skill in the daily plant environment. The third represented the distribution of skill that he believed the plant would require in the future. In between the two, he drew a curve representing how well the plant operated at night. He believed that the skill level was significantly greater at night, when the absence of managers freed operators to express and develop their intellective capabilities. There were many managers and operators who agreed with that assessment.

When people at Tiger Creek reflected on their involvement with the Expense Tracking System and on the controversy surrounding their accomplishments, they tended to see the system of imperative control as the critical barrier to a fuller exploitation of that system's potential. They had come to the conclusion that a system like ETS needed to be introduced in the context of more extensive organizational change if that potential was ever to be mined.

> We now believe that social systems' change will be necessary if something like the ETS is to be fully utilized. But in our planning we did not deal with those issues. We were focused on how we could save money.

An operator with seventeen years in Tiger Creek reflected:

> We are like reeds in the wind. The extent to which we can do anything is determined by what kinds of pressure the managers exert.

If learning is a pivotal experience in the effort to utilize the value of new information, then the autonomous dynamics set into motion by a technology that informates will not be sufficient to achieve its full realization. Learning requires a learning environment if it is to be nurtured as a core organizational process. Based upon what we have seen of life at the data interface, a learning environment would encourage questions and dialogue. It would assume shared knowledge and collegial relationships. It would support play and experimentation, as it recognized the intimate linkages between the abstraction of work and the requirements for social interchange, intellectual exploration, and heightened responsibility.

If the technology cannot shoulder the entire burden of strategic change, it nevertheless can set into motion a series of dynamics that present an important challenge to imperative control and the industrial division of labor. The more blurred the distinction between what workers know and what managers know, the more fragile and pointless any traditional relationships of domination and subordination between them will become.

The explication of meaning that is so central to the development of intellective skill requires that people become their own authorities. The communicative demands of abstract work compel once implicit and largely silent know-how to become psychologically active and individually differentiated. Without the consensual immediacy of a shared action context, individuals must construct interpretations of the information at hand and so reveal what they believe to be significant. In this way, authority is located in the process of creating and articulating meaning, rather than in a particular position or function. Under such conditions, it is unlikely that a traditional organization will achieve the efficiencies, standards of quality, or levels of innovation that have become mandatory in an environment marked by the competitive challenges of global markets and deregulation.

Recent studies of advanced computer-based technologies in manufacturing support this view. For example, the National Research Council sponsored two surveys of advanced manufacturing installations in order to determine the managerial practices associated with successful utilization of new technologies, such as computer-aided manufacturing, computer-aided design and engineering, and computer-integrated manufacturing. The conclusions were consistent in both studies. These new technologies require organizational changes, attitudinal and cultural shifts, creative initiatives from managers, cooperation, integration, involvement, less hierarchical organizational structures, and higher levels of skill in the operating work force. In both studies, it was clear that some plant managers were beginning to recognize these demands but did not have a well-developed understanding of the means to fulfill them.[2] In other words, the effects of the technology's informating power, together with its dysfunctional consequences for the traditional approach to organization, were being felt. However, there was as yet little evidence of a conscious strategy designed to fully exploit the new opportunities offered by an informating technology. In another study of flexible manufacturing systems, researchers at Boston University found that companies implementing advanced automation systems typically failed to exploit their potential benefits because they had failed to implement practices that would develop a flexible and knowledgeable work force, even when they had recognized the need for such practices.[3] Other researchers have also found that successful utilization of intelligent systems requires maximizing the cognitive capacity and learning ability of the work force.[4]

The informating process may not be sufficient to transform authority, but it does appear to erode the pragmatic claims that have lent force and credibility to the traditional managerial role. If allegiance to the faith that sustains imperative control takes precedence over effectiveness, then that faith will inevitably find itself attempting to draw life from withered roots. These lessons drawn from the manufacturing sector would seem to be of even greater importance for service organizations like Global Bank Brazil, where market pressure, extremely undetermined processes, and the disastrous consequences of systems errors are each acute. There is far less likelihood of settling upon automated systems for the development and delivery of new products and services in an organization like Global Bank Brazil, because such efforts clearly require innovative thinking and an acute understanding of the changing nature of the bank's markets and functions. The visionaries who worked to achieve a data-base environment are likely to encounter many of the dysfunctional consequences they predicted from the intrinsic features of an informating technology. Whether or not these dysfunctional dynamics are ever transformed by a conscious informating strategy will continue to depend upon the contingencies of managerial choice.

A redistribution of authority is both the basis upon which intellective skill development can proceed and the necessary implication of its success. Unless informating is taken up as a conscious strategy, rather than simply allowed to unfold without any anticipation of its consequences, it is unlikely to yield up its full value. The centerpiece of such a strategy must be a redefinition of the system of authority that is expressed in and maintained by the traditional industrial division of labor. As long as organizational members are unwilling to critically examine their faith in this system, individuals at every level will remain like reeds in the wind, able to do only as much as their roles prescribe, seeking the psychological equivalent of the graveyard shift in order to test one's wings, only to be pulled back daily by the requirements of the faith.

Without a capacity to envision an alternative, it is likely that our work organizations will continue to reproduce relationships that impede a powerful understanding of the economic and social potential of new technology. Philip Green used the classic terms of political economy when he posed this problem for the manufacturing sector:

> The traditional proletariat is in severe decline in advanced capitalist societies . . . but those societies continue to reproduce the proletariat as though it were still the motor force of production. What is reproduced, therefore, is an obsolescent class whose social cost (to reproduce and to maintain) is far beyond its productive capacities in a "post-industrial" or "knowledge" society. . . . The proletariat, or at the very least its children, ought to be joining the knowledge class and thus expanding the sphere of the new technology, in planned conjunction with the phasing out of the old technology.[5]

The experience of Global Bank Brazil argues that this lesson need not be framed exclusively in the language of class relations. The resistance in that organization to opening up knowledge and developing the skills with which to master information crippled the productive capacity of many organizational members at every level and hampered the bank's ability to fulfill its strategic ambitions.

The informating process sets knowledge and authority on a collision course. In the absence of a strategy to synthesize their force, neither can emerge a clear victor, but neither can emerge unscathed.

PART THREE

TECHNIQUE:
THE MATERIAL DIMENSION
OF POWER

TECHNIQUE IS THE MATERIAL DIMENSION OF POWER

In the previous chapters, authority was defined as the spiritual dimension of power because it depends upon some reasonable degree of shared faith in the values that determine rank. This faith must be renewed in daily experience in order to heighten the probability that commands will elicit obedience. Effective authority requires a continual effort to shape organizational experience in ways that replenish legitimacy. For example, Piney Wood's managers used the new technology to create patterns of daily experience that perpetuated the credibility and necessity of managerial authority. Even so, imperative control is a delicate human mechanism. Those who command and those who obey are locked in a mutual dependency that is infused with shared meaning. Command is ever vulnerable to the vagaries of changing values, conflicting experiences, and diverse interests.

Managers are often unnerved by the chronic uncertainties associated with the dependence of the superior upon the subordinate. When authority fails, or appears fragile, managers frequently look toward a second dimension of power: its material aspect, which I shall refer to under the general rubric of "technique." The techniques that comprise the material dimension of power concern the concrete practices that can shape and control behavior and so can be harnessed to the interests of those who employ them. Techniques of control, are used for monitoring, surveillance, detection, or record keeping. They can be a source of comfort and relief to those in a position of authority because they offer ways to shore up or circumvent the imperfections of imperative control.

Techniques of control protect authority by diminishing the likelihood of disobedience, which is sometimes accomplished merely by increasing the probability that acts of disobedience will be detected. They betray doubt in the unity of command and obedience, and reveal a crisis of confidence in the system of faith that ought to constrain behavior. Such techniques constitute a fail-safe system running alongside authority and casting a safety net beneath it.

When a feudal king worried about the robustness of his authority, he used a variety of techniques to detect and counter his vulnerability. He paid unexpected visits to parts of his realm in order to reinforce his authority; he made abrupt and arbitrary decisions in order to instill fear and to test for obedience; he insisted that authority could be delegated for only a short period. The ruler might exclude officials from responsibility over areas in which they had personal ties, or even take their sons or other relatives as courtiers, retainers, or hostages so that the official would fear for their safety.[1]

Managers, too, have used a wide variety of techniques to safeguard their authority and increase the certainty of their control. Part 3 explores how information technology makes itself available as such a means. First, chapter 9 illustrates how the informating capacity of the new technologies can heighten the transparency of workers' behavior as both the substance of work *and* the way it is performed become part of the new electronic text. In chapter 10 we see computer technology used as a communications medium by professionals and managers who unwittingly expose their daily dialogues to an unprecedented degree of hierarchical scrutiny. Both chapters examine how managers discover and decide to exploit the new opportunities for control that are laid open by information technology and how the consequences of their choices tend to be manifested.

CHAPTER NINE

THE INFORMATION PANOPTICON

Home
Returning to earth after his life
of weightlessness, the astronaut cannot
lift the small bouquet of flowers the child gives him.
He cannot raise his head off the pillow, pulled down
by the gravity of a dream.

He remembers nothing, no sound,
in the absolute zero of deep space,
the wild pounding of his baffled heart. He lifted
a building in one hand and a pencil in the other.
This was what he wanted: the world
like a worn stone cast into the water.
He wanted to break the promise of the body
to the earth, to stop the long descent of everyone
he loved under the ground. He wanted
to rise, an angel
in a paradise of exact data.

He spills his milk on his shirt. The earth
has darkness, and then light. The earth has birds
bickering over the last seeds. His fork slips
clattering on the plate. The road is shining.
The magnolia is shameless in the rain.

—JOHN WITTE

THE TEXTUALIZATION OF WORK BEHAVIOR

It was 3:00 A.M. when the phone rang in the home of Cedar Bluff's plant manager. The production coordinator was calling to inform him that a tank had exploded—there was one minor injury. The night crew had begun cleaning and repairs, and production was certain to be affected for several days. The next day, managers began to unravel the causes of the explosion. To do this, they summoned up data from the Overview System, which had been built to read and record key instrument values throughout the plant (more than 2,500 pieces of data) every five seconds. These values could be organized by unit or summarized to provide a bird's-eye view of the total operation. The data were available on-line for three days and then were stored indefinitely. This meant that it was not necessary to know in advance what data might be important or why; the data could be retrieved and analyzed at a later date, giving rise to ever new interpretative possibilities. People learned more about what they had been doing as they found new ways to engage with this voluminous history of minute events.

> The system fulfills an important need because our plant is so interdependent. I can't imagine managing without it. It captures history. If a screwup happens, you can go to the precise moment in time to see what happened. It helps you troubleshoot and coordinate data to figure out how to solve a problem.

The Overview System had been designed for these purely technical purposes—to accumulate, monitor, and analyze comprehensive data reflecting each moment of the production process. Once the system was in place, managers discovered that another parallel history was also being captured. This was the history of human decisions at the data interface, the history of operators' attentional behavior, the history of operator problem solving. Managers had learned to use the objective record as a means of deducing this behavioral history. One manager explained:

> Most of the key promotional criteria, including leadership in problem solving, use of discretionary time, training others, being a resource to peers, correcting problems, understanding the interdependencies of the process, project work, and hard number results are all derivable, at least to some extent, from information in the Overview System. The system gives you a larger and more objective data base for making technically related assessments of performance.

As another manager put it:

> This computer is like X-ray vision. It makes the people who operate the process very unfriendly. It's like lifting up the rock and letting

the roaches scurry out. If the employee blows it, it's clear right away.
You can know who didn't do what. If a person stops concentrating,
you know it from the data.

When the tank blew up, managers turned to the Overview System, pour-
ing through each minute of the last several days in order to see exactly
what process values had changed up until the moment of the explosion.
This information in turn would enable them to deduce the cause: had some
piece of equipment or instrumentation failed, had an operator made a poor
decision, or had an operator simply failed to take notice?

Some managers appreciated the system because it provided a powerful tool for accelerating individual learning and improving the plant's
performance. It could help a manager determine who needed more
training and in what areas; it could be a source of instructive feedback
with which operators could refine their understanding.

> The manager should use the data to say, "I've got some data for you,
> am I off calibration or did you do something incorrectly?" The person
> would then receive the data and make the right move. The manager
> is motivated by the need to know what's going on in his or her area—
> that's their responsibility. The system is a way managers can learn
> what operators need without taking their confidence away.

That vision of a cool, unruffled, nonthreatening partnership in the
data was not shared by all managers, however. Others recognized that
although using the system as a learning tool sounded like a good idea,
the path of least resistance tended to point in another direction.

> With the Overview System, I can find out everything you did except
> for what went on in your head. This can be good or bad. It becomes
> easier to catch people in judgment situations if you have some data
> to use as a basis. It makes feedback easier and more effective. But if
> someone makes an obvious mistake, the tendency is to feel that it is
> easier to fire them than to help train them.

As managers tried to unravel the tank catastrophe, operators waited
uneasily, wondering if the "hard facts," the "straight scoop," the "real-
time reality" available from the data captured in the Overview System
would mean that one of them would soon be without a job.

It is 8:00 A.M., and a craftsworker for Metro Tel reports to work
on the outskirts of town in a fortress-like building that houses the

telephone-switching circuits for a portion of the city. Not many years ago, entering the building meant reporting in to the foreman and exchanging greetings with several other craftsworkers. The foreman distributed assignments, pertinent information was discussed, and the craftsworkers set to their tasks. Sometimes they would discover problem circuits, and they would put aside their assignments in order to address the more urgent problem. At times, they sought out one another or the foreman to confer over a task, which they referred to as a "trouble."

On this morning, the building is empty. The only sounds the craftsworker hears as he enters the work area are the low hum of the electronic equipment and his own footsteps moving across the yellowed linoleum floor. He moves toward a computer terminal and enters his password, time, and location. Within seconds, the screen is filled with his assignments for the eight-hour workday. The assigned tasks are listed in the order in which they are to be undertaken, and each task is accompanied by a "price"—the amount of time in which it is to be completed. As he finishes each task, the craftsworker checks in with the computer terminal to note the completed assignment and the amount of time it actually took to do the work. He also checks to see if his work load for the rest of the day has been altered in any way. If he was unable to solve a problem, he may indicate that the task was not completed, and it will be passed along automatically to a worker on the next shift. Sometimes a task will take longer to complete than its assigned time. This may have been because the craftsworker dawdled or because he simply wasn't able to figure out the trouble. Usually it is because a very complicated assignment was underpriced. Once a price is assigned by the system, it cannot be altered, except by a foreman who is identified by a special password. Managers in the central office want to know how workers perform against the prices they are assigned. The system uses these ratios to compute "efficiency ratings" for each worker, ratings that are later used to evaluate performance and that become part of the managerial data base used for determining prices, assigning work loads, and judging organizational efficiency.

Today this worker is concerned. Three of his assigned tasks were complex and required more than the allotted time. Rather than finish the day with a poor efficiency rating, he decides to change the original prices designated for each of these jobs. He feels fortunate to know the foreman's password, which will allow him to enter the system and alter the prices; he wonders, briefly, if anyone will notice.

*   *   *

An informating technology textualizes the objects, events and processes that constitute an organization's work. The factories and offices described in the previous chapters have illustrated how this textualization process engenders new possibilities for the production and distribution of knowledge, and finally challenges a system of managerial authority that has depended on exclusive control of the organization's knowledge base. Conversely, managers can choose to design and deploy the technology in ways that reproduce old experiences of limited access to information. Because knowledge is becoming ever more dependent upon intellective mastery, this approach both preserves and extends the distance that has separated workers from managers.

In each of the organizations I studied, information technology had textualized not only the content of work but also the task-related behaviors of the men and women who engaged with the data interface. This parallel text presented managers with a new set of divergent choices. To what extent was it the occasion for organizational members to more fully grasp their own reflections, learn from what they could now see, and increase their opportunities for autonomous action? To what extent would the text be treated as a technical convenience enabling more assiduous behavioral control? Was the text to be the keystone of a new learning environment, or would the increased visibility of behavior be exploited in the service of managerial control as an antidote to the pressures of uncertainty?

PANOPTIC POWER AND THE DISCIPLINARY SOCIETY

Techniques of control in the workplace became increasingly important as the body became the central problem of production. The early industrial employers needed to regulate, direct, constrain, anchor, and channel bodily energies for the purposes of sustained, often repetitive, productive activity. Still struggling to establish their legitimate authority, they invented techniques designed to control the laboring body. The French historian Michel Foucault has argued that these new techniques of industrial management laid the groundwork for a new kind of society, a "disciplinary society," one in which bodily discipline, regulation, and surveillance are taken for granted.

This type of power is in every aspect the antithesis of the mechanism of power which the theory of sovereignty described. . . . The latter is linked to a form of power that is exercised over the Earth and its products, much more than over human bodies and their operation. The theory of sovereignty is something which refers to the displacement and appropriation on the part of power, not of time and labour, but of goods and wealth. It allows discontinuous obligations distributed over time to be given legal expression but it does not allow for the codification of a continuous surveillance. It enables power to be founded in the physical existence of the sovereign, but not in continuous and permanent systems of surveillance. . . . This new type of power . . . which lies outside the form of sovereignty, is disciplinary power.[1]

The Panopticon was an architectural innovation developed by the moral philosopher Jeremy Bentham. In Foucault's view, it is both a sign of and metaphor for this new disciplinary society. Bentham extolled the Panopticon as a technological triumph capable of exploiting the productive potential of those who had flouted, thwarted, or otherwise escaped social authority. His initial targets were convicts and paupers, though he did not fail to see the potential usefulness of the Panopticon for students, asylum inmates, and workers.

The architectural plan conceived by Bentham was first constructed by his brother Samuel, an engineer, in 1787 for a factory at Critchef in Russia. It was later adapted to the problems of housing convicts and paupers. The structure consisted of a twelve-sided polygon formed in iron and sheathed in glass in order to create the effect of what Bentham called "universal transparency." A central tower, pierced with wide windows, opened onto the inner wall of the surrounding polygonal structure, which itself was divided into narrow cells extending across the width of the building. Each cell had a window on both the inner and outer walls, allowing light to cross it and illuminate all the inhabitants to an observer in the central tower, while that observer could not be seen from any one of the cells. Mirrors were fixed around the tower to direct extra light into these apartments.

The external skin of small glass panes was held in a mesh of leadings, in a web of mullions and transoms, in a ladder of iron columns and lintels, without one inch of walling. . . . The function of inspection was greatly enhanced by the use of these materials. With masonry, nothing like the same panorama could have been achieved.[2]

The Panopticon's genius was that illumination and visibility provided the possibility of total control.

> Hence the major effect of the Panopticon: to induce on the inmate a state of conscious and permanent visibility that assures the automatic functioning of power. So to arrange things that the surveillance is permanent in its effects, even if it is discontinuous in its action; that the perfection of power should tend to render its actual exercise unnecessary; that this architectural apparatus should be a machine for creating and sustaining a power relation independent of the person who exercises it; in short, that the inmates should be caught up in a power situation of which they are themselves the bearers. . . . Bentham laid down the principle that power should be visible and unverifiable. Visible: the inmate will constantly have before his eyes the tall outline of the central tower from which he is spied upon. Unverifiable: the inmate must never know whether he is being looked at at any one moment; but he must be sure that he may always be so. . . . In the peripheric ring, one is totally seen, without ever seeing; in the central tower, one sees everything without ever being seen.[3]

The Panopticon represents a form of power that displays itself automatically and continuously. Panoptic power lies in its material structure and presence; the Panopticon produces the twin possibilities of observation and control. It functions independently of the observer in the central tower and is meant to function effectively without an observing presence. It can achieve results independent of the motives, intentions, or ideologies of the observer.

The allure of the panoptic world view is, above all, the promise of certain knowledge based upon the totality of observation it affords. The psychological effects of visibility alone are enough to ensure appropriate conduct. Certainty can be achieved even without observational effort. "He who is subjected to a field of visibility, and who knows it, assumes responsibility for the constraints of power; he makes them play spontaneously upon himself; he inscribes in himself the power relation in which he simultaneously plays both roles; he becomes the principle of his own subjection. By this very fact the external power may throw off its physical weight. . . . It is a perpetual victory that avoids any physical confrontation and which is always decided in advance."[4]

Bentham's Panopticon relied upon the materials and techniques of his day to create a structure that could autonomously reproduce an individualized social control, providing a central authority with certain knowledge of an institutional population through the architectural invention of "universal transparency." Bentham's extensive plans for the reform of prison management created both controversy and interest within the British Parliament.[5] Though his management proposals were not implemented, the central principle of continuous observation made possible by technical arrangements was to influence the administrative and architectural orientation of bureaucratic organizations from schools, to hospitals, to workplaces in which individuals are taken up as unique problems to be managed and measured against appropriate norms:[6] "Panopticism is the general principle of a new 'political anatomy' whose object and end are not the relations of sovereignty but the relations of discipline. . . . What are required are mechanisms that analyze distributions, gaps, series, combinations, and which use instruments that render visible, record, differentiate and compare. . . . It is polyvalent in its application. . . . Whenever one is dealing with a multiplicity of individuals on whom a task or a particular form of behavior must be imposed, the panoptic schema may be used."[7]

THE PANOPTIC POWER OF INFORMATION TECHNOLOGY

Information systems that translate, record, and display human behavior can provide the computer age version of universal transparency with a degree of illumination that would have exceeded even Bentham's most outlandish fantasies. Such systems can become information panopticons that, freed from the constraints of space and time, do not depend upon the physical arrangement of buildings or the laborious record keeping of industrial administration. They do not require the mutual presence of objects of observation. They do not even require the presence of an observer. Information systems can automatically and continuously record almost anything their designers want to capture, regardless of the specific intentions brought to the design process or the motives that guide data interpretation and utilization. The counterpart of the central tower is a video screen. The web of windows is replaced by procedures for data entry such as microprocessors built into operating equipment, or the control interfaces that record operator inputs at

Cedar Bluff, or the daily system updates provided by the craftsworkers in their remote field sites at Metro Tel.

What is the allure of panoptic power? Why do some managers look toward information technology as a way of achieving control, when the same results might be accomplished by simply managing the authority relationship? The manager's world is an interpersonal vortex of relentless demands upon personality, ego strength, and empathy. Managers face the continual problem of getting others to do what the organization requires of them, and the manager's action-centered talents in the service of *acting-with* are a crucial factor in determining the likelihood of success. With the professionalization of management, a vast body of literature has generated a mountain of sometimes contradictory advice on how managers can cope most effectively with this central and often terrifying requirement of face-to-face engagement with an "other." Managers are exhorted to revamp their methods of communication, invite feedback, give feedback, listen, coach, facilitate, manage by objectives, encourage autonomy, provide vision, et cetera.

These demands are further complicated by the mutual dependency of the authority relationship, which is based upon reciprocity and so requires mutually advantageous conduct. Mutual dependency derives from the fact that both the manager and the managed have the means with which to counter the behavior of the other. Reciprocal relations are not mechanical—they must be continually nurtured and cultivated if reciprocity is to be adequately fulfilled—and they are inherently uncertain because reciprocity also can be withheld. Managers can wish to avoid reciprocal relationships because of the psychological effort they require and the necessary ambiguity they entail. Under these conditions, any alternative that promises to achieve managerial objectives while sidestepping these uncertainties may be irresistibly attractive.[8]

Techniques of control and the panoptic power they convey offer one such alternative. Information systems can alter many of the classic contingencies of the superior-subordinate relationship, providing certain information about subordinates' behavior while eliminating the necessity of face-to-face engagement. They can transmit the presence of the omniscient observer and so induce compliance without the messy conflict-prone exertions of reciprocal relations.

As an informating technology textualizes a wide range of workplace behaviors, new patterns of conduct and sensibility emerge from the heart of the panoptic vision—the secret comfort of the one-way mirror, the yearning for omniscience in the face of uncertainty, the conformity-inducing power of involuntary display. The panoptic power of information systems was evident at both Cedar Bluff and Metro Tel, and the social-psychological dynamics unleashed by these information panopticons unfolded with clockwork consistency across each organization.

Panoptic Power at Cedar Bluff

Though managers at Cedar Bluff were frequently drawn to the advantages of the information panopticon, the systems they relied upon to achieve universal transparency had not been developed for that purpose. For example, the Overview System received real-time data from the plantwide control system. It was referred to as a "snapshot of what's happening"—one glance at the summary screen and the operations of the entire plant were visible. The system had been developed as a solution to problems that were pragmatic, immediate, and technical: to achieve better process control, to achieve higher levels of reliability, and to have better information for the purposes of process optimization and improvement. Once in place, these technical systems offered opportunities to better cope with some of the chronic exigencies of the managerial predicament, particularly the felt need for certainty as a form of release from the personal risk, exertion, and dependency associated with the authority relationship. The techniques of panoptic power were typically developed after the fact, by coincidence and by accident, as managers discovered ways to colonize an already functioning portion of the technological infrastructure and use it to satisfy their felt needs for additional certainty and control. The plant manager admitted:

> Our information capability did not evolve this way consciously. The evolution of the system was not seen as an opportunity to gather total information; rather, it was seen as an opportunity to create better process control. We are a giant laboratory; everything is new and up for grabs. We don't have the answers.[9]

To be sure, some managers saw the enhanced certainty of their information about subordinates as an opportunity to accelerate learning and improve performance. They found that the data from the Overview System made it possible to survey a wide range of behavior for evidence of irregularities. To the extent that the sources of such irregularities could be discovered, the data could be used to "coach" subordinates and to help them realign their behavior within acceptable standards. One manager recounted:

> We have tremendous amounts of information about people in our computer, and there are positive reasons for it. It can be used for coaching. When a person goes to the storeroom, he will give his employee number when he takes something out. If a person consistently seems to get the wrong work order number or charge to the wrong department, we can give them coaching as to why it's important to give the right data, how we are going to use that data, et cetera. Right now, we only know that certain individuals aren't giving the right coding information, but we don't know the reason. . . . Is it a problem in knowledge or in execution? We don't know if they are trying to pervert the system or sabotage it, or just don't understand how the data can be used later. By finding out who the individuals are and who we need to coach, we stand a better chance of resolving the situation.

On the other hand, many of Cedar Bluff's managers were more interested in the possibility of obtaining foolproof data than in the opportunity of using such data for coaching. In the context of a conventional technology, managers had to rely on their subordinates for valid information. The quality of the data they received was likely to be a function of the quality of the reciprocal relationship they had established. In contrast, an informating technology could provide valid information under any conditions.

> When I managed in the older plant, we depended on our hourly people keeping logs. We had to rely on the operators' putting true numbers in the logs. The computer takes away this need to rely on someone's integrity. People were very apt to fudge the numbers to cover their own ass. Now we no longer have that problem because the computer doesn't lie, at least not intentionally.

This capability is more than just a matter of convenience. It alters familiar contingencies in the process of management and creates new ones. The computer can be less an aid to supervision than a substitute for the supervisory function. For example, in most organizations, termination decisions are considered grave enough to require exhaustive documentation. It has become increasingly important for managers to document carefully the examples of an employee's behavior that might warrant separation from the company, because supervisors can be accused of bias in their assessment. Such evidence might take a year or longer to compile. During that period, the employee would be likely to learn of the effort and perhaps even receive feedback that may help to improve his or her behavior. In the Cedar Bluff "laboratory," managers discovered that the impartiality and detail of data from the Overview System provided an ironclad basis for some difficult personnel decisions that in a conventional context would have taken months or years to execute. As the plant manager described it:

> We have disciplined and terminated people based on information from the Overview System. It provided information on incidents which showed that the individual was not performing to basic knowledge requirements. By recording what happens to all of the instrumentation in a given part of the process on a five-second basis, we can see exactly what was done, what should have been done, and what was not done. Since you know the people that were there, you know what they did or did not perform. This becomes independently verifiable because the system knows it.
>
> You can take a piece of paper right out of the Overview System and put it into someone's performance file, and this contributes to their promotion. It can be used for counseling, for guidance, for promotion, and for discipline. Without the information coming from the system, it would be difficult to have absolute proof of poor performance. If the poor performance had occurred on shift, maybe it would have been picked up. In general, it would have been deduced at some point through greater accumulation of incidents. Therefore, the termination might have occurred a year later because a case would have had to be built, and it would have cost the company a lot more.

Some managers who observed the tendency to use the Overview System as a substitute for personal supervision believed that it allowed managers to distance themselves from the kind of qualitative knowledge about one's subordinates that was so vital in maintaining good reciprocal relations.

> If I didn't have the Overview System, I would walk around and talk to people more. I would make more phone calls and digress, like asking someone about their family. I would be more interested in what people were thinking about and what stresses they were under. When I managed in another plant without it, I had a better feeling of the human dynamics. Now we have all the data, but we don't know *why*. The system can't give you the heartbeat of the plant; it puts you out of touch.

They realized that the computer system could not tell why an operator made an error or what failures of commitment or comprehension contributed to poor decisions and missed opportunities for process improvement. Such insights could be gathered only in direct interaction. Whether managers experienced panoptic power as an unfortunate crutch or as an invaluable solution seemed to depend on their tolerance for uncertainty and the degree of confidence they felt in the interpersonal skills that could assure reasonable levels of control through healthy reciprocal relations.

Cedar Bluff was an organization committed to participative management and thus was characterized by a better-than-average ability to tolerate ambiguity. Still, the interdependency of the production process, the systemic and costly consequences of human error, the responsibilities felt by managers to have the answers, and the psychological exertion of the face-to-face relationship conspired to make universal transparency irresistible for many of its managers. As a result, panoptic power was slowly transforming the administrative assumptions and practices of the managerial hierarchy.

Panoptic Power at Metro Tel

Metro Tel was part of a large and highly centralized telecommunications company. Both technology and work organization were standardized across all the firm's operating companies. While many of the men and women at Metro Tel had worked together for as long as fifteen years, the lines between workers and managers were firmly drawn. Workers were unionized, members of the Communications Workers of America. Though there was little overt hostility, subtle adversarial relations and mutual suspicion pervaded the organization. Some managers admitted that evaluations of workers were biased according to "who we want to become part of our group." In their turn, many workers seemed intent on limiting their effort to fulfilling only the minimum standards of adequacy.

In Metro Tel, the drift toward increased reliance on panoptic power was given a boost with the computer-based centralization of telephone-switching functions in the 1960s. Just as operators at Piney Wood had closely interacted with discrete pieces of equipment before the advent of centralized computer control, telephone-switching craftsworkers had worked in buildings that housed switches (switching stations) for a particular sector of the city, and an individual had primary responsibility for a small group of switches. Each craftsworker was a member of a crew assigned to a single building and headed by a foreman. Like the operators at Piney Wood, the telephone craftsworker's eyes, ears, and hands were essential to accomplishing good work. Some said that hearing was the most important ability of the craftsworker, that they could troubleshoot the switches based solely on what they heard. "The worst sound of all in the switching office would be the sound of total silence. If you didn't hear a lot of clackitty clack, you knew something was gravely wrong." Other craftsworkers were known for their ability to "run their fingers over a bank of switches and feel the one switch that was off."

The computerization of switching brought with it centralized control in switching control centers (SCCs). The SCCs were established to integrate monitoring and control of the switching functions from a number of electronic switching stations (ESSs) over an extended geographical area. Information from the computerized switches was sent directly by computer to a central office to be analyzed by a second level of computers and monitored by a new breed of craftsworkers known as "analyzers." Centralization meant that instead of having crews assigned to an ESS, it was now possible to dispatch individual craftsworkers to a given ESS with instructions as to which switches were out of order and what remedies they required. Foremen, who constituted the first level of management, could now rotate between field and SCC assignments. Field foremen might supervise as many as seven ESSs, while center foremen supervised the analyzers and assigned work loads to craftsworkers in the field.

The centralization of operations in the SCC created a series of perplexing administrative problems. The SCCs were "drowning in paperwork" as they now were required to administer a range of craftsworkers dispersed across a wide area with complicated assignments and follow-up procedures. With centralization, the methods of work administration had become far more specific and complex. Before, a foreman decided what had to be done in his or her building and assigned the tasks to a craftsworker. Now, analyzers used computerized information to determine the work load for each switching station. These tasks were then prioritized, and clerks, under the supervision of SCC foremen, were responsible for assigning them to a particular craftsworker. An elaborate pricing guide, based on thousands of cases, specified how much time each job would require. Thus, computerization had meant an absolute increase in paperwork, as well as the centralization of these administrative functions in the SCC.

A second problem involved the difficulties of remote supervision. Craftsworkers were dispersed among a variety of locations, and they usually worked in isolation. A foreman could drive around to each of the buildings under his or her supervision, but this was the only means of determining what each worker was actually doing. Did the worker report to the building? How efficiently was the worker accomplishing his or her work? What problems might require further effort? The only data on work load completion available in the SCC were the paper tickets submitted by each craftsworker at the close of the day. Bins corresponding to each ESS were crammed with these paper tickets, and in order to get an overview of work in progress, it was necessary to spread out these bits of paper and "eyeball" them for a sense of task completion, outstanding work, priorities, overtime hours worked, scheduling, potential roadblocks, quality of troubleshooting, et cetera.

Collapsing under the new paperwork demands and the logistics of remote management, the SCCs clamored for a new kind of information system, one that would allow them to effectively centralize the administration of the work force, just as the SCC had centralized the administration of switching equipment. The system developers' response to this demand was dubbed the Work Force Supervisory System (WFSS). The WFSS integrated two major data bases: one that contained information on the work to be done in each ESS and a second that contained information on the work force available for these assignments. The pricing guide was automated, so the system determined the hours and minutes necessary for each task. With the integration of the two data bases, the computer system could respond to a work identification number with calculations on the amount of time the job would require and its priority status. Each job would then automatically be assigned to a worker according to an algorithm that created up to an eight-and-one-half-hour workday, while minimizing travel time. Each craftsworker who reported to an ESS began the day logging on to the WFSS computer, which printed out the day's assignments, their sequence, and their price. Workers would then update the system as they completed their tasks. Any work not completed would be reloaded automatically to the next shift, with an increment in its priority rating. Foremen in the SCC could now review workers' progress at any time of day or night. This meant real-time monitoring of work behavior: "what is pending and what is in jeopardy. The computer is the foreman's eyes and ears." Managers were now able to "monitor things that they could not even dream of before." As one foreman put it:

We direct him on what to do and when to do it at all times. He
doesn't do what he wants to do when he wants to do it.

The system had also absorbed a number of vital supervisory decisions.
For example, the WFSS's designers described the days of heated discussion that went into finding the algorithm that would automatically form
a work load for the craftsworker. The data base was built to include
information on site location, travel time, and even the number of floors
in each building. This made it possible to create work loads that minimized the amount of travel by car and by elevator during the workday.
Decisions were made as to how jobs would be reloaded automatically
if someone called in sick. Another important decision involved how to
load the worker for an eight-hour day. Suppose that while loading a
worker with the highest priority items, the computer had a choice of
forming a seven-and-one-half or an eight-and-one-half-hour work
load? Should it create a load for eight-and-one-half hours or scan the
priority list until it found a less important half-hour job in order to
total exactly eight hours? One of the system's designers described the
decision-making process this way:

> There were hundreds of gutsy human issues that had never been
> faced down before which were necessary to tackle in order to auto-
> mate these decisions. You can't believe how many hours we argued
> about this. Finally, we reached a consensus. The idea was to drive the
> craftsperson as hard as possible. Instead of going down to the next
> lowest priority, take that one-hour job. This way, we end up with an
> eight-and-one-half-hour load, but if we push them, they will do the
> work and probably do many of the jobs in less time than we have
> assigned. Unfortunately, this process was completely undocumented.
> We have no record of what these issues were or why we made these
> decisions. When the people who made them leave, no one will know
> why we designed it this way.

When analyzers in the SCC sat down in front of their computer terminals, the data they viewed was received directly from the computer-
based switching equipment in the field stations. When they noticed
"troubles" (problem switches requiring craft attention), these were recorded as work requests and downloaded into the WFSS computer. The
WFSS in turn transformed these work requests into work loads assigned
to each craftsworker in the field. Work loads could be altered as often
as fifteen minutes before the start of a new shift. Sometimes, emer-

gencies meant that a work load would have to be adjusted during the shift, but such adjustments could be made only by the foremen in the SCC whose special password allowed him or her to enter the WFSS and alter the work assignment or its price.

Computerization meant that the work itself—the condition of the switches—had become transparent. The WFSS meant that workers' behavior was now almost as visible as their work. Gone were the bins filled with paper "trouble tickets"; gone were the ledger books and files. All the information was "at your fingertips" in a moment. The foremen were full of praise:

> I can know if the work is getting loaded properly and if the craft has done his job right. You can see roadblocks instantly. I can look each day and see everything that I have loaded, if it's done, if not, why not. I can know everything in an instant.

> It is beautiful now. I can track my people's work. All I have to do is type the craft's initials in and see how he is progressing and see what his total work load was. What is his productivity? Before, we had to judge people more on hearsay. Now we have it in black and white.

The system automatically computed efficiency ratings for each worker by comparing the amount of time it took to complete a job with the amount of time for which it had been priced. Such calculations could have been generated only by a computer system, since "we could never have enough clerks to compute these kinds of ratios." The ratings were considered management information and were not accessible to the craftworkers. Many foremen cautioned against taking the ratings at face value. The most experienced craftsperson frequently was loaded with the most difficult assignments. That individual might show the worst efficiency rating simply because his or her assignments were the most complex and required more than the assigned time. Some foremen argued that the only effective way to evaluate their workers was to compare data from the WFSS to the output from the SCC computers.

> By what he told me on the WFSS about how long it took him and what he did, I can look back at the machine and see what he did in order to best evaluate him. With these two pictures, one of the machine and one of the man, I can know what he did, the exact time, how long it took. Everytime he does something to the machine, no matter what he does, I can see it and usually the reasons why. Even if I was out there visiting the buildings, I could never see all of this.

Other foremen were more cynical about the way in which WFSS was used. There seemed to be something compelling about the "black-and-white" information from the system. Because uncompleted work would be reassigned automatically, these foremen were less motivated to dig into background data in order to verify or understand the causes of the workers' behavior.

> People see that someone did not do the job, but they would never go back and see why; whereas if you were there in the building with the guy, you would know. No one seems to backtrack to find out why or when, because it will get done eventually and it is all in the computer. You tend to get away from questioning.

In fact, many of the foremen believed that the WFSS had usurped their role as the primary supervisors of the craftsworkers. There was less room for individually negotiated accommodations between foreman and craftsworker. Earlier reciprocities—you help me out now, and I'll take care of you later—had no place in a world of unilateral computerized instructions.

> Before, craft and management cared about each other if they could be useful to each other. Now the computer could care less about who you are. A person can be dealt with, but not a computer.[10]

Just as the architecture of the Panopticon was designed to accomplish supervision without the direct engagement of the observer and the observed, the architecture of the WFSS absorbed supervisory functions and diminished the necessity of, and the opportunities for, face-to-face engagement. Most foremen acknowledged that they sometimes found themselves "supervising" workers whom they had never seen. In these cases, their evaluations were based solely on data from the WFSS. The consequence, they felt, was a new impersonality and formality. Even foremen who had known many of their crew members for several years found that they now rarely interacted with their crew and knew far less about their personal problems and needs—precisely the sort of information upon which reciprocity depends.

> In the old environment, the supervisors would arrive at the same building as the craft and greet you in the morning. He would be able to walk around and talk to you, and he would see how you were doing. You had that camaraderie of communication through the visual. Now you are basically just dealing with computers and checking

on people. I can't see my men in the field now, because I look through the computer. If someone has a problem, I can't work it out with him like I used to. Does he need some time off? The computer doesn't know his problems. It doesn't want to know if his kid just passed away or if his wife has problems. Maybe I need to lay off him for a while and then later I'll know I can count on him.

The foreman's job had become one of monitoring the new text of worker behavior and responding to major gaps, inconsistencies, problems, or evidence of lagging skills.

The manager's job has had several components. There is the face-to-face part—giving orders, direction, organizing, using the manager's authority. Then there is administration, and then developing and evaluating people. A lot of the face-to-face stuff has been built into the WFSS, which increases the administration aspect. Even though it's a face-to-face job, I don't have to do it face-to-face. The computer is being my face. It's telling them what to do.

The computer is programmed to do all the thinking for me. . . . It figures out vacation time and scheduling. It calculates the time a person gets paid for. The WFSS is not a tool. It has become my job. Now I track their work to see what they are doing. Now I can see where there are problems and spend more time training people.

The computer has become an extension of the supervisor. It is the law now, black and white. There is no question there about what you have to do.

Some foremen argued that taking that extra step to engage with the craftsworker in a more direct fashion would result in better performance. They spoke of the value of periodic site visits. These foremen believed that it was important to maintain the personal relationships that would provide leverage for valuable reciprocities. Others stressed the importance of personal contact so that the craftsworker would not feel like an anonymous number in an indifferent organization.

I don't have to see the people anymore, but I think if you disregard people, they will feel like just a number. Most people will rebel if they are made to feel that way. So I think it's important to call them up once in a while and say, "Hey, I've been looking over all your reports, and I see that you are doing a good job." This way, he won't think all of his interaction with the computer is just wasted. At least you make the person feel a little more connected to something. They know that someone is paying attention.

Despite these insights into the authority relationship that punctuated the foremen's reflections, most agreed that there was a distinctive shift toward less interaction, less engagement, and more impersonally administered relationships. Once, knowledge of workers' behavior depended upon the interpersonal effort associated with maintaining the reciprocities of the authority relationship through face-to-face engagement. Centralized administration had increased the difficulty of direct supervision, and the textualization of behavior accomplished by the WFSS now made it possible to circumvent interpersonal effort entirely. Interaction had become an option rather than a necessity. Under these conditions, many foremen seemed irresistibly drawn to the WFSS for a respite from the uncertainties and personal terrors associated with managing reciprocities. They felt more comfortable knowing that they could rely on the computer to give orders.

> Back in the old days, if a guy says he didn't want to do something, you had to start trading favors with him. Now it doesn't work that way. The computer says, "Bingo—you got this assignment Tuesday night. Here is the information, do it!"

There were still cases when people failed to fulfill the instructions passed on to them through WFSS. Managers then had to decide whether to confront these individuals or avoid the confrontation, letting them slide by until so much objective documentation had been accumulated that the union would have to respond to management's complaints. One motive to avoid confrontation was that a subordinate with an aggressive personality could make life unpleasant.

> There are a lot of people we do not want to confront. If it is the kind of person that may give you a hard time, you can just ignore it. The computer is such a buffer to me as a manager that I can call up the more pleasant people and deal with them. If the others do not do their work, I will know it from the computer. I can go around their back and write things about them and turn them in and never really have to confront them.

Others wanted to avoid potential conflicts that might lead to union flare-ups or grievances. They complained that it was not worth the aggravation to go after the shirkers, because they were sure to accuse management of harassment and invite union involvement. When that happened, a foreman could not be certain of support from his or her own peers or from other workers. The tendency, then, was to take advantage of the technical buffer as a means of exercising formal control without risking the threat of ostracism associated with personal confrontation.

> If you confront a guy, even if he's a poor worker, you become the bad guy. You are alone. They come back at you with the union.

Foremen could afford to avoid such confrontations because they knew the system would automatically bump any uncompleted tasks along to the next worker. This meant that difficult assignments would repeatedly drift to the best workers, and poorer performers would be able to float through the system, at least for a while. The system could make low performers visible, but it could not ensure that they learned from that visibility or that organizational performance benefitted from their transparency. For many foremen, transparency instead had become one way to avoid managing, even as it tightened the reins of technical control.

> If I don't confront a man because he didn't do the job, who is going to know? The men know among themselves, and they become disgruntled. Yet it's a big game with the computer between us. You can keep pushing the work to the people who will do it. The other group, they can just keep going through the computer, not being confronted by anyone. No questions are asked. The top people stay at the top of the rating, and the bottom never moves. People are protected by the system because nobody wants to confront them. You know who really benefits from it? Nobody. That man is allowed to do what he wants, and I am allowed to not do my job.

System designers were aware that the WFSS made it possible for foremen to avoid face-to-face conflict with their craftsworkers. They were proud of having designed the system to accomplish just that. For example, the union limited the degree to which foremen could specify which worker would receive which assignment. The goal was to protect the top workers from always being assigned the most complicated tasks. Designers had programmed the WFSS so that each task was categorized according to its level of complexity and each worker was given a corresponding designation based on assessments of his or her ability. The system then automatically matched difficult tasks with excellent workers. Workers receiving these assignments had no way of knowing that the program was biased in its method of distributing the work. As one designer explained:

> We have been able to use the computer this way with a high degree of refinement. We can have any number of designations we please, which really works out to being able to have a designation for every person if we want to. This allows us to get around our problems with the union.

Another designer recognized that programming choices were made that would have increased the potential for conflict in a face-to-face situation. The designers felt comfortable making choices that "pushed the craftsworker harder than usual," knowing that the technical buffer would muffle conflicts that might have erupted in a more personal atmosphere. For example, one designer explained how he programmed the computer to load a worker for up to eight-and-one-half hours.

> There might be a different set of algorithms that we would have developed on the basis of people-to-people interaction than the ones we developed on the basis of envisioning computer-to-people interaction. Without the computer, we might not have deliberately decided to load eight-and-one-half-hours' worth of work, because if you did that, the craft might call you up and yell at you. With the computer, you can avoid friction. It doesn't go away, even if you ignore it—it will keep banging away, day in and day out. We knew they could not yell at the computer.

In the information panopticon, many managers are tempted to circumvent the exertions of the authority relationship—the responsibility for decisions that help shape the work life of subordinates, the perpetual effort required to nurture reciprocity, the emotional demands of face-to-face engagement with its attendant risk of conflict and confrontation. They seek other means of increasing the certainty that subordinates will produce desired behaviors. In Metro Tel, many managers relied on the technology to make behavior transparent in the belief that people are more likely to do what they are told when they know their actions will be translated instantly and displayed as electronic text. That behavioral text then becomes incontrovertible proof of obedience or neglect; this kind of proof can overpower reciprocities and bolster the manager's claim to control.

Under these circumstances, managers confront the electronic text not only in the service of their substantive tasks but also as a medium of administration. Intellective skill demands appear to crowd out an earlier reliance on action-centered skill, as managers must interpret behavior from the text rather than observe it directly. Managers at Cedar Bluff and at Metro Tel had become adept at using the data from the behavioral text to make inferences and informed evaluations. Their oral culture, highly charged with attractions and antagonisms, seemed to be giving way to a different kind of workplace. As one manager at Metro Tel described it:

> There are fewer arguments now, hardly any at all. There is less friend-ship, too. We were once a tight little group. Now we are mechanized. It is impersonal now. You are no longer close to the people you work closely with.

Still, the textualization of behavior has raised some intriguing questions that have not yet been answered sufficiently. There were at least some managers who saw the potential of the behavioral text as an instrument of learning and improvement. What are the organizational conditions under which that potential might be exploited? The answer requires a closer examination of the information panopticon. What is the extent of the transparency it promises? Does it in truth accomplish its intended effect—to induce conformity with the foreknowledge of certain and involuntary self-display?

HIERARCHY IN THE INFORMATION PANOPTICON

One way that the information panopticon departs from Bentham's principles is that it is hierarchically organized. At every level of the organization, the observer is as likely to be a target of technical control as its vehicle. Observation is double-edged: observer and observed are enmeshed in one body but are of two minds.

In the American Paper Company, networks of information systems linking plants to divisional and corporate headquarters were in the early stages of implementation. Many corporate executives had yet to become involved in using information systems, but there were already significant numbers of executives who enthusiastically anticipated access to a real-time data base that would reflect the organization's entire business. One of the top leaders in APC's corporate management voiced his expectations for the development of the corporate information system capability:

> My vision is that one wall of my office will be a screen. I can hit buttons and see my reports or any other data I want. The data base will integrate the entire organization, and all the data will be in agreement. We'll all have the same numbers. I'll be able to manipulate the data, and much of it will be of a quality that doesn't yet exist. We must have the whole company looking at data the same way. I want the president of the company to have a screen on his wall. We should be able to look at the data on a minute-by-minute basis, and the screen should be continuously updated. That way, we can see how different businesses are doing and who needs help.

Work was under way to integrate divisional offices with plant operations through real-time information systems. One divisional manager explained how he envisioned utilizing information systems to improve management results:

> With the new integrated systems we are developing, I can push the button and in one minute see which of the plant managers has the situation in control. I can manage by exception. I anticipate a screen on the plant manager's desk that flashes when something goes out of control or flags exceptions at the end of each day. The systems allow us to supplement all the bullshit with the real thing. I can call up some screens and see where something is wrong and walk right to that place. Then I can talk from real data, not just things that they are dishing up. I can use that to coach them in how they are managing their business. It gives you that check at the bottom level—are they doing what they should be?

Throughout the division, plant managers discussed their concerns about becoming transparent to their divisional hierarchy, even as divisional executives seemed insulated from the mounting anxiety. A senior manager from corporate headquarters who had been tracking the controversy described it this way:

> The plant managers are worried. They know the divisional executives want to have total on-line real-time access to the raw data from the mills, and they don't want this to happen. They have jokingly tried

to communicate this to the divisional vice president, but he hasn't heard it. There are others trying to head it off, but the push for it is very strong.

Early in the implementation process, Cedar Bluff's plant manager, the same man who coolly admired the Overview System's capacity to increase the objectivity of performance evaluation, spoke with disdain for and suspicion of the plans for a divisional information system:

> They want to have access to real-time data from the mills. But as plant manager, I do not want to be second-guessed. I don't want them breathing down my neck or wasting their time on the nitty-gritty from the shop floor. Right now, I have some flexibility in terms of deciding what data they see, when they see it, and how it is presented. If I lose control over that, it is an important piece of my job over which I will have less control.

In the course of a long discussion, he began to appreciate the irony of his case. He discovered the extent to which he was animated by the same fears, irritations, and mistrust that characterized many members of the work force. With a wide grin and nervous laughter, he let me know that he was aware of the incongruity and apparent hypocrisy of his position. In a tone of self-mockery, he reflected:

> Well, of course, when my people say it, it doesn't matter, but when I say it, it really is a problem.

As the first stages of implementation were completed, the new divisional capability began to alter the plant manager's daily life:

> When the vice president calls me at 9 A.M. from his office over five hundred miles away to ask what happened last night because he has spotted something irregular in the data, I have to have the answers for him. This means that I must get in and ask the questions earlier. He would not be calling if it were not for the information power we have—instant access. The mere presence of the information makes you ask the questions.

Some months later, he discussed Cedar Bluff's new Data Access System. He spoke with enthusiasm of the access he would have to an integrated data base reflecting the totality of plant operations and business functions. He looked forward to programming the system to flag deviations from the strategic plan, to check budget expenditures against the forecast and to portray unit productivity, reliability, absenteeism, overtime, et cetera.

> I expect the information will let me keep closer track of the units and will mean that I will do more following up with my subordinates. It will mean additional pressure on them. I plan to use the data to track my managers. My belief is that this will push them to become more computer literate, which will become increasingly crucial to our success.

Panoptic power had also found its way through every level of the Metro Tel organization. While foremen observed their craftsworkers, the second level of management used the WFSS as a means of measuring and evaluating foremen, particularly those foremen assigned to the field. During the earlier phase of centralization, which had culminated in the SCC organization, a rivalry had developed between the foremen who rotated among field sites and those who were assigned to the SCC. Work load assignments were supposed to originate in the SCC and could be altered only by an SCC foreman. However, "the field foreman didn't like not being the one who told the guys what to do, because that meant he was no longer thought of as 'The Boss.' " Without that authority, field foremen had lost the basis for reciprocal relations with their craftsworkers. They responded to this situation by frequently "breaking the load" that had been assigned from the central office. Upper levels of SCC management considered this one of the biggest obstacles to maintaining efficient operations. The WFSS, which provided a record of how many times a load was broken, was seen as a way to combat the problem. Because changing a load required entering a password, it was easy to determine whether the load had been changed from the central office or by a field foreman. These data were now considered an important indicator of the quality of work force management in a switching control center and were monitored by upper levels of management. Metro Tel's second-level managers relied on these numbers, noting that "now we can see what is going on." They also insisted that their own managers should have no use for the WFSS and the varieties of data it provided:

> I don't think my boss should get involved with it. . . . If anything is wrong, he can come and ask me. I don't think he should be involved with the nitty-gritty of running the job on my level.

Despite their concerns, the third-level manager was an avid user of the WFSS. He claimed to want a terminal on his desk in order to be able to sit in his office and punch up data that would indicate how the work in the SCC was being performed. The principal system designer had agreed to collaborate with him. As he put it, "We took care of each other. We had a secret pact, and we worked together to understand what those measures meant." The systems designer described the various ways that the third-level manager had learned to use the system:

> He was after the *Playboy* magazines and the sleeping bags—all the guys who take advantage of the night shift in our remote locations. He would compare the night- and day-shift statistics and try to use those to get the night people to do more work. He would use the data to look for the broken load and go right to that field foreman and ask for an explanation. He used the measures to look at the analyzer's job—that is, the person who spots troubles on the SCC screen and creates work requests for the craft. If you find a group of workers who say they can't find the trouble they are supposed to fix, and they are all getting their requests from the same analyzer, then we have to ask, does this person know his job?

Part of the collaborative agreement between this manager and the systems designer included protecting the manager from scrutiny at higher levels: "We agreed that the work being tracked by the WFSS would not go any higher than the third level. I didn't want the computer to show that he was doing a crappy job. He promised never to bad-mouth WFSS, because it was my system." Still, it seemed only a matter of time before higher levels of Metro Tel management would have access to similar forms of data. Their interest was not in measuring craftsworkers or foremen but in developing aggregate indicators of the effectiveness of third- and fourth-level management. Another system designer described the growing pressure for such data:

> The vice presidents of Metro Tel see they have an opportunity to increase levels of measurement of the SCC. They want us to add new dimensions to the WFSS so that they can measure on a district or regional basis and assess the effectiveness of managerial decisions at the third- and fourth-level and potentially right on up the hierarchy. This introduces a whole new set of terrors.

THE PSYCHOLOGY OF VISIBILITY

At each level of these organizations, people searched for ways to adapt to the intense illumination of the information panopticon. There was less room for interpersonal ploys or negotiated solutions and fewer hidden corners in which to enjoy anonymous repose or indulge in overtly negative behavior. To some, it seemed that only the human heart retained its privacy, out of reach and recalcitrant.

Cedar Bluff's operators recognized the Overview System's supervisory power and tried to adapt themselves to the fact of involuntary display.

> Managers use the system to see how we are doing. It's a good thing, unless you are trying to hide something. You can't hide mess-ups from the system. There are no fibs with this system.

> When I do something, it shows up on the Overview System, so I have to think about what I tell the boss. The system can give a manager information of anything that happened. Usually there is no punishment. We have a lot of pride, too, because they can also see if you straightened something out.

> There are only a few standard operating procedures we can cheat on because it can't be traced. When they can't trace it, we feel more freedom.

Some operators had discovered that the truth value of the data could also work in their favor. There were examples of operators using the data from the Overview System to prove to managers that they were not to blame for a particular problem. There were other cases where managers used the data to protect their own subordinates from being blamed for an error. Finally, operators wondered how far managers would go in their reliance upon the Overview System as the basis for decisions regarding how rewards and punishments should be distributed. Would the data be used as a guide to termination, promotion, or pay? Would this lead to an unbearable work environment or a more just organization?

Maintaining reciprocal relations also required psychological exertion on the worker's part. Some operators hoped that the new data-rich environment would remove the burden of interpersonal effort, substituting objective facts for political skills.

> There must be a reason for them to save all of this data, but I am not
> sure what it is. As the plant begins to run more smoothly, I think
> managers will start to use the data more. They will get to managing
> at a greater level of detail because of the Overview System. Will they
> start to manage against the system? How long will it be before they
> start to use it for performance verification? If they do, some people
> will probably do better as judged by objective data instead of having
> to excel at the political stuff of getting along and getting over.

As the operators pondered the implications of universal transparency, Cedar Bluff's head of systems development was grappling with
the prospect of the plant's sudden visibility to divisional management.

> We don't want them to second-guess our minute-to-minute deci-
> sions. We want them to evaluate us based on our ability to meet our
> monthly goals. So our concern is that they will be on our backs and
> we will all end up with ulcers.

His search for a solution ricocheted back and forth between the two
dimensions of power—authority and technique. First, he appealed to
the inherent rationality of authority and the covenant implied in the
structure of imperative control.

> Those at higher levels in the hierarchy know their jobs, and they
> know that we are doing our job. They shouldn't be spending their
> time on these data, and I think they know that. I am sure these issues
> can be worked through with objectivity.

According to this view, managers would be expected to rely on the
binding power of imperative control rather than on their capacity to
view subordinates in an ever-present electronic text. It assumes that
decency and rationality will prevail among those who are joined by a
common faith in the values that rank them and that ensure their mutual
dependency. Yet, as the discussion unfolded, this manager revealed his
own misgivings about the civility with which the issue would be handled. "You have to deal with the politics of it too," he added confes-
sionally. "We will have to push back all the way up the hierarchy."
What is the method for "pushing back"? His second solution was a
technological one: the plant's systems engineers would make sure that
the plant retained ultimate control over divisional managers' access
to data.

> It's OK for them to have an on-line capability if we control what they see. All they will have is a terminal designed for the purpose of receiving what we release to them. They will not have a keyboard. If they ask for more, then we tell them we don't have the technical capability to do what you asked for. Our technological solution includes the idea that we will transmit to them, and they will never request data from us. This way, we can control what they look at, and they could not just come in and snoop.

This example illustrates how a lack of confidence in the shared values of the authority relationship can lead to a new reliance on technical means of promoting group interests. Once superiors reveal their lack of trust in the power of legitimate authority to guide behavior, then subordinates are alerted to the danger of a broken covenant. When superiors betray a tenuous faith in the hierarchy, then subordinates will develop means of self-protection. When superiors doubt their own legitimacy and so turn to technique as a means of enforcement, subordinates, too, cast about for "extralegitimate" techniques of defense.

The adversarial vocabulary of "us" and "them" invaded the language of operators toward their managers, and plant managers toward divisional executives. This mistrust was not rooted in a perception of evil or malicious intent. It was, instead, the feeling evoked in the silent dance of the observer and the observed. To be visible in this way evokes a sense of vulnerability and powerlessness. The person observed begins to wonder, "Am I exposed in some way that I would not choose to be? How can I be certain about precisely what I have exposed? What is it that they might see?"

The resistance to such exposure reflects in part an effort to retain a sense of self-control and to avoid feelings of shame. What is shame and how is it activated in this context? The developmental psychologist Erik Erikson has described shame in the following way:

> Shame supposes that one is completely exposed and conscious of being looked at—in a word, self-conscious. One is visible and not ready to be visible; that is why in dreams of shame we are stared at in a condition of incomplete dress, in night attire, "with one's pants down." Shame is early expressed in an impulse to bury one's face out of sight, or to sink, right then and there, into the ground.[11]

One way to minimize the risk of shame would be to look for ways to circumvent the observer, to thwart the power of the panopticon.

This motivates managers who seek a technological solution that will ensure some measure of shadow, of privacy, and thus of self-control, in the increasing glare of the information panopticon.

These feelings rarely surface directly. Instead, they must be read from tactics, innuendo, and humor. For example, a small group of engineers at Cedar Bluff met to discuss a new automation project. The conversation proceeded in an entirely "rational" mode until the subject of real-time divisional access to the new automated data base was raised. The mood in the group shifted abruptly. The men began to giggle and to send one another sidelong glances, like schoolchildren who had hidden a frog under the teacher's desk. They attempted a few statements that paralleled the head of systems development's earlier comments on the rationality of authority. Suddenly there was a crack in the facade. One member of the group looked around and, with a sly smile, announced, "Look, if it gets to the point that they really want access, we'll just make sure it doesn't work. Right, fellas?" The group's response was immediate and unequivocal—"Right!" At that moment an awareness of the feelings they had just revealed flashed across their faces, and as if choreographed, they returned just as abruptly to an emotionless discussion of their engineering plans.

> Too much shaming does not result in a sense of propriety but in a secret determination to try to get away with things when unseen.[12]

There is another tactic for avoiding the experience of shame. The behavioral expectations of the observer can be so keenly anticipated by the observed that the foreknowledge of visibility is enough to induce conformity to those normative standards. Anticipatory conformity is a tactic for avoiding the dread associated with the possibility of shame. It accepts visibility and adapts to it by producing behavior that minimizes the risk of unwanted discovery. As the immediate environment is saturated with measurement, the pressure of visibility begins to reorganize behavior at its source, shaping it in conformity with the normative standards of the observer. On one pulp-drying machine, a microprocessor recorded each time there was a break in the sheet of pulp. The operators discovered that if the machine could be brought up in less than thirty seconds, the break would not register. As a group of managers recalled:

> The operators began to really race to beat the clock. They started to
> beat it regularly, so we changed the programming to give them only
> fifteen seconds. We found out that when they tried to beat the thirty
> seconds, they were getting too sloppy and the overall number of
> breaks increased.

An operator on the pulp-drying machine explained:

> With this information on the computer, there has been a psychologi-
> cal effect. We know there is something that will tell on us exactly.
> We can't fudge it now, so we hustle more.

Though Cedar Bluff was struggling with the challenge to managerial
authority provoked by the informating process, its commitment to
team-based participative management within the hourly work force and
its highly informated task environment had generated a policy of open
access to a wide range of operating data. Managers used the Overview
System to monitor their workers, but the workers had access to these
data as well. The plant manager believed that universal access would
create joint ownership of the data and thus joint responsibility for the
behavior it reflected.

> As long as operators get more information, too, why should they care
> that I have the data? They should expect we will question them for
> purposes of improvement. It is not my data. It is our data, all of it. It
> is OK for you in the pulping unit to question someone in woodyard.
> We want to build in a healthy contesting nature. If it is a legitimate
> business question in an area that you have some control over, you
> have to respond to questions, no matter who puts it to you. . . . Lead-
> ership should be functional, not hierarchical.

In such a view, anticipatory conformity is not only a response to the
threat of being shamed by the boss but also a method for managing
one's appearance to peers and minimizing the pressure they are likely
to exert. That pressure derives in part from internalizing management's
goals and values, and it is fueled by the functional interdependence of
production units. No single group can fulfill the normative standard
independent of the others; mutual visibility becomes an additional
mechanism for ensuring the viability of that interdependence. Universal access, as a correlate of universal transparency, diminishes the feeling of oppressive surveillance. Many of Cedar Bluff's operators voiced
feelings that did indeed reflect a sense of collective responsibility:

> Everything that anyone does is documented. Anything you do that interfaces with the equipment is recorded. It is our data, even if we don't have a need for most of it or wouldn't even know how to use it. Because we all have access, it is like we are all watching each other, not just like management watching us.

> With these systems, there is no doubt. The results are the truth. They bring the truth to management. This means managers can really see what is happening, and they have to buckle down and focus on problems. It creates a joint awareness. We end up working together more than fighting over what really happened.

There was considerable evidence that operators used their access as a way of asserting control within their own spheres of influence. When they observed peers making mistakes, they felt the right and the obligation to respond.

> One time, a guy from another area looked at this screen and caught a problem and told me about it. If another group acts crazy, we can see what's happening right on our screen. You can tell what your buddies are doing right quick. Having the system like this makes for better communication. We use the screens and that eliminates word of mouth. You don't have to have a conversation; you just pull up the screen. It's a way we provide each other with checks and balances.

Though many of Cedar Bluff's managers were determined to limit divisional access to their data, they also reacted differently when data was treated as a communal resource. They believed that the truth value of the data tended to reduce the amount of bickering involved in establishing the facts and to eliminate the feelings of resentment or frustration that typically followed such disagreements. The information system was experienced as putting the facts on a higher plane. Cedar Bluff's plant manager claimed:

> In those areas of the plant that are most highly penetrated with automated information, there are fewer interpersonal problems. Those areas that don't have it complain about management judgment. Where I have less objective data, I have to deal with emotions. With data, I am able to get around the emotions. In those areas with less data, there is only individual subjective judgment, and they have a more difficult time resolving their differences.

As their traditional forms of influence began to languish, subjected to increasingly closer scrutiny and measurement, and faced with a growing sense of the ineffectiveness of their functional roles, many managers found the new data-rich environment to be a humbling experience. *Humility* was a word repeated countless times to express the sense of muted subjectivity engendered by the presence of so much "objective" information. It comes from the Latin *humus*, meaning soil, and it expresses the sense of a new groundedness and realism, a fall from a grace that had drawn upon faith in the rightness and necessity of managerial control. The information panopticon tended to expose the managers' territory, preempting opportunities to fashion his or her own methods of illumination and thus construct a portrait of "what is." The panopticon also enabled managers to see more of the processes and behaviors that affected their areas, without necessarily making it any easier to influence or control those events. The heightened awareness of these contingencies increased the complexity of managerial data, while the skills they had developed, the constraints imposed by the definition of their roles, and the criteria by which they continued to be evaluated limited their capacity to respond. These parallel experiences—a felt loss of control and a heightened awareness of complexity—often left a manager feeling more diminished than augmented.

> If you assume you don't know all the right answers, you can handle it. But if you like to control, then it is frustrating. Data opens up the organization. Everyone has to be more humble, modest, open.

The role requirements associated with managerial authority have demanded that managers have the answers and be in control. The spiraling complexity and intense illumination afforded by the information presence conspire to create new contingencies for influence and success. In the midst of transition, these contingencies are only dimly understood, and the skills, roles, and structures that would define the new middle-management function are not yet apparent. Like the operators they are supposed to direct, many of these managers felt robbed of the familiar ways in which they have experienced mastery, with little to embrace as a substitute.

This feeling of diminished importance may be a necessary prelude to a new kind of augmentation. The yearning for omniscience that exploits technology to create the information panopticon represents a craving for truth as much as a need for more predictability and control. The all-seeing eye is not satisfied with a welter of detail; rather, those who observe usually believe that out of the particularity of real-time reality

the contours of some essential truth will emerge. Given the right methods of observation, the right way to know, the data can be made to open
up their center, the still point where the one best way, the summary of
all that is rational, will be revealed. Humility is the price one pays for
revelation. The individual is weaker than the force of truth that shines
through the facts. If one is willing to endure temporary humiliation,
then the prize may be a truth more vast and comprehensive than one
individual's efforts could ever obtain. Many of Cedar Bluff's managers
expressed this reverence for the truth value of their data.

> With the kind of data base we are developing, the problems should
> jump out at you from the data base, not from someone jumping on
> you after the problem has occurred. When everybody looks at the
> data base, it should be obvious—data becomes the focus, not the
> people. People hear words differently, but with the right data, we
> have something objective beyond what each person hears.

> With all of this data, you can be more objective and less subjective.
> You don't have to debate; you can see what is true.

This perception of the truth value conveyed in the information system brings organization members together as brethren in the data. The
world that is disclosed comes closer to Frederick Taylor's dream of
mutuality born of a perfect science than anything the time-study experts ever conceived. The information panopticon creates the fantasy
of a world that is not only transparent but also shorn of the conflict
associated with subjective opinion. Many who now dwell in that transparency suppose that reasonable individuals confronting the same data
will find the same truth revealed, and that in this way the system will
eliminate disagreement about "what is." Their attitudes betray an urgent desire for light without heat. Thus rationalized, human energy can
be turned toward the implementation of solutions whose appropriateness is amply demonstrated by the "facts."

The powerful, conformity-inducing effects of shared information
had not been lost on those divisional executives most actively involved
in supporting new information systems to link the plant with divisional
headquarters. As they developed their plans for the future design and
utilization of such systems, several executives recognized the technology as an opportunity to increase conformity to management's expectations. Individuals would learn to respond to the silent, calm, steady,
and unalterable "information presence" once they understood the in-

evitability of their own transparency. In order to achieve this effect, the same data would have to be equally accessible to each level of the organization. In this vision, the data base would become a shared reality—the grounds upon which to establish consensus as to "what is really going on." The system would communicate senior management's expectations clear down to the shop floor. This could be accomplished by establishing parameters, to define the desired range for various outcomes, and by designing the information system to flag deviations from these parameters. Everyone with access to the system would be able to identify the sources of deviance, whether human or mechanical. Individuals would be able to see their own behavior reflected in the system, while knowing that others (peers, subordinates, and superiors) could see it as well. The system would also include industry data in order that everyone might share the frame of reference from which management's expectations were derived. In this way, the real-time system could both communicate the normative standard and measure its fulfillment. As one divisional executive put it:

> The plants will be able to see industry data, and this will make me believable. I will have put it at their fingertips and said, "Here is the basis for my expectations." They will know what we know. They will be able to judge themselves in real time, see their record compared to industry and the real-time impact of their actions. You set a norm for what your expectations are, and then they know what is acceptable.

This tactic relies upon individual internalization of the evaluation process. People would be able to see where they fell short of the norm and would know that everyone else could see it as well. The potential for experiencing shame under these conditions would fuel individual energies toward anticipatory conformity. Executives discussed this dynamic in the language of "exception management." The system could be used to flag exceptions, activities that fell too far outside the norm, and to focus the organization's efforts on those problem areas in order to bring them into alignment with corporate expectations.

> The system will make different levels of exception management possible. As an organization, we will be able to target the exceptions and work on where the pain is. These exceptions might be at the individual, group, or plant level. The information system will force awareness of exceptions down into the organization.

The knowledge that one could show up as an "exception" was considered by this executive to be an important motivator in ensuring anticipatory conformity. The beauty of the arrangement lay in its bloodless automaticity.

> From my desk I can look at any plant. They all know what I am looking at. They can see it, too, and how they stack up. They will compare themselves internally, and this creates a certain level of competition. It can extend all the way down to the individual. The hourly worker will know that if this exception goes up the line, it will come right back to him. Once he learns that he is going to be questioned on it, he will manage his own responses more effectively. A worker under these conditions does not need to be controlled—you simply expect him to respond to the information the same way you do.

This rendering of panoptic power reflects an important evolution of the original concept. It rests on a new collectivism in which "the many" view themselves and each views "the other." Horizontal visibility is created even as vertical visibility is intensified. The model is less one of Big Brother than of a workplace in which each member is explicitly empowered as his or her fellow worker's keeper. Instead of a single omniscient overseer, this panopticon relies upon shared custodianship of data that reflect mutually enacted behavior. This new collectivism is an important antidote to the unilateral use of panoptic power, but it is not a trouble-free ideal. Horizontal transparency breeds new human dilemmas as well, many of which will be discussed in more depth in the conclusion.

Metro Tel did not share this collective orientation; thus, there was little to mitigate the oppressive sense of unilateral surveillance. There were a few workers who welcomed computer-mediated remote management because it increased their sense of autonomy.

> I prefer feeling self-sufficient. Obviously, I am not—there are many invisible reins on me—but I like the idea of being given tasks and accomplishing them as quickly as I can. I like the invisible presence of a foreman. I know he's there, but I don't have to deal with him unless I need him. At least there is some imagined independence involved.

Most of the craftsworkers reacted differently. One man recently had been promoted to foreman after many years as a craftsworker, and his reaction to the WFSS represented that of many workers in the field.

> I hated it. It was too close. I could no longer hide anything. Management could monitor me hour by hour, and that was kind of scary.

It seemed that the system generally had succeeded in inducing a considerable degree of conformity to work standards. Foremen noted that the majority of workers could be counted on to finish the work load they were assigned. For the high achievers, this might mean doing less work than usual, but for the mediocre workers, it meant doing more: "People do what is expected of them now, so there is an equalization between those who used to do more, and those who did less."

On the surface, the situation seemed orderly enough. The WFSS computed daily efficiency ratings, which were accessed by all of the management hierarchy for a variety of evaluative purposes. Below the surface, however, things were not as tidy. The culture of adversarialism and the emphasis on the WFSS as a means of unilateral control also stimulated barely latent antagonisms and evoked a generous display of sly, subversive, and frequently imaginative adaptations. For many, surveillance represented an exciting challenge: "Go ahead, try and catch me." The goal was to thwart management's efforts at omniscience.

Some workers called this approach "passive resistance." They chose to ignore one or more work requests, later insisting that it simply had not been included in their work load assignment. "The computer missed it," they would argue. "The computer isn't perfect yet." Workers also reported that they had worked on a trouble without being able to fix it. This meant their time was accounted for, but they might have been sleeping or reading a book during the hour or two the system recorded them as working on the problem. If a worker took this approach only once every five or six days, he or she was unlikely to be detected. A third approach involved learning how to "wheel and deal" with the WFSS. This meant figuring out how to accomplish an eight-hour work load in less time in order to garner the extra hours for relaxation. As one man put it, "Now I am starting to realize this system can work for me, not only me working for the system."

The techniques of panoptic power applied at Metro Tel differed in some important respects from those used at Cedar Bluff. One significant difference involved the dependence on worker's data entry in order to maintain the WFSS. In Cedar Bluff, the control interface and computerized equipment registered data regardless of the operators' intentions, but the WFSS at Metro Tel required workers to access the system for their daily work load and to update it throughout the day as those work loads were completed. It was this dependence on worker input that created the opportunity for the most cunning adaptations. Some craftsworkers had learned how to "snow the computer" in order to "make yourself look like a star." Instead of conforming to the standards it conveyed, they had figured out how to make the data look good regardless of their actual behavior. How? "All you need is a terminal and a password, and if you are smart enough, you can change things." These workers had come into possession of their foreman's password, and they used it to change the prices they were assigned. For example, if a job priced for one hour actually took two, the worker would receive a 50 percent efficiency rating—not very flattering. By changing the price to two hours, the rating would be 100 percent. How did these workers come to have the passwords that would allow them to alter the original price? In many cases, their foremen had given them these passwords just for this purpose. Why? Some foremen did it out of a sense of justice. If a worker had put in the time to do a job well, why should he or she be penalized with a poor efficiency rating? One foreman agonized:

> If a man puts the time in and the computer makes him look bad, where is the justice? We have to manipulate the computer to show how good or bad people are trying.

Typically, however, when foremen shared their passwords with workers or when they themselves changed the prices in order to "clean up" the ratings, it was because they feared the conclusions their own bosses would draw when they noticed poor efficiency ratings on the WFSS reports. These foremen believed that if the boss questioned their ratings, it would mean a "black mark against my name" or that the boss would conclude that the foreman did not have things "under control" in his or her area and, therefore, "must be doing the job wrong." Because they did not trust their managers to interpret the data correctly, and because they did not trust their own ability to explain the data adequately, foremen preferred to manipulate the data so that it reflected something even more meaningful than behavior—the still unmeasurable intentions, commitments, and aspirations of the foremen and their workers. As one foreman explained:

> If we let the computer run us, we look bad, so we manipulate the computer. We are not trying to cheat anybody or steal. We are trying to deal with the human element involved.

A small fish is eaten by a bigger one, which is in turn swallowed by an even larger fish: there was some evidence that second-level managers knew of, and quietly condoned, the price changes because they, too, were being evaluated by third-level managers on the efficiency of their areas. As one foreman recollected:

> It is a vicious cycle. If my boss sees that he did not meet his boss's productivity, can't he change the data too? He wants everybody's printout to look good. How much cheating is going on? Who knows?

The WFSS had been designed as a technical means by which to control workers' behavior and increase managers' certainty about what was actually occurring in remote field locations. It was a classic example of what organizational theorists James March and Herbert Simon called an "uncertainty absorber"—a vehicle for transmitting and legitimating "facts" to levels of the organization that no longer have contact with the concrete realities this abstracted information is meant to represent.[13] What is even more striking is that the WFSS was able to fulfill its role as a mitigator of uncertainty, even when many individuals had cause to either reject or suspect the validity of these "facts." These managers colluded in treating the behavioral text as a legitimate reflection of the workplace, because it could continue to fulfill their emotional and pragmatic requirements for certainty.[14]

Each level of the hierarchy at Metro Tel chose to emphasize the opportunities for increased unilateral surveillance provided by the new behavioral text. The message communicated throughout the organization was one of tenuous faith in the binding strength of the authority relationship. Nurturing reciprocities had become less important than these more certain means of control. Each level responded to its managers in a similar fashion, as they developed extralegitimate techniques of defense to protect themselves from involuntary display. Even as technique battled technique and faith gave way to cynicism, the emerging conditions of work bore the stubborn mark of universal transparency. How much cheating was really going on? No one could be sure, but it seems that relative to the earlier work environment, there were indeed fewer shadowy corners. According to Metro Tel foremen, "cheating" had been a persistent characteristic of their adversarial, measurement-prone organization, regardless of the technology involved. The crucial point is not just that people continued to find ways to subvert measurement, but that almost everyone agreed with the new information systems it was becoming increasingly more difficult to do so. Several foremen recognized this trend:

> People were cheating before on paper—it was called a pencil whip. That meant you take a monthly report and lie with the numbers. That went to the boss, he signed it, and everyone believed that was "reality." Now once people get skilled with the computer, it's harder. Cheating can't even be done on certain levels because they have terminals and can monitor you.

They were right. The systems designers already had wind of the efficiency ratings scam and were preparing their own response.

> There are ways that people in the field will find to get around measurements. But what you want to do with the system is to continually look for ways to trap people by recording their actions. If the craft are trying to get around their efficiency ratings by changing the price, all I have to do is start measuring how often they change the price and use that as a performance measure.

MANAGING COLLECTIVE RESPONSIBILITY IN THE INFORMATION PANOPTICON

The information panopticon adds another dimension to the informating process. It enables organizational processes, in addition to production or business-related processes, to be explicated by information technology. Who does what and how well they perform can be translated into "objective" data, along with the hundreds of variables that describe the production process or other business functions. In many cases, this means that managers' subjective judgments and personal sources of influence lose some of their force, while the intellective skills required to competently address the electronic text become more important.

The system of imperative control permitted the middle manager a fair degree of latitude to exercise personal judgment in operating his or her own area of responsibility. The development of the techniques represented by the information panopticon were intended to protect and preserve that authority. However, as Cedar Bluff's middle managers began to discover, the objective information presence enshrines rationality over authority. Reality is codified independent of those who would benefit from it or be ill-served by it. Now an autonomous domain of "facts" can be used to check the command structure.

Techniques of universal transparency, even when their goal is to elicit anticipatory conformity, do not benignly serve the interests of authority. Because rationality has no guile, it can also work to limit authority. Workers and managers together can find themselves "focused on the data rather than the people," as one manager put it. The ambiguity of reciprocal relations and the subjective quality of behavioral data are displaced by a new sense of "black-and-white" certainty. Ambiguity has worked for and against both managers and workers. It has allowed managers to be more arbitrary and powerful; it has allowed workers to find ways to exert some control over their immediate environment. The price of that ambiguity has been that the manager's word counted for more than the worker's. The informating process has not only provided workers with the language to confront their managers but also equalized their respective realities, since the objective record stands as final arbiter of what has happened.

For the textualization of organizational processes represented in panoptic power to have this effect, two elements are absolutely necessary, though in the longer term not sufficient, to engender a new framework of relations. One element involves egalitarian access to the emerging electronic text as it increasingly represents the full spectrum of organizational functioning. The second element involves the presence of a sufficient depth of intellective skill so that those who have access to data also have access to their meaning.

The very distinct dynamics engendered by an emphasis on collective, as opposed to hierarchical, panoptic power indicate the central importance of the rules that govern access to the data base. As the electronic text becomes the symbolic surrogate for the organization's vital activities, access rules become the functional equivalent of organization structures. As in the case of Metro Tel, these rules can mirror the hierarchy as they enable unilateral observation. Alternatively, universal access provides a structure in which a redistribution of authority becomes possible. One operator at Cedar Bluff summarized this neatly when he said, "If I can control my own access to data, I can control my own learning." It is this learning, more than anything else, that explodes the confines of the worker's conventional role.

Not one of the organizations I studied had yet confronted this crucial issue. Rules of access were being constructed ad hoc, as individual managers were motivated to dip into data normally reserved for their subordinates and as subordinates found it in their interests to restrict or impede their superiors' access. Most people said that it would "take a lot of guts" for their organizations to develop a clear policy for data access.

Cedar Bluff's plant manager reflected on his and others' use of the Overview System. He recognized the growing tendency to use the system in ways that contradicted the collaborative spirit of the plant.

> Now that total information is possible, it requires management discipline not to ask for information. The effort at limiting information will be greater than the effort to generate information. It is very hard for a top manager to have information and not want to do something about it. If you give me the data from that system, I will make more decisions. What is the right level of problem for each level of the organization?

Managers throughout these organizations returned repeatedly to this theme of management discipline in the face of the vast new capability afforded by information systems. They seemed to be searching for some code of discipline that managers would use to restrain their enthusiasm for information, but most wondered how this discipline could be mustered. Why should a fourteenth-century author of a primer on etiquette compose a lengthy discussion on the evils of blowing one's nose into the tablecloth, if it were not for the fact that many people routinely did just that? Similarly, the volume of commentary on the need for managerial discipline is likely to point to the frequency with which managers are in fact tempted by panoptic power.

The elusiveness of a managerial code of information discipline and the difficulty of explicitly confronting the policy issues related to access rules may stem in part from the fact that there is no longer an obvious rationale to justify the choices one makes regarding the appro-

priateness of information at each level of the organization, and therefore the manager's optimum span of control. Historically, the criteria
used to establish such norms were shaped in part by a recognition of
what was actually feasible in the daily press of organizational affairs. It
is clearly inappropriate for a divisional vice president to have real-time
operating data from the manufacturing site when acquiring such data
would engage extreme amounts of time and resources. The process
of such acquisition would be ridiculously awkward. Would the vice
president spend days in the plant? Would he or she have someone continually available by telephone? Would the vice president ask to read
operator logs?[15]

Technology radically alters the context of what is possible. How
different it is for a high-level executive to sit in his or her office and
use a desktop terminal to view summaries of operating data or to review
exceptions to optimal ranges of performance. It is still reasonable to
argue that such an executive should not spend time responding to data
that others are better positioned to manage. Once the awkwardness of
the data acquisition process is eliminated, however, the immediate face
validity of such arguments is diminished.[16]

As the material circumstances of the enterprise evolve, so do the demands on the manager. In a highly informated organization such as Cedar
Bluff, the autonomy of the data base and the extent of both vertical and
horizontal channels of access to the data added considerable weight to
the already severe pressures that middle managers felt. Traditionally, the
middle manager's role has been largely defined by the collection, analysis, and dissemination of information. The most skilled aspects of the job
involved nonroutine information, usually culled in face-to-face interactions and through personal networks. The less skilled aspects were those
that concerned routine information associated with a particular bureaucratic position or function. Both Metro Tel's and Cedar Bluff's managers
discovered that the power of their information systems had undercut
both dimensions of their job. Personal sources of information once
lodged in informal networks were now deemed less important. Their
control over the information related to their own functions had been
severely curtailed. At Cedar Bluff, managers said:

> Our systems now require a difference in how people interact with
> each other and what role they play. Things no longer must be filtered
> from the top down. Our information and control systems make infor-
> mation automatically available. Unless someone destroys the system

or pulls the plug, it all exists independently now. The operators can go to the data and bypass the manager. It's even data that managers have never had.

Managers don't collect and assimilate data themselves. It is a lost luxury. This means more communication at night via the telephone to managers while things are happening. I don't want to be surprised in the morning when my manager needs answers because his manager is trying to respond to the divisional VP who already has data on how we ran last night. I don't want to be caught cold. The subordinate used to control the size of the supervisor's window. Now the information system does it.

Both the skilled and the semiskilled aspects of the middle managers' job had been invaded by the information presence. Remember Chester Barnard's definition of a communications system in chapter 3? He viewed it as managers placed around the organization who came together to discuss what they knew. How different it is to consider communication in the context of a comprehensive real-time system, such as the systems at Metro Tel or Cedar Bluff, where information constituted an autonomous domain independent of those who once gathered, recorded, analyzed, discussed, and stored it. The familiar forms of influence associated with these activities were losing much of their force; yet, for most managers caught in this transformation, new sources of influence remain undefined.

Much of the manager's sense of artistry is derived from the manner in which he or she garners and communicates information. One consequence of the new electronic text is that it diminishes the sense of personal style, initiative, and art that many managers had felt. A manager at Cedar Bluff expressed it this way:

The more automated the information becomes, the more managers perceive themselves to have less choice, less opportunity for artistry or initiative. The information will be more integrated, and it will be more obvious what has to be done, and different people will know data from different parts of the organization, so the data won't be owned by a single manager.

At Metro Tel, a manager explained:

I had ways of doing things that other people never knew about. My own approach to administration—getting and storing information. Other people had their own, but I always felt mine was better. That

was my skill. Now my administrative skill is not required, because
everything comes out of the computer.

The integrative nature of the data base, together with its increased
scope and complexity, also created new questions about the utility of
the categories that defined managerial functions. There was a widespread feeling in Cedar Bluff that the amount of data now widely available to the management group demanded a more team-centered,
problem-solving orientation. Like the employee at the data interface,
these managers faced a broad array of data that integrated disparate
production, business, and organizational processes. Their capacity to
deal adequately with such data seemed to require interactive discussion
and analysis as observed in the control rooms as well as a new interdependence among the various business and operations functions.

Some managers believed that the conventional logic of middle-
management functions not only was outmoded but also had become a
dangerous barrier to constructive use of the data. Just as it was no
longer useful to occupy an operator with data pertaining to only one
piece of equipment, or for workers at Metro Tel to have responsibility
for only one set of telephone switches, so there was also the risk that
managers who regarded the data base from a narrow functional perspective would misinterpret or overlook important information.

> There is a great opportunity for misinterpretation of data when ev-
> eryone can see what is happening but their narrow perspective means
> that they can't tell why it is happening. Most people have a one-
> sided, functionally oriented sense when they look at the data. It gets
> worse in that the technology lets you look down that data tunnel at
> lightening speed—then the tunnel turns into a dot. You end up with
> one number, one reason, and you react to it.

Maintaining the faith that undergirds imperative control is hard
work—psychologically demanding, time-consuming, and inevitably
prone to ambiguity. It requires action-centered skills oriented toward
nurturing reciprocity among those bound together in the mutual dependency of direction and execution. Sometimes technologies appear
to offer an easier way to secure managerial objectives, and alternatives
that promise more certain results are difficult to resist. Managers are
frequently persuaded to employ these techniques of control to satisfy
their conceptions of their own roles ("I must have the answers") or as
a means of circumventing the emotionally risky and sometimes fright-

ening exertions of face-to-face engagement. It is in this context that managers can choose to "automate" their own action-centered skills and to build managerial functions into machines that convey instructions and tirelessly display even minute behavioral events. When these techniques are accompanied by an emphasis on unilateral surveillance, the triumphs of enhanced certainty and control come at some cost.

Unilateral techniques of control tend to evoke techniques of defense from subordinates who resent their own involuntary display. While these defensive measures can be thwarted, they also can contaminate the validity of data. Even more important this battle of techniques of control versus techniques of defense signals the erosion of reciprocal relations as information becomes the field upon which latent antagonisms are set loose.

When managers choose to automate the action-centered skills involved in managing reciprocities and in gathering and disseminating information, they increase their dependence upon the electronic text, not only as a means of accomplishing substantive tasks but also as a medium of administration. The electronic text can so insulate managers from the felt realities of their workplaces that they will no longer have available the means with which to rekindle reciprocities if they should want to. Paradoxically, that very insularity increases the vulnerability of the text to contamination while it simultaneously heightens the requirements for valid objective data. Thus insulated, managers often collude in ignoring the ever more slender relationship between their data and the organizational realities that they are meant to reflect.

The horizontal dimension of Cedar Bluff's information system suggests another view of panoptic power. Shared universal transparency can create a sense of mutual participation in and responsibility for operational and behavioral events. Joint access to the behavioral text can mean opportunities for joint learning. While key dimensions of managers' action-centered skill may be absorbed by the information system, new skill demands emerge. Prominent among these is the capacity to understand the business more broadly: in Cedar Bluff, functional designations seemed as outmoded as job classifications that once assigned a man to watch a single furnace for his entire work life. Managers also are likely to face new communicative demands—for sharing interpretations, problem-solving, and making sense of complex and interdependent forms of data about people and events.

CHAPTER TEN

PANOPTIC POWER

AND THE SOCIAL TEXT

For the sake of common worship
they've slain each other with the sword.

—FYODOR DOSTOEVSKY
The Brothers Karamozov

IT WAS a misty evening in early May when thirty-five professionals—chemists, systems specialists, statisticians, and research-and-development managers—met in Zito's Bar to toast the "end of innocence" at DrugCorp. The bittersweet bonds between them had been forged four years earlier when they pioneered the discovery and adaptation of new methods of communication made possible by DrugCorp's considerable investment in computer-conferencing technology. The excitement and promise of the first years now had given way to cynicism and anxiety. The communications technology with which they had so cheerfully elaborated and extended their networks of relationships, access to information, thoughtful dialogue, and social banter had also provided a quantum increase in their visibility to DrugCorp's managerial hierarchy.

DrugCorp's professionals had enthusiastically adapted their communicative behavior to the computer medium, believing that they were merely improving the efficacy of their oral culture. In time, it became clear that they had also unwittingly exposed once evanescent and intangible aspects of their social exchange to an unprecedented degree of hierarchical scrutiny. Their computer-mediated exchanges had created a new electronic text that not only greatly enriched the professional learning environment with an unprecedented amount of information sharing and new opportunities for developing collegial relationships but also provided DrugCorp's managers with a new window onto the organization and challenged basic premises regarding the boundaries between work and sociality. Managers' critical and sometimes punitive attitude had stung the more innovative participants in the system and gradually succeeded in shifting the emphasis of the new medium from one of inquiry and dialogue to one of perfunctory messages and routine electronic mail. The textualization of sociality accomplished in the service of learning and innovation had opened the firm to a rich new array of possibilities for the organization of communicative behavior. Gradually, that text was subverted by managers' need to impose their own conception of appropriate work behavior. How this occurred and what was learned in the process provides another illustration of the informating power of computer technology and the choices confronting those who use it.

COMPUTER CONFERENCING AT DRUGCORP

The impetus to develop a computer-conferencing system at DrugCorp originated in its research and development (R & D) division. During the late 1970s, R & D's management had sponsored a number of studies to analyze and improve the innovation process. These studies repeatedly converged on a single theme: interpersonal communication provided researchers with their most important channels of access to information and stimulation for new ideas. One study explored how channels of communication made a difference in successful projects and determined that personal communication was the crucial factor in 80 percent of the cases. Formal resources, such as publications, libraries, or computerized data retrieval systems, contributed only 5 percent to 20 percent of the knowledge useful to a project. Because of the vital importance of personal communication networks, managers in R & D believed they had a responsibility to facilitate individual efforts to develop communication opportunities. However, there were barriers. One report indicated that people sometimes were reluctant to approach an expert because of "the anticipated humiliation that would be sustained if a person's questions were to be met with a critical rebuff." Others cited the prerequisites for trust and respect that determine the breadth and effectiveness of an individual's network, or the difficulty of identifying appropriate experts for a given problem.

During the same period, a small group of researchers had begun experimenting with a commercially available computer-conferencing system. While the product proved to be too inflexible for their needs, the experience alerted them to the potential of this medium for facilitating the kind of communication that seemed most vital to the R & D division. By late 1978, a group from the systems development division had begun to build an in-house version of computer conferencing, one that would accommodate the varied and far-flung members of the R & D community. The leader of that team, who was to be the major force behind what would become one of corporate America's largest computer-conferencing systems, recalled their compelling, almost spiritual, vision:

> We wanted to create a "universal mind" that would span time and distance. It would be like ESP; people would be in touch with knowledge across cultures and time.

Computer conferencing is a communications medium that offers an alternative to the constraints of geography and time associated with face-to-face meetings or telephone conversations while avoiding the formality of written correspondence. It requires a continually operating computer system, which allows participants to send and receive messages at their own convenience. A conference consists of any defined subgroup of members who want to exchange information, share ideas, or collaborate on a particular subject. Messages on that subject typically are addressed to the conference as a whole, and in many cases, participants can conduct a dialogue for weeks, months, or even years, depending upon their interests.

The conferencing system developed at DrugCorp, known as DIALOG, was structured so that each conference was initiated by an organizer, who was responsible for admitting and deleting its members. A conference was organized around a specific topic, and the organizer was required to specify an "open" or "closed" status, which defined access to the file as well as reading and writing privileges. A "closed" conference could be accessed only by its members. Nonmembers could read only those messages associated with an "open read" conference and could send messages only to those conferences with an "open write" status.

Individuals who enrolled in the DIALOG system were given a password and an account number. Training was impromptu, usually provided by acquaintances who were already familiar with the system. A manual distributed to all participants outlined the basic procedures for operating the system, provided guidance related to message composition, and described the role of the conference organizer, who would lead the conference discussion to its business purpose "much like they might do in a face-to-face meeting after the people get socialized with one another and the meeting site." The software permitted interactive processing—that is, participants could communicate directly with each other at the same time. Alternatively, messages could be read at any time a person entered the system. Because the system preserved a record of all DIALOG entries, previously seen messages also could be retrieved at a later date. After three months, messages were removed from the active system and stored in an "electronic file cabinet" under the name of the conference organizer. The costs of using the system were charged to the unit of the company in which the participant worked, embedded in its total monthly computing costs.

DIALOG was first made available to DrugCorp's employees in January 1979, and two years later, there were over 1,200 people enrolled. Membership and conferences sprouted informally, by individual initiative. Conference topics ranged from technical subjects having to do with the development and testing of new pharmaceuticals to organizational issues. For example, one conference called "The New Office" was devoted to understanding and improving the DIALOG system. One year after the system began operating, an evaluation survey found that heavy participants (who averaged four-and-one-half hours per week) saved ten hours a week of verbal communications time. Respondents said that DIALOG seemed to facilitate the kind of group communication which "supports learning" but that "the most frequent indication of ineffective use occurred when conferences were organized on the basis of formal organization."

By early 1981, computer conferencing was costing the company $506,000 annually: 1,224 employees spent an average of one hour each week processing fifteen messages. About 20 percent of the participants sent a majority of the messages, while many others were predominantly readers. The average participant consumed $8.00 of computing resources each week, or $0.53 per message. Initially, the majority of participants were from R & D, but membership had come to represent all parts of the company, including systems development, engineering, and both international and domestic manufacturing. DrugCorp's top management, which had already initiated a variety of companywide cost-cutting drives in response to new pressures from international competition, decided to undertake a comprehensive review of the DIA-LOG system. Was the system worth the expense? If so, should enrollment remain voluntary, or should whole portions of the company, perhaps even the entire worldwide operation, be automatically enrolled and encouraged to communicate through this medium? If computer conferencing were to be embraced as a dominant communications medium, what implications might it have for the organization, its culture, and the nature of professional work at DrugCorp?

THE DIALOG EXPERIENCE

The corporate review stimulated participants across the company to reflect upon their use of the system and to assess its value. There was widespread enthusiasm, for DIALOG's participants had found that the conferencing medium helped create a new culture of information sharing and discussion, one that provided a stark contrast to the corporation's norms of information exchange. Though DrugCorp was a leader in developing innovative work systems for hourly employees within its domestic manufacturing plants, the managerial and professional sectors of the corporation were known for their formality and respect for the chain of command. Channels of communication tended to be narrow and highly structured. One internal report described corporate information exchange norms in the following way:

> Specific information about the way the company and each division are organized is carefully controlled so that employees in one division may not have a clear picture of other divisions or the company in its entirety. Official communication is handled hierarchically. Negotiations between divisions are made "from the top down." The mid- and upper-level managers are usually the most skilled commu-

nicators in the organization; they are in charge of executing cross-divisional work. In general, management of communication is an important aspect of the job. There are periodic warnings about only sharing information on a "need-to-know" basis.

The DIALOG system provided a new kind of access to people and places. Participants used the system to extend their communication networks beyond the group of acquaintances to which they otherwise might have been restricted. People who had never seen each other formed close working relationships. Many people began to experience a sense of the company as a whole and to develop feelings of belonging to an organization that was increasingly familiar and accessible.

> DIALOG gives me a better awareness of the company as a whole. Now I know it's not just me, myself, and I in a small group—I'm in a whole company.

> Now I use DIALOG to stay in touch with folks that I don't see as part of my job. We do information sharing about what's happening—who was transferred, left the company, what new policy developments are in the works. It's like being tapped into the grapevine. I hear about what's happening in the organization more quickly. Through DIALOG, I know how the organizational system works and how to get things done.

The DIALOG system also provided more effective access to the vast informational resources of the company. It was possible to address a question to a conference and receive responses from those with knowledge pertinent to the problem at hand. For example, one R & D division researcher encountered a problem in programming a statistical software package for which there were no known experts in the company. He entered a message into the "Mathematics and Statistics" conference explaining the problem and asking for help. Within two days he had received two messages and three telephone calls from five individuals who each provided similar but not identical answers. With that, he not only was able to solve his problem but also felt that he had learned even more about the software package from analyzing the differences between those answers. In another case, a group of plant technicians formed a conference to discuss density problems in the manufacture of a new ointment. The conference reduced the duplication of unsuccessful experiments and more quickly diffused the results of problem-solving accomplished in each plant. Participants found themselves receiving vitally important data from others whom they otherwise would not have known to contact. All of this occurred at the convenience of each participant and without travel expenses or a cumbersome series of telephone calls.

Many of these benefits appeared to accrue even to those who tended to read messages more often than they wrote them. These participants used the conferences as a way to increase their familiarity with a wide range of subjects and to learn from "watching how others' minds work." While participants initially resented readers, they gradually came to the conclusion that DIALOG was like a large-group meeting in which some people spoke and many others sat and listened, only occasionally making a contribution to the discussion.

Many of DIALOG's participants thought that the medium worked most effectively in facilitating the examination of issues from a range of perspectives. They spoke of using the system for thinking rather than for taking positions, and they found that it encouraged divergence and inhibited convergence on a single line of reasoning. Some people likened conferences to brainstorming sessions in which expression is encouraged within a supportive environment. This was precisely the kind of cross-functional communication that had become necessary for Cedar Bluff's managers in chapter 8 as they confronted their own informated task environment. Such exposure to a range of perspectives prevented the kind of narrow, specialist's approach that was increasingly dysfunctional when it came to the ever more complex, integrated, and data-rich product development and production processes. As one R & D division researcher framed it:

> It's the process of looking at something from different angles that I find so valuable. That is a fundamental piece of how you become creative with data. You ask, "How else can I look at these data? What do they teach me that I didn't know I could learn here?"

Others found that the system allowed them to make decisions more effectively. For example, one systems analyst in corporate headquarters was a support consultant to a network of manufacturing-oriented computers at plants across the United States. He was required to design and implement uniform software changes in all plants. Before the existence of DIALOG, he would circulate a memo describing the options for altering the computer program. Responses would be received during a two-to-three-week period, either by written memo, prearranged telephone calls, or joint meeting of plant managers, who would have to fly to headquarters. DIALOG changed all this. All the plants were enlisted in a single conference to discuss program modifications. If a given suggestion met with favorable responses, it could be implemented immediately. If there was disagreement, the systems analyst would propose an approach and give other participants one week to respond. His assessment?

> DIALOG leads to less arbitrary and single-minded decisions based on limited data. You don't have to arrange finding all the right people at a convenient time. There is no travel or adjustment of schedules involved. Before you are called on, you have the opportunity to see what others have said, think about it, organize your thoughts, and marshal your arguments. With DIALOG, the thought-interactive process is spread out over a week or two rather than an hour or two before reaching a decision. You have more back burner stewing time to consider all the aspects. Without DIALOG, there would be less interaction among the respondents. That is where we benefit a lot.

Most of DIALOG's participants viewed the conferencing medium as an opportunity to extend and elaborate the oral culture in which they conducted their professional work. This orientation was reflected in the DIALOG manual, which emphasized the colloquial character of a conference message—messages were described as typically short, informal (spelling or grammatical errors were acceptable), and "more like verbal dialogue than a memo or report." As they reflected on their DIALOG experiences, many people saw the conferencing medium as comparable to face-to-face interactions. "It doesn't have to be precise," they said. "It's like a conversation."

> You have to be highly verbal to use DIALOG. Spelling and grammar really don't matter. They did at first, but nobody cares anymore. We learned to separate formal from informal.

Many people believed that messages in the conferencing system were more substantive than in other media. Because messages were unencumbered by considerations of grammar, etiquette, or organizational position, they were seen as reflecting the writer's opinion, in a blunt yet trustworthy form. Others compared meandering through the conferences to hallway conversations, experiencing the same degree of serendipity and stimulation.

> The spark for innovation is usually unexpected—in the hallway or
> over lunch. DIALOG is the closest thing I know to running into some-
> one in the hallway. It has the potential for that kind of spontaneity,
> which is so often the source of new ideas. When you walk down the
> halls of DIALOG, you know you'll meet somebody.

Yet there were other ways in which the experience of communicating through DIALOG seemed to contrast with the fluidity and convivial-
ity of oral culture. Some people noted the psychological security that
came with being able to take the time "to say what you really mean,"
unflustered by the pressures of face-to-face engagement. Many participants felt that they could be more honest in this medium than in any
other. Messages were composed in solitude, which engendered feelings
of privacy and even invulnerability. Yet these same messages were conveyed in informal language and often evoked immediate responses
from other conference members. The unusual combination of isolation
and connectedness stimulated many people to "sit and pour their souls
out at the keyboard." More than one person wistfully expressed the
wish to communicate with family members through the computer medium. Many people felt less inhibited with the conferencing system
than in direct interaction because of the absence of any palpable sense
of the people they addressed.

> When I discuss something on DIALOG, in the back of my mind I
> know somebody else is going to hear it, but it isn't as obvious as if
> we were all in one room. It's like I know the tape recorder is running,
> but I kind of block it out.

These factors also contributed to a general sense that the conferencing
medium made it easy to disagree with, confront, or take exception to
others' opinions.

The remote and textual qualities of the conferencing medium contrasted with oral communication in another crucial way. The conference brought together individuals from different functional areas and
diverse social backgrounds, and eliminated the entire set of skill demands traditionally placed upon the white-collar body. Face-to-face
engagement places a premium on the body as an instrument of *acting-
with*. The body's composure, stance, gestures, beauty, attire, color, and
gender can each influence how utterances or nonverbal behaviors are
received and responded to. The computer medium eliminated these
sources of advantage or disadvantage. People who regarded themselves

as physically unattractive reported feeling more lively and confident when they expressed themselves in a computer conference. Others with soft voices or small of stature felt they no longer had to struggle to be taken seriously in a meeting. DIALOG was referred to as a "sociological event" because it brought together in "conversation" people who otherwise would be separated by position or prejudice.

> DIALOG lets me talk to other people as peers. No one knows if I am an hourly worker or a vice president. All messages have an equal chance because they all look alike. The only thing that sets them apart is their content. If you are a hunchback, a paraplegic, a woman, a black, fat, old, have two hundred warts on your face, or never take a bath, you still have the same chance. It strips away the halo effects from age, sex, or appearance.

As the political skills related to *acting-with* were deemphasized, the mastery of one's subject area and the ability to share knowledge effectively became recognized as new sources of power and influence. DIALOG's participants built reputations based on the quality of their messages and their helpfulness in sharing information. People became known as experts in their subject areas based on the content of their contributions, and less attention was paid to their formal job designation.

> Lots of people have power that is not knowledge-based; it is forceful and based on their personality or position. In DIALOG, the power lies in the ability to communicate and pass on knowledge. I have extended my power base through my knowledge rather than through intimidation or style. It is strictly now the quality of your ideas, the way you put things in words, or your sensitivity to what others say that now determines your influence.

Mastery of these new skills required inventing communicative devices that conveyed some of the same emotions and nuances as oral expression. New textual conventions began to emerge and were quickly adopted by the entire network. For example, stars around a phrase indicated anger; melancholy was expressed by using small letters, even when it was appropriate to capitalize; people shouted by using CAPITAL LETTERS; and the symbol ">)" was used to indicate "tongue in cheek." With practice, people began to "speak electronicese," which was defined as a "fluency for using the electronic medium for communication." As one skilled "speaker" pointed out:

> DIALOG is a conversation. It's like learning a new language. You
> develop an electronic intonation by the method and format in which
> you type information. You need an ability to formulate messages ex-
> temporaneously—like in a conversation.

(A sample DIALOG transcript appears opposite.)

THE NEW VISIBILITY OF SOCIAL EXCHANGE

By early 1982, there were 2,400 participants in the DIALOG system,
75 percent of whom were from three staff divisions—R & D, systems
development, and engineering. The corporation reaffirmed its commitment to computer conferencing with a decision to transfer responsibility for the maintenance and expansion of the DIALOG system from the
research and development division to the operations department within
the systems development division. New cost-accounting procedures
made it possible to identify the precise usage levels of each participant.
A report issued shortly after this transfer outlined recommendations
for DIALOG's future development and concluded that while informal
communication should be preserved, the system should be upgraded to
provide for more formal communication as well. It also stressed the
importance of expanding DIALOG to include more middle managers,
as that group was "relatively disadvantaged compared to senior managers who have more and faster communications resources at their dis-
posal and who also have the authority to get quick responses."

Expanding the managerial presence in DIALOG engendered new
difficulties, however. The majority of communications on the DIALOG
system were conducted among peers, rather than between subordinates
and superiors. DIALOG had deepened and extended the horizontal dimensions of the organization, but most people agreed that vertical
communication still depended upon a good deal of face-to-face interaction if a subordinate was to be able to reliably decipher the boss's
intentions. The nuanced messages of the boss's body were still considered an indispensable resource in the highly charged game of managing
upward.

> Your manager tells you to do a lot of things, but only in face-to-face
> interaction can you figure out what it is he really wants you to do.

(121) From: JM 2:53 PM

Fascinating discussion about the isms. HS, your message about origins of discrimination is right on and sociologically recognized. The coinage of the term classism to describe some of what people are expressing I believe is accurate and has always been applicable to non-exempts. Just being defined as a non-anything (although this is a government description) puts a person in a one down category to begin with.

I also find it fascinating and extremely interesting that our serious conference to discuss the non-seriousness of DIALOG has led around very quickly to this discussion. What that says to me is there are a lot of energy and a lot of pain being felt in this area, and we are needing a place to vent, express and share ideas about this. I also find it interesting that a computer-based tool such as DIALOG can be used and is being used to vent and work a very personal emotionally charged issues. This is interesting in light of the research being done in that the computer is often accused or seen as potentially dehumanizing people and systems, whereas this is an example of a usage where just the opposite is happening. We are able to vent our very human kind of reactions and feelings to what is perceived to be discrimination through a computerized tool that offers us the space and time to gather our thoughts and work them in a cool medium which may even help to defuse what could potentially be an explosive issue. By the use of the cool medium we can gather our thoughts and determine any action if indeed we need or want to take any in a cool way rather than in a heated kind of get together that might not be as productive.

(122) From: HS 3:47 PM

Intriguing observation, JM! Our laboratory experience teaches us that one of the most effective ways of dealing with, or defusing, an emotiaonlly charged issue is to get people to talk about it rationally and objectively. To put it another way, the key is to change a predominantly right-brain experience into a left-brain experience.

DIALOG actually forces this transition to happen because of the nature of the technology. Screaming, shouting, cursing, kicking, and playing sexual attraction games don't have my impact on a computer terminal!

(123) From: DG 3:59 PM

True, HS. But I think this company is too damn left brain as it is.

> Some things are ideas, and some things they want done yesterday. It
> is hard to tell which it is over DIALOG.

Managers also encountered difficulties communicating with their
subordinates through the computer medium. They found that their every opinion was treated as a direct request or a policy statement, rather
than as simply another contribution to the conference. Some managers claimed that even when they wanted to engage with others outside
of the hierarchical relationship, their subordinates made it difficult to
do so.

> The problem is that everything I say comes out like it is policy. When
> I type a message, it is in print and people will act on it. Ideally,
> we should be equals. I once fired back an answer in the Artificial
> Intelligence conference, and they took action on it immediately. I
> just about died!

There were at least a few examples of managers who had encountered some success at using conferencing to improve their decision
making. The head of the systems development division reported a frustrating experience when in the aftermath of an inconclusive face-to-
face meeting with a group of technicians responsible for the security
of the DIALOG system, he organized a conference and asked each person to state their position. A week later he had yet to receive a single
message. In frustration, he sent out a new message that said, "Goddam-
mit—get back to me on this subject!" It was only a few days before he
had a stream of printouts that stretched back and forth across his office
floor. He scissored the messages, piled them into response categories,
and used the data as the basis for his decision. Subsequent discussions
with his subordinates indicated that even those who disagreed with the
outcome felt comfortable because he had "listened" to all points of
view.

The leaders of the DIALOG systems development effort insisted that
it had been designed for peer relationships and that vertical communication would cast a death pall on the collegial environment it had
fostered.

> Conferencing between managers and subordinates will never work.
> You have to be careful about what you say to one person in the pres-
> ence of others. When you deal laterally, none of those issues are

operative. Managerial politics kill the medium, because they bring too much pressure.

Much of the discussion about the future development of the system revolved around perceived differences between the professional and managerial cultures that coexisted within the same organization. Professionals were technically oriented and tended to draw their status from their knowledge-based disciplines. One systems analyst betrayed the latent animosity between the two groups when he said, "Systems development is an organization of professional people managed by office workers." Many complained that professionals were treated like second-class citizens within the company, though the formal organization chart indicated that they occupied hierarchical positions comparable to managers involved in administration and finance. Others (many of whom were professionals with managerial responsibilities) tried to understand the origins of the differences between the two groups. Their insights attempted to lift the discussion above personal conflict and antagonism in order to identify the functional responsibilities that forced professionals and managers to operate differently. Professionals were trained to use ambiguity as a way of uncovering new data, whereas managers were required to minimize the amount of uncertainty in their plans and projects.

> As professionals, we are trained to avoid taking firm positions on any subject unless and until we have the data to support our positions. It is quite all right for me to say, "I don't know," to acknowledge my ignorance or uncertainty, when I am acting in my professional role. But the realities of our social and business worlds are such that taking no decision is oftentimes seen as more damaging than the risks of being wrong. As professionals, we are not overly troubled by ambiguity and uncertainty. They are part and parcel of the process of learning. As managers, even of our personal lives, ambiguity and uncertainty are deadly foes, and we take umbrage at anyone who tries to tell us otherwise. Managers will act on beliefs as though they were truths rather than accept the paralysis of being uncertain.

It was the very ambiguity at the heart of professional activity that made social exchange so vital. The intellectual stimulation associated with social interaction provided an ambiance in which ideas came together in often fruitful but not altogether predictable ways. Sometimes conversations were explicitly work-related and sometimes they were not. This loose structure distinguished professional work in an important way from other kinds of white-collar activity. Exchanges over coffee or in the lunchroom were as likely to be laced with job talk as social banter. Relationships forged in these exchanges provided future resources in the professional's information network and helped to create the sense of psychological freedom that motivates and renews professional life.

The boundaries that delimit dutiful work behavior from social exchange have always tended to be hazy when it comes to professional work life, and it is likely that this is necessarily the case. Just as professionals do not cease to be professionals after work hours, the psychological self and the organizational self are also likely to be closely aligned during the workday. Thus, ambiguity is associated with professional work behavior as well as with work tasks. It can be tolerated in a large organization in part because it is invisible. The social exchanges that surround professional work help constitute an oral culture; they vanish without a trace when the coffee break is over, when a group rises from the lunch table, when people part in the hallway, when the telephone receiver is replaced on its hook, when the meeting room empties.

Computer conferencing transformed this transient talk into a concrete presence. It was as if the ether of sociality that once filled the hallways had suddenly congealed. Now there were printouts that could be touched, carried about, and carefully examined. Through participation in DIALOG, a great deal of the sociality that infuses professional exchange was committed to text and so made concrete and visible in a wholly new way. It was this textualization of sociality that, more than any other single factor, activated the simmering antagonisms between professionals and managers and helped provoke a fundamental alteration in the character of computer conferencing at DrugCorp.

Many of the consequences associated with the textualization of sociality are vividly illustrated in the case of a conference known as the Computer Coffee Break (CCB), which was organized shortly before the announcement of the corporate evaluation of DIALOG. The title of the conference alluded to the possibility that people would spend their work breaks communicating on the electronic medium. The CCB was organized by a researcher from the R & D area, with the support of the systems developer who was in charge of the DIALOG effort. The rationale for the conference was articulated this way:

> Companies are willing to set aside floor space and electricity for soda machines, candy machines, smoking areas, and break areas because they recognize the need for breaks and humor during the course of a workday. If that's okay, then it is just as appropriate for computer-based workplaces to have a computer-based coffee break.

Founding members of the conference recognized that some in the company might question the legitimacy of their activity, but they insisted that the CCB was a valid analogue to conversations in hallways and lunchrooms. The conference was organized as a "closed read," which meant that only members had access to the CCB text, but it was "open title" and "open write" so that others could find out about the conference and write messages to it. There were only two rules for membership: nothing in a message was to be taken seriously and each member had to make at least one contribution each month. The CCB quickly became the most popular conference in DIALOG. By March 1981, three months after it had begun, there was an average of twenty messages sent each day, and more than two thousand messages had been posted, accounting for 20 percent of all DIALOG traffic.

The new conference began to absorb many of the social activities of its members, activities that had once constituted their oral lives together. Instead of chatting in the cafeteria for half an hour or cruising down the hallway, participants claimed that the CCB was a more efficient way to take a break.

> CCB is better than a planned break because you never know who you are going to bump into or what you are going to read. You can stay as long or as short as you like. It is a kind of neat, self-managed, self-controlled break, but it has all the same means of getting away from work—talking to other people. You have total control over how long you decide to stay. So you don't really insult anybody by leaving.

Like coffee break chatter, the CCB conveyed its share of off-color humor and complaints about the problems of daily work life in Drug-Corp. Many people used the conference as a place to "blow off steam," and some characterized the CCB as

> a counterculture to some small degree. A lot of people use it as a safety valve for the frustrations of dealing with the company. It used to come through in cocktail party conversations.

Others claimed that spending their free moments conferencing in the CCB was even more fun and rewarding than a "real" coffee break. They saw participation in the CCB as the bright spot of their day and felt that it stimulated their resourcefulness, creativity, and enthusiasm in ways that spread to other areas of their work.

> I look forward every day to getting on CCB. It has given me a renewed enthusiasm for being at work that sometimes shows up as creativity that has spilled over into another conference or project.

While CCB members recognized that some in the company might question the appropriateness and even legitimacy of their conferencing activity, they were prepared to defend the rationale for CCB by insisting that "the company gets slightly less out of me directly, but indirectly, they get more." (A sample CCB transcript appears opposite.)

As the management of DIALOG shifted from R & D to the operations department within the systems development division in 1982, and efforts continued to expand the system and include more managers, the halcyon world of the CCB faced a series of new and severe threats. The first incidents demonstrated the still-fragile state of the computer system on which DIALOG was maintained. In one case, a manager in a European branch office was teaching his secretary how to enter the DIALOG system when a screenful of "foul" and "embarrassing" messages inexplicably appeared on the terminal screen. The manager was furious and raised the issue with his superiors—how could such "dialogue" possibly be justified with company resources on company time? As word of the CCB spread, other managers engaged in "deliberate surveillance." One entered the CCB using his secretary's identification number and password (remember, it was "closed read"). Angered by what he saw there, he ordered his secretary to make hard-copy transcripts and to highlight all the names of participants from his own division. The material was sent to the division head along with scathing memos to those who maintained the DIALOG system. Other managers began to take similar action, and rumors circulated that participation in the CCB was being considered a sign of "nonproductivity" and a "negative element" in performance evaluations.

The situation became intolerable when printouts of CCB transcripts began circulating throughout the company. Some CCB members received their messages through interdepartmental mail, instead of from a computer terminal. Employees operating the printer at the corporate

```
*  *  *  *  *  *  *  *  *  *  *  *  *  *  *  *  *  *  *  *  *  *  *  *
*  *                                                              *  *
*  *        Transcript of the Computer Coffee Break               *  *
*  *                                                              *  *
*  *  *  *  *  *  *  *  *  *  *  *  *  *  *  *  *  *  *  *  *  *    *  *
*  *                                                              *  *
*  *  (2739) From: (GS) Gordon Schulz          06/17/81   7:51 AM *  *
*  *  I am reminded of the latest R&D POLICY & PROCEDURES for EARLY RETIRE- *  *
*  *  MENT due to the reducting in R&D Div. workload.             *  *
*  *  i'm sharing them on this conference in case they haven't been implemented yet *  *
*  *  in the other divisions:                                     *  *
*  *                                                              *  *
*  *  As a result of automation as well as a declining workload, Management must, of *  *
*  *  necessity, take steps to reduce our work force. A reduction in force plan has *  *
*  *  been developed which appears the most equitable under the circumstances. *  *
*  *                                                              *  *
*  *  Under the plan, older employees will be placed on early retirement, thus permitting *  *
*  *  the retention of employees who represent the Future of the Company. *  *
*  *                                                              *  *
*  *  Therefore, a program to phase out older personnel by the end of the current fiscal *  *
*  *  year via early retirement will be placed into effect immediately. The program shall *  *
*  *  be known as Retire Aged Personnel Early (RAPE).             *  *
*  *                                                              *  *
*  *  Employees who are RAPEd will be given the opportunity to seek other jobs within *  *
*  *  the Company, provided that while they are being RAPEd they request a review *  *
*  *  of their employment status before actual retirement takes place. This phase of *  *
*  *  the operation is called Survey of Capabilities of Retired Early Workers (SCREW). *  *
*  *                                                              *  *
*  *  All employees who have been RAPEd and SCREWed may also apply for a final *  *
*  *  review. This will be called Study by Higher Authority Following Termination *  *
*  *  (SHAFT).                                                    *  *
*  *                                                              *  *
*  *  Program Policy dictates that employees may be RAPEd once and SCREWed *  *
*  *  twice, but may get the SHAFT as many times as the Company deems *  *
*  *  appropriate.                                                *  *
*  *                                                              *  *
*  *  *  *  *  *  *  *  *  *  *  *  *  *  *  *  *  *  *  *  *  *    *  *
*  *  *  *  *  *  *  *  *  *  *  *  *  *  *  *  *  *  *  *  *  *    *  *
```

data center would watch for CCB humor, photocopy it, and post it on the computer lab bulletin board or send it to friends in other parts of the company. Though CCB participants were outraged when they discovered that their confidentiality had been violated, they could not stem the mounting tide of criticism as more nonmembers came in contact with CCB transcripts.

There were senior managers who attempted to defend the CCB concept and preserve the openness and informality of the conferencing medium. They believed that the proven value of informal communication among professionals warranted the risk of certain "conversational excesses" that sometimes characterized CCB exchanges. These managers insisted that the hierarchy should use DIALOG only as a way of keeping better informed about "organizational living," or what they called the "soft stuff" in the organization. One such manager used DIALOG to observe how well the company was operating but insisted that it could not be used as a basis for evaluating or second-guessing others' actions. He reflected:

> If information from DIALOG is used in a punishing way, then these rich sources of data about the organization will dry up, and we will be left with only formal and less-reliable reflections of company life. It is a question of having trust in the organization or simply using DIALOG to multiply our surveillance capability. DIALOG is analogous to every other information pipeline we have. If we abuse it, we know that ultimately they will rig it, and it will be useless.

Other managers noted a hypocritical element in the hierarchy's attitude toward the CCB. The same behavior that was acceptable in a meeting of all male managers was spurned when it showed up in the CCB. One top manager related an episode that had occurred in a recent executive meeting. One of the executives had remarked that he only had time to tell a few jokes before departing for the airport.

> He then told two of the dirtiest jokes I have ever heard to the whole group. We all chuckled, and he left. Later, the subject of dirty jokes in the CCB conference was raised. Everyone was against it. So I confronted them with the man's behavior who had told the jokes and left our meeting. The only difference was that in CCB, it is written and spread all around the place.

The only difference, indeed. The sexual stories told around the meeting table, no matter how harsh, disappeared along with whatever discomfort or titillation they evoked from listeners. The content of the CCB—the spontaneous pun, the off-color joke that seemed acceptable late Friday afternoon, the sometimes wistful sometimes insistent efforts to communicate with unseen colleagues—all of these had been reborn as text, unwittingly but remorselessly documented. Gradually, DIALOG participants began to realize that their enthusiastic use of the conferencing medium as a means of extending oral culture had seriously miscalculated the consequences of its textualizing power. Their efforts to use this remote electronic medium to construct and manage complex social exchanges had inadvertently reified and exposed the most delicate and sometimes questionable facets of their organizational lives.

> We are used to face-to-face interaction where words disappear. We assume that over the phone, too. We don't stop to think that someone is recording what we say. How does electronic communication fit with the stuff we're used to? I assumed keyboard communication was like a letter or a phone call, but now I understand that it doesn't disappear. The social aspects of confidentiality and security haven't been thought through.

> The myth is that electronic communication is invisible. No one acknowledged the visibility of the medium because it was abstract. Input is abstract; output is concrete.

DIALOG's robust peer orientation was attenuated when managers gained access to conferences that were supposedly "closed." Participants in the CCB adapted to their new awareness of involuntary display in much the same way as workers at Metro Tel and Cedar Bluff. First, they opted for some kind of anticipatory conformity. They tried to maintain their participation in the CCB, but they "toned down" the character of their comments. By the second half of 1982, however, one-and-a-half years after the inception of the conference, they decided that the Computer Coffee Break "must die." That decision brought with it a new opportunity to use the technology as an instrument of revenge. With 8,500 messages already posted in the conference, there was a rush to put in another 1,500 messages in order to see if they "could break the computer system with a five-digit message number."

Finally, new techniques of defense came into play. Soon after CCB was eliminated from the conferencing system, a group of twenty former participants began a new and secret conference called the Innovative Communications conference. The title was meant to signal, to anyone who might inquire, the legitimate purpose of the conference as "an experiment on the value of people using networks." During the next two years, the new conference grew to a membership of over fifty persons and entailed a number of unwritten rules to ensure privacy. The existence of the conference could not be acknowledged publicly by any member. The conference was "closed read," "closed write," and "closed title." Membership was permitted only by invitation from current members after nomination, seconding, and review by other current members. Messages had to be received either on the terminal screen or in hard copy from a printer at the member's desk. Everyone had to check into the conference at least once every two weeks. No one was to refer to the conference in any other messages or conferences.

Managers' tendency to exploit the new transparency of social exchange as an opportunity to augment their panoptic power was not confined to the Computer Coffee Break. As their incursions spread, so did the efforts to cope with the threat of surveillance. One conference had been organized precisely to discuss the issues related to defining legitimate work behavior. Participation trailed off as the perception grew that members "risked trouble" if managers read the messages and deemed them unrelated to business. A core of diehards sustained the conference, while the number of browsers (people who only read messages) grew.

> There are now a lot more readers than contributors for any conference perceived to be somewhat risky. You can read it without managers knowing because you aren't billed for watching—only for the number of lines you contribute. There is no way to deny you spend time in the conference if you say something.

One year after the demise of the CCB, another innovative conference was initiated. It was called "Women's Professional Improvement" so that "when managers hear about it, they will view it as a way to increase productivity." Again, to ensure privacy, the conference was both "closed read" and "closed write"; only members could review and respond to its content. The conference quickly became one of the most popular, with 130 members sharing information aimed at "helping professional women cope with life in a male-dominated corporation." The conference often addressed issues related to the conflicting demands of work and family life. Many women described it as "our effort to build our own 'old boy's network.' "

The "old boy's network" drew a good deal of its power from its invisibility, but the Women's Professional Improvement conference, despite its technical precautions, was all too visible. A number of incidents in the conference created a stir within the management hierarchy. In one case, a member had posted information about affirmative action in the conference. In another case, some members discussed a personal issue with little business relevance.

The head of systems development, the division responsible for maintaining DIALOG, received complaints from the industrial relations division concerning the possibility of female employees organizing a union and from the legal department complaining that the women might file affirmative action suits. He responded by compiling hard copies of conference transcripts and a list of members. A group of participants was called into his office and asked to explain the "legitimate business purpose" of the conference. While the group's rationale was accepted, they were told to exert more leadership in directing the discussion to business issues. In the aftermath of these events, conference membership dwindled. Many continued to observe the discussions, but far fewer women contributed messages. "The organization has given everyone a signal," the women agreed. "DIALOG is too public for real day-to-day support."

The electronic text that had become an interpersonal and intellectual resource for many of DrugCorp's professionals, had also become an enduring witness to their social behavior. The latent antagonisms between managers and professionals, which derived from distinct values and conceptions of authority, swelled as managers tried to counter behavior that seemed to threaten the preeminence of imperative control. Though some managers earnestly wanted to "keep the faith," to trust their subordinates, and to use the new text of social behavior only as an opportunity to learn more about their organization, most managers found it difficult to forego the panoptic power the text offered. The new visibility of sociality had provided a technical means by which managers could attempt to control and channel what had always been the most ephemeral aspects of subordinates' behavior.

Many DIALOG participants lamented the lack of trust and absence of shared values that these events had betrayed. They complained that management was dishonest to have allowed some conferences to be designated as "closed," when in fact their content was available for unilateral screening. The situation had left the professional employees feeling fearful and insecure.

> If we knew that managers trusted our allegiance to the company, or if we could believe that messages were really private, then we wouldn't be so paranoid. But now we know that if they want to look, they can. Nothing is closed, nothing is private.

In 1983 a new computer was brought on-line to supplant the earlier system. By now, the corporation had decided to expand its use of electronic communication but to refashion the character of this usage. The new system was known as Total Office Network Integration (TONI). A new policy of automatic enrollment was instituted, in contrast to the earlier procedure of enrolling only those who expressed interest. Within a year, there were 6,300 people registered in TONI, most of whom had not been participants in DIALOG. TONI was seen as a support device for formal communications and administrative services, rather than as the creative medium once envisioned by DIALOG's pioneers. It improved overseas communications and made it possible to transmit documents rapidly. Most people felt that the kind of informal communication once encouraged in DIALOG was no longer permissible in TONI. Though conferencing was still a feature offered by the new system, there were fewer conferences and far fewer participants. Routine electronic mail and short, technically oriented messages were now predominant.

The new awareness that electronic communication provided a documentary record of formal communication also shaped the way in which it was used for business correspondence and organizational communication. The accommodations to panoptic power continued to spread as participants began to "manage" the text that would ultimately reflect their social behavior. Some people admitted that they avoided fully stating their position on a given topic within the electronic medium so as to not leave any "written tracks." In other cases, the system was used as a way of going "on record." Individuals would post long documents that were unrelated to the particular questions raised in a conference but that served instead to draw attention to their presence in the conference. Everyone involved agreed that the new emphasis was one of formality, self-consciousness, and self-protection.

There were dramatic differences of opinion as to the future of electronic communications in DrugCorp. On one side were those managers who emphasized the need for efficiency and control. DrugCorp was not an "intellectual democracy," they said, and it never would be. Some senior managers confessed that they viewed the spreading of DIALOG "like a disease that must be walled off and contained." The head of the systems development division, though battered by these pressures, recognized that shutting down electronic communications was no more possible than eliminating the telephone system.

> Management has not been able to appreciate how the electronic network improved morale. The company hierarchy does not have a very good understanding of the social and emotional needs of people to communicate. They have become preoccupied with security, cost, and counterculture/egalitarian issues.

On the other side were those professionals (some of whom also had managerial responsibilities) who believed that mounting competitive pressures would finally place such a premium on the free flow and creative use of information that it would be necessary to return to the earlier goals of the DIALOG system. They recognized that managers traditionally depended upon controlling the flow of information as an important device for exercising control. These "obsolete organizational formulas," they claimed, would not survive in a world where significant advantages accrue from a more effective internal sharing of information in the service of learning and innovation. Like their counterparts in Global Bank Brazil, they believed that the technology would unleash an irreversible trend toward collective access to, and shared ownership of, information. In the absence of a management strategy to exploit this new potential, they maintained their enthusiasm for the autonomous power of an informating technology.

> There will be a significant change in how information is moved in the company. Some managers protect their ass by protecting information. Those people will have a tough time. You cannot have a lock on information with this technology. I am frustrated now, but the changes are coming. Even if they wanted to, nobody could screw it up. The system is moving on its own. It is inevitable.

The founding vision of the DIALOG system had been one of a "universal mind . . . like ESP," an ethereal gossamer net pulsating with pure thought. There were moments when it seemed they had achieved this. Knowledge displayed itself as a collective resource; nonhierarchical bonds were strengthened; individuals were augmented by their participation in group life; work and play, productivity and learning, seemed ever more inseparable. However, the informating technology that translated and displayed the form and content of these exchanges also transformed a local oral reality into an unwavering text. The horizontal dimensions of organizational life that had flourished in DIALOG were no match, at least in the short run, for the vertical pressure exerted by DrugCorp's managers.

The fate of DIALOG recalls again the interplay between essence and choice in the computerized workplace. Transparency, integration, remote relationships, abstraction—these are the compelling propensities of an emerging work milieu. How will they be managed, and to what end? Is it inevitable that managerial needs for certainty will colonize the new behavioral text and finally convert it into another opportunity for enhanced control? We have seen how the old world tries to suffocate the new—its successes and its failures. Now is the time for an alternative vision. What will managing the informated organization entail? What fresh dilemmas will be encountered?

CONCLUSION

MANAGING THE
INFORMATED ORGANIZATION

What defines humanity is not the capacity to
create a second nature—economic, social, or
cultural—beyond biological nature; it is
rather the capacity of going beyond created
structures in order to create others.

—MAURICE MERLEAU-PONTY
The Structure of Behavior

TECHNOLOGY IS A PLACE

Put your eye to the kaleidoscope and hold it toward the light. There is
a burst of color, tiny fragments in an intricate composition. Imagine a
hand nudging the kaleidoscope's rim until hundreds of angles collapse,
merge, and separate to form a new design. A fundamental change in an
organization's technological infrastructure wields the power of the
hand at the turning rim. Technological change defines the horizon of
our material world as it shapes the limiting conditions of what is possible and what is barely imaginable. It erodes taken-for-granted assumptions about the nature of our reality, the "pattern" in which we dwell,
and lays open new choices. When the telephone makes it possible to
pursue intimate conversations without bodies that touch or eyes that
meet, or when the electric light rescues the night from darkness, the
experience is more than simply an element within the pattern. Such
innovations give form and definition to our worldly place and provoke

a new vision of the potential for relatedness within it. It is in this sense that technology cannot be considered neutral. Technology is brimming with valence and specificity in that it both creates and forecloses avenues of experience.

History reveals the power of certain technological innovations to transform the mental life of an era—the feelings, sensibilities, perceptions, expectations, assumptions, and, above all, possibilities that define a community. From the social influence of the medieval castle,[1] to the coming of the printed book,[2] to the social and physical upheaval associated with the rise of the automobile[3]—each specific example serves to drive home a similar message. An important technological innovation is not usefully thought of as a unitary cause eliciting a series of discrete effects. Instead, it can be seen as an alteration of the material horizon of our world, with transformative implications for both the contours and the interior texture of our lives. Technology makes the world a new place—a conception expressed by Fernand Braudel when he wrote:

> It was only when things went wrong, when society came up against the ceiling of the possible, that people turned of necessity to technology, and interest was aroused for the thousand potential inventions, out of which one would be recognized as the best, the one that would break through the obstacle and open the door to a different future. . . . In this sense, technology is indeed a queen: it does change the world.[4]

Yet the metaphor of the kaleidoscope is finally a limited one. Those pretty fragments align themselves at random, but change in human societies is not quite as blind. Between the turning of the rim and the emergence of a new pattern, there is another force that infuses the final configuration of elements with meaning: the human activity of choice. Though intentions do not always predict consequences, humans do attempt to proceed by constructing meaning; assessing interests; and, with varying degrees of awareness, making choices. As the ceiling of the possible is newly defined, opportunities for choice are multiplied. Should I fly or drive or take a train? What is my destination? Should I use the telephone to maintain intimate contact with friends I rarely see? Whom should I call? How often? For how long should we speak? It is here in the realm of choice that technology reveals its indeterminacy. Though it redefines the possible, it cannot determine which choices are taken up and to what purpose.

Some theorists have attributed systematic and purposeful agency to the managerial use of technology. They argue that managers are interested exclusively in technology as a means of controlling, limiting, and ultimately weakening their work force.[5] The data I have presented suggest a more complicated reality. Even where control or deskilling has been the intent of managerial choices with respect to new information technology, managers themselves are also captive to a wide range of impulses and pressures. Only rarely is there a grand design concocted by an elite group ruthlessly grinding its way toward the fulfillment of some special and secret plan. Instead, there is a concentration of forces and consequences, which in turn develop their own momentum. Sometimes these lines of force run in predictably straight paths. At other times, they twist and spiral, turn corners, and flow to their opposite. Activities that seem to represent choices are often inert reproductions of accepted practice. In many cases, they are convenient responses to the press of local exigencies. In some instances, they may actually reflect a plan.

To fully grasp the way in which a major new technology can change the world, as described by Braudel, it is necessary to consider both the manner in which it creates intrinsically new qualities of experience and the way in which new possibilities are engaged by the often-conflicting demands of social, political, and economic interests in order to produce a "choice." To concentrate only on intrinsic change and the texture of an emergent mentality is to ignore the real weight of history and the diversity of interests that pervade collective behavior. However, to narrow all discussion of technological change to the play of these interests overlooks the essential power of technology to reorder the rules of the game and thus our experience as players. Moreover, these two dimensions of technological change, the intrinsic and the contingent, need to be understood, not separately, but in relation to one another. The same innovation that abstracts work and increases its intellectual content, thus enhancing the learning of lower level employees (remember the operators at Tiger Creek and their experience with the new expense-tracking system described in chapter 7), can also, within the context of the choices by which it is adapted, be experienced as a new source of divisiveness and control (as Tiger Creek's managers perceived a threat to their roles and resisted the potential for change).

The dilemmas of transformation that have been described are embedded in the living detail of everyday life in the workplace as it undergoes computerization. They are dilemmas precisely because of the way they reveal the subtle interplay between essence and choice. Information technology essentially alters the contours of reality—work becomes more abstract, intelligence may be programmed, organizational memory and visibility are increased by an order of magnitude beyond any historical capability. Individuals caught up in this newly configured reality face questions that did not need to be asked before. New possibilities arise and require new deliberations. The duality of information technology—its capacity to automate and to informate—provides a vantage point from which to consider these choices. The relative emphasis that organizations give to these capacities will become the foundation for a strategic conception of technology deployment and so will shape the way the dilemmas are confronted and resolved.

The organizations described in this book have illustrated how the need to defend and reproduce the legitimacy of managerial authority can channel potential innovation toward a conventional emphasis on automation. In this context, managers emphasize machine intelligence and managerial control over the knowledge base at the expense of developing knowledge in the operating work force. They use the technology as a fail-safe system to increase their sense of certainty and control over both production and organizational functions. Their experiences suggest that the traditional environment of imperative control is fatally flawed in its ability to adequately exploit the informating capacity of the new technology.

In these organizations, the promise of automation seemed to exert a magnetic force, a seduction that promised to fulfill a dream of perfect control and heal egos wounded by their needs for certainty. The dream contains the image of "people serving a smart machine," but in the shadow of the dream, human beings have lost the experience of critical judgment that would allow them to no longer simply respond but to know better than, to question, to say no. This dream brings us closer to fulfilling Hannah Arendt's dreadful forecast of a world in which behaviorism comes true:

> The last stage of the laboring society, the society of jobholders, demands of its members a sheer automatic functioning, as though individual life had actually been submerged in the over-all life process of the species and the only active decision still required of the individual were to let go, so to speak, to abandon his individuality, the still individually sensed pain and trouble of living, and acquiesce in a

dazed, "tranquilized," functional type of behavior. The trouble with modern theories of behaviorism is not that they are wrong but that they could become true, that they actually are the best possible conceptualization of certain obvious trends in modern society. It is quite conceivable that the modern age—which began with such an unprecedented and promising outburst of human activity—may end in the deadliest, most sterile passivity history has ever known.[6]

That managers may give themselves over to this dream because of inertia and convenience rather than cogent analysis is all the more disturbing. Organizations that take steps toward an exclusively automating strategy can set a course that is not easily reversed. They are likely to find themselves crippled by antagonism from the work force and the depletion of knowledge that would be needed in value-adding activities. The absence of a self-conscious strategy to exploit the informating capacity of the new technology has tended to mean that managerial action flows along the path of least resistance—a path that, at least superficially, appears to serve only the interests of managerial hegemony.

Yet what would seem to be a maddeningly predictable story line has its share of surprises, false starts, dead ends, trap doors, tarnished hopes, and real failures. The seeds of an informating strategy were apparent in each of the organizations described here, especially in Cedar Bluff, Global Bank Brazil, and DrugCorp. In the absence of a comprehensive strategy, no single organization fully succeeded in exploiting the opportunity to informate.

The interdependence of the three dilemmas of transformation I have described—knowledge, authority, and technique—indicates the necessary comprehensiveness of an informating strategy. The shifting grounds of knowledge invite managers to recognize the emergent demands for intellective skills and develop a learning environment in which such skills can develop. That very recognition contains a threat to managerial authority, which depends in part upon control over the organization's knowledge base. A commitment to intellective skill development is likely to be hampered when an organization's division of labor continuously replenishes the felt necessity of imperative control. Managers who must prove and defend their own legitimacy do not easily share knowledge or engage in inquiry. Workers who feel the requirements of subordination are not enthusiastic learners. New roles cannot emerge without the structures to support them. If managers are to alter their behavior, then methods of evaluation and reward that encourage them to do so must be in place. If employees are to learn to operate in new ways and to broaden their contribution to the life of the business, then career ladders and reward systems reflecting that change must be designed. In this context, access to information is critically important; the structure of access to information expresses the organization's underlying conception of authority. Employees and managers can hardly be partners in learning if there is a one-way mirror between them. Techniques of control that are meant to safeguard authority create suspicion and animosity, which is particularly dysfunctional when an organization needs to apply its human energies to inventing an alternative form of work organization better suited to the new technological context.

The interdependence among these dilemmas means that technology alone, no matter how well designed or implemented, cannot be relied upon to carry the full weight of an informating strategy. Managers must have an awareness of the choices they face, a desire to exploit the informating capacity of the new technology, and a commitment to fundamental change in the landscape of authority if a comprehensive informating strategy is to succeed. Without this strategic commitment, the hierarchy will use technology to reproduce itself. Technological developments, in the absence of organizational innovation, will be assimilated into the status quo.

THE DIVISION OF LABOR AND THE DIVISION OF LEARNING

Organizational theorists frequently have promoted a conception of organizations as "interpretation systems."[7] The computer mediation of an organization's productive and administrative infrastructure places an even greater premium upon an organization's interpretive capabilities, as each organizational level experiences a relatively greater preponderance of abstract cues requiring interpretation. This is as true for the plant manager as for the pulp mill worker, for the banker as well as for the clerk. In each case, oral culture and the action-centered skills upon which that culture depends are gradually eroded, and perhaps finally displaced, by the incursions of explicit information and intellective skill.

As bureaucratic coordination and communication become more dependent upon mastering the electronic text, the *acting-with* skills of the white-collar body are subordinated to the demands associated with dominating increasing quantities of abstracted information. In many cases, traditional functional distinctions no longer reflect the requirements of the business. When managers increase their engagement with the electronic text, they also risk a new kind of hyperrationalisn and impersonalization, as they operate at a greater distance from employees and customers.

When the textualizing consequences of an informating technology become more comprehensive, the body's traditional role in the production process (as a source of effort and/or skill in the service of *acting-on*) is also transformed. The rigid separation of mental and material work characteristic of the industrial division of labor and vital to the preservation of a distinct managerial group (in the office as well as in the factory) becomes, not merely outmoded, but perilously dysfunctional. Earlier distinctions between white and blue "collars" collapse. Even more significant is the increased intellectual content of work tasks across organizational levels that attenuates the conventional designations of manager and managed. This does not mean that there are no longer useful distinctions to be made among organizational members, but whatever these distinctions may be, they will no longer convey fundamentally different modes of involvement with the life of the organization represented by the division of abstract and physical labor. Instead, the total organizational skill base becomes more homogeneous.

In the highly informated organization, the data base takes on a life of its own. As organizations like Cedar Bluff develop mechanisms that allow data to be automatically generated, captured, and stored, they begin to create their own image in the form of dynamic, detailed, real-time, integrated electronic texts. These texts can provide access to internal operations as well as external business and customer data; they can be designed with enough reflexivity to be able to organize, summarize, and analyze aspects of their own content. The electronic text becomes a vast symbolic surrogate for the vital detail of an organization's daily life. Such data constitute an autonomous domain. They are a public symbolization of organizational experience, much of which was previously private, fragmented, and implicit—lodged in people's heads, in their sensual know-how, in discussions at meetings or over lunch, in file drawers, or on desktops.

The textualization process moves away from a conception of information as something that individuals collect, process, and disseminate; instead, it invites us to imagine an organization as a group of people gathered around a central core that is the electronic text. Individuals take up their relationship toward that text according to their responsibilities and their information needs. In such a scenario, work is, in large measure, the creation of meaning, and the methods of work involve the application of intellective skill to data.

Under these circumstances, work organization requires a new division of learning to support a new division of labor. The traditional system of imperative control, which was designed to maximize the relationship between commands and obedience, depended upon restricted hierarchical access to knowledge and nurtured the belief that those who were excluded from the organization's explicit knowledge base were intrinsically less capable of learning what it had to offer. In contrast, an informated organization is structured to promote the possibility of useful learning among all members and thus presupposes relations of equality. However, this does not mean that all members are assumed to be identical in their orientations, proclivities, and capacities; rather, the organization legitimates each member's right to learn as much as his or her temperament and talent will allow. In the traditional organization, the division of learning lent credibility to the legitimacy of imperative control. In an informated organization, the new division of learning produces experiences that encourage a synthesis of members' interests, and the flow of value-adding knowledge helps legitimate the organization as a learning community.

The contemporary language of work is inadequate to express these new realities. We remain, in the final years of the twentieth century, prisoners of a vocabulary in which managers require employees; superiors have subordinates; jobs are defined to be specific, detailed, narrow, and task-related; and organizations have levels that in turn make possible chains of command and spans of control. The guiding metaphors are military; relationships are thought of as contractual and often adversarial. The foundational image of work is still one of a manufacturing enterprise where raw materials are transformed by physical labor and machine power into finished goods. However, the images associated with physical labor can no longer guide our conception of work.

The informated workplace, which may no longer be a "place" at all, is an arena through which information circulates, information to which intellective effort is applied. The quality, rather than the quantity, of effort will be the source from which added value is derived. Economists may continue to measure labor productivity as if the entire world of work could be represented adequately by the assembly line, but their measures will be systematically indifferent to what is most valuable in the informated organization. A new division of learning requires another vocabulary—one of colleagues and co-learners, of exploration, experimentation, and innovation. Jobs are comprehensive, tasks are abstractions that depend upon insight and synthesis, and power is a roving force that comes to rest as dictated by function and need. A new vocabulary cannot be invented all at once—it will emerge from the practical action of people struggling to make sense in a new "place" and driven to sever their ties with an industrial logic that has ruled the imaginative life of our century.

The informated organization is a learning institution, and one of its principal purposes is the expansion of knowledge—not knowledge for its own sake (as in academic pursuit), but knowledge that comes to reside at the core of what it means to be productive. Learning is no longer a separate activity that occurs either before one enters the workplace or in remote classroom settings. Nor is it an activity preserved for a managerial group. The behaviors that define learning and the behaviors that define being productive are one and the same. Learning is not something that requires time out from being engaged in productive activity; learning is the heart of productive activity. To put it simply, learning is the new form of labor.

The precise contours of a new division of learning will depend upon the business, products, services, and markets that people are engaged in learning about. The empowerment, commitment, and involvement of a wide range of organizational members in self-managing activities means that organizational structures are likely to be both emergent and flexible, changing as members continually learn more about how to organize themselves for learning about their business. However, some significant conceptual issues are raised by the prospect of a new division of learning in the informated organization. The following discussion of these issues does not offer a rigid prescription for practice but suggests the kinds of concrete choices that define an informating strategy.

MANAGERIAL ACTIVITIES IN THE INFORMATED
ORGANIZATION

As the intellective skill base becomes the organization's most precious resource, managerial roles must function to enhance its quality. Members can be thought of as being arrayed in concentric circles around a central core, which is the electronic data base. The skills required by those at the core do not differ in kind from those required at a greater distance from the core. Instead of striking phenomenological differences in the work that people do, the distance of any given role from the center denotes the range and comprehensiveness of responsibilities, the time frame spanned by those responsibilities, and the degree of accountability for cross-functional integration attached to the role. The data base may be accessed from any ring in the circle, though data can be formatted and analyzed in ways that are most appropriate to the information needs of any particular ring of responsibility.

On the innermost ring, nearest to the core, are those who interact with information on a real-time basis. They have responsibility for daily operations, and the level of data they utilize is the most detailed and immediate. Because intellective skill is relevant to the work of each ring of responsibility, the skills of those who manage daily operations form an appropriate basis for their progression into roles with more comprehensive responsibilities.

The jobs at the data interface become increasingly similar to one another as the informating process evolves. In the advanced stages of informating, these become "metajobs," because the general characteristics of intellective skill become more central to performance than the particular expertise associated with specific production-related functions. Expertise either is available from on-site specialists or is built into information systems. For example, at Cedar Bluff, top managers believed that they would solve the problem of vanishing artistry by building that expertise into the information system capability. The know-how of managers with years of experience could be systematized and made available to operators who would never have the same degree of involvement in the action contexts that had developed the personal and specific knowledge associated with action-centered skill.

This relationship between general intellective skills and expertise in specific areas was also illustrated in the case of the calculator models at Cedar Bluff, discussed in chapter 7. Operators needed the kind of understanding that would allow them to know when and how to use a model, and when to be critical of its assumptions or outputs. That quality of understanding did not depend upon being able to match the expertise that went into the models' calculations. The operator with a conceptual approach to the process, skilled in data-based reasoning, and familiar with the theory that links elements in the production process, may not be able to reproduce the knowledge of an individual with years of hands-on experience or expert training. Nevertheless, he or she should be able to understand the conceptual underpinning of a problem well enough to select among potential analytic strategies and to access the expert knowledge that is required. Intellective skill is brought to bear in the definition of the problem for analysis, the determination of the data that is required for analysis, the consideration of the appropriateness of an analytical approach, and the application of the analysis to improved performance.

The activities arrayed on the responsibility rings at a greater distance from the core incorporate at least four domains of managerial activity: intellective skill development, technology development, strategy formulation, and social system development. For example, the crucial importance of the intellective skill base requires that a significant level of organizational resources be devoted to its expansion and refinement. This means that some organizational members will be involved in both higher-order analysis and conceptualization, as well as in promoting learning and skill development among those with operational responsibility. Their aim is to expand the knowledge base and to improve the effectiveness with which data is assimilated, interpreted, and responded to. They have a central role in creating an organizational environment that invites learning and in supporting those in other managerial domains to develop their talents as educators and as learners. In this domain, managers are responsible for task-related learning, for learning about learning, and for educating others in each of the other three domains.

A new division of learning depends upon the continued progress of informating applications. This managerial domain of technology-related activity comprises a hierarchy of responsibilities in addition to those tasks normally associated with systems engineering, development, and maintenance. It includes maintaining the reliability of the data base while improving its breadth and quality, developing approaches to system design that support an informating strategy, and scanning for technical innovations that can lead to new informating opportunities. Members with responsibility for the development of technology must be as concerned with the use of technology (Do people understand the information? Do they know how to use it?) as they are with other aspects of design and implementation. This kind of technological development can occur only in the closest possible alignment with organizational efforts to promote learning and social integration. Technology develops as a reflection of the informating strategy and provides the material infrastructure of the learning environment.

Learning increases the pace of change. For an organization to pursue an informating strategy, it must maximize its own ability to learn and explore the implications of that learning for its long-range plans with respect to markets, product development, new sources of comparative advantage, et cetera. A division of learning that supports an informating strategy results in a distribution of knowledge and authority that enables a wide range of members to contribute to these activities. Still, some members will need to guide and coordinate learning efforts in order to lead an assessment of strategic alternatives and to focus organizational intelligence in areas of strategic value. These managers lead the organization in a way that allows members to participate in defining purpose and in supporting the direction of long-term planning. The increased time horizon of their responsibilities provides the reflective distance with which they can gauge the quality of the learning environment and can guide change that would improve collective learning.

There is considerable interdependence among these four domains of managerial activity (intellective skill development, technology development, strategy formulation, and social system development). For example, activities related to intellective skill development cannot proceed without the social system management that helps to foster roles and relationships appropriate to a new division of learning. Activities in either of these domains will be frustrated without technological development that supports an informating strategy. Integration and learning are responsibilities that fall within each domain, because without a shared commitment to interdependence and the production of value-adding knowledge, the legitimacy of the learning community will suffer. Business outcomes such as cost, efficiency, quality, product development, customer service, productivity, et cetera, would result from coordinated initiatives across domains. Managerial work would thus be team-oriented and interdisciplinary, and would promote the fluid movement of members across these four domains of managerial activity.

The concentric structure depends upon and promotes both vertical and horizontal organizational integration. There are no predetermined boundaries between any rings within the organizational sphere or between the domains of managerial authority. The skills that are required at the data interface nearest to the core of daily operating responsibilities provide a coherent basis for the kind of continual learning that would prepare people for increasingly comprehensive responsibilities. The relative homogeneity of the total organizational skill base suggests a vision of organizational membership that resembles the trajectory of a professional career, rather than the two-class system marked by an insurmountable gulf between workers and managers. The interpenetration between rings provides a key source of organizational integration.

Some observers of the emerging technological environment have predicted an increasingly bifurcated distribution of skills in the workplace.[8] On the other extreme, the operators at Piney Wood, whose discussion of the future opened our Introduction, believed that in the future all factory workers would be college graduates. The concentric organizational structure suggests that the solution to future skill requirements need not be as drastic as either of these scenarios implies. While it is probable that entry-level requirements will become more demanding, the increased homogeneity of skills and the continuity between organizational rings entails an ongoing commitment to training and education in order to facilitate career progression. The shape of skill distribution thus is more likely to represent a curve than the discontinuous step function that characterizes the traditional hierarchy, with its more rigid distinction between managers and the managed.

THE BODY'S NEW WORK: MANAGING THE INTRICACY OF POSTHIERARCHICAL RELATIONSHIPS

The vision of a concentric organization is one that seems to rely upon metaphors of wholeness—interdependency, fluidity, and homogeneity each contribute to organizational integration. What is required of man-

agers in such a workplace, where learning and integration constitute
the two most vital organizational priorities? How is the social system
of such an organization to be managed?

As we have seen, the abstract precincts of the data interface heighten
the need for communication. Interpretive processes depend upon creating and sharing meaning through inquiry and dialogue. New sources
of personal influence are associated with the ability to learn and to
engender learning in others, in contrast to an earlier emphasis upon
contractual relationships or the authority derived from function and
position.

What new patterns of relationships will characterize this kind of
learning environment? What will replace the familiar map that the
model of imperative control has provided? The answer to this question
derives from one of the most significant dialetics of an informating
strategy. In a conventional organization, managers' action-centered
skills are geared toward the politics of interpersonal influence, princi-
pally as they pertain to maintaining reciprocities, managing superiors,
and gathering or disseminating information. These skills are shaped by
the demands of achieving smooth operations and personal success under conditions of hierarchical authority. People develop their expectations about how to treat one another largely in reference to rank and
function. An informating strategy does place severe demands upon
managers' action-centered skills in the service of *acting-with* but in a
very different context. The relationships to be managed are both more
dynamic and more intricate than earlier patterns. The shape and quality
of relationships will vary in relation to what people know, what they
feel, and what the task at hand requires. Relationships will need to be
fashioned and refashioned as part of the dynamism of the social processes, like inquiry and dialogue, that mediate learning. Such relationships are more intricate because their character derives from the spe-
cifics of the situation that are always both pragmatic—what it takes
to get the work done best—and psychological—what people need to
sustain motivation and commitment.[9]

In the information panopticon, managers (like those at Metro Tel)
frequently tried to simplify their managerial tasks by displacing face-
to-face engagement with techniques of surveillance and control. As a
consequence, they became isolated from the realities of their organizations as they were increasingly insulated by an electronic text that in
turn was even more vulnerable to workers' antagonisms. The demands

of managing intricate relationships reintroduce the importance of the sentient body and so provide a counterpoint to the threat of hyperrationalism and impersonalization that is posed by computer mediation. The body now functions as the scene of human feeling rather than as the source of physical energy or as an instrument of political influence. Human feeling operates here in two ways. First, as members engage in their work together, their feelings are an important source of data from which intricate relations are structured. Second, a manager's felt sense of the group and its learning needs is a vital source of personal knowledge that informs the development of new action-centered skills in the service of *acting-with*.

The demands of a learning environment can reduce the psychological distance between the self and the organization because active engagement in the social processes associated with interpretation requires more extensive participation of the human personality. In a traditional approach to work organization, employees could be treated as objectively measurable bodies, and in return, they could give of their labor without giving of their selves. The human being as wage earner and the human being as subjective actor could remain separate. In an environment of imperative control, managers can remain indifferent to what their subordinates feel, as long as they perform adequately. This "is" was eventually translated to "ought," as incursions of private feeling into the workday came to be seen as squandering the organization's time. It was this view that ultimately triumphed over the professionals at DrugCorp who had unwittingly textualized their own playfulness. As they struggled with their notions of legitimate work behavior, DrugCorp's managers tried to define the self out of the workday. But when work involves a collective effort to create and communicate meaning, the dynamics of human feeling cannot be relegated to the periphery of an organization's concerns. How people feel about themselves, each other, and the organization's purposes is closely linked to their capacity to sustain the high levels of internal commitment and motivation that are demanded by the abstraction of work and the new division of learning.

The relationships that characterize a learning environment thus can be thought of as posthierarchical. This does not imply that differentials of knowledge, responsibility, and power no longer exist; rather, they can no longer be assumed. Instead, they shift and flow and develop their character in relation to the situation, the task, and the actors at hand. Managing intricacy calls for a new level of action-centered skill, as dialogue and inquiry place a high premium on the intuitive and imaginative sources of understanding that temper and hone the talents related to *acting-with*. The dictates of a learning environment, rather than those of imperative control, now shape the development of such interpersonal know-how.

The seeds of this new intricacy are already evident in several of the organizations I have described. The managers at Cedar Bluff who learned to join their workers in asking questions and searching for answers were already engaged in forging patterns far more intricate than the simpler prescriptions derived from faith in managerial authority. The professionals of DrugCorp, normally divided by function, professional discipline, and organizational rank, had invented new modes of relationships based upon a valued exchange of information, shared inquiry, and play. At Global Bank Brazil, bankers and operations managers were groping for new relationships that would reach beyond turf and hierarchy in order to better serve their customers. At Tiger Creek, managers and workers reached and stumbled as they attempted to shift the logic of their relationship from one based on hierarchy to one shaped by the pragmatic opportunities offered by a redistribution of knowledge. In each of these cases, organizational members were confronted with rich new possibilities engendered by an informating technology. In each case, they discovered that exploiting these new opportunities required new forms of relationships governed by the necessities of learning and performance rather than by the rules of an older faith—rules that sort, rank, and separate.

DISSENT FROM WHOLENESS

Is there a dark side to this vision of a wholistic organization with its emphasis on relationships that are intricate, dynamic, and constructed ad hoc? What new psychological costs might it imply? What new mechanisms might be required to ensure justice and equity? To answer these questions, we need to return to the voices of the mill workers as they lived through the transition to an informated environment.

One source of insight into the potential pitfalls of the wholistic organization comes from those workers at Piney Wood who drew strength from the institutional arrangements of a traditional work system. When workers at that plant anticipated the future, they saw computer-based technology as a catalyst for new work systems that would be more flexible, collaborative, and socially integrative than anything they had known. Many were curious and even enthusiastic about such a prospect, but there were others who dissented from this vision of wholeness. Their perspective reminds us of how a certain breed of American worker has found psychological sustenance in the norms of the industrial workplace. It can also alert us to what might be lost in the transformation to a new form of organization and asks that we think carefully about what was best in the old arrangement and should be preserved.

Though the corrosive effects of an adversarial environment cannot be denied, there are those who found an important source of psychological freedom in the rigorously defined contractual relationships that characterized Piney Wood. In such a workplace, the union contract defines binding arrangements—jobs are meticulously defined, and seniority rules guide pay and promotion decisions. Individual workers know exactly what is required of them and, in return, what rights they possess. The worker's first obligation is above all to the job—to perform it competently and completely. As long as individuals uphold their end of the employment contract, their rights are protected. These protections provide them a status under the law that is equal to that of their employer. If the contract is violated, then there are institutionalized mechanisms of due process, invested ultimately with the legitimate authority of the state, through which a person can redress a grievance or seek to influence the policies that inform the labor-management relationship.

The organizing principle of such a workplace is based on the individual. People are held accountable for their particular jobs, and these jobs are treated as distinct elements that must be assembled in order to accomplish the work of the organization. That one's obligation is first of all to the job, rather than to the enterprise, creates a certain psychological distance between the self and the organization. Living up to the terms of the employment contract leaves a wide range of behavior that is unspecified and noncontractual. A worker need not buy into the purposes or values of the organization in order to perform competently and enjoy the rewards that he or she has earned. There is no pressing need to be liked by those around you, either superiors or peers, when one's primary obligation is to fulfill the demands of a narrow job description.

These arrangements can provide the worker with a measure of independence and autonomy. They make it possible to feel that one is, as the idiom goes, one's "own man." U.S. labor relations reflect a conception of equality in which parties each seek advantage through negotiation. Neither party must buy into the worldview of the other. A pluralism of values and interpretations may coexist, so long as the job gets done.[10]

When the workers in such an organization consider their managers, they see a very different world. Those who most value the psychological distance and autonomy provided by the contractual relationship, view managers with a certain pity. They believe that managers are at the mercy of a system that can make unlimited demands, because the boundaries that define the manager's job are vague and permeable. Managerial jobs themselves are abstract enough to be subject to diverse interpretations. Managers might well ask themselves, have I done my job? If the job is that abstract, then it is also easy for peers and superiors to question what a manager has done and to formulate their own evaluations of his or her performance. Without a collective contract, the manager is vulnerable and dependent; he or she must surrender to the organization's purposes and values. Instead of the feistiness and pluralism that characterize the labor-management relationship, many workers see in the managers' world overbearing demands for ideological unity, loyalty, and the submergence of the self. In other words, managers may seek to control their subordinates, but they are not in control of their own work lives.

There is a breed of American worker who cherishes the autonomy and sense of self-control afforded by his or her skills and protected by the union contract. When these workers contemplate the prospect of the socially integrated high-technology workplace, they feel despair. They anticipate a loss of their unique identities, of freedom and autonomy, and of well-defined rights and responsibilities. They fear that without the traditional sources of protection provided by their job descriptions and their contract, they will become prey to every capricious whim of their superiors. They understand that the managers' world requires the body as a political instrument for self-presentation and influence, but they know that these are talents they have not developed and toward which they feel more than a little distaste.

> They say that with this new technology we need a more flexible sys-
> tem, one that will make us competitive. They figure it works for
> management, so why not for the blue-collar worker. If a manager
> hasn't saved money, he won't get his extra one hundred dollars a
> week. If he doesn't produce, he's out the gate. But right now, I don't
> have anything to worry about except doing my job and doing it well.
> I don't have to be friends with people in order to move up. I don't
> have to use anybody. In the management world, you have got to be a
> salesman to a certain extent. You have go to know how to manipulate
> the human system. If I am like management, it means I will have to
> be doubly nice to you whether I like you or not. You have to see
> everybody as a stepping-stone.

Other operators believe that in a fluid, socially integrated workplace, without clear job descriptions and contracts, they would lose the clarity of rights and obligations that currently offer an important sense of personal control. Without such definition, how will one know what to expect each day and how will it be possible to manage the extent of one's own exertion? They fear flexible arrangements that would change according to the needs of the total organization, in place of discrete task assignments on an individual basis. Their "have-skills-will-travel" image is a kind of emotional insurance policy, but an enterprise-centered approach to task distribution would make each individual more dependent upon and integrated with the organization.

> They say the new technology will require a flexible system. But under
> a flexible system, you have no choice but to go where they send you,
> when they send you. You can get to earn high pay, but you have no
> choice about what your job is, and you can't have your own job. You
> never know what to wear to work—do you wear your good Levi's or
> do you wear your greasy ones?

This statement represents the operators' worst fears—that the loss of control over one's work would invade the most intimate and ordinary details of everyday life. Stumbling around the bedroom on a dark morning, trying to get ready in time to have a cup of coffee before leaving for the plant, the worker must ask, What do I wear? What kind of day should I look forward to? What is in store for me today? Will I feel good about the things I am asked to do? Without the capacity to set one's expectations, it is difficult to locate oneself emotionally. It is easy to feel helpless, as if one is at the mercy of others.

The disquiet these workers feel culminates in a frank concern over power. In a workplace in which divisions among workers and between workers and managers are minimized, where all members are supposed to pull together in the service of the organization, what rights will individuals have? How will these rights be specified? What mechanisms will ensure that individuals have a voice in and influence over the policies and practices that shape their work life? Who will have the power to define the circle of legitimate behavior by which all members are evaluated?

> They say that in a new flexible system the criteria for advancement are fitness and ability instead of seniority. But who gets to say you are fit? Who decides what is fit? It will turn out to be that if you are nice to your supervisor, if you do what your supervisor wants you to do, that is what makes you fit.

When these workers consider an organizational system that puts a premium on wholeness, they also see a system that will require manipulation, ingratiation, and conformity. They envision a new approach to the work system without also having considered the changes in the distribution of authority that would be necessary for an informating strategy to fully succeed. However, their concerns do warn of the potential for tyranny in a flexible and socially integrated organization. There are two immediate implications of this warning. First, there presumably will continue to be individuals for whom psychological distance and contractualized responsibilities are very important. To a certain extent, such persons might simply choose to avoid membership in a wholistic informated organization. Viewed in another way, the perspective offered by such individuals probably would be healthy for any learning community. They provide a sensitive barometer for organizational processes that violate respect for the individual or somehow endanger the balance that must exist between individual and organizational interests. A second crucial issue involves the need for mechanisms that can ensure equity and due process within the informated organization. Labor-management contracts grew out of a need for workers to protect themselves from the unilateral authority of their employers. I have already suggested that a new division of labor will not thrive in nor easily tolerate unilateral authority. Nonetheless, informated organizations will have to pay careful attention to developing a constitutional infrastructure that legitimates public debate and mutual influence. The clarity of individual rights within the enterprise is likely to become extremely important to the extent that the learning community requires the participation of the "total person" in its endeavors. Because such a system will exert considerable pressure on an individual's psychological boundaries, it will require mechanisms that can arbitrate competing interpretations of rights and obligations.

The notion of a wholistic informated organization must be qualified in still another way. I have offered a vision of organization in which there are no a priori designations of managers and managed. Instead, people move from the operating core to increasing responsibility and comprehensive influence based upon the degree to which they excel in the skills required by an informated task environment. The intellective skills developed at the data interface provide an important part of the basis for later movement to further rings in the concentric structure. These intellective skills are unlikely to be equally distributed, and the variation in their distribution can become a new source of hierarchical distinctions within even the most fluid organization. For example, at Cedar Bluff, new shades of meaning that began to appear in everyday language foretold the implicit criteria according to which some members would be more highly valued and so implied new sources of conflict as well. These ranking rules were expressed in the metaphorical devices most commonly used in discussions of the new technological environment. Typically, spatial designations were used to convey the worth of people and activities.[11] Consider these interrelated and most often repeated uses of the spatial metaphor:

1. Formal intelligence is up; experiential know-how is down.

    A low-IQ operator will not accept a computer on the job. He will ignore the data in favor of his own way of doing things.

    At Piney Wood, digital instruments seem like black magic, but at Cedar Bluff, operators are more educated. They average one to two years of college instead of just tenth grade. It's a higher, more advanced type of person.

2. Young is up; old is down.

    Younger people find it easier to grasp the computer stuff because they are a higher caliber. Installing new technology is a message to the older operators. It says you must have computer and electronic skills. Some want to retire when they hear this.

    We will be displacing older people who cannot qualify for the new jobs we are creating. They have to lift themselves up to standard.

3.   Abstract work is up; manual work is down.

> With this technology, we are bringing people to a higher level
> intellectually. It is more demanding, so you have to treat them
> differently. The physical demands are gone. There are no hammers
> and wrenches. To deal with problems now is more complex. The
> computer operators are going to be higher than the man on the
> floor, because the physical is easier to train that the brain.
>
> We need a higher caliber of people now. They have to use their
> heads now, not just what comes below the neck. Not just do things.

Cedar Bluff's plant manager recounted their efforts to recruit a
"high" caliber work force suited to the demands of "high" technology:

> We believed that having a number of people with higher levels of
> understanding would create group dynamics effects that would result
> in better problem solving. A high level of knowledge, a high level
> of intelligence, will result in a higher individual contribution to
> the business. We need people to be able to optimize our use of the
> technology.

Workers had been promised a completely computerized operation
and believed their jobs would be "push-button easy" with no "nasty
work" to leave them soiled and exhausted at the end of the day. The
reality was somewhat different, requiring a fair amount of interaction
with the operating equipment, particularly in the first years as operators
learned their way around the mill. Though their direct involvement
with equipment was substantially less than it would have been in a
conventional mill, their only frame of reference was that initial promise
of "workless" work. Subtle hierarchical pressures began to take shape
within this work force that had been so painstakingly recruited and
primed for teamwork. People began to believe that the best and the
brightest were those who excelled at the data interface, while others
gravitated (or were nudged) toward maintenance work. A manager
described this subtle sifting process:

> We need our most-qualified people manning the computer screens.
> The people who really know what the equipment feels like and
> sounds like are becoming second-class citizens. In a traditional sys-
> tem, you spent your whole life developing that feel, and your liveli-
> hood depended on it. But the new generation must trust the com-
> puter screen. A new pecking order emerges. The computer screen

takes more mental skills, and we reward those skills. Maybe the work in the field is intrinsically as valuable, but people around here don't see it that way.

There was a great deal of resentment when a crisis such as a pulp spill pulled the control room operators "out into the process" with tall rubber boots and shovels. Operators called these kinds of tasks "nasty work," a designation that clearly demarcated such activities from their "real" work at the data interface and provided a sense of psychological distance from the role of the laboring body. The special label signaled their preferred self-conception as people who could keep their collars clean:[12]

> If there is nasty work here, it means someone made a mistake. We don't like to get nasty. They told us all we would do is run computers.

The resentments that surround physical exertion once defined the boundary between managers and workers but now were felt within the operating work force. Subtle conflicts erupted among operators as they struggled to balance the satisfactions of intellective virtuosity against the comforts of group solidarity. Several operators at Cedar Bluff told of incidents in which they had made a special effort to break new ground in their understanding of the theoretical and practical aspects of the relationships among the process variables under their control. In each case, their discoveries had made it possible to solve a chronic problem and to generate significant savings. These operators became the target for derisive chiding from their peers. One man told of spending several months studying a problem that concerned the operation of the boiler. He conducted experiments, ran tests, monitored data, and read theories. He finally concluded what was wrong with the way they had been controlling the boilers. He wrote up the material in the format of a proficiency exam, supplying all the answers to the questions with the material he had amassed.

> I wanted to share it with the team, to learn it better by teaching them. They said, "I don't want to hear that shit!" They didn't even want to see the book.

Another told of a similar experience. His discovery was of such economic value that he was sent to divisional headquarters to present his findings to the engineering staff.

They had me talk to a VP about it, so I got recognized. In fact, it embarrassed me that I got so much recognition. I would have liked less because of the peer pressure I got. None of my peers would go along with it from the beginning. So I had to go to all the shift coordinators instead. My peers treated me like someone who thinks they know it all, a company man. They said I was getting too close to management. That was tough to work with on a day-to-day basis. I learned how to work it now—just play it low key.

One explanation for this behavior is that it repeats the game of self-protection so well known to generations of industrial workers. Gloria Schuck has labeled it "intellective rate busting": any worker who excels at the data interface increases the demands on the whole group.[13] Another interpretation is that the barriers that separate managerial from operating jobs have been maintained but simply pushed down to a lower level of the organization. A gulf continues to exist; what has changed is the distribution of members on each side.

The reactions of these disgruntled operators does not take into account the possibility of a change in the logic of imperative control—a logic that sustains the necessity of managerial authority and perpetuates adversarial feeling. In the context of that logic, workers learn that they cannot learn, and managers learn that they must already know. Thus, the interests of each group remain divergent, even as they are locked in the fitful interdependence of imperative control.

In contrast, an informating strategy implies a discontinuity in the logic of imperative control. The new division of learning should organize experience in ways that help perpetuate belief in a synthesis of interests and thus legitimate a learning environment that presupposes relationships among equals. Only under such conditions can knowledge be shared in a way that strengthens the collective effort. Barriers between information-intensive and non-information-intensive responsibilities limit equality and inhibit the spirit of inquiry that animates the informated organization, thus inviting adversarial games of self-protection and domination.

The problem appears to be that not every job in even the most informated organization is likely to require intellective skills. Certainly in the near term, most organizations will continue to have some tasks that either are physically demanding or involve highly routinized versions of information handling. How such jobs are distributed becomes a crucial question for any organization that would commit itself to a new division of labor. Does the fact of these persistent differences between tasks lead inevitably to a reproduction of the labor-management caste system?

It is important to reiterate here that the presupposition of relations of equality does not imply a correlative assumption that all organizational members are exactly alike. In any organization, there will be some individuals who reject the demands of intellective work. Not everyone will contain in equal measure the internal commitment, motivation, or cognitive style associated with the responsibilities of life at the data interface. Some will be repelled by the mental stress of such work and find it too perplexing or anxiety-inducing. Others will prefer to conduct their work lives in motion, drawing sustenance from using their bodies to accomplish their tasks. There were many such operators in the Piney Wood Mill. One expressed his anxiety about his place in the emerging organization when he asked:

> What will happen to the blue-collar man, the little man, who did his job and did not take it home with him at the end of the day. . . . When a man has reached his limits, are they going to get rid of him?

There was a smaller but still significant subset of workers at Cedar Bluff who felt deeply uncomfortable with the work available to them in the control rooms, despite the importance and prestige attached to it.

> The work in the control room is mental. It isn't as hard as out in the process, but I would rather be out on the floor working. I am moving out there. I don't like to be cramped up with no room to breathe. If they padded this room, I would have my body indented in the walls from bouncing off them all the time.

While some degree of hierarchy is inevitable in any social group, the values and beliefs that animate these distinctions can operate very differently from the traditional assumptions of imperative control. In the informated organization, there is no reason why these individuals could not elect to align themselves with the jobs best suited to their sensibilities or talents. The difference here lies in the voluntary, nonarbitrary, and reversible nature of their decisions. Instead of facing rigid and practically irreversible designations that are reinforced by virtually every aspect of organizational experience, these individuals could be free to self-select into or out of the more abstract forms of work.

The freedom of self-selection can be maintained as long as institutional arrangements ensure the full participation of these members in the political life of the learning community. There are several mechanisms through which this could be accomplished. First, these individuals, like other members, would have broad access to the streams of circulating information within the organization. Were they to so choose, they could be rotated into positions that provided a greater opportunity for the development of their intellective potential. Second, the close coordination and integration of the various aspects of the production process would require these members to keep abreast of critical information from daily operational issues to changes in the business context, or a new direction in the strategic plan. Finally, the rewards available for their work would be commensurate with their value to the production process and not undervalued as a matter of course.[14]

THE INFORMATED ORGANIZATION AND RECENT TRENDS IN WORK ORGANIZATION

As the years passed at Cedar Bluff, managers began to confront more openly and honestly the challenges to their skills that had been unleashed by the informating process. It was not untypical for organizations pursuing high commitment strategies to feel the strains of participative management and to experience a good bit of conflict concerning the limits of managerial prerogatives. At Cedar Bluff, however, the demands on managers had become relentlessly insistent. The knowledge requirements of the data interface, the vulnerability of plant performance to variations in operator skill and motivation, and the broad accessibility of data had lent new urgency to questions about the skills, roles, and structures that should define the organization. This was vividly illustrated by the turmoil that surrounded the development of a new pay and promotion system for hourly workers. The operators had become increasingly proficient in operating the plant, and after several years of producing pulp at far below the equipment's true capacity, production levels began to climb. As operators' skills improved, so did their dissatisfaction with the pay and promotion system. They believed that it arbitrarily limited the amount of learning for which they could be rewarded. Amid mounting dissension, a committee consisting of operators and managers from the various areas of the plant was appointed to gather data on the problem and to recommend new policies. The plant had reached production levels of more than nine hundred tons a day, but as the committee went into session, operators were heard to say, "That's the last nine-hundred-ton day this plant will see until the pay and promotion problems are resolved."

In the months that followed, their predictions came true; the plant returned to earlier production levels. Cedar Bluff's managers were especially frustrated because they could not identify the causes of the downturn. Only rarely could a manager point to something that operators were doing incorrectly that might be contributing to poor production. They concluded that the disappointing performance could be attributed, not to what operators *were* doing, but to what they *were not* doing. The operators' errors were sins of omission—an underutilization of the data interface resulting from their refusal to notice, to think, to explore, to experiment, or to improve. In other words, the power of the new technology was going to waste. Managers felt helpless to alter the situation. It was only when the new pay and promotion system was finally developed and accepted by a majority vote that production levels began to climb once again.

There are several lessons to be learned here. First, the requirements of an informating strategy support existing work-improvement efforts, such as the high commitment approach to work force management, with its emphasis on self-managing teams, participation, and decentralization. Organizations that are already pursuing this approach are more likely to have developed both the ideological context and the social skills necessary to plan and implement an informating strategy. In this regard, Cedar Bluff provides an important contrast not only to Piney Wood but also to organizations, like Global Bank Brazil, that have minimal experience with work-system innovation. Second, the demands for a redistribution of knowledge and the consequent challenge to the managerial role that can be unleashed by the informating process are likely to exacerbate the growing pains associated with participative management and to accelerate the need for positive change. Third, organizational innovations designed to create high commitment work systems typically have focused upon the hourly work force. In most cases, and Cedar Bluff is one example, the managerial hierarchy has remained relatively intact, while team organization and pay-for-skill systems have been designed for the operational work force. In contrast, an informating strategy suggests the need for a more wholistic reconceptualization of the skills, roles, and structures that define the total organization. Partial change efforts, as at Tiger Creek, or technology-driven initiatives, as at Global Bank Brazil, are unlikely to result in the kind of learning environment necessary for an ongoing and robust approach to the informating process. Finally, managing in an informated environment is a delicate human process. The ability to use information for real business benefit is as much a function of the quality of commitment and relationships as it is a function of the quality of intellective skills.

The words of the clerk at Global Bank Brazil continue to echo: "Will things be any different now?" In response, we can say that the opportunity is there, and we now know more about what it will take. An informating strategy requires a comprehensive vision based upon an understanding of the unique capacities of intelligent technology and the opportunity to use the organization to liberate those capacities. It means forging a new logic of technological deployment based upon that vision. A coherent rationale will be necessary, particularly when the tide of conventional thinking and familiar assumptions on this subject can submerge many important choices regarding basic technological design and management. Cedar Bluff's plant manager foresaw this danger:

> The technology is going in the direction that says one person operates the master controls. Is the technology right? We don't believe it is, and we are working hard to convince our vendors to leave the design flexible enough so that it does not preclude the uses we want to make of it.

The informated organization does move in another direction. It relies on the human capacities for teaching and learning, criticism and insight. It implies an approach to business improvement that rests upon the improvement and innovation made possible by the enhanced comprehensibility of core processes. It reflects a fertile interdependence between the human mind and some of its most sophisticated productions. As one worker from Tiger Creek mused:

> If you don't let people grow and develop and make more decisions, it's a waste of human life—a waste of human potential. If you don't use your knowledge and skill, it's a waste of life. Using the technology to its full potential means using the man to his full potential.

THE SCOPE OF INFORMATION
TECHNOLOGY IN THE
MODERN WORKPLACE

Information technology is a label that reflects the convergence of several streams of technical developments, including microelectronics, computer science, telecommunications, software engineering, and system analysis. It is a technology that dramatically increases the ability to record, store, analyze, and transmit information in ways that permit flexibility, accuracy, immediacy, geographic independence, volume, and complexity. Information technology has a unique capability to restructure operations that depend upon information for the purposes of transaction, record keeping, analysis, control, or communication.

There is hardly a segment of the U.S. economy that has not been penetrated by some form of computer-based technology. The core of this technology is the silicon-integrated circuit, or "chip." The equivalent of hundreds of thousands of transistors can be built on a silicon chip measuring no more than a fraction of an inch. The astonishing reductions in the cost of these microprocessors, coupled with their equally impressive performance levels, have been exhaustively documented. During the past thirty years, the price per second of instruction has decreased dramatically: a computation that now costs one dollar would have cost about $30,000 in 1950.[1] Porter and Millar calculate that the cost of computer power relative to the cost of manual information processing is at least eight thousand times less than the cost thirty years ago. Between 1958 and 1980, the amount of time needed for one electronic operation fell by a factor of 80 million. They also cite Department of Defense studies that show that the error rate in recording data through bar coding is one in 3 million, compared to one error in three hundred manual data entries.[2] During the past fifteen years, the memory capacity of an integrated circuit has increased by a factor of one thousand, as has its reliability. As another writer remarked, "If the automotive industry had paralleled the advances that the computer industry has experienced in the last 25 years, a Rolls Royce would cost 50 cents and would deliver 15 million miles to the gallon.[3]

Numerous studies by economists and industry analysts have concluded that computer-based information technologies will profoundly affect the structure of the U.S. economy.[4] One analyst estimates that in 1980, approximately 10 million Americans interacted daily with a video display terminal and that this number would increase to 25 million by 1990.[5] Another estimates that by the year 1990, 50 million American office workers will spend a significant portion of their workday interacting with a computer terminal of some sort.[6] Another expert predicts that in 1990, 65 percent of all professional, managerial, technical, and administrative workers (a group that now constitutes almost half the labor force) will depend upon computer-based workstations.[7] The Congressional Office of Technology Assessment has predicted that there will be at least one computer terminal for every two or three office workers by 1990.[8] One recent survey of 530 employees representing every organizational level in twenty-six companies offers some accurate, if more limited, findings. Respondents were divided according to occupational groups: executives, managers, professionals, technicians, secretaries, and clerks. Averaging across all categories, researchers found that 67 percent of all the respondents interacted directly with a computer during the regular course of their work and that 26 percent expected to do so in the near future. When executives (for whom the figures were 36 percent and 46 percent, respectively) are eliminated from this average, the figure for current usage jumps to 74 percent. Of these same respondents, about half reported using the computer during 30 percent or less of their working time, another quarter of the group reported spending up to 70 percent of their time at the terminal, while the final quarter spent up to 100 percent of their workday at the computer terminal. Such figures suggest the degree to which information technology is affecting everyday life across a broad spectrum of the work force.[9]

THE SERVICE SECTOR

Information technology has different applications in the service and manufacturing sectors of the economy. In the service sector, the technology has been used primarily to meet the mushrooming demands of handling information. Businesses now are faced with the task of controlling 400 billion documents, a number that is expected to increase at the rate of 72 billion per year.[10] As the technology develops, clerks working with documents in the back office can enter data directly into terminals linked to a computer mainframe, which does the actual processing. In many cases, even the documents have disappeared; clerks are able to perform all their transactions through the electronic medium. Such on-line applications began to be widespread in the early 1980s and have become a prominent trend in most large service organizations.

The early 1980s also saw new applications of information technology for professionals, managers, and technical workers. The introduction of small, stand-alone word processors, microcomputers, and personal computers made it easier for nonspecialists to use databases, to manipulate text and quantitative data, to generate tables and graphic displays, to utilize analytical software, and to communicate with one another through a computer network. Today, microcomputers are being linked to one another as well as to central computers so that they can be used independently or in conjunction with corporate data bases. These emerging systems also can be linked to external data bases and communications networks; further, they can cross organizational and national boundaries.

Most large information-processing organizations, such as banks and insurance companies, still require a sizeable clerical work force to enter data and perform routine transactions on a computer system. Many such organizations are searching for ways to circumvent this massive clerical effort and at the same time increase the continuity of their operations. An increasingly popular solution is to incorporate the data-entry function in operations that are external to the organization. For example, when a customer uses an automated teller machine, the data-entry function is accomplished automatically without clerical input. A hospital computer may send bills directly to the health insurer's computer, which in turn instructs the bank's computer to transfer funds. An inter-organizational computer system thus can eliminate routine clerical work in several organizations.

Technologies that were once relatively distinct now have begun to converge. The functions once accomplished by typewriters, printing presses, copying machines, telephones, files, calculators, and mail sorting systems, are becoming either subsumed within or linked to the functioning of the comprehensive computer-based network. Software is more powerful and easier to use. New procedures allow people to interact with the computer in ways that encourage more familiarity and immediacy, such as touch-sensitive screens and voice-activated programs.[11]

THE MANUFACTURING SECTOR

Applications of computer technology in the manufacturing sector have developed along distinct lines in discrete parts manufacturing (for example, automobiles, farm equipment, electronics) and in the continuous-process industries (for example, oil refineries, chemical processors, food and beverages, paper and pulp), which each face different problems in manufacturing process. Continuous-process production typically involves a flow of material that can pass through several stages before emerging in its final form. The production process manipulates the composition of materials by chemical reaction, purification, and blending of component materials. At each stage, different operations are performed, such as heating, cooling, mixing, chemical reaction, distillation, drying, or pressurization. This requires continual measurement and control of variables like time, temperature, raw material characteristics, steam pressure, chemical levels, densities, viscosities, liquid levels, flow rates, et cetera. Twenty percent of all industrial computers, and 40 percent or more of all minicomputers and microcomputers, are accounted for by continuous-process applications designed for monitoring, analysis, control, and optimization. Process computers evolved from simple data recording devices: they collected real-time operational data and set off alarms under critical conditions.

The next phase of development produced "open loop" systems, in which operators rely on either first-hand observations of the process or data generated by microprocessor-based sensors and programmable logic controllers built into operating equipment. With this information, they can use the computer system for mathematical analysis to help them adjust process conditions. The computer also becomes the medium through which operators can manipulate process variables and parameters to meet the desired conditions. Most recent developments include supervisory process-control systems that can be programmed to receive information directly from instruments monitoring the process, to set control points, to perform computations, and to adjust control variables to continually approximate optimum levels of functioning. Theoretically, such systems mimimize the need for operator involvement, except in upset conditions.

As plants apply these control systems to their operations, the amount of physical interaction with the production process is reduced and workers typically operate from remote control rooms, where they monitor video terminals that display data reflecting the state of the production process. In some process industries, such as oil refining or steel production, where the various steps of the conversion from raw material to output are well understood, there has been considerable progress in developing supervisory control systems. These were among the first industries to comprehensively apply microprocessor-based control technology. In other process industries, such as paper and pulp or food and beverages, the manufacturing process has not yet been entirely explicated, and there are no adequate sensing devices to measure all key variables. These industries have been slower to adopt the technology and face more difficulty in programming supervisory control.[12]

In discrete parts manufacturing, the problems are more geometric in nature, involving the placement of parts and equipment in relation to one another, as well as their movement from one stage of assembly to another. Typical applications of information technology in discrete parts manufacturing include computer-aided design (drafting and engineering), computer-aided manufacturing (robots and numerically controlled machine tools), flexible manufacturing systems, automated material handling, and automated storage-and-retrieval systems. Computer-aided design systems facilitate the use of previous designs and allow more rapid design changes. They can improve the design process by allowing engineers to try out a dozen or a hundred different variations, when they previously might have been limited to building three or four prototype models. It is estimated that in 1983, there were thirty-two thousand computer-aided design workstations being used in the United States.[13]

Robots are mechanical manipulators that can be programmed to move workpieces or tools along a prescribed path. While most robots today can perform only relatively well-defined and repetitive tasks, efforts are under way to incorporate more intelligence and sensory capacities within these machines. There are many differing estimates as to the extent of robotization in manufacturing. The Robot Institute of America indicates that in 1983, 66 percent (31,900) of the world's robots were operating in Japan and 13 percent (6,301) were in the United States.[14] Nobel-prize-winning economist Wassily Leontief has predicted a 30 to 40 percent annual growth rate in the market for industrial robots between 1985 and 1990.[15]

Computer-numerically-controlled machine tools fashion metal according to programmed instructions that indicate the desired dimensions of a part and the sequence to be followed in the machining process. Since the late 1970s, these machines have been equipped with microprocessors or dedicated minicomputers and frequently include a screen and keyboard for writing or editing the programs that guide the equipment. These devices are the basis for "direct numerical control machines," in which a larger mini-computer or mainframe computer is used to program and run more than one numerically controlled tool simultaneously. The Congressional Office of Technology Assessment reports that as the price of small computers has declined, these machine tools are being equipped with microcomputers that can be linked to one another and to a central controlling computer, thus creating a hierarchy of computer control.[16] Many observers have remarked upon the relatively slow diffusion of these applications due to their high capital cost and the bottlenecks in developing and maintaining software programs. In 1983, numerically controlled machine tools represented only about 5 percent of the machine tools in U.S. metalworking, but this may change rapidly.[17] For example, General Motors Corporation has stated that by the end of the 1980s, 90 percent of all new capital investments will be in computer numerically controlled machines.[18]

Flexible manufacturing systems integrate these more discrete applications of technology. They consist of computer-controlled machining centers that sculpt complicated metal parts at high speed and with great reliability, robots that handle the parts, and remotely guided carts that deliver materials. These components are linked by computer-based controls that dictate what will happen at each stage of the manufacturing sequence. Many consider the great advantage of these systems to be their ability to achieve low-cost production in small volumes, without having to rely on the economics of scale associated with mass production. "A flexible automation system can turn out a small batch or even a single copy of a product as efficiently as a production line designed to turn out a million identical items."[19] These systems are complex and costly, and thus still relatively rare. Reliable statistics are difficult to obtain because of conflicting definitions of precisely what level of integration and control constitutes "flexibility." However, *Fortune* magazine recently counted thirty such systems operating in the United States and considerably more in Japan. According to their report, one Japanese firm alone, Toyoda Machine Tool Co., has thirty such systems in operation.[20] Despite the still-modest number of such systems in the United States, *Fortune* estimates that by 1990, the sales of equipment to support flexible manufacturing—robots, computer controls, material-handling devices, et cetera—will rise to $30 billion annually from 1982 levels of $4 billion.

While information technologies in these two manufacturing domains—discrete parts and continuous-process—have developed separately in order to address distinct types of problems, their differences are increasingly diminished by new developments that use computer systems for comprehensive production management. This approach, known as computer-integrated manufacturing, increases the continuity of the production process in discrete parts manufacturing, thus bringing it closer to the "optimal model" of manufacturing in which continuity and controllability are maximized.[21] Under these conditions, workers' tasks begin to look very similar to those of operators in the continuous-process environment, as they come to emphasize monitoring and control (though the types of variables and procedures continue to differ). A recent study published by the National Academy of Sciences points to the integration of computer-aided design and manufacturing with manufacturing resource planning (software that translates demand for products into the parts needed to produce them and then orders the parts from inventory or from suppliers) and computer-aided process planning (software that routes parts through the factory to maximize operating time and to eliminate bottlenecks). "The four technologies are increasingly 'speaking' to each other through local-area networks, and formerly isolated applications are being linked as computer-integrated manufacturing.[22]

Experts continue to disagree on the ultimate consequences of these developments for employment in the manufacturing sector. Some believe that computer-integrated manufacturing will provide the basis for nearly unmanned factories; others insist that automation rarely can be complete and that people will be needed to monitor, control, maintain, manage, and plan these processes, although at lower levels of employment than have characterized older technologies. Whether the unmanned factory is a likely scenario in some cases or not, the coming decade will continue to see manufacturing operations that depend upon people, not just computers. These organizations will become more alike as they are able to increase the continuity and controllability of production through computer integration.

NOTES ON FIELD-RESEARCH

METHODOLOGY

Behind every method lies a belief. Researchers must have a theory of reality and of how that reality might surrender itself to their knowledge-seeking efforts. These epistemological fundamentals are subject to debate but not to ultimate proof. Each epistemology implies a set of methods uniquely suited to it, and these methods will render the qualities of data that reflect a researcher's assessment of what is vital. I believe that researchers ought to indicate something about their beliefs, so that readers can have access to the intellectual choices that are embedded in the research effort.

My own commitment to understanding social phenomena has been fundamentally shaped by the study of phenomenology and, in particular, its application to sociology and psychology. I want to understand the dialectical interchange between human responsiveness (feeling, perceiving, behaving) and what philosophers call the "life-world" or the "life-field." On the one hand, the human body and its responsiveness actively structure the world, but that world in turn shapes and selects forms of human responsiveness. It is in this perpetual interchange that human meanings take shape and find their expression in feeling and behavior. My shorthand for this perspective is to say that "feelings are the body's version of a situation." The interior, preconceptual, felt texture of human responsiveness is an immensely rich source of critical insight into the situation that a person is living. While this level of responsiveness provides for individual variation, the constellation of commonly felt meanings can be a powerful critique of a shared situation. This epistemological perspective is best expressed in works such as Merleau-Ponty's *The Structure of Behavior*, George Herbert Mead's *Mind, Self, and Society*, or Eugene Gendlin's *Experience and the Cre-*

ation of Meaning.[1] These general beliefs led me to certain conclusions about the kind of data I wanted and the methods best suited to my endeavor. As a trained social scientist, I also wanted to employ methods that would be rigorous and systematic. As a field researcher, I understood the importance of opportunism and serendipity. These three considerations shaped each aspect of my methodology.

THE FIELD RESEARCH

Site Selection

I began with some general criteria for site selection. First, because I was determined to search for generic themes in this technological transformation, I wanted sites that represented occupational diversity and that would provide access to different levels of the organization. I wanted to include both manufacturing and service industries, and I wanted to encompass blue-collar workers, clerical employees, managers, and professionals. I wanted sites where one or more of these groups had experienced a fundamental reorganization of their tasks as a result of computer-based technology, and where people were confronting these new task conditions for the first time. In general, I looked for sites where those same individuals had prior task experience with a more traditional medium, though this was not true in every case. For example, in Cedar Bluff, most of the work force had no prior experience in the pulp industry. As a result, I was also able to establish some comparisons between those workers who made the transition to computer mediation and those who were introduced to their work tasks with computer technology already on the scene. I wanted to study organizations that were known to be technological leaders in their industry. My reasoning was that the themes that emerged in those organizations would be most likely to characterize a wide range of organizations in the future. Finally, the roles of serendipity and opportunism in site selection cannot be denied. For example, while on a tour of the Tiger Creek Mill, things seemed pretty placid until I overheard two operators discussing their intention to use the "graveyard" shift for experimentation with the Expense Tracking System in order to avoid managerial interference. I veered away from the formal tour and instead tried to learn more about why the operators felt as they did. These explorations resulted in my choosing to study Tiger Creek's new Expense Tracking System in more depth.

The kind of research process I envisioned was field intensive and longitudinal. It required a considerable degree of organizational largesse to permit me access over a period of time and to a wide range of people. In most cases, this involved several preliminary meetings with managers and workers in order to determine if the site fit my criteria and whether they stood to learn something from the new knowledge that would be produced. In the end, the firms that agreed to participate in my study did provide me with generous access to people and places, and each of them fulfilled my criteria in all the most crucial respects. In all cases, the contract developed with these companies allowed me to operate as an independent researcher with complete ownership of the data I collected. I was asked to respect company rules regarding proprietary material and to disguise the company's identity in my subsequent writing. In some cases, management asked me for informal feedback regarding the nature of my findings, which I conducted in a way that was careful to protect the anonymity of my informants. As my data began to take shape, I used a combination of literature review and short visits to additional firms in order to test informally the general applicability of my findings. These efforts have convinced me that the conceptual map presented here is highly relevant to a broad range of organizations experiencing the transition to information technologies.

Sampling

While my goal was to understand the living meaning of a collective situation, much of my data gathering focused on individuals and what they felt and did. As a result, it was extremely important to apply the principle of triangulation, which calls for a continual juxtaposition and comparison of data culled from distinct sources that purport to describe the same phenomenon. In most organizations, my research focused on the people whose work had been affected by a new technological application; for example, the stock transfer system, the dental claims system, the computer-conferencing system, or the Expense Tracking System. In these cases, I tried to conduct interviews and discussions with all of those who were directly affected, in addition to observing them at work. I also explored the views and experiences of mid-level and senior-level managers as well as the relevant members of the technical community. When it was not possible to engage each individual, I applied two methods of sampling: First, I selected a random group for interviews, and second, I selected those individuals who were known to be particularly involved, candid, or well informed. This provided both a sense of the overall distribution of attitudes and themes, as well as the benefit of the most articulate informants.

The nature of the sampling process had to be tailored to meet the constraints imposed by the site and the kind of work in question. For example, in Consolidated Underwriters Insurance or Universal Technology, I was able to hold large group meetings with a random sample of clerks and then invite the most candid informants back for an individual interview. In the pulp mills, my access to workers was through the control rooms. I remained in a control room for several shifts and thus met a variety of people assigned to that part of the mill. The more control rooms I visited, the more workers I had access to. I then interviewed the majority of line managers and technicians with relevant responsibilities.

Data-Gathering Techniques

I used a range of techniques to gather data; the choice among them depended a great deal on the site and the constraints it imposed. In the two clerical organizations, I conducted small-group discussions over a period of several weeks. The most candid and articulate individuals were invited back for more probing discussions. In general, I tried to tape-record these discussions, though I always gave my informant the option of rejecting the recorder or turning it off at any point. In these organizations I also conducted either small-group or one-on-one interviews with supervisors, managers and technicians. In Global Bank Brazil, Metro Tel, and DrugCorp, I relied on individual interviews, and on occasion, small-group discussions were held with either managers or employees. When it was not possible to tape-record, my procedure was to write down literally everything that was said. These verbatim notes proved to be as reliable as taped transcripts. In the three mills, my discussions with workers evolved more informally. Sometimes, I was able to conduct intensive individual interviews; at other times, I spoke with groups of workers in the control rooms. I conducted individual interviews with managers and technical people, but I also attended many management meetings, where I was able to observe the discussion, and sometimes ask questions.

In all of the sites, I also used the techniques of participant observation: living in the organizations and spending time observing and/or working side-by-side with employees. We took lunches and coffee breaks together, I was invited to workers' homes for dinner, and I sometimes invited groups of people out for drinks at the close of the day. These informal gatherings always deepened my appreciation of their experience and helped to nurture a level of trust that allowed them to explore their experience with me. As an observer in the workplace, I kept notes that included both verbatim accounts and descriptive observations. I also recorded my observations of my own learning and discovery process. My involvement as a participant observer was most extensive in the mills, which I visited repeatedly over a five-year period. The data from DrugCorp also developed over a four-year period. In the other organizations, my visits tended to cover a time frame of about two years. Each organization provided me with complete access to files, documentation, and reports that bore upon my interests.

Interview Procedures

I began this project with a range of themes I wanted to explore and an extensive interview protocol designed to translate those themes into appropriate questions. As I accumulated more experience, and my conceptual map became both more comprehensive and more differentiated, I developed a more precise understanding of the issues I wanted to explore and, for each issue, dozens of field-tested ways of asking questions that would evoke the level of data I was after.

In all cases I informed those with whom I engaged of the nature of my research project. People knew I was working on a book and that I had been invited into their organizations, not as a consultant, but as an independent researcher. Each informant was assured that the content of our discussions would remain confidential and anonymous. I felt a genuine commitment to producing new knowledge that could improve management practice and policy, and I asked people to engage with me in this process. It was clear to me that if I was going to learn anything, it would depend on my informants' capacities as teachers, and I told them so. In order to understand the nature of their interior experience in the context of new technology, it was necessary to ask people to engage in a quality of discussion that required a high degree of trust and openness. My belief was that only a spirit of mutual collaboration in search of deeper understanding would merit the kind of generosity I sought.

In my interviews and discussions, I practiced a non-judgmental form of listening informed by two different methods. First, I was interested in that aspect of people's experience that was still implicit—not yet converted into words or frozen in clichés. I used Gendlin's listening techniques as a way of focusing on the implicit, felt sense of an issue and of helping people through the process of finding words for it.[2] Sometimes, when people had difficulty finding words, I asked them to draw pictures that conveyed their felt sense of the work situation before and after the introduction of new technology. The process of describing the pictures served to free up their ability to find words for their experience. Second, I was interested in the nature of people's reasoning about the problems they confronted. Here, I was also influenced by the interview techniques developed by researchers in the area of cognitive and moral development, such as Piaget, Kohlberg, and Gilligan.[3] This interview approach is designed to explore the boundaries of an individual's cognitive paradigm by calling attention to puzzles, contradictions, or alternative interpretations.

Almost without exception, I was struck by the goodwill, sincerity, and generosity of those with whom I spoke. I learned that people have a great deal to say about their work, but there is rarely anyone around to listen. I felt lucky to be the recipient of so many riches. There were many examples of mill workers, office clerks, and managers so engaged in the discovery process that they collected articles for me or wrote down further thoughts that they mailed to me. Several times I returned to an organization to find that people had been collecting observations or writing down their feelings, waiting for my return in order to share these treasures.

Data Analysis

If there is any single word to describe my analytical method, it is *inductive*. I tried to treat the data much as I treated individual informants—by listening to what they had to say without imposing a preconceived judgment. I spent months puzzling over patterns that I did not understand or that seemed to contradict the concepts I had already developed. During the second year of field work, I thematically coded approximately 1,500 pages of field notes and transcripts. With the themes that emerged, I began to build a conceptual map of the territory, and each subsequent visit was used to elaborate, challenge, confirm, and clarify the emerging material.

I tried to elucidate the range of perspectives on any given issue and to triangulate these perspectives as a way of constructing an image of the organizational system. The quotations that I have included in the text and the verbatim notes that informed my own conclusions represent the main trend of responses on the subject in question. They illustrate both the content of thought and the style of expression of the larger group to which that informant belongs. I have included unusual responses or minority opinions only where there is a substantive reason to do so, and these are clearly indicated in the text. Naturally, an analysis of the scholarly literature that bears upon my subject, primarily in the fields of history, cognitive psychology, social theory, and the sociology of work, was an additional resource in the overall effort to interpret the field data.

NOTES

Introduction Dilemmas of Transformation
in the Age of the Smart Machine

1. See, for example, Michael Piore and Charles F. Sabel, *The Second Industrial Divide: Possibilities for Prosperity* (New York: Basic Books, 1984).
2. Alfred Schutz described the problem this way: "As long as the once established scheme of reference, the system of our and other people's warranted experiences, works, as long as the actions and operations performed under its guidance yield the desired results, we trust these experiences. . . . It needs a special motivation, such as the eruption of a "strange" experience not subsumable under the stock of knowledge at hand or inconsistent with it, to make us revise our former beliefs" (*The Problem of Social Reality, Collected Papers*, vol. 1 [The Hague: Martinus Nijhoff, 1962], 228).
3. Susan Sontag, *On Photography* (New York: Farrar, Straus & Giroux, 1973), 97.

PART ONE KNOWLEDGE AND COMPUTER-MEDIATED WORK

Chapter One The Laboring Body: Suffering and Skill in Production Work

1. Fernand Braudel, *The Wheels of Commerce: Civilization and Capitalism 15th–18th Century*, vol. 2 (New York: Harper & Row, 1982), 466.
2. Ibid., 485.
3. Jacques Legoff, *Time, Work, and Culture in the Middle Ages* (Chicago: University of Chicago Press, 1980), 69–70.
4. Keith Thomas, "Work and Leisure in Pre-Industrial Society," *Past and Present* 29 (1965): 38.
5. Legoff, *Time, Work, and Culture*, 71–97.
6. Thomas, "Work and Leisure," 57.
7. From Sir Thomas More's *Utopia*, quoted in Frank Manuel, "Toward a Psychological History of Utopias," *Daedalus* (Spring 1965): 300.
8. Norbert Elias, *The Civilizing Process: The History of Manners*, vol. 1 (New York: Urizen Books, 1978), and *The Civilizing Process: Power and Civility*, vol. 2 (New York: Pantheon, 1982).
9. Ibid., 1: 56.
10. Ibid., 2: 7–8.
11. Stanislas Fontaine, "The Civilizing Process Revisited: An Interview with Norbert Elias," *Theory and Society* 5 (1978): 248.
12. Ibid., 245.

13. See the discussion in Elias, *Civilizing Process*, 2: 270–300.

14. Ibid., 2: 271–72.

15. Braudel, *Wheels of Commerce*, 495, 499.

16. A. P. Wadsworth, and Julia Mann. *The Cotton Trade and Industrial Lancashire 1600–1780* (Manchester: Manchester University Press, 1931), 395–401.

17. Stephen A. Marglin, "What Do Bosses Do? The Origins and Functions of Hierarchy in Capitalistic Production," *Review of Radical Political Economics* 6 (1974): 60–112.

18. Sidney Pollard, *The Genesis of Modern Management* (Cambridge: Harvard University Press, 1965), 160–73.

19. Sebastion DeGrazia, *Of Time, Work and Leisure* (New York: The Twentieth Century Fund, 1962), 197.

20. Pollard, *Genesis of Modern Management*, 161.

21. Ibid., 182.

22. Douglas Reid, "The Decline of Saint Monday 1766–1876," *Past and Present* 71 (1976): 79.

23. Ibid., 78.

24. Ibid., 80.

25. Ibid.

26. Pollard, *Genesis of Modern Management*, 182.

27. Herbert Gutman, *Work, Culture, and Society in Industrializing America: Essays in American Working-Class and Social History* (New York: Alfred A. Knopf, 1976), 20.

28. Ibid.

29. Ibid., 38.

30. Pollard, *Genesis of Modern Management*, 189. Sidney Pollard has classified these measures in three categories: the negative sanctions for particular behaviors, the positive inducements toward particular behaviors, and the general effort to create a "new ethos of work order and obedience." An 1833 Factory Commission survey asked employers how they disciplined their child laborers. Negative measures were reported 575 times and included everything from dismissal to degrading dress. Positive measures were reported 34 times and included kindness (two cases), promotion, and rewards.

31. Ibid., 184.

32. J. L. Hammond, and Barbara Hammond, *The Town Labourer* (London: Longmans, Green, and Co., 1918), 19–20.

33. Rhodes Boyson, *The Ashworth Cotton Enterprises* (Oxford: Oxford University Press, 1970), 95.

34. See Hammond and Hammond, *Town Labourer*; see also the discussion in Pollard, *Genesis of Modern Management*, 181–92.

35. Daniel Rodgers, *The Work Ethic in Industrial America: 1850–1920* (Chicago: University of Chicago Press, 1978), 161.

36. Ibid.

37. Ibid., 163.

38. Ibid.

39. See: Reid, "Decline of Saint Monday"; David Landes, *The Unbound Prometheus* (Cambridge: Cambridge University Press, 1972); see also an important qualification of this point in Raphael Samuel, "The Workshop of the World: Steam Power and Hand Technology in Mid-Victorian Britain," *History Workshop* 3 (1977): 6–72.

40. Wadsworth and Mann, *Cotton Trade*, 385.

41. E. J. Hobsbawn, "Custom, Wages, and Work-Load." in E. J. Hobsbawn, *Laboring Men: Studies in Labor History* (New York: Basic Books, 1964), 349, 351.

42. Daniel Nelson, *Managers and Workers: Origins of the New Factory System in the U.S., 1880–1920* (Madison: University of Wisconsin Press, 1975), 42.

43. Ibid., 46; see also John Bodner, *Immigration and Industrialization: Ethnicity in an American Mill Town, 1870–1940* (Pittsburgh: University of Pittsburgh Press, 1977), 38.

44. Sumner Slichter, *Union Policies and Industrial Management* (Washington, DC: 1941); Lloyd Ulman, *The Rise of the National Trade Union* (Cambridge: Harvard University Press, 1955).

45. David Montgomery, *Workers' Control in America, Studies in the History of Work, Technology, and Labor Struggles* (Cambridge: Cambridge University Press, 1979), 15.

46. Samuel, "Workshop of the World."

47. Ibid., 21.

48. Ibid., 26.

49. Ibid., 27.

50. Ibid., 32.

51. Joan Wallach Scott, *The Glassworkers of Carmaux: French Craftsmen and Political Action in a Nineteenth-Century City* (Cambridge: Harvard University Press, 1974), 82.

52. Samuel, "Workshop of the World," 34.

53. Ibid., 43.

54. David Hounshell, *From the American System to Mass Production, 1800–1932* (Baltimore: The Johns Hopkins University Press, 1984), 67–124, 153–88.

55. John Fitch, *The Steelworkers* Philadelphia: William F. Fell, (1911), 102.

56. Ibid., 11.

57. Ibid., 11–15.

58. Nelson, *Managers and Workers*, 42. The same process for the early British factory is described in Pollard, *Genesis of Modern Management*, 125.

59. Nelson, *Managers and Workers*, 42; see discussion.

60. For an early collection of essays, see Clarence Bertrand Thompson, ed., Scientific Management (Cambridge: Harvard University Press, 1922). A good analytical discussion can be found in Craig R. Littler, "Understanding Taylorism," *British Journal of Sociology* 29 (1978): 185–207. Harry Braverman's discussion of Taylorism has been an influential one. See his *Labor and Monopoly Capital* (New York: Monthly Review Press, 1974). A fascinating study of Taylor's personality is available in Sudhir Kakar's *Frederick Taylor: A Study in Personality and Innovation* (Cambridge: MIT Press, 1970).

61. Daniel Nelson, *Frederick W. Taylor and the Rise of Scientific Management* (Madison: University of Wisconsin Press, 1980), 96.

62. Nelson, *Managers and Workers*, 72; Alfred Chandler, *The Visible Hand: The Managerial Revolution in American Business* (Cambridge: Harvard University Press, 1977), 276–77.

63. Nelson, *Frederick Taylor* 201; see also the discussion in Chandler, *Managerial Revolution*, 276–83.

64. Lieut. G. J. Meyers, "The Science of Management," in Clarence Bertrand Thompson, ed., *Scientific Management* (Cambridge, Harvard University Press, 1914), 134.

65. Forrest Cardullo, "Industrial Administration and Scientific Management," in Thompson, *Scientific Management*, 62.

66. Henry P. Kendall, "Unsystematized, Systematized, and Scientific Management," in Thompson, *Scientific Management*, 121.

67. Nelson, *Managers and Workers*, 74; Nelson, *Frederick W. Taylor*, 147.

68. Siegfried Giedion, *Mechanization Takes Command* (New York: Norton, 1969), 101.

69. One of the best examples of this dynamic is the case of the Watertown Arsenal, where a strike was ignited by the imposition of Taylorism. See: Hugh Aitken, *Taylorism at the Watertown Arsenal: Scientific Management in Action, 1908–1915* (Cambridge: Harvard University Press, 1960); see also the discussion in Daniel Rodgers, *Work Ethic in Industrial America*, 167; Montgomery, *Workers' Control in America*, 115.

70. See the discussion in Littler, "Understanding Taylorism."

71. Nelson, *Managers and Workers*, 75; Montogomery, *Workers' Control in America*, 116.

72. Montgomery, *Workers' Control in America*, 116.

73. Rodgers, *Work Ethic in Industrial America*, 168.

74. Giedion, *Mechanization Takes Command*, 115.

75. Stephen Meyer, *The Five Dollar Day: Labor Management and Social Control in the Ford Motor Company, 1908–1921* (Albany: State University of New York Press, 1981), 22.

76. Ibid., 26; see also Stephen Meyer, "Adapting the Immigrant to the Line: Americanization in the Ford Factory, 1914–1921," *Journal of Social History* 14 (Fall 1980): 67–82.

77. See the discussion in Hounshell, *From the American System*, 217–62.

78. It must also be noted that the intensification of effort associated with the "machine-driven" character of assembly-line work has remained an important feature of work in these production environments, despite the introduction of labor-saving (and skill-absorbing) technology. A variety of recent studies have documented the physically depleting nature of assembly-line work and the social divisiveness to which it gives rise. See, for example, William Faunce, "Social Stratification and Attitude Toward Change in Job Content," *Social Forces* 39 (December 1960): 140–48; R. Blauner, *Alienation and Freedom* (Chicago: University of Chicago Press, 1964); Stephen Cotgrove, "Alienation and Automation," *The British Journal of Sociology* 23 (1972): 437–451; Michael Fullan, "Industrial Technology and Worker Integration in the Organization," *American Sociological Review* 35 (1970): 1028–39; C. R. Walker and R. Guest, *Man on the Assembly Line* (Cambridge: Harvard University Press, 1952); and Robert Linhart, *The Assembly Line* (Amherst: University of Massachusetts Press, 1981).

79. James Bright, *Automation and Management* (Boston: Harvard Business School Press, 1958); Harry Braverman, *Labor and Monopoly Capital* (New York: Monthly Review Press, 1974).

80. Bright, *Automation and Management*, 10.

81. Ibid., 199–200.

82. Ibid., 205.

83. Ibid., 203.

84. Ibid., 211.

85. C. F. Braverman, *Labor and Monopoly Capital*, 231: "The 'progress' of capital-

ism seems only to deepen the gulf between worker and machine and to subordinate the worker ever more decisively to the yoke of the machine."

86. For a current example, see two recently published studies of the printing
industry in which similarly divergent conclusions are reached: Frank Hull,
Nathalie Friedman, and Theresa Rogers, "The Effect of Technology on Alienation From Work," *Work and Occupations* 9, (1982): 31–57; Michael Wallace and
Arne L. Kalleberg, "Industrial Transformation and the Decline of Craft: The De-
composition of Skill in the Printing Industry, 1931–1978," *American Sociological
Review* 47 (1982): 307–24.

87. Ely Chinoy, *Automobile Workers and the American Dream* (Boston: Beacon
Press, 1965), 70.

88. Bill Goode, "The Skilled Auto Worker: A Social Portrait, *Dissent* (Fall 1976):
392–97.

89. Robert Schrank, *Ten Thousand Working Days* (Cambridge, The MIT Press,
1978), 79.

90. Ibid., 88.

91. Chinoy, *Automobile Workers*, 47.

92. Blauner, *Alienation and Freedom*, 124.

93. Ibid., 138.

94. Ibid., 147.

95. Ibid., 159.

96. E. R. F. W. Crossman, "Automation and Skill," in Elywn Edwards and
Frank P. Lees, eds., *The Human Operator and Process Control* (London: Taylor &
Francis, 1974), 5–6.

97. Ibid., 8.

98. Blauner, *Alienation and Freedom*, 144–45.

99. Michael Fullan, "Industrial Technology and Worker Integration," 1028–
39; Barbara Kirsch and Joseph Lengermann, "An Empirical Test of Robert
Blauner's Ideas on Alienation in Work as Applied to Different Type Jobs in a
White Collar Setting," *Sociology and Social Research* 56 (1971–72): 180–94; Ste-
phen Cotgrove, "Alienation and Automation"; Ruth Tenne and Bilha Mann-
heim, "The Effect of the Level of Production Technologies on Workers' Orienta-
tions and Responses to the Work Station," in M. R. Haug and J. Dofny, eds.,
Work and Technology (London: Sage Publications, 1977), 61–79; Alan Touraine,
"The End of the Road for the Skilled Worker," in Edward Shorter, ed., *Work and
Community in the West* (New York: Harper & Row, 1974).

100. Serge Mallet, *La Nouvelle Classe Ouvriere* (Paris: 1969); Braverman, *Labor
and Monopoly Capital*; Duncan Gallie, *In Search of the New Working Class* (Cambridge: Cambridge University Press, 1978).

101. Blauner, *Alienation and Freedom*, 102.

102. Ibid., 179.

Chapter Two   The Abstraction of Industrial Work

1. It should be noted that there are other motivations that could account for
an operator's inarticulateness in the face of such questioning. Operators, like
generations of craftspeople before them, know that as their activities become

more explicit, their skills seem less significant. Explication means a loss of power. However, my work in this mill over several years led me to believe that although many operators were aware of these political dynamics, they tended to choose methods of resistance and counteroffense other than deliberately undermining the process engineer's efforts. In most cases I was convinced that operators were not withholding information but, rather, that they had really reached the limits of their explicit understanding.

2. Surrealist painters such as Magritte and Dali have developed this technique to an extreme. In another vein, David Smith's Voltri series uses hand-tool-like objects to similar effect.

3. M. T. Clanchy, *From Memory to Written Record: England, 1066–1307* (Cambridge: Harvard University Press, 1979), 202.

4. Ibid., 232–33.

5. J. R. Clammer, *Literacy and Social Change: A Case Study of Fiji* (Leiden, The Netherlands: E. J. Brill, 1976), 67.

6. Karl Weick discusses the importance of triangulating data from different sources when work depends primarily on computerized information; see: "Cosmos vs. Chaos: Sense and Nonsense in Electronic Contexts," *Organizational Dynamics* (Autumn 1985): 51–64.

7. Howard Gardner has suggested that such mental imagery may be related to a form of intelligence he labels "spatial." He suggests that there are likely to be individual differences in the degree to which this intelligence is developed. See his discussion in his book *Frames of Mind: The Theory of Multiple Intelligences* (New York: Basic Books, 1983), 174–76; for a different and more technical perspective on this mental capacity, see Stephen Kosslyn, *Ghosts in the Minds Machine: Creating and Using Images in the Brain* (New York: W. W. Norton & Co., 1983), 177–205.

Chapter Three   The White-Collar Body in History

1. Sidney Pollard, *The Genesis of Modern Management* (Cambridge: Harvard University Press, 1965), 104.

2. Reinhard Bendix, *Work and Authority in Industry* (Berkeley: University of California Press, 1974), 211.

3. Alfred Chandler, *The Visible Hand* (Cambridge: Harvard University Press, 1977), 414.

4. This quote is found in Joanne Yates, "From Press Book and Pigeonhole to Vertical Filing: Revolution in Storage and Access Systems for Correspondence," *The Journal of Business Communication*, 19 (1982): 8.

5. Seymour Eaton, *How To Do Business As Business is Done in Great Commercial Centers* (Philadelphia: P. W. Ziegler & Co., 1896), 254–55.

6. An interesting discussion of mental arithmetic can be found in Patricia Cline Cohen's *A Calculating People: The Spread of Numeracy in Early America* (Chicago: University of Chicago Press, 1982), 116–38.

7. See the discussions in Pollard, *Genesis of Modern Management*, 122–23; Chandler, *Visible Hand*, 414; Bendix, *Work and Authority*, 212.

8. Chester Barnard, *The Functions of the Executive* (Cambridge: Harvard University Press, 1938), 235.

9. Ibid., 217.

10. Ibid., 224.

11. John Kotter, *The General Managers* (New York: Free Press, 1982).

12. My discussion of Daniel Isenberg's work is based upon a recent article entitled "How Senior Managers Think," *Harvard Business Review* (November–December 1984): 81–90. see also his "Strategic Opportunism: Managing Under Uncertainty" (Harvard Graduate School of Business Administration, Working Paper 9-786-020, Boston, January 1986).

13. The human organism registers untold amounts of data about the situations it experiences, and these data make themselves known as vague feelings. This is what people mean when they say they have a "gut feeling" or a "felt sense" of a situation or person. Thus, the executive's intuitive feel is the result of experiencing the past and present action context. It is the sedimentation of many years of first-hand exposure to a "repertoire of familiar problematic situations" and an experience base in which patterns of responses have become linked to particular kinds of situations. An elaborated view of this perspective on human feeling can be found in Jean-Paul Sartre, *The Emotions* (New York: Philosophical Library, 1948); Maurice Merleau-Ponty, *The Structure of Behavior* (Boston: Beacon Press, 1963); and Eugene Gendlin, *Experiencing and the Creation of Meaning* (New York: Free Press, 1964).

14. Ibid., 89.

15. Ibid., 85.

16. Kanter, *Men and Women.*

17. Henry Mintzberg, *The Nature of Managerial Work* (New York: Harper & Row, 1973).

18. Ibid., 61.

19. Ibid., 149.

20. Ibid., 78.

21. Ibid., 90.

22. Ibid., 38.

23. Ibid., 38; see also Rosemary Stewart, *Managers and Their Jobs* (London: Macmillan, 1967); John Kotter, *The General Managers.*

24. Mintzberg, *Nature of Managerial Work*, 38, 44.

25. Ibid., 34.

26. Ibid., 174.

27. Barnard, *The Functions of the Executive*, 222.

28. Mintzberg, *Nature of Managerial Work*, 145, 150.

29. The outstanding example is found in Harry Braverman, *Labor and Monopoly Capital* (New York: Monthly Review Press, 1974).

30. Bendix, *Work and Authority*, 212.

31. Chandler, *Visible Hand*, 381.

32. Peter Drucker, *Management* (New York: Harper & Row, 1973), 381.

33. Mary Parker Follett, "Management as a Profession," in Harwood Merrill, ed., *Classics in Management* (New York: American Management Association, 1960), 317–20.

34. Harry Arthur Hopf, "Management and the Optimum," in Merrill, *Classics in Management*, 374–75.

35. Ibid., 363–64.

36. Nathaniel C. Fowler, Jr., *The Boy: How to Help Him Succeed* (Boston: Oakwood Publishing Co., 1902), 101–2.

37. Toni Pierenkemper, "Pre–1900 White Collar Employees at the Krupp Steel Casting Works: A New Occupational Category in Germany," *Business History Review* 58 (1984): 401.

38. Janice Weiss, "Educating for Clerical Work: The Nineteenth Century Private Commercial School," *Journal of Social History* 14 (1981): 415.

39. Bendix, *Work and Authority*, 303.

40. Barnard, *Functions of the Executive*, 121.

41. Kanter, *Men and Women*, 134.

42. Ibid., 48.

43. Ibid., 61.

44. See for example, E. A. Fleishman, "The Description of Supervisory Behavior," *Journal of Applied Psychology* 37 (1953): 1–6; R. H. Guest, "Of Time and the Foreman," *Personnel* 32 (1955): 478–86; L. R. Sayles, *Managerial Behavior* (New York: McGraw-Hill, 1964); C. R. Walker et al., *The Foreman on the Assembly Line* (Cambridge: Harvard University Press, 1956).

45. B. G. Orchard, *The Clerks of Liverpool* (1871), quoted in David Lockwood, *The Black-Coated Worker* (London: George Allen & Unwin, 1958), 19.

46. Pollard, *Genesis of Modern Management*, 125.

47. Pierenkemper, "Pre–1900 White Collar Employees," 391.

48. Cindy Aron, "To Barter Their Souls for Gold: Female Clerks in Federal Government Offices, 1862–1890," *The Journal of American History* 67 (1981): 850.

49. Ibid., 852.

50. Elyce Rotella, *From Home to Office: U. S. Women at Work, 1870–1930* (Ann Arbor, MI: UMI Research Press, 1981), 69–70.

51. See particularly the data in Rotella, *From Home to Office*; and Weiss, "Educating for Clerical Work."

52. Weiss, "Educating for Clerical Work," 411, 413.

53. In conjunction with a description of this historical process, Rotella, *From Home to Office*, 166–68, offers a cogent explanation based on human capital theory; for related discussions, see Veronica Beechey, "The Sexual Division of Labour and the Labour Process: A Critical Assessment of Braverman," in S. Wood, ed., *The Degradation of Work* (London: Hutchinson, 1982), 54–73; and Janet M. Hooks, *Women's Occupations Through Seven Decades*, U.S. Department of Labor, Women's Bureau, Bulletin no. 218 (Washington, DC: U.S. Government Printing Office, 1947).

54. Yates, "From Press Book," 17.

55. Michel Crozier, *The World of the Office Worker* (Chicago: University of Chicago Press, 1971), 16. This process may be repeating itself in current efforts to further rationalize managerial work using advanced information technology. It has been widely assumed that new forms of office technology would displace managerial functions. These views typically extrapolate from the consequences of automation for skilled workers. The logic of my argument implies that such extrapolations cannot account for the relationship between managerial activities and rationalization. Instead, new information technology in the office would be expected to increase the demands for monitoring, analysis, and coordination. While some clerical jobs may be displaced, it is less likely that managerial functions will be displaced. Rather, they would be expected to undergo further differentiation—on the one hand, integrating some formerly clerical responsibilities and, on the other, branching out as new domains of information are made more explicit and therefore require more management. There is some re-

cent evidence to suggest that this is indeed the case. Between 1978 and 1985, blue-collar productivity is estimated to have increased by 13 percent, and the number of blue-collar jobs was reduced by 1.9 million, to a total of 30 million. During the same period, white-collar productivity declined by 10 percent, and the number of white-collar employees grew by 10 million (21 percent), to a total of 58 million. In an effort to explain these trends, several analysts have pointed to the actual effects of information technology in many firms. When information systems are used to create new products, as is frequently the case in the financial services industry, they also tend to create new jobs with responsibility for creatively utilizing the new information. For example, accounting is now one of the most automated functions of a modern organization, yet accountants have not been displaced by new technology. The number of accountants has increased by one-third between 1978 and 1985. A similar trend holds for other financial service occupations, such as stockbroking. See the discussion in "Is American Business Being Managed to Death?" *The Economist*, 13 December 1986, 71.

56. In 1909, The System Company published a volume entitled *Business Administration: The Principles of Business Organization and Systems, and the Actual Methods of Business Operations and Management*, which was one of the first studies to explicitly compare the office to the factory; another influential volume was Lee Galloway, *Office Management: Its Principles and Practice* (New York: 1918).

57. William Henry Leffingwell, *Office Management* (Chicago and New York: A. W. Shaw Co., 1925), 333.

58. Ibid., 357, 359.

59. For an example of such "enriched" clerical work that illustrates its reintegration with the evolutionary path of managerial coordination, see Richard Matteis, "The New Back Office Focuses on Customer Service," *Harvard Business Review* (March-April 1979).

60. International Labour Organization, "Effects of Mechanization and Automation in Offices: III," *International Labour Review* 81, no. 4 (1960): 351–52.

61. Ibid., 353–55.

62. James Duncan, "Clerical Work Needs Engineering," *The Office* (July 1969): 30–34.

63. "Measuring How Office Workers Work," *Business Week*, 14 November 1970, 54.

64. Ibid., 60.

65. In *A Guide to Office Clerical Time Standards for Manual Operations* (Association for Systems Management, 1972).

66. Kanter, *Men and Women*, 75, 80.

Chapter Four   Office Technology as Exile and Integration

1. Several studies document the industrializing effects of office automation: Joan Greenbaum, *In the Name of Efficiency* (Philadelphia: Temple University Press, 1979); Evelyn Glenn and Rosalyn Feldberg, "Proletarianizing Clerical Work: Technology and Organizational Control in the Office," in Andrew Zimbalist, ed., *Case Studies in the Labor Process* (New York: Monthly Review Press, 1978): 51–72. Rosalyn Feldberg and Evelyn Nakano Glenn, "Technology and Work Degrada-

tion: Effects of Office Automation on Women Clerical Workers," in Joan Roths-child, ed., *Machina Ex Dea: Feminist Perspectives on Technology* (New York: Pergamon Press, 1984), 59–78; Mary Murphee, "Brave New Office: The Changing World of the Legal Secretary," in K. Sachs and D. Memy, eds., *My Troubles Are Going to Have Trouble With Me: Everyday Trials and Triumphs of Women Workers* (New Brunswick, NJ: Rutgers University Press, 1984), 140–59.

2. This success in achieving productivity increases was not without financial cost. The unit cost of a claim transaction had increased from $3.50 before the conversion to $5.00 afterwards. This unanticipated increase was due to the high costs of data processing. Accounting procedures allowed the corporation to absorb data-processing costs in order that the field office could show a lower unit cost than was technically the case. The expenditure for building and implementing the system was 400 percent over budget and totaled $30 million.

3. Paul Adler discusses this paradoxical quality of automated clerical work in: "Rethinking the Skill Requirement of New Technologies" (Harvard Graduate School of Business Administration, Working Paper 84-27 Boston, October 1983).

4. See Lucy Suchman and Eleanor Wynn, "Procedures and Problems in the Office," *Office: Technology and People* 2 (1984): 133–54. which describes the relationship between this unspecific knowledge characteristic of *acting-with* and the technical knowledge associated with the substance of the formal task. Informed by the pioneering intellectual work of the ethnomethodologist Harold Garfinkle, these researchers set out to document the observable course of practical action in which clerks engage in order to produce as an outcome, work that can be held accountable to the formal procedures publicly acknowledged as the "rules" by which work is to be done. Suchman and Wynn realized that it was the formal procedures said to specify office work that are taken up as a template upon which to design systems to automate the office. This approach cannot account for the kind of unspecific but vital interpersonal work that has traditionally enabled the formal procedures to appear meaningful. As a result, computerized systems tend to organize out of the office routine the underlying practical activities upon which smooth operations have depended. Their studies of office settings have led Suchman and Wynn to conclude that "the accomplishment of procedures is tied to the contingencies of actual cases, the work of managing those contingencies involves ongoing consultation and negotiation, and the work is grounded in the material environment of the office setting." See also Lucy Suchman, "Office Procedure as Practical Action: Models of Work and System Design," *ACM Transactions on Office Information Systems* 1 (1983): 320–28.

5. This formulation helps to explain why so much of the literature on office automation has focused on issues related to physical distress. For an excellent overview of this literature, see: "Office Automation and the Quality of Worklife," in *Automation of America's Offices, 1985–2000*, U.S. Congress, Office of Technology Assessment, no. OTA-CIT-287 (Washington, DC: U.S. Government Printing Office, December 1985), 125–68.

Recently, the Center for Disease Control concluded that psychological disorders (affective disturbances, behavioral problems, psychiatric disorders, and somatic complaints) are one of the ten most widespread work-related diseases. Its study notes that adverse working conditions tend to be reported most frequently by workers using new office technology, such as video display terminals. The study concludes that "some of these conditions have been linked to chronic stress-related disorders." See Center for Disease Control, "Leading Work-Related Diseases and Injuries," *Morbidity and Mortality Weekly Report* 35 (1986): 613–14.

6. To restate an earlier point, automating and informating are not opposites; rather, they coexist in a relationship of hierarchical integration. Informating depends upon an automated base of operations—a technological infrastructure whereby events, activities, objects, and processes can be translated into information. For many organizations, a key challenge lies in how to create such an automated infrastructure. One route is to have a small army of clerical workers performing data-entry functions that are eventually integrated across wider areas of the organization. There are costs to this approach. The jobs themselves can be stressful and without compensatory rewards in skill development, pay, or the quality of the working environment. Labor costs remain high, and the organization must grapple with how to effectively manage jobs with the inherent contradictions of responsibility for on-line data integrity; sustained concentration; and routine, repetitive, isolating tasks.

The technological infrastructure of the pulp mills operated very differently. Data was generated without human intervention as microprocessors translated the physical production process into information. Many nonmanufacturing organizations have begun to develop ways to provide an automated infrastructure that would circumvent, or at least limit, the dependence on a massive clerical data-entry function. One prominent approach that is being developed involves new interorganizational information systems. Data-entry operations that are now repeated in several interdependent organizations (for example, the customer company, the health care provider, and the insurance company) can, with the support of interorganizational systems, be completed once and fed into each organization's data base. For a discussion of interorganizational systems, see James Cash and Benn R. Konsynski, "IS Redraws Competitive Boundaries," *Harvard Business Review* (March–April 1985).

Another complementary approach to building an automated infrastructure involves lodging data-entry functions at the very point at which the data is generated. A well-known example is the automated teller machine, where data entry is built into the customer's self-service activities. Powerful software can eliminate much of the risk associated with input errors, though some staff is still required to monitor the quality of the data and to correct inconsistencies.

7. Eileen Applebaum, "Technology and the Redesign of Work in the Insurance Industry" (Stanford University School of Education, Institute for Research on Educational Finance and Governance, Project Report no. 84-A22, Stanford, CA, November 1984), 7–8.

8. For a discussion of recent trends in the banking industry, see: Eduard Ballarin, *Commercial Banks Amid the Financial Revolution* (Cambridge, MA: Ballinger Publishing Co., 1986); also, "The New Shape of Banking," *Business Week*, 18 June 1984, 104–10.

9. Touche Ross International, *The Impact of Technology on Banking: World Summary* (1985), 2. In 1985 Touche Ross International conducted a worldwide study of the impact of technology on the banking industry and found that the prior decade had seen massive investments in technology that bankers predicted would increase still more sharply by 1990. The study concluded that those banking organizations that had reported the greatest success in utilizing technology to improve their competitive positions or their cost structure had done so by

effectively linking technology and marketing strategies: "Hardware has achieved almost commodity status and is available in smaller units. The scarce resources for bankers in most countries have become people with software development expertise. The most effective management of these resources is from market-driven organizations or service units. In addition, fourth generation software and prototype tools permit the flexibility for systems professionals and users to define and develop their own systems."

10. James Martin, *Managing the Data Base Environment* (Englewood Cliffs, NJ: Prentice-Hall, Inc., 1983), 5. Computer expert James Martin defines data-base technology as a "shared collection of interrelated data designed to meet the needs of multiple types of end users. It can be defined as a collection of data from which multiple different end-user ideas can be derived. The data are stored so that they are independent of the programs that use them." On page 3, he exhorts his executive readers:

A task of executives of all types in the years ahead is to assist in the building of the computerized corporation. In the age of microelectronics, fast response to customers, fast reaction to problems, and fast response to information needs will be increasingly vital for competitive survival. Data-base usage is the key to flexible employment of computers and their transmission networks. How well the data-base environment is managed affects executives in all areas of a corporation.

11. The central liabilities unit (CL) was part of a chain of procedures that began when an account officer requested a line of credit for a customer. The credit department checked if the transaction was within the bounds of current policy and procedures, and then completed a credit approval (CA) form based on information supplied by the account officer. If the application was for a client who had previously done business with the bank, the credit clerk asked CL for the outstandings (that is, credit already used) and the client history. The official CA form was described as "complex" and had to be neatly typed, so most clerks preferred to use an "easier" form called the "take-down ticket." The CA or take-down ticket was sent back to the account officer, who attached a defense of the credit risk and submitted it to the Credit Approval Committee, which was composed of three senior credit officers, for approval. If approved, Committee members signed the CA and returned it to the credit department, where it was verified as correct (for example, with proper authorization signatures). The CA was stamped "correct, approved, and verified," and sent to CL in operations. CL did a "double check" to verify that it was correct and entered the data on ledger cards.

Chapter Five   Mastering the Electronic Text

1. Milman Parry, *The Making of Homeric Verse* (Oxford: Clarendon Press, 1971); Eric Havelock, *The Greek Concept of Justice* (Cambridge: Harvard University Press, 1978); Harold Innis, *The Bias of Communication* (Toronto: University of Toronto Press, 1951); Marshall McLuhan, *The Gutenberg Galaxy* (Toronto: University of Toronto Press, 1962); Walter Ong, *The Presence of the Word* (New Haven: Yale

University Press, 1967); id., *Interfaces of the Word* (Ithaca, NY: Cornell University Press, 1977); id., *Orality and Literacy* (London and New York: Methuen, 1982).

2. Ong, *Orality and Literacy*, 43.

3. Ibid., 43.

4. New scanning technology is developing rapidly. Graphics and text scanning are being merged, which will enable more organizations to translate paper files directly into the computer data base. See Erik Sandberg-Diment, "The Executive Computer: Curling Up with a Good Novel," *The New York Times*, 2 November 1986.

5. Ernst Cassirer, *The Philosophy of Symbolic Forms*, vol. 3 of *The Phenomenology of Knowledge* (New Haven: Yale University Press, 1957), 114. The philosopher Cassirer has discussed this power of the symbol to transcend the limitations of the present tense:

> Only where we succeed, as it were, in compressing a total phenomenon into one of its factors, in concentrating it symbolically, in "having" it in a state of "pregnance" in the particular factor—only then do we raise it out of the stream of temporal change; only then does its existence, which had hitherto seemed confined to a single moment in time, gain a kind of permanence: for only then does it become possible to find again in the simple, as it were, punctual "here" and "now" of present experience a "not-here" and a "not-now." Everything that we call the identity of concepts and significations, or the constancy of things and attributes, is rooted in this fundamental act of finding-again. Thus it is a common function which makes possible on the one hand language and on the other hand the specific articulation of the intuitive world.

6. Havelock, *Greek Concept of Justice*, 220–21.

7. Ibid., 224; see also David Olson, "From Utterance to Text: The Bias of Language in Speech and Unity," *Harvard Educational Review* 47: 278. In a similar vein, Susan Sontag has pointed out that the camera freed painting for abstraction; see: *On Photography* (New York: Farrar, Straus & Giroux, 1973), 94.

8. This discussion is based on Elaine Scarry's analysis in *The Body in Pain* (New York: Oxford University Press, 1985), 151–52; see also: William H. McNeil, *The Pursuit of Power* (Chicago: University of Chicago Press, 1982).

9. Michael Polanyi, *The Tacit Dimension* (New York: Doubleday & Co., 1967), 4.

10. Ibid., 18.

11. Ulric Neisser, "Toward a Skillful Psychology," in D. Rogers and J. A. Sloboda, eds., *The Acquisition of Symbolic Skills* (New York: Plenum Publishing Corp., 1983), 1–17.

12. J. J. Gibson, *The Ecological Approach to Visual Perception* (Boston: Houghton Mifflin Co., 1979).

13. Neisser, "Toward a Skillful Psychology," 3.

14. George Stelmach and Barry Hughes, "Does Motor Skill Automation Require a Theory of Attention?" in Richard Magill, ed., *Memory and Control of Action* (Amsterdam: North Holland Publishing Co., 1983), 67–92.

15. John Anderson, *Cognitive Psychology* (New York: W. H. Freeman & Co., 1985), 40–47, 57–70.

16. Walter Schneider and Arthur D. Fisk, "Attention Theory and Mechanisms for Skilled Performance," in Richard A. Magill, ed., *Memory and Control of Action* (Amsterdam: North Holland Publishing Co., 1983), 119–42; E. J. Langer and L. Imber, "When Practice Makes Imperfect: Debilitating Effects of Over-Learning," *Journal of Personality and Social Psychology* 37 (1979): 2014–24.

17. M. I. Posner and C. R. R. Snyder, "Attention and Cognitive Control," in R. C. Solso, ed., *Information Processing and Cognition*. The Loyale Symposium (Hillsdale, NJ: Lawrence Erlbaum, 1975); J. H. Lingle and T. M. Ostram, "Principles of Memory and Cognition in Attitude Formation," in R. E. Petty, T. M. Ostram, and T. C. Brock, eds., *Cognitive Responses in Persuasion* (Hillsdale, NJ: Lawrence Erlbaum, 1981), 399–420; P. E. Tetlock and A. Levi, "Attribution Bias: On the Inconclusiveness of the Cognition-Motivation Debate," *Journal of Experimental Social Psychology* 18 (1982): 68–88.

18. R. E. Petty and J. T. Cacioppo, "Issue Involvement Can Increase or Decrease Persuasion by Enhancing Message-Relevant Cognitive Responses," *Journal of Personality and Social Psychology* 37 (1979): 1915–26; R. E. Petty, et al., "Personal Involvement as a Determinant of Argument-Based Persuasion," *Journal of Personality and Social Psychology* 41 (1981): 847–55; A. M. Tybout and C. A. Scott, "Availability of Well-Defined Internal Knowledge and the Attitude Formation Process," *Journal of Personality and Social Psychology* 44 (1983): 474–91.

19. Andersen, *Cognitive Psychology*, 104–6, 142–46.

20. Ibid., 107–12, 114.

21. A. Newell and H. Simon, *Human Problem Solving* (Englewood Cliffs, NJ: Prentice-Hall, Inc., 1972).

22. G. Namikas, "Vertical Processes and Motor Performance," in Magill, ed., *Memory and Control*, 95–119.

23. The nomenclature varies among researchers—terms such as "motor" or "action" skills cover a domain that is generally similar to what I have defined as action-centered skill; "cognitive" or "symbolic" refers to the general territory defined as intellective skill. See the discussions in Neisser, "Toward a Skillful Psychology"; M. T. Turvey, "Constructive Theory, Perceptual Systems, and Tacit Knowledge," in W. B. Weimer and D. S. Palermo, eds., *Cognition and Symbolic Processes* (Hillsdale, N J: Lawrence Erlbaum, 1974), 165–79; J. A. Adams, "On Integration of the Verbal and Motor Domains," in Magill, ed., *Memory and Control*, 3–13; M. J. Posner, "Coordination of Internal Codes," in W. Chase, ed., *Visual Information Processing* (New York: Academic Press, 1973): 35–73.

24. Howard Gardner, *Frames of Mind: The Theory of Multiple Intelligences* (New York: Basic Books, 1983), 8–9.

25. Ibid., 232.

26. Ibid.

27. Ibid., 164.

28. Scribner and Cole make a related point in their work on the psychology of literacy. They found that abstract skills developed in school were strongest while people were in school and diminished with increased distance from the school experience. Thus, skill in abstract thinking is not a permanent achievement but something that requires practice. See: Michael Scribner and Sylvia Cole, *The Psychology of Literacy* (Cambridge: Harvard University Press, 1981), 130–31. The data from Global Bank Brazil also alert us to the danger of oversimplifying the identification of intellective competence and formal education. While

formal education may predict potential competence, the skill demands of everyday life at work do not necessarily call up that potential or further develop it.
Thus, even well-educated bankers could be referred to as "concrete" thinkers.
They were uncomfortable when it came to reasoning abstractly about their business, in large measure because that is not what the daily experience of their
work had required.

29. Ibid., 221.

30. Karl Weick provides an excellent discussion of many of these aspects of
problem-solving in his article, "Cosmology Episodes," *Organizational Dynamics*
(Autumn 1985): 51–64.

31. For a discussion of the Three Mile Island accident from a "human factors"
point of view, see Charles Perrow, "Normal Accident at Three Mile Island,"
Society 18 (1981): 17–26.

32. Basil Bernstein, *Class, Codes and Control: Theoretical Studies Towards a Sociology
of Language* (New York: Schocken Books, 1975), 125, 128. On a psychological
level, the codes may be distinguished by the extent to which each facilitates
(elaborated code) or inhibits (restricted code) an orientation to symbolize intent
in a verbally explicit form.

33. Walter Ong has also observed this relationship between Bernstein's work
and the oral/written culture distinct in Ong, *Orality and Literacy*, 106.

34. Bernstein, *Class, Codes and Control*, 177–78.

35. Ibid., 143. For an extensive, empirically based discussion of the relationship between the "substantive complexity" of work and its effects on individual
intellectual ability and personality, see Melvin Kohn and Carmi Schooler, *Work
and Personality: In Inquiry into the Impact of Social Stratification* (Norwood, NJ: Ablex
Publishing Corp., 1983); and Joanne Miller, Kazimierz Slomcynski, and Melvin
Kohn, "Continuity of Learning-Generalization: The Effect of Job on Men's Intellective Process in the United States and Poland," *American Journal of Sociology* 91,
(1985): 543–615.

36. Bernstein, *Class, Codes and Control*, 175. Consider Bernstein on this
subject:

> We can see that the class system has affected the distribution of knowl-
> edge. Historically, and now, only a tiny percentage of the population
> has been socialized into knowledge at the level of the meta-languages
> of control and innovation, whereas the mass of the population has been
> socialized into knowledge at the level of context-tied operations. A tiny
> percentage of the population has been given access to the principles of
> intellectual change, whereas the rest have been denied such access.
> This suggests that we might be able to distinguish between two orders
> of meaning. One we could call universalistic, the other particularistic.
> Universalistic meanings are those in which principles and operations
> are made linguistically explicit, whereas particularistic orders of mean-
> ing are meanings in which principles and operations are relatively lin-
> guistically implicit. If orders of meaning are universalistic, then the
> meanings are less tied to a given context. . . . Where meanings have
> this characteristic then individuals have access to the grounds of their
> experience and can change the grounds. Where orders of meaning are
> particularistic . . . such meanings are . . . more context bound, that is,
> tied to a local relationship and to a local social structure. Where the

meaning system is particularistic, much of the meaning is embedded in the context and may be restricted to those who share a similar contextual history. Where meanings are universalistic, they are in principle available to all because the principles and operations have been made explicit, and so public.

PART TWO AUTHORITY:
THE SPIRITUAL DIMENSION OF POWER

1. Max Weber; *The Theory of Social and Economic Organization* (New York: Free Press, 1964), 152–53.
2. The fact of authority should be sufficient to elicit obedience. As Hannah Arendt has put it:

Authority . . . is incompatible with persuasion, which presupposes equality and works through a process of argumentation. Where arguments are used, authority is left in abeyance. . . . The authoritarian relation between the one who commands and the one who obeys rests neither on common reason nor on the power of the one who commands; what they have in common is the hierarchy itself, whose rightness and legitimacy both recognize and where both have their predetermined stable place (Hannah Arendt, "What Was Authority?" in Carl J. Friedrich, ed., *Authority* [Cambridge: Harvard University Press, 1958], 82).

Peter Blau makes a similar distinction between authority and persuasion in *The Dynamics of Bureaucracy* (Chicago: University of Chicago Press, 1963), 219.
3. Arendt, "What Was Authority?" 83.
4. Indeed, the term *religion* itself referred to the reverential bonds one maintained with the past, with the wisdom of those who had laid the foundation for all that would follow:

Religion literally meant *religare*: to be tied back, obligated, to the enormous almost superhuman and hence always legendary effort to lay the foundations, to build the cornerstone, to found for eternity. To be religious meant to be tied to the past (ibid., 99).

5. An empirical demonstration of this dynamic can be found in Nicole Woolsey Biggart and Gary G. Hamilton, "The Power of Obedience," *Administrative Science Quarterly* (December 1984): 540–49.

Chapter Six   What Was Managerial Authority?

1. Max Weber, *The Protestant Ethic and the Spirit of Capitalism* (New York: Charles Scribner's Sons, 1958), 172.
2. John Child, *British Management Thought* (London: George Allen and Unwin, 1969), 33.

446   Notes

3. George Cabot Lodge, *The New American Ideology* (New York: Alfred A. Knopf, 1975), 116.

4. Thorstein Veblen, *The Theory of Business Enterprise* (New York: Charles Scribner's Sons, 1923), 73.

5. As Reinhard Bendix put it: "The doctrine of self-help proclaimed that employers and workers were alike in self-dependence, and that regardless of class each man's success was a proof of himself and a contribution to the common wealth. . . . By bidding the people to seek success as they did themselves, the employers manifested their abiding belief in the existence of a moral community regardless of class, for they proposed to measure the worth of each man by the same standard" (Reinhard Bendix, *Work and Authority in Industry* [Berkeley: University of California Press, 1974], 115).

6. Daniel Rodgers, *The Work Ethic in Industrial America: 1850–1920* (Chicago: University of Chicago Press, 1978), 9–10.

7. Sidney Pollard, *The Genesis of Modern Management* (Cambridge: Harvard University Press, 1965) 123–26.

8. Rodgers, *Work Ethic*, 21; Herbert Gutman, *Work, Culture, and Society in Industrializing America: Essays in American Working Class and Social History* (New York: Alfred A. Knopf, 1976), 20, 37, 58.

9. See the discussion in Frank W. Fox, "The Genesis of American Technology 1790–1860," *American Studies* 17 (Fall 1976): 29–48.

10. Pollard, *Genesis of Modern Management*, 107–118.

11. Ibid., 157.

12. Ibid., 150.

13. Bendix, *Work and Authority*, 230–31.

14. Ibid., 256–58.

15. Sir Francis Galton in Britain, Bertillon in France, Lombroso in Italy, the criminologist Arthur MacDonald in the United States, and the psychologists Louis Terman, James Watson, and Hugo Munsterberg, were leaders in developing "anthropometric" systems of identification, which they argued could discern moral and intellectual qualities: "Trying to develop a new science of social and psychological selection to substitute for the old work ethic touched off sharp debate. . . . The possibility of reclassifying a citizenry on a basis of physical qualities offered scientific confirmation of what many people assumed to be true. The criminal had a low and vulgar aspect; the lower classes were weaker and smaller physically than the upper classes; blacks and immigrants were racially, intellectually, and morally inferior to native whites; genius was a variety of mental disease just as epilepsy was a physical disease" (James B. Gilbert, *Work Without Salvation: America's Intellectuals and Industrial Alienation, 1880–1910* [Baltimore: The Johns Hopkins University Press, 1977], 154–157). In England, Francis Galton had published his work on *Hereditary Genius*, arguing that intellectual capacity was strictly determined by inheritance. Havelock Ellis followed up on Galton's work with his own original classification scheme. His *A Study of British Geniuses* was published in the United States in 1900 by *Popular Science Monthly*. In it, he claimed that, with the exception of painters, men of genius derived exclusively from Anglo-Norman upper-class stock. He concluded that there was no reason to believe "that the education of the proletariat will lead to a new development of eminent men" (ibid., 159).

Magazines such as *Popular Science Monthly* frequently contained debates on the psychological and sociological implications of physical features such as skull size, eye color, jaw formation, height, and other physical characteristics. Another influential and popular book published in 1916 was called *Analyzing Character*. In it, the authors proposed a new science of social placement and vocational selection. With this method of self-analysis based on physiognomic classification, "individuals might be able to discover what position in society they should occupy—where they belonged in the complex and confusing new social order" (ibid., 162).

16. C. R. Henderson, "Business Men and Social Theorists," *American Journal of Sociology* 1 (1896): 385–86.

17. Edward C. Kirkland, *Business in the Gilded Age* (Madison: University of Wisconsin Press, 1952), 35. Charles Gerstenberg, the head of the Department of Finance at New York University's School of Commerce, published a textbook, *Organization and Control*, in a well-known series entitled *Modern Business*, edited by the dean of that institution. Early in the text, in a discussion of sole proprietorship, he took special pains to explain success in the marketplace with reference to intimate biological "truth." He titled the section "Survival of the Fittest": "The struggle for existence is severe; it insures a speedy elimination of the unfit. . . . There is a degree of certainty about the selection of the fit among individual proprietors. . . . John Brown's voice, his handshake, his face, even his gait, make me like or dislike him and helps to determine whether or not I shall make my purchases in his store" (Charles W. Gerstenberg, *Organization and Control* [New York: Alexander Hamilton Institute, 1918], 30–31).

Patricia Cline Cohen provides another example of the increased biologisms of social thought during this period. She notes that during the eighteenth century, girls were rarely exposed to formal education. When they were sent to school, arithmetic was not included in their curriculum because it was believed they would not need it. By the end of the nineteenth century, the disparity in arithmetic skills came to be seen as an intrinsic difference between the sexes. See *A Calculating People: The Spread of Numeracy in Early America* (Chicago: University of Chicago Press, 1982), 140.

18. Child, *British Management Thought*, 54.

19. Quoted in Melvyn Dubofsky, *Industrialism and the American Worker, 1865–1920* (New York: Thomas Y. Crowell, 1975), 82.

20. Samuel Haber, *Efficiency and Uplift: Scientific Management in the Progressive Era 1890–1920* (Chicago: The University of Chicago Press, 1964), 89.

21. Ibid., 165.

22. Ibid.

23. Sanford M. Jacoby, *Employing Bureaucracy: Managers, Unions, and the Transformation of Work in American Industry, 1900–1945* (New York: Columbia University Press, 1985), 128.

24. J. Anton DeHaas, *Business Organization and Administration* (New York: Gregg Publishing Co., 1920), 1–6.

25. Jacoby, *Employing Bureaucracy*, 129; Child, *British Management Thought*, 59–60; Alfred Chandler, *The Visible Hand: The Managerial Revolution in American Business* (Cambridge: Harvard University Press, 1977), 464–68.

26. For example, in 1922 H. H. Goddard wrote in a popular new book of "practical psychology": "The number of people of relatively low intelligence is vastly greater than is generally appreciated . . . this mass of low-level intelligence is an enormous menace to democracy unless it is recognized and properly treated

. . . the intelligent group must do the planning and organizing for the mass" quoted in Bendix, *Work and Authority*, 305.

27. Alan Fox, "Managerial Ideology and Labour Relations," *British Journal of Industrial Relations* 4, no. 3 (November 1966): 367.

28. Howell John Harris, *The Right to Manage: Industrial Relations Policies of American Business in the 1940s* (Madison: University of Wisconsin Press, 1982), 97.

29. Ibid., 98.

30. Bendix, *Work and Authority* 323; see Fox, "Managerial Ideology," 369; for a more extensive discussion of this point see Shoshana Zuboff, "The Work Ethic and Work Organization," in Jack Barbash, ed., *The Work Ethic: A Critical Analysis* (Madison, WI: Industrial Relations Research Association, 1983), 165–73.

31. Elton Mayo, *The Social Problems of an Industrial Civilization* (Boston: Harvard University Graduate School of Business Administration, 1945), 120, 122.

32. Harris, *Right to Manage*, 102.

33. Bendix, *Work and Authority* 326–28.

34. Alexander Heron, *Sharing Information with Employees* (Stanford, CA: Stanford University Press, 1942), 22.

35. W. Lloyd Warner and James C. Abegglen, "The Social Origins and Acquired Characteristics of Business Leaders," in W. Lloyd Warner and Norman Martin, eds., *Industrial Man* (New York: Harper and Brothers, 1959), 105.

36. Eli Ginzberg, "The Professionalization of the U.S. Labor Force," *Scientific American* 240, no. 3 (March 1979): 418.

37. James N. Baron and William T. Bielby, "Workers and Machines: Dimensions and Determinants of Technical Relations in the Workplace," *American Sociological Review* 47 (1982): 185.

38. For example, Nicos Poulantzas in "On Social Classes," *New Left Review* (1978) and in *Classes in Contemporary Capitalism* (Atlantic Highlands, NJ: Humanities Press, 1975).

39. Claus Offe, *Industry and Inequality: The Achievement Principle in Work and Social Status* (New York: St. Martin's Press, 1977).

40. James B. Atleson, *Values and Assumptions in American Labor Law* (Amherst: University of Massachusetts Press, 1983), 13. As Atleson put it: "The deeper reasons for the assumption of managerial exclusivity are hidden, but explanations often rely upon notions of property rights and the need for capital mobility. . . . Moreover, behind the notion of reserved rights is the belief that these are prerogatives that "management must have to successfully carry out its function of managing the enterprise. . . . Certain rights are necessarily vested exclusively in management or are based upon an economic value judgment about the necessary locus of power" (ibid., 9, 123).

41. Ibid., 176; see also Philip C. Lederer, "Management's Right to Loyalty of Supervisors," 32 (Fall 1981): 83–104.

42. Barnard, 220; see the discussions on the subject of loyalty in Rosabeth Kanter, *Men and Women of the Corporation* (New York: Basic Books, 1977), 49–51, 53, 63–66; C. Wright Mills, *White Collar*, (London: Oxford University Press, 1951), 77–112, 229–235.

43. Atleson, *Values and Assumptions*, 176.

44. Robert Schrank, *Ten Thousand Working Days* (Cambridge: The MIT Press, 1978), 226.

45. Ely Chinoy, *Automobile Workers and the American Dream* (Boston: Beacon Press, 1965), 47.

46. Ibid., 48.

47. Richard Sennett and Jonathan Cobb, *The Hidden Injuries of Class* (New York: Alfred A. Knopf, 1972), 78.

48. See Daniel Bell's discussion in "The New Class: A Muddled Concept," *Society* (January-February 1979): 22, and more generally as reflected in his essays *The Cultural Contradictions of Capitalism* (New York: Basic Books, 1976).

49. Theodore Caplow et al., *Middletown Families* (Minneapolis: University of Minnesota Press, 1982), 15; see for contrast Robert S. Lynd and Helen Merrell Lynd, *Middletown: A Study in American Culture* (New York: Harcourt and Brace, 1929).

50. Ginzberg, "Professionalism of U.S. Labor Force," 50.

51. For a more extensive discussion, see Zuboff, "Work Ethic," 166–68.

52. U.S. Department of Health, Education, and Welfare, *Work in America* (Cambridge: The MIT Press, 1973), 13–23.

53. Zuboff, "Work Ethic," 169–71.

54. Some recent descriptions of Quality of Work Life philosophy and efforts can be found in Edward Lawler III, *High-Involvement Management* (San Francisco: Jossey-Bass, 1986); Jerome Rosow, ed., *Teamwork: Joint Labor Management Programs in America* (New York: Pergamon Press, 1986); Robert Zager and Jerome Rosow, eds., *The Innovative Organization: Productivity Programs in Action* (New York: Pergamon Press, 1982); Thomas A. Kochan, Harry C. Katz, Robert B. McKersie, *The Transformation of American Industrial Relations* (New York: Basic Books, 1987); Richard Walton, "From Control to Commitment in the Workplace," *Harvard Business Review* (March-April 1985): 77–84; Robert Schrank, ed., *Industrial Democracy at Sea* (Cambridge: The MIT Press, 1983); Rosabeth Kantor, *The Changemasters* (New York: Simon & Schuster, 1984).

55. Kochan, Katz, McKersie, *Transformation of American Industrial Relations*, 146–77.

56. See, for example, Richard Edwards, *Contested Terrain: The Transformation of the Workplace in the Twentieth Century* (New York: Basic Books, 1979); John Witte, *Democracy, Authority and Alienation at Work* (Chicago: University of Chicago Press, 1980); Edward Greenberg, "The Consequences of Worker Participation," *Social Science Quarterly* 56 (1975): 191–209.

57. Richard Walton, "The Topeka Work System," in Zager and Rosow, eds., *Innovative Organization*, 284.

58. Richard Walton, "From Control to Commitment," 78, 84.

59. Kochan, Katz, McKersie, *Transformation of American Industrial Relations*, 176.

Chapter Seven   The Dominion of the Smart Machine

1. Jonathan Z. Smith, "The Bare Facts of Ritual," in *Imagining Religion: From Babylon to Jonestown* (Chicago: University of Chicago Press, 1982): 53–65.

2. As Smith puts it:

Ritual represents the creation of a controlled environment where the variables (i.e., the accidents) of ordinary life may be displaced precisely because they are felt to be so overwhelmingly present and powerful. *Ritual is a means of performing the way things ought to be in conscious tension to the way things are in such a way that this ritualized perfection is recollected in the ordinary, uncontrolled, course of things.* . . . It provides the means for demonstrating that we know what ought to have been done, what ought to have taken place. . . . Ritual provides an occasion for reflection and rationalization in the fact that what ought to have been done was not done, what ought to have taken place did not occur (ibid., 63).

3. A paper machine crew is composed of one machine tender, who is the informal crew boss; one back tender, who operates the front end of the machine; and one third hand, an entry-level position.

4. A centerline is the point at which all variables are aligned for optimum equipment utilization.

5. *Iron Age*, 25 February 1983.

6. Personal communication.

7. Ramchandran Jaikumar, "Postindustrial Manufacturing," *Harvard Business Review* (November–December 1986): 69–76.

8. David F. Noble, *Forces of Production: A Social History of Industrial Automation* (New York: Oxford University Press, 1986); see particularly 144–92.

9. Harley Shaiken, *Work Transformed: Automation and Labor in the Computer Age* (New York: Holt, Rinehart & Winston, 1985), 264.

10. Robert Howard, *Brave New Workplace* (New York: Viking, 1985); see particularly 15–35.

11. The psychiatrist R. D. Laing used the term "knots" to describe the complexities of interpersonal communication and understanding. See his *Knots* (New York: Pantheon Books, 1970).

Chapter Eight   The Limits of Hierarchy in an Informated Organization

1. The tendency to rely on social and subjective criteria in the face of uncertain standards or in the evaluation of abstract phenomena has been well documented in social psychology. For example, in an early article, Leon Festinger noted "the less 'physical reality' there is to validate the opinion or belief, the greater will be the importance of the social referent, the group, and the greater will be the forces to communicate" ("Informal Social Communication," *Psychology Review* 57 [1950]: 273). More recent empirical confirmation of this tendency can be found in Michael Kelley, "Subjective Performance Evaluation and Person-Role Conflict Under Conditions of Uncertainty," *Academy of Management Journal* 20, no. 2 (1977): 301–14; Jeffrey Pfeffer, Gerald Salancik, and Huseyin Leblebici, "The Effect of Uncertainty on the Use of Social Influence in Organization Decision Making," *Administrative Science Quarterly* 21 (1976): 227–45.

2. National Research Council, Committee on the Effective Implementation of Advanced Manufacturing Technology, *Human Resource Practices for Implementing Advanced Manufacturing Technology* (Washington, DC: National Academy Press, 1986); National Research Council, Manufacturing Studies Board, *Toward a New Era in U.S. Manufacturing* (Washington, DC: National Academy Press, 1986).

3. Margaret B. W. Graham and Stephen R. Rosenthal, "Flexible Manufactur-

ing Systems Require Flexible People" (Manufacturing Roundtable, Research Report Series, Boston University School of Management, Boston, 1985).

4. Ramchandran Jaikumar and Roger E. Bohn, "The Development of Intelligent Systems for Industrial Use: A Conceptual Framework" and "The Development of Intelligent Systems for Industrial Use: An Empirical Investigation" (Harvard Business School Working Papers 9-786-024 and 9-786-025, Boston University Graduate School of Business Administration, May 1986); see also the discussion in Larry Hirschhorn, *Beyond Mechanization* (Cambridge: The MIT Press, 1984).

5. Philip Green, "Considerations on the Democratic Division of Labor," *Politics and Society* 12 (1983): 451.

PART THREE TECHNIQUE: THE MATERIAL DIMENSION OF POWER

1. Reinhard Bendix, *Kings or People: Power and the Mandate to Rule* (Berkeley: University of California Press, 1978), 220-21.

Chapter Nine The Information Panopticon

1. Michel Foucault, in Colin Gordon, ed., *Power/Knowledge: Selected Interviews and Other Writings 1972-1977* (New York: Pantheon, 1980), 104-5.

2. Robin Evans, "Regulation and Production," *Lotus* (September 1976): 11.

3. Michel Foucault, *Discipline and Punish: The Birth of the Prison* (New York: Vintage Books, 1979), 201-2.

4. Ibid., 202-3.

5. See the discussion in Gertrude Himmelfarb, *Victorian Minds* (Gloucester, MA: Peter Smith Publisher, 1975), 32-82.

6. For additional discussion of Bentham's invention and its fate in the British Parliament, see Ron Harrison, *Bentham* (London: Routledge & Kegan Paul, 1983), 127-31; Robert Alan Cooper, "Jeremy Bentham, Elizabeth Fry, and English Prison Reform," *Journal of the History of Ideas* 42, no. 4 (October-December 1981): 675-90; Thomas A. Markus, "Pattern of the Law," *Architectural Review* 116 (October 1954): 251-56.

7. Foucault, *Discipline and Punish*, 205, 208.

8. For additional discussion of the significance of uncertainty avoidance as a feature of organizational life and the attraction of uncertainty avoidance mechanisms, see Heinz Eulau, "Technology and the Fear of the Politics of Civility," *Journal of Politics* 35 (1973): 367-85; James D. Thompson, *Organizations in Action* (New York: McGraw-Hill, 1967); Richard M. Cyert and James G. March, *A Behavioral Theory of the Firm* (Englewood Cliffs, NJ: Prentice-Hall, Inc., 1963), 119; Russell Stout, Jr., *Management or Control?* (Bloomington: Indiana University Press, 1980); Donald Gerwin and Jean Claude Tarondeau, "Case Studies of Computer-Integrated Manufacturing Systems: A View of Uncertainty and Innovation Processes," *Journal of Operations Research* 2 (1982): 87-99.

9. Foucault framed this aspect of the materiality of power when he wrote:

> Let us not look for the headquarters that presides over its (power's) rationality. . . . The rationality of power is characterized by tactics that are often quite explicit at the restricted level where they are inscribed, tactics which, becoming connected to one another, attracting and propagating one another, but finding their base of support and their condition elsewhere, end by forming comprehensive systems: the logic is perfectly clear, the aims decipherable, and yet it is often the case that no one is there to have invented them, and few who can be said to have formulated them: an implicit characteristic of the great anonymous, almost unspoken strategies which coordinate the loquacious tactics whose "inventors" or decision makers are often without hypocrisy (Michael Foucault, *The History of Sexuality*, vol. I [New York: Vintage Books, 1980], 95).

10. In their discussion of "institutional control," Rob Kling and Suzanne Iacono found that computerization produced a highly structured environment in which there was reduced reliance on negotiations and greater emphasis on the discipline of keeping accurate records; see "Computing as an Occasion for Social Control," *Journal of Social Issues* 40 (1984): 77–96.

11. Erik H. Erikson, *Identity: Youth and Crisis* (New York: W. W. Norton & Co., 1968), 110.

12. Ibid.

13. See the discussion in James G. March and Herbert Simon, *Organizations* (New York: John Wiley & Sons, 1958), 165–66.

14. Martha S. Feldman and James G. March have discussed these symbolic uses of information in "Information in Organizations as Signal and Symbol," *Administrative Science Quarterly* 26 (1981): 171–86; see also the discussion in Geert Hofstedl, *Culture's Consequences: International Differences in Work-Related Values* (Beverly Hills, CA: Sage Publications, 1980), 159–60.

15. "Span of control" has been a notoriously problematic concept. Early formulations were often derived from military experience (for example, Napoleon, Clausewitz). Others used rule-of-thumb notions or personal experience as the basis for categorical normative statements regarding how many people one manager should supervise directly. The first theoretical formulation came from V. A. Graicunas in 1933. He based his reasoning on some now-questionable assumptions regarding brain capacity and attention span. The concept is also closely associated with the administrative theorist L. F. Urwick, who drew upon his own military experience as a source of validity. Though many authors have tried to formalize and quantify a rationale for span of control, empirical support has been slow to follow and is often contradictory. In general, these rationales have been based on considerations that are either material (for example, geographic dispersion) or psychological (for example, the necessity of face-to-face supervision and discussion). Even in 1956, when Urwick published a *Harvard Business Review* article to defend his concept from repeated attack, his arguments were based on these considerations. For example, he argued that: "with no strict limits on the executive's span of authority, subordinates will line up in his secretary's office and will be constantly frustrated when they want a word with him." The point is, information systems, and the emerging administrative environ-

ment in an informated organization, alter the material and psychological grounds upon which even rule-of-thumb assessments have relied. For further discussions of the "span of control" concept, see Lt. Col. L. F. Urwick, "V. A. Graicunas and the Span of Control," *Academy of Management Journal* 17 (1974): 349–54; "The Manager's Span of Control," *Harvard Business Review* (May–June 1956): 39–47; David D. Van Fleet, "Span of Control: A Review and Restatement," *Akron Business and Economic Review* (Winter 1974): 34–42; David D. Van Fleet and Arthur Bedian, "A History of the Span of Management," *Academy of Management Review* (July 1977): 356–72; William G. Ouchi and John B. Dowling, "Defining the Span of Control," *Administrative Science Quarterly* 19 (1974): 357–65; Harold Koontz, "Making Theory Operational: The Span of Management," *The Journal of Management Studies* 3 (October 1966): 229–43; Davis Entwisle and John Walton, "Observations on the Span of Control," *Administrative Science Quarterly* (1961): 522–33; David D. Van Fleet, "Span of Management Research and Issues," *Academy of Management Journal* 26 (1983): 546–52; Paul Neuman, "What Speed of Communication Is Doing to Span of Control," *Administrative Management* 39 (1978): 30–31.

16. There is already some empirical evidence to suggest that managers use information on the basis of its accessibility rather than on considerations of its quality or "appropriateness"; see: Charles A. O'Reilly III, "Variation in Decision Makers' Use of Information Sources: The Impact of Quality and Accessibility of Information," *Academy of Management Journal* 25 (1982).

Conclusion   Managing the Informated Organization

1. Michel Bur, "The Social Influence of the Motte-and-Bailey Castle," *Scientific American* (May 1983): 132–40.

2. See, for example, Lucien Febvre and Henri-Jean Martin, *The Coming of the Book: The Impact of Printing 1450–1800* (London: NLB, 1976); Amanda Wood, *Knowledge Before Printing and After: The Indian Tradition in Changing Kerala* (Oxford: Oxford University Press, 1985); Elizabeth Eisenstein, *The Printing Press as an Agent of Change* (Cambridge: Cambridge University Press, 1979).

3. See for example James J. Flink, *The Car Culture* (Cambridge: MIT Press, 1975); and James J. Flink, *America Adopts the Automobile: 1895–1950* (Cambridge: MIT Press, 1970).

4. Fernand Braudel, *The Structures of Everyday Life: Civilization and Capitalism 15th–18th Century*, vol. I (New York: Harper & Row, 1981), 435.

5. The classic formulation of this point of view can be found in Harry Braverman's *Labor and Monopoly Capital* (New York: Monthly Review Press, 1974); see also David Noble, *The Forces of Production* (New York: Oxford University Press, 1984); Harley Shaiken, *Work Transformed* (New York: Holt, Rinehart & Winston, 1984).

6. Hannah Arendt, *The Human Condition* (Chicago: The University of Chicago Press, 1958), 322.

7. See, for example, Richard C. Daft and Karl E. Weick, "Toward a Model of Organizations as Interpretation Systems," *Academy of Management Review* 9 (1984): 284–95; Aaron Wildarsky, "Information as an Organizational Problem," *Journal of Management Studies* 20 (1983): 29–40.

8. See for example Robert Kuttner, *The Economic Illusion: False Choices Between Prosperity and Social Justice* (Boston: Houghton Mifflin Co., 1984).

9. I refer the reader to a recent critique of ego functions and social relationships in the postmodern era written by the psychologist-philosopher Eugene T. Gendlin. He argues that contemporary relationships are more "intricate" than can be accounted for by our nineteenth-century models of authority—models upon which Freud's concept of psychic structure was based. I borrow the term *intricate* from Gendlin's usage, as his formulation provides the general context within which these alterations in workplace relations are a salient example. See Eugene T. Gendlin, "A Philosophical Critique of the Concept of Narcissism: The Significance of the Awareness Movement," in D. M. Levin, ed., *Pathologies of the Modern Self: Postmodern Studies* (New York: New York University Press, 1987), 251-304.

10. For a more elaborate discussion of this view of traditional work organization, see Shoshana Zuboff, "I Am My Own Man: The Democratic Vision and Workplace Hierarchy," in Robert Schrank, ed., *Industrial Democracy at Sea: Authority and Democracy on a Norwegian Freighter* (Cambridge: The MIT Press, 1983), 171-92.

11. In their analysis of ordinary language, Lakoff and Johnson define the function of metaphor as "understanding and experiencing one kind of thing in terms of another." Because human thought processes are largely metaphorical, the use of metaphor in everyday language provides a window onto the conceptual system that people use to structure and interpret experience. They refer to such metaphors as "metaphorical concepts." Unlike most metaphors, which structure images or concepts in terms of other images or concepts, "orientational metaphors" based on spatial designations actually organize whole systems of concepts with respect to one another. The psychological power of these orientational metaphors is further illustrated in Barry Schwartz's study of vertical classification. He demonstrates what appears to be a universal tendency to classify social relationships along a vertical axis where "up" conveys dominance, power, authority, and goodness. Exploring a wide range of evidence in order to explain the salience of vertical classification in social relations, Schwartz argues that the use of the spatial metaphor to represent a moral or social relation is derived from the conditioning built into primary object relations; that is, every infant depends upon and looks up to an adult who is bigger and higher. The adult is the source of protection and gratification. Being held and suckled is an experience in going "up," while separation, or going "down," can be experienced as punishment or deprivation. For further discussion, see George Lakoff and Mark Johnson, *Metaphors We Live By* (Chicago: University of Chicago Press, 1980), 14-21; Barry Schwartz, *Vertical Classification: A Study in Structuralism and the Sociology of Knowledge* (Chicago: University of Chicago Press, 1981), 36-43, 73-74, 104.

12. Sociological studies of "dirty work" designations have revealed similar patterns. For example, Everett Hughes notes that work becomes "dirty" when it in some way "goes counter to the more heroic of our moral conceptions." Another recent study suggests that "dirty work designations comprised a way in which workers economically expressed to observers that the task at hand should not be taken to exemplify the nature of either the work or the worker." See Everett C. Hughes, *The Sociological Eye* (Chicago: Aldine Publishers, 1971), 343;

Robert M. Emerson and Melvin Pollner, "Dirty Work Designations: Their Features and Consequences in a Psychiatric Setting," *Social Problems* 23 (1976): 252.

13. Gloria Schuck, "Intelligent Technology, Intelligent Workers: A New Pedagogy for the High-Tech Workplace," *Organizational Dynamics* (Autumn 1985): 66–79.

14. The political philosopher Philip Green confronted a similar problem in his analysis of a "democratic division of labor." He wondered whether a society that encouraged individuals to explore the full range of training and employment opportunities and allowed, by virtue of its institutional arrangements, "genuinely uncoerced" occupational choice would be faced with a glut of experts and leaders, with no one to follow or execute the less intellectually complex work. His argument leads to a similar conclusion:

> The assertion that all people innately have the same motives and ambitions is unbelievable. If socialists and utopians have been too prone to make that assertion over the past two centuries, it has been out of a laudable desire to point out that the ways individuals behave in capitalist societies should not be taken as revelations of their "natures." Of course that is correct. It is a wholly unwarranted deduction, though, that no one is very lazy, slow-moving, unambitious, or driven. Given the most absolutely equal opportunity imaginable, and the permanent eradication of all social stereotypes, there is still no reason to believe that all people would want, for most of their lives or even at all, to work at the most demanding, most responsible, most intellectually or technically complex, or most prestigious kinds of work. I suspect that the truth lies much more in the opposite direction: that the problem for egalitarian institutions would be to be able to find enough people willing to do the burdensome, anxiety-creating jobs, without instituting sharp graduations of reward and reintroducing a strong version of the social division between mental and material labor. But that is a danger egalitarians would cheerfully face up to, as an alternative to having never made the effort in the first place (Philip Green, "Considerations in the Democratic Division of Labor," *Politics and Society* 12 [1983]: 467).

Appendix A   The Scope of Information Technology in the Modern Workplace

1. Gavriel Salvendy, "Human-Computer Communication with Special Reference to Technological Development, Occupational Stress, and Educational Needs," *Ergonomics* 25 (1982): 435.

2. Michael Porter and Victor Millar, "How Information Gives You Competitive Advantage," *Harvard Business Review* (July-August 1985): 152.

3. Sara Kiesler, "Organizational Efforts of Robotics and Manufacturing Technology," (Carnegie-Mellon University, Committee on Social Science Research in Computing, Working Paper Series, Pittsburgh, October 1983), 2.

4. Wassily Leontief, "The Choice of Technology," *Scientific American* 252 (June 1985): 37–45.

5. Salvendy, "Human-Computer Communication, 436.

6. Tora K. Bikson et al., *Computer-Mediated Work* (Santa Monica, CA: The Rand Corporation, 1985).

7. David Terrie, Senior Office Systems Analyst, International Data Corporation, quoted in "How Computers Remake the Manager's Job," *Business Week*, 25 April 1983, 68–70.

8. U.S. Congress, Office of Technology Assessment, *Automation of America's Offices*, OTA–CIT–287 (Washington DC: U.S. Government Printing Office, December 1985), 15.

9. Tora K. Bikson and B. A. Gutek, "Advanced Office Systems: An Empirical Look at Utilization and Satisfaction" (Santa Monica, CA: The Rand Corporation, February 1983).

10. U.S. Congress, Office of Technology Assessment, *Automation of America's Offices*, 307.

11. For more detail, see U.S. Congress, Office of Technology Assessment, "The Technology of Office Automation," in *Automation of America's Offices*, 307–329.

12. Robert Ouellette et al., *Automation Impacts on Industry* (Ann Arbor, MI: Ann Arbor Science Publishers, 1983), 8; see also, Lawrence Evans, "Impact of the Electronics Revolution on Industrial Process Control," *Science* 195 (March 1977): 1146–51.

13. U.S. Congress, Office of Technology Assessment, *Computerized Manufacturing Automation: Employment, Education, and the Workplace*, OTA–CIT–235 (Washington, D.C.: U.S. Government Printing Office, April 1984), 46.

14. Cited in ibid., 52.

15. Leontief, "Choice of Technology," 39.

16. U.S. Congress, *Computerized Manufacturing Automation*, 59.

17. Ibid., 54.

18. Leontief, "Choice of Technology," 37.

19. Gene Bylinsky, "The Race to the Automatic Factory," *Fortune*, 21 February 1983, 54.

20. Ibid., 58.

21. See the discussion in John Bessant and Keith Dickson, *Issues in the Adoption of Microelectronics* (London: Frances Pinter, 1982), 36–52.

22. National Academy of Sciences, Committee on the Effective Implementation of Advanced Manufacturing Technology (Richard Walton, Chairperson), *Human Resource Practices for Implementing Advanced Manufacturing Technology* (Washington, DC: National Academy Press, 1986), 9.

Appendix B   Notes on Field-Research Methodology

1. Eugene Gendlin, *Experience and the Creation of Meaning* (New York: Free Press, 1964); George Herbert Mead, *Mind, Self, and Society* (Chicago: The University of Chicago Press, 1934); Maurice Merleau-Ponty, *The Structure of Behavior* (Boston: Beacon Press, 1963).

2. Eugene Gendlin, *Focusing* (New York: Everest House, 1978), 115–43.

3. Jean Piaget, *The Moral Judgement of the Child* (New York: The Free Press, 1965); Lawrence Kohlberg, "Stage and Sequence: The Cognitive Developmental Approach to Socialization," in *Handbook of Socialization: Theory and Research*, ed. D. Goslin (New York: Rand McNally, 1969), 347–480; Carol Gilligan, *In a Different Voice* (Cambridge: Harvard University Press, 1982).

INDEX